For a
Socially Engaged Faith

For a
Socially Engaged Faith

Felix Wilfred

2024

For a Socially Engaged Faith — published by the Indian Society for Promoting Christian Knowledge (ISPCK), Post Box 1585, 1654, Madarsa Road, Kashmere Gate, Delhi-110006.

ISBN: 978-81-19434-07-7

Cover Design:
Mere knowledge of society and societal dynamics is inadequate. Faith comes in to provide the enlightenment to see our experiences - individual and social - differently and in a new light. This new light of seeing the social realities through engagement is represented by the eye. The Third Eye is also a metaphor of compassion as in the Buddhist tradition. The idea is expressed in Tamil classics as "*Kadaikan*" meaning compassionate eye.

Socially Engaged Faith as the Third Eye of Enlightenment and Compassion

Laser typeset by

ISPCK, Post Box 1585, 1654, Madarsa Road, Kashmere Gate, Delhi-110006
• *Tel:* 23866323/22

e-mail: ashish@ispck.org.in • ella@ispck.org.in
website: www.ispck.org.in

Printed at Saurabh Printers, NOIDA.

This dedication, a humble tapestry of words,

A symphony composed with profound appreciation and gratitude

To my cherished students and esteemed colleagues at

St Paul's Seminary, Tiruchirappalli and

Department of Christian Studies, University of Madras

CONTENTS

LIBERATION

DEMOCRACY AND HUMAN RIGHTS

CHURCH RENEWAL

PUBLIC THEOLOGY

POST-PANDEMIC THEOLOGY

PREFACE

A Chinese sage unveils the inevitable truths of the ageing process. In this enlightening voyage, we discover that life is akin to a grand theatrical performance. In our youth and middle age, we take centre stage playing the vibrant roles of actors on the stage. However, as we advance in years, we transition from the spotlight to a position of respect on the front row. This shift signifies a transformation from an active participant to a mere observer. Personally, I am deeply grateful for the divine grace that enables me to continue playing a small role on the theological stage rather than being a passive bystander.

Amidst the current state of the world and society, there is a compelling call for conscientious believers to embrace their responsibility in driving transformation and fostering positive change. Inspired by the yearning for the Reign of God, our faith transforms into a vigorous force, propelling us into the heart of society. This work represents a humble attempt to reflect on what it means to be a socially engaged Christian in the context of contemporary times.

Much like some of my earlier endeavours, the present work represents the culmination of reflections, shared experiences, and conversations held on various occasions and with diverse audiences in response to distinct requirements. Nevertheless, there exists a unifying theme that connects them all. This common thread revolves around the pivotal notion that faith must yield tangible outcomes through the transformation of the world and society, accompanied by an ongoing process of conversion and personal maturation. I have included an appendix in the volume providing background information to enable readers to grasp and interpret the content with the specific contexts of their creation and evolution.

This work is dedicated to my students and colleagues at St Paul's Seminary, Tiruchirappalli, and at the Department of Christian Studies, University of Madras. Many of my past students have embraced active social roles and demonstrated pastoral creativity in Tamil Nadu and other regions of the country. Others have taken up the mission of dedicated theologians giving intellectual leadership, nurturing a new generation of students with theological vision and insights leading to transformation. The accomplishments of my students fill me with immense pride. I wish to extend my heartfelt appreciation to them, with a special mention to Dr R.K. Samy, Msgr L. Anthuvan, Dr M. Arockiasamy Xavier S.J. and Dr T. Sagayaraj. Their gesture of organizing a felicitation event in my honour on 21 June 2023, in Tiruchirappalli, serves as a testament to their affection. This event provided a splendid opportunity to reconnect with my former students, and for that, I am truly grateful.

Countless scholars and friends from India and beyond have contributed their wisdom, enriching the pages of this volume. I would like to acknowledge a few of them by name while expressing my heartfelt gratitude to everyone involved. Dr Mary John went through the entire manuscript with his eye for details and pointed out errors, and made suggestions for improvement. He also helped in preparing the index to the volume. Dr Amirtharaj Arockiam, Mr Leo Fernandez and Mr Rudolf Fernandez read with critical eyes the manuscript and gave several insightful suggestions for improvement and addition. I also wish to thank Dr Namrata Chaturvedi, Dr James

Ponniah, Dr Antony Lawrence, Dr Merlin Ambrose, and Dr Johnson Silvuaipillai for their feedbacks.

I am thankful to Dr Ashish Amos, Dr Ella Sonawane and the ISPCK team for their deep interest in my writings and for their excellent publishing work of yet another volume of mine.

Without Ms Nirmal, this work would not have seen the light of day. I am immensely grateful to her for her diligent efforts, unwavering commitment, and exceptional support right from the inception of this work, especially in the final editing of the manuscript.

May this modest work serve as a beacon, guiding religious believers, especially the Christian communities, to deepen their social commitment, and illuminating the path for students and faculty to align their theological vision with the pressing issues of our contemporary world and society.

Felix Wilfred

Asian Centre for Cross-Cultural Studies (ACCS)
Chennai
2 August 2023

INTRODUCTION

The Developing Crisis

Understanding the ongoing worldwide crisis, especially in the context of India, requires an attentive exploration of key concerns like the decline of democratic principles, the surge of populism and authoritarian tendencies, and the regrettable departure from noble ideals and values in political and economic spheres. The strength of a robust democracy is rooted in its democratic establishments, and the crisis of these institutions presents a noteworthy obstacle that affects everyone, not the least religious adherents.

Traditionally, the political realm has been a space for deliberating the common good, where resources are pooled and utilized to achieve righteous goals. Regrettably, in recent times, politics has deviated from this lofty purpose and instead become a battleground for power struggles. Rather than focusing on the greater good, individuals involved in politics seek personal gains and advantages, undermining the essence of true democratic representation.

This shift towards populism and authoritarian tendencies has further exacerbated the crisis. Populist leaders often exploit public sentiment and fears to gain support, sometimes at the expense of democratic principles. On the other hand, the rise of authoritarianism threatens the very foundation of democracy by concentrating power in the hands of a select few, stifling dissent, and marginalizing the voices of the people.

Regarding the economy, the ideal expectation is for it to harness the resources of nature to meet the needs of every individual without excessive exploitation and destruction of nature. Unfortunately, the current state of affairs depicts an economy that is primarily influenced by market interests and profit motives, resulting in the accumulation and control of wealth by a privileged few. This monopolistic trend poses a threat to the economic well-being of the less privileged, further aggravating social and economic inequalities.

Contemporary culture, on its part, is grossly conditioned by the digital world and networking. People become simply nodes in large net works and get progressively de-personalized. Unfortunately, a significant portion of the population remains excluded from this digital landscape, while human relationships are increasingly governed by technological codes. The result is an "administered world" that diminishes human agency and freedom. In this process, human actions and choices are reduced to predictable algorithms, undermining the spontaneity and uniqueness of individual expression.

Challenging Times

In the West, secularism has often been interpreted as the separation of religion from public affairs. However, global developments, particularly in Asian countries and other developing nations, reveal a different trend - the rise of religious-nationalist states disguising themselves with a thin democratic façade. While outwardly maintaining democratic appearances, these political powers seek to suppress potential threats and consolidate absolute and unchecked authority.

A prominent example of this trend is the deliberate suppression of civil society movements and the engagement of Non-Governmental Organizations (NGOs). This stands in stark contrast to the situation in the 1980s and 1990s, when non-governmental groups, including faith-motivated organizations, were regarded by the state as agents and instruments working towards the realization of a welfare state.

The current shift reflects a departure from the ethos of empowering NGOs and faith-based groups. Instead, the focus now appears to be on consolidating state power and limiting the influence of independent civil society actors. This poses significant challenges to democracy and highlights the growing complexities of political landscapes, especially in South Asia.

Regarding religion, their dynamic involvement in social issues has been demonstrated through their engagement in welfare and charitable activities. This involvement, as we noted, was well-received, like in the case of NGOs, and even encouraged by the ruling establishment, as it complemented the state-led welfare initiatives. To support the efforts of faith-based groups, the state even provided funding, recognizing their dedication and efficacy, often surpassing the capabilities of state institutions and channels. A notable example of this cooperation was observed during the period of rehabilitation after the Tsunami, where faith-based groups collaborated closely with the state to bring about positive outcomes.

In all these endeavours, there was an attempt to depict, define, and align social action with social engagement. However, it is essential to acknowledge the existence of another less conspicuous current, one that drew inspiration from faith but adopted a more critical stance towards the prevailing societal structures, including the state. This stream presented an alternative vision, urging society to reflect on its current state and work towards a more inclusive and transformative path. Understanding this form of social engagement requires recognizing and appreciating the complexity and challenges it entails.

Changing Landscape

Social engagement by faith-based groups and movements is perceived today as a direct challenge to the state's authority. The prevailing sense of insecurity has led increasingly authoritarian states to restrict the public sphere from any involvement by faith-motivated groups. Disturbingly, new laws and regulations are implemented to hinder the activities of socially engaged religious groups, severely curbing their ability to make a positive impact.

The state operates with an alarmist mentality, seeing potential threats to its political power everywhere. This approach is sustained by an ideology that empowers the state to regulate religious practices and interactions. Religions are expected to comply unquestioningly with state-enacted laws, even if their legality and fairness are questionable, as these laws are ultimately designed to protect the political power of the state.

The current situation has created significant obstacles in upholding the dignity of human beings, striving for the common good, and promoting equality and justice. In the face of these political challenges, socially committed Christians – and this can be extended to engaged members of other religious traditions – may find themselves disheartened by the weight of oppression and may be tempted to conform to the prevailing status quo.

Religious groups deeply attached to preserving their traditions, rituals, and institutions, often equating them with their faith, can succumb to fear, much like the political powers challenging them. This fear leads them to withdraw and seek safety within their own circles, creating a cocoon of isolation. Regrettably, this withdrawal, frequently concealed behind convenient ideologies, results in an inability to provide a prophetic witness.

As a result, we witness several Church leaders advocating for "building bridges" with political authorities, using the pretext of practising the gospel's teaching to love one's enemies. Not infrequently, they cowardly adopt the views of the state on complex issues to avoid any trouble for themselves. For these leaders, fulfilling the Christian obligation of social engagement is over with performing charitable works through organizations like "Caritas" or diocesan social service societies. This narrow interpretation of social engagement tends to overlook the broader issues of addressing systemic injustices and advocating for transformative change in society.

We find ourselves in new and evolving political and social frontiers, but unfortunately, many Christians and Church leaders seem unaware of the implications of these developments. They appear disconnected from the birth and impact of grassroots movements dedicated to social transformation, where numerous Christians and Christian groups actively participate, driven by their faith and its relevance to public life.

These engaged individuals and groups view their involvement as a means of contributing to the humanization of society. Their commitment lies with the welfare of the subalterns and marginalized sections of society. This stands in contrast to the historical development-orientation of the Church, which was aligned with the ideal of nation-building. In the past, collaborating with the state to foster the development of Asian nations was seen as a way to affirm the Church's Asian identity. Nonetheless, the concept of nation-building has evolved, and its significance should be reevaluated in the context of contemporary circumstances. The agenda of nation-building remains pertinent, but it now requires understanding in new terms and adapting to the changing realities of our times.

The unfolding developments have sparked reflections on the concept of public theology, which involves addressing public issues in their political, social, economic, and cultural complexities, with a particular focus on the concerns of the subalterns and historically excluded groups. Public theology delves into the profound political significance of the Christian faith and emphasizes the vital role of faith in offering prophetic insights during critical times.

Socially conscious Christians are urging the Churches to direct their attention towards the emerging questions that demand immediate consideration. These include migration, refugees, land alienation faced by tribal communities, the plight of the poor and marginalized, trafficking of women and children, exploitative tourism, clinical trials involving vulnerable populations, the displacement of indigenous people, caste and ethnic conflicts, the challenges faced by farmers and fisherfolk, and environmental destruction disguised as development.

These pressing issues are inherently linked to politics, and thus, the South Asian Churches face an increasing challenge to become politically conscious in their social engagement. Rather than shunning politics, they are encouraged to view it as a crucial arena for effecting societal transformation guided by their faith. Embracing this perspective can empower the Churches to address these complex challenges and contribute to a more just and equitable society in the light of their religious belief.

The Shifts in Understanding Social Engagement

The aforementioned observations must be situated within historical context in order to comprehend the development of social involvement within South Asian Churches. Upon reflection, noteworthy milestones in this progression become evident. During the colonial era of missionary efforts, the focus of social engagement was directed towards eliminating superstitious and perceived "uncivilized" practices entrenched in South Asian societies. Examples of such practices include *sati* (widow burning), child-marriage, and the prohibition of widow-remarriage. Missionaries assumed a pivotal role in driving this transformation. They regarded the modernization of colonized societies as a necessary groundwork for their mission and the dissemination of the gospel. This approach was frequently denoted as the "civilizing mission."

Subsequently, during the peak of the development ideology, the Church's social engagement shifted towards involvement in projects, schemes, and welfare initiatives aimed at alleviating poverty and leading communities towards a development model akin to that of western developed nations. The Catholic Church, for instance, showed support for such an agenda at the global level through Pope Paul VI's encyclical, *Populorum Progressio* (Development of Peoples), especially during the post-decolonization period.

These historical contexts provide valuable insights into the changing perspectives of social engagement within the South Asian Churches, reflecting how their understanding and approach have evolved over time in response to various societal and global influences.

However, we have witnessed a shift in the Church's development agenda due to changing political dynamics. As religious nationalism and right-wing extremism have gained momentum, what was once seen as the Church's contribution to the nation has been misinterpreted and twisted. The Church's genuine efforts towards social engagement, often centred around welfare and development, came under critical scrutiny and faced unfounded allegations of harbouring ulterior motives, specifically religious conversion.

This situation echoes historical suspicions that date back to the eighteenth and nineteenth centuries when social reforms initiated by missionaries were perceived as a means to destabilize traditional societies in collusion with Christian colonial rulers. The Church's intentions were tainted by "guilt by association." The present context showcases a similar pattern, where the genuine social engagement of the Church is misconstrued and undermined by baseless accusations of hidden agendas. These misconceptions threaten to overshadow the positive impact the Church seeks to make in society and hinder its efforts towards genuine social progress.

There is another aspect to the resistance against Christian social reform. In a broader context, the introduction of modernity through education and western medicine, along with the care provided to orphans and widows, was warmly welcomed by marginalized groups such as Dalits, tribals, and women. Christians played a crucial role as catalysts of modernity, particularly in various parts of Asia, notably in South Asia.

Among the upper castes and classes, there is a begrudging acknowledgement of Christianity's social contributions. However, this recognition is often seen through the lens of the traditional caste system, which assigns specific duties (*dharma*) to each of the four *varnas* based on birth. From this perspective, the service (*seva*) provided by Christians through their social work is equated to the duty assigned to the *shudras*, the lowest caste in the hierarchy. Consequently, Christians are perceived by the upper castes and classes as fulfilling their dharma of service to society, much like a fictional group of *shudras*. The services of Christians are taken for granted since service is taken to be their *dharma*.

Sadly, this view does not lead to Christians becoming an inspiration or model for others in the eyes of the upper castes and classes. Ironically, however, the fear of Christian social and welfare activities triggering to conversions has acted as a catalyst for several Hindu groups to initiate their own welfare and philanthropic endeavours. This unintended consequence demonstrates how the apprehension regarding conversion has inadvertently spurred positive social action among other religious communities.

Social Teachings

During the modern period of Catholic social teaching, the issue of workers took centre stage due to the impact of the industrial revolution. Over time, the Church's social teaching expanded to encompass a wide range of topics, including human dignity, rights, ecology, politics, and economic matters. Additionally, many Protestant Churches have also issued courageous statements on various social issues. However, a fundamental weakness in these well-intended social teachings and statements is their reliance on the notion that applying principles to specific situations will resolve social conflicts and issues. While principles certainly hold importance, a mere application of ethical principles has not proven to be highly effective in bringing about meaningful change. It necessitates a deeper approach, one that involves true social conversion and a transformation of attitudes and behaviours. It demands devising ways and means to initiate genuine societal change and transformation. Moreover, some critical and long-standing local social issues, such as casteism in the context of South Asia, have not received adequate attention in these social teachings.

To create lasting and impactful change, social teachings must be accompanied by efforts to foster true social conversion and promote a shift in people's attitudes and behaviours. Additionally, addressing region-specific issues is essential to ensure the relevance and effectiveness of these teachings in addressing the unique challenges faced by local communities. It is equally important to insert the social teachings of the Church in the social history of the concerned region or people.

Fortunately, there are vibrant Christian responses emerging from the grassroots level, which play a pivotal role in directing Christian engagement towards genuine social conversion. One notable and influential document is the *Kairos Document,* which originated from the struggles against apartheid and has served as an inspiration for social commitment not only in South Africa but also in other parts of the world.

In Latin America, profound reflections on the mystery of the cross amidst dehumanization and oppression have led to the perception of the poor and marginalized as a crucified people. This perspective views Christian involvement as an effort to alleviate the suffering and injustice faced by the crucified, providing an antidote to social indifference and apathy.

The essence of social teachings should be to encourage Christians to transform themselves into caring and compassionate neighbours, exemplified in the parable of the Good Samaritan. However, this aspect of personal and spiritual transformation should not be the endpoint. Social teachings must delve deeper into analyzing the structural dimensions of each issue and inspire Christians to respond to them effectively. Regrettably, many Christian social practices lack this structural approach.

On the contrary, grassroots faith-inspired movements are characterized by a strong structural approach. They understand the need to address not only individual experiences of suffering but also the underlying systemic injustices that perpetuate social problems. By adopting a structural perspective, Christian social engagement can become more effective and far-reaching in bringing about lasting positive change in society.

The Pitfalls Within

In contrast to the socially inspired grassroots movements within Christianity, we observe another phenomenon, particularly prevalent in the Catholic Church. This phenomenon involves a hesitancy to confront those in positions of power, juxtaposed with a growing interest in new spiritual movements. These movements within the Catholic Church have experienced a remarkable expansion, capitalizing on the infantile and gullible faith of many believers.

The new movements led by "spiritual" celebrities serve the Church establishment in various ways. For, these movements are skilled at mobilizing large numbers of devotees to partake in popular devotions within their respective movements. However, this comes at the cost of taming and domesticating the power of faith, making the masses more compliant and receptive to the Church leaders. These movements often showcase extravagant ceremonial spectacles, presenting an exhibition of the Church's "spiritual" prowess. Unfortunately, these trends tend to anesthetize the Christian social consciousness, diverting focus away from critical reflection on burning issues in society.

Moreover, such movements and mega churches can inadvertently serve as a cover-up for numerous improprieties within the Church involving its clergy and leaders. Due to the lack of critical reflection, some of these movements are plagued with scandals related to money and sexual misconduct.

Similar developments are seen in Protestant Churches, where the focus shifts towards the Bible and its fundamentalist interpretation. Furthermore, on a global scale, we witness the rise of mega churches, which closely resemble the church-movements within the Catholic Church mentioned earlier. These mega churches adopt a consumer-capitalist approach, providing spiritual goods to religious consumers.

Similar to the Catholic "spiritual" movements, they are highly visible and have considerable appeal and attraction.

The Waning of Social Consciousness

The waning idealism and declining social commitment, accompanied by a surge in "spiritualism," can be better understood within the context of today's capitalism and neoliberalism. The overwhelming influence of capitalism, the market-driven economy, and an excessive reliance on technology for governance has numbed the consciousness of the middle class. Once fervently involved in India's struggle for independence and social reforms, this middle class, now, seems preoccupied with consumerism, driven by a constant pursuit of personal gain and seeking better opportunities. Consequently, the necessity of making compromises with those in power becomes inescapable.

While a few brave individuals persist in civil society activism, their efforts resemble an oasis in a vast desert of apathy and indifference towards the plight of the poor. The social activism is progressively waning, leaving a void in advocating for the marginalized and disadvantaged.

Furthermore, many of today's "spiritual movements" fail to establish a connection between faith and the oppressive realities surrounding us. Instead, these movements primarily cater to the needs of a middle class that, as I mentioned earlier, is gradually losing its social consciousness and commitment. The middle class's spirituality tends to be individualistic, with a focus on personal salvation and seeking divine blessings for a prosperous life, often through imploring God and saints.

On a global scale, the so-called "prosperity gospel" has captured the imagination of Christians who perceive wealth as a sign of God's favour and its absence as a consequence of sin. This raises fundamental questions about what it truly means to be a Christian in the present day. The command to love one's neighbour is central to Christian teachings, and the entire Bible is written from the perspective of the oppressed and marginalized. Jesus' teachings revolve around caring for the poor and proclaiming God's Good News of the Kingdom of God.

Living as a Christian in the twenty-first century requires being attuned to the realities of the world and our societies. We must read the signs of the times and learn from God's continuing revelation through history. Embracing a socially engaged faith practice calls for seeking insights from other disciplines to comprehend and interpret various aspects of life, including the social, political, economic, and cultural realms. This deeper understanding will inspire us to intervene in the world, fuelled by our faith and its guiding energy.

In this pursuit, we must also attend to another aspect, namely recognizing that actions and circumstances are not solely the outcomes of individual agency. Socio-political realities significantly influence our lives, and adopting a more comprehensive and structural approach is crucial to grasp the complexities of various issues. Understanding this dynamic will shape our responses to the challenges we face, motivated by a faith that embraces compassion, justice, and solidarity.

A faith that draws wisdom from various disciplines will transcend an individualistic perspective and allow believers to perceive that many aspects we typically attribute to the goodness or sinfulness of individuals are, in fact, interconnected with broader societal dynamics. Emile Durkheim, considered the father of modern sociology, highlights this understanding through his study on suicides. He demonstrates that this phenomenon cannot be fully explained solely from the perspective of individual psychology, as it is profoundly influenced by social forces and broader cultural structures.

In this light, faith informs us to recognize that our actions and circumstances are not isolated occurrences but are intricately intertwined with the larger fabric of society. By acknowledging these interconnected factors, we can gain a deeper comprehension of the complexities that shape human behavior and experiences, leading to a more holistic and empathetic understanding of the world around us. This broader perspective nurtures with deeper wellspring of compassion and a heightened sense of responsibility in tackling societal issues and actively striving for meaningful and constructive change.

Within the Church, there is a prevailing tendency to overlook the intricate web of forces at play in every socio-political and cultural phenomenon. This inclination often results in viewing reality through a binary lens, categorizing situations into opposing extremes: light and shadow, good and evil, saint and savage. Unfortunately, this oversimplified approach leads to a superficial understanding of complex problems and hasty moral judgments.

To counter such tendencies, it becomes crucial to adopt a more studied approach. The document "*Gaudium et Spes*" from Vatican II acknowledges the importance of conducting research and study for the development of effective pastoral policies and practices. By delving deeper into the complexities of various issues, the Church can gain a more nuanced understanding of the world and its challenges. This approach will enable the Church to navigate the intricacies of contemporary realities, address societal issues more effectively, and engage in meaningful dialogue and action for the common good. In short, a more profound understanding of the world and a faithful response emerge when we adopt a complex and structural approach.

For instance, the issue of caste discrimination can be viewed simplistically as a matter of prejudice that can be overcome through education and personal transformation. However, such simplistic explanations fail to acknowledge that caste is deeply entrenched even among highly educated individuals. This realization compels us to examine how caste operates within societal structures, creating systems of exclusion. To address caste discrimination effectively, we must, therefore, confront and dismantle the deeply embedded social structures that perpetuate it.

It becomes evident that relying solely on the institutional Church to effect change in caste discrimination may not be sufficient. In the United States, for example, attending church does not automatically lead to overcoming racism. On the contrary, research shows that white racism tends to be stronger among white evangelical frequent church goers, while it is less prevalent among those who attend church rituals not so frequently. This indicates that the issue of racism is influenced by broader social and cultural factors beyond individual religious practice. This is also very much true of casteism.

In India, a similar phenomenon can be observed where individuals deeply attached to the institutional Church, its clergy, and hierarchy may display less sensitivity towards caste discrimination compared to others. Drawing attention to this issue, I would like to share the conclusion of an M.Phil. student of mine who conducted a study on the attitudes of Catholic youth towards other religions in a specific diocese in Keralam. The empirical findings revealed that the more the young people were attached to the parish and its clergy, the less open they were to engaging in dialogue with people of other faiths, in contrast to their peers in the diocese.

In short, embracing a more comprehensive and structural approach allows us to grasp the intricate interplay between individual actions and the wider socio-political context. Understanding and addressing complex societal issues, such as caste discrimination and racism, require concerted efforts that extend beyond personal transformation and involve challenging and transforming the underlying social structures and systems.

Commitment to transforming the world must draw inspiration from the fundamental principles of the Bible and the life and teachings of Jesus. It should arise from a mature and engaging adult faith that goes beyond the confines of the Church's institutional boundaries.

In the past, Catholics, Protestants, and other denominations were often in conflict with each other, reflecting a legacy of western Christianity. However, today, a new alignment is emerging across denominational divides, comprising those who view faith and Christian identity through the lens of social engagement, and others who uphold traditional normativity as the foundation of Christian identity. This shift reflects the changing dynamics of contemporary Christianity, where a growing number of believers prioritize social involvement and embrace a holistic approach to living out their faith.

Faith at the Social Frontiers

The Solidarity movement in Poland, the anti-apartheid movement in South Africa, and more recent movements like the sanctuary movement in support of migrants, the civil rights movements of the black Church, and the Black Lives Matter movement against racism in the USA were all deeply influenced and inspired by faith. Their leaders drew inspiration from religious resources and history, making these movements ethics in practice. Rather than deriving moral behaviour from mere codes, the flame of faith kindled a transformative practice that challenged prevailing social norms, earning religion a "disruptive role."

Historically, religious movements played pivotal roles in advocating for social justice and change. The Social Gospel Movement in the nineteenth century was a pioneering example, placing faith at the forefront of social struggles. Even earlier, religious abolitionists in Protestant circles denounced slavery as a national sin, highlighting the integration of religious fervour with enlightened approaches to understanding social realities.

In South Asia, the bhakti movement spanning over a millennium exemplifies the potential of faith to transcend deeply entrenched traditions, such as caste, and foster a perspective that sees human beings beyond their religious affiliations. In contemporary times, Asia has witnessed resistance against dictatorial regimes in several countries like Korea, Indonesia, Myanmar, and The Philippines. Faith and religious resources served as the inspiration for these movements, leading to the re-establishment of democracy. The Umbrella Movement in Hong Kong, challenging the oppressive Communist Party of China (CCP), was notably led by young Christians who bravely endured prison sentences for their activism.

In summary, throughout history and in recent times, faith has been a powerful force driving social movements, challenging injustices, and inspiring people to work for positive change and greater equality.

Social Mysticism

The social teachings of the Roman Catholic Church and ecumenical organizations like the WCC present a wealth of principles concerning justice, human rights, ecology, and gender issues. Nevertheless, merely applying these principles falls short of bringing about significant transformation. What is needed is a social mysticism that permeates everyday life, surpassing superficial adjustments and delving into the realms of mindset, values, and methods, and the very approach to social engagement.

Mysticism essentially entails an encounter with unity, where all apparent divisions dissolve, and everything that seems distinct becomes intertwined and interlinked. For Christians who draw inspiration from social mysticism, their involvement in the world becomes an intrinsic aspect of their faith-driven existence. The basis of social mysticism in Christianity finds its roots in the mystery of the incarnation. The humanity of Jesus carries enduring significance, enabling us to grasp and encounter the divine through human relationships, while simultaneously illuminating human existence in the divine radiance. Consequently, all dichotomies and dualities, be it God versus humanity or earth versus heaven, are transcended and melded in harmonious unity, surpassing the often-perceived binary distinctions.

This perspective has sparked vigorous discussions, especially in light of the rise of a liberating and socially-oriented understanding of the gospels within liberation theology. Detractors contend that those who actively address social matters might overlook the spiritual and individual aspects of faith. Nonetheless, practitioners of social mysticism underscore that despite their immersion in worldly affairs, they remain intimately linked to the spiritual core of their faith. Their deeds are directed by a profound recognition of being interconnected and unified with God and humanity.

There is another aspect to social mysticism we need to explore. From a Christian perspective, engaging in society reflects a deep love for one's neighbour, serving as a visible expression of love for God. These two loves are intertwined and indivisible, forming a unified love that manifests in diverse ways. Embracing this unity of the love of God and love of neighbour leads to a life guided by social mysticism, recognizing the importance of understanding salvation as more than just a private, individualistic spiritual journey. Rather, it entails a communal and social dimension, where each individual takes responsibility for the welfare and wholeness of all.

Just as humans are "*capax Dei*" or capable of God, so a comparable potential exists for authentic universal brotherhood and sisterhood transcending beyond narrow barriers like caste, tribe, nation, or religion. Part of this potentiality is the ability to empathize with others and willingly endure suffering on their behalf. While martyrdom was once hailed as a testament to one's faith, present-day perspectives highlight the significance of everyday martyrdom fuelled by love for others, especially the marginalized ones.

Social mysticism takes into account the fact that Christian engagement unfolds within a world marked by violence, conflict, betrayal, and contradictions, presenting a significant challenge to committed Christians dedicated to transformative efforts. The Old Testament story of Joseph and his brothers serves as a paradigm, illustrating how reconciliation and fraternity can emerge even after a complex history of discord (Gen. 37-50).

The arduous struggles and selfless sacrifices undertaken to foster a world and society founded on fraternal principles bring about a profound realization and celebration of the divine fatherhood and motherhood. This transformative journey enables individuals to grasp a deeper understanding of the divine aspects of nurturing and parental care. In the pursuit of social engagement, hope for the future becomes indispensable—a belief in the possibility of creating a world characterized by universal brotherhood and sisterhood. Christian faith embraces this hope, casting its influence over every social involvement.

For Christians to be impactful in society, they must possess a keen awareness of the vulnerability endured by the oppressed and marginalized while also acknowledging their own vulnerabilities. This perspective shapes a Christian's role in social transformation, not as a saviour for others, but as someone who experiences the impact of the same systems that create victims. These individuals aim to collaborate with others through open dialogue, active participation, and a shared dedication to nurture collective change. In doing so, they blur the lines between social actors and objects of social action, fostering a profound sense of unity and cooperation.

Further, Christians who embrace social mysticism reject the notion of engaging in society solely for personal gain or reciprocity. Today's world often prioritizes self-interest, but social mysticism liberates the socially engaged Christian from such toxic motivations. When deeply reflecting on their social commitment, a Christian realizes that it is a sacred duty, an obligation to utilize the gifts, talents, and resources bestowed by God for the betterment of the community, especially its vulnerable and marginalized members. Acting in favour of those who cannot reciprocate represents a divine act, calling for deep spiritual and mystical experiences. Engaging in unreciprocated giving for the benefit of those in need liberates both the giver and the receiver. It frees the giver from any sense of condescending charity and the receiver from being viewed as a passive recipient of handouts.

Christian anthropology underpins social mysticism at an even deeper level. In the Christian worldview, the self is not an isolated entity with a fixed identity. Instead, the self exists within the interconnected world of the community and society. Thus, it holds true to say, "I am because we are." The other individuals in the community become an integral part of the self's identity.

Building on this idea, the Christian tradition of the Middle Ages expanded the concept by recognizing the poor not just as fellow human beings but also as representatives of Christ – *vicarius Christi*.

This perspective adds an intense spiritual dimension to the act of aiding the needy, as it is akin to serving Christ himself.

Finally, in social mysticism, we need to pay attention to the transformation of the self through the experience of inner freedom. Freedom serves as the pivotal concept that bridges the realms of spirituality and society. The historical figure of Jesus embodies a divine revelation of freedom, symbolizing liberation from the confines of self and exemplifying authenticity. Authenticity arises when one breaks free from attachments that bind the self. A person who achieves inner freedom becomes a potent force for social transformation. This transformation does not follow a strict chronological sequence where personal change must precede social change. Instead, there exists a correlation between the two—a unified movement of freedom that liberates the self and empowers one to liberate others, each aspect reinforcing the other.

Integrating Role of Theology

The concept of social mysticism brings to light the unifying and mystical essence of all theology. Ultimately, a theology dedicated to integration naturally becomes a faith at social frontiers. The impact of fragmentation is evident across various domains of life, affecting politics, economy, society, culture, bureaucracy, and disciplines of knowledge. In this world of fragmentation, theology should play a crucial role in fostering integration and helping individuals perceive a sense of wholeness.

This contrasts with the traditional role of theology, which aimed at offering comprehensive explanations through its doctrines. In the past, theological explanations encompassed everything from birth to death and all aspects of human life in between, creating what postmodernism termed "metanarratives." These theological explanations were all-inclusive, leaving nothing outside their purview and explanation. However, the contemporary view emphasizes the importance of theology facilitating integration rather than imposing rigid and all-encompassing frameworks.

Given the current landscape, theology's role must undergo a transformative shift. In a world and society marked by extensive disintegration, theology assumes a crucial role in facilitating the linkage and amalgamation of ostensibly disconnected and disjointed facets. The loss of a sense of wholeness and an exhilarating experience of integration can lead to serious personal and societal challenges. Living amidst fragments often feels like being trapped in a dark and isolated tunnel, and the remedy lies in forging ever-closer connections within the intricate web of relationships that bind society, the world, nature, and the entire universe.

The experience of wholeness and integration represents a mystical journey toward salvation and completeness. Rather than merely expounding traditional doctrines, theology will strive to identify the extensive network of interdependencies that unite people and reality beyond borders and boundaries. This approach seeks a truth without walls, fostering unity and understanding across diverse perspectives and domains. Theologies emerging from these perspectives will inspire Christians to involve themselves in society and discover the deeper layers and meanings of faith.

Regrettably, in the Global North, there is a growing tendency to abandon theology, arguing that it lacks "scientific" validity and that its primary function is to provide explanations. As a result, there is an increasing shift towards "religious studies," which is perceived as more scientific and respectable. However, if theology attempts to conform to traditional scientific standards, it risks becoming just another fragment amidst the vast array of fragmented knowledge.

Hence, both in the North and the South, it becomes essential to reevaluate theology's role as a science of integration. Rather than striving to align itself with a specific scientific paradigm, theology should embrace its unique identity and mission: to contribute to a holistic and integrated worldview. This approach holds immense healing power, setting theology apart from other sciences that tend to thrive by dissecting and isolating their objects of study.

In essence, by fulfilling its mission of progressive integration, theology becomes a healing science—a form of medicine—rather than a detached system of abstract explanations with no connection to real-life issues. The failure to interconnect various aspects of existence can lead to perilous personal and societal ailments, making theology's focus on unity and integration all the more crucial.

Theologian as a Public and "Organic" Intellectual

In the present day, it is crucial for theology to be closely intertwined with "disruptive" social movements that are fostered by a distinct vision of the world and society. A theology that remains confined to intellectual exercises alone offers little in terms of driving change and transformation. The crisis of faith experienced in the Global North can, in part, be attributed to theology's failure to address real issues and questions faced by individuals and societies, leading to a decline in church attendance.

Antonio Gramsci, the well-known Italian thinker, made a distinction between traditional intellectuals and organic intellectuals. The power-establishment often surrounds itself with traditional intellectuals who align with and reinforce its stability and objectives. They can be likened to the mandarins of the Chinese imperial court. On the other hand, organic intellectuals play a critical and creative role. They envision a different and alternative order of things compared to the prevailing establishment.

Similarly, within the Church, there are traditional theologians who merely echo and amplify the pronouncements of authority. However, what is truly needed in the face of mounting crises are organic theologians whose creativity and engagement serve the Kingdom of God. These theologians adopt a critical approach to both the Church and the larger world. Drawing inspiration from scriptures, tradition, and contextual, cultural resources, they generate insights that can shape the future trajectory of the Church and society as a whole. Their creative vision offers a fresh perspective on the challenges and opportunities confronting humanity in these turbulent times.

Signs of Hope

The millennials, born between 1981 and 1996, constitute the largest demographic group worldwide, followed by Generation Z, born between the late 1990s and early 2000s. Considering the future of the world and society, it is crucial to understand the orientation and vision instilled in these generations. Thankfully, there are encouraging signs among these young people. While they are concerned about their own careers and future, many of them also demonstrate a strong sensitivity towards issues of justice, equality, climate change, women's dignity, and the rights of marginalized communities. They support the cause of women and actively resist racism and casteism while valuing inclusion, diversity, and transparency.

Growing up in a highly interconnected and technologically advanced world, the millennials and Generation Z possess immense potential to harness the power of digital platforms, technology, and social media to advocate for justice, equity, and the inclusion of marginalized groups. With proper guidance and orientation, these young generations can become the driving force behind significant social changes in contemporary times. Their awareness, knowledge, and passion can be channelled to create a positive impact on global issues and contribute to a more just and equitable world.

The presence of such values and activism among the younger generations is indeed heartening, especially in contrast to the decline in social consciousness and activism among the middle class, which we mentioned earlier. However, to ensure the continuity of the youth's idealism and their vision for a better world presents a significant challenge for religious figures, particularly educators and theologians. As we highlighted, these individuals must assume the role of public intellectuals, aiding the young generation in interpreting their experiences and connecting their faith with the aim of transforming the world and societies.

The budding social activism displayed by the youth bodes well for the future, but it also presents numerous challenges for our society. Nurturing and supporting this new generation in their pursuit of positive change requires collective effort and dedication from religious agents and all members of society. By providing guidance, encouragement, and a platform for their ideas and actions, we can help the young generation contribute significantly to shaping a more just and compassionate world.

The Structure of the Book and Major Themes

The book is structured into six distinct sections. A compelling opening section comprising three chapters delves into the theme of mission and evangelization. These initial chapters hold profound importance in comprehending and reimagining the interplay of faith in today's critical context. The bedrock of social dedication rests on what we understand by salvation and mission, and who are our partners in this endeavour.

The opening chapter takes a different perspective on other religions, viewing them not as targets of our mission, but rather as co-participants in the divine mission to save humanity and nature. Achieving this collective mission across all religions might be challenging in current conditions without integrating the interplay between faith and politics. The second chapter precisely underscores the significance of political engagement by all participants in catalyzing the transformation of the world and society. The third chapter of this segment centres on mission within the framework of South Asia. Commencing with a reflection on distinct theological underpinnings for mission, this chapter explores the intricacies of evangelization within the region. It tackles the necessity for an evangelization pedagogy that fosters transformation.

The subsequent section of the book explores the theme of liberation, intricately linked with the concept of evangelization. It begins with a chapter that tackles the raw truth of exclusion, a core element in the multifaceted aspects of poverty—both in its traditional and modern forms. The chapter that follows examines closely the issue of women's liberation in South Asia, accomplished through an intertextual analysis that aligns biblical narratives with one of the renowned literary creations by the poet Kalidasa, the celebrated "Śakuntalā."

In the final chapter of this section on liberation, the focus shifts to the phenomenon of cities in present-day South Asia and the hardships faced by the poor, Dalits, and marginalized populations as they strive for space and survival within urban settings. It becomes evident that a project centred on cities with a focus on the liberation of the poor differs greatly from an idealized "smart city" concept that primarily caters to the elites and the modern bourgeoisie. This chapter explores the urgent need to prioritize the well-being and liberation of marginalized urban dwellers to address the prevalent social inequalities and injustices.

The third section of the book, titled *"Democracy and Human Rights,"* comprises two chapters. For anyone devoted to social causes, the human rights regime serves as an essential and powerful reference point, acting as a defense for the rights of the poor and marginalized. The Universal Declaration of Human Rights, proclaimed in 1948, has evolved significantly. Originally centred on civil and political rights, it later expanded to encompass social and cultural rights. A third generation of human rights has emerged, focused increasingly on the rights of the excluded, migrants, refugees, individuals with physical and mental challenges, and the elderly, among others. As the human rights regime continues to progress, it becomes imperative for socially engaged Christians to embrace these developments in their faith-based initiatives.

One critical aspect that demands attention today is whether a rational or natural law foundation alone is sufficient to inspire and motivate the practical implementation of human rights. History and experience have shown that a mere rational and theoretical recognition of human rights does not automatically translate into their effective practice. Faith plays a crucial role in igniting the fire that drives the implementation of human rights. Without the fervour of faith, human rights might remain nothing more than ashes and embers, lacking the transformative power required to bring about real change in society. It is the fusion of faith and action that can empower individuals to uphold and promote human rights effectively.

In the following chapter within this third segment, a comprehensive assessment is conducted regarding democracy, democratic values and human rights in Indian Christianity, with a specific focus on Catholicism. This examination revolves around the application of democracy and human rights. The Indian Catholic Church grapples with two significant legacies that impact its approach to these issues. Firstly, there has been a historical negation of democracy in Catholic social thought during modern times. Secondly, the pervasive influence of casteism has seeped into the life and governance of the Indian Catholic Church. The adherence to democratic values is heavily influenced by how these two traditions have manifested in practicality. The chapter also delves into the role played by the participatory structures introduced by Vatican II and examines their effectiveness in addressing the aforementioned legacies. It further explores the claims of Oriental Churches to be synodal and participatory, particularly highlighting the absence of Dalit representation, especially at higher levels of decision-making within the Catholic Church. Democracy is presented in this chapter as a vocation and mission, prompting reflection on how the Indian Catholic Church engages in the realm of political democracy within the secular context. The chapter raises critical questions about the Church's involvement in shaping and promoting political democracy in India.

The fourth section of the book is titled *"Church Renewal,"* and it commences with a chapter centred around the currently much-discussed issue of synodality. The chapter contextualizes this topic with Indian experiences and argues the importance of canonical reforms in the Church for a lasting renewal and change. It contends that synodality must not remain a mere wish or exhortation; instead, it needs to be translated into the daily life, mission, and governance of the Church. The subsequent chapter in this section focuses on Pope Francis, who is regarded as a crusader of reform within the Catholic Church. The chapter examines the issues, difficulties, and critiques he encounters as he strives to transform the Church from a fortress into a compassionate "field-hospital," reaching out and serving everyone.

The reader will note that the spirit and concern of public theolog is present throughout the book. It is treated in second chapter speaking of the relationship between mission and politics. However, it is the fifth section that addresses more elaborately the topic of "*Public Theology*" in Asia, particularly South Asia, situating it within the broader development of Asian theology over the past few decades. In the first chapter of this segment, public theology is presented as the way forward for the future of theology in the Asian continent. The following chapter explores Pope Francis' "*Fratelli Tutti*" as an exemplar for developing a subaltern public theology.

Given the significant impact of the Covid-19 pandemic on the global world, the seventh and final section of the book focuses on "Post-Pandemic Theology." It starts with a critical examination of the hidden and implicit aspects of the pandemic experience and analyzes the various responses to it. The final chapter of the book reflects on the implications of the Covid-19 experience for theology and points out the dangers present in the current social, political, economic, cultural, and technological directions. It calls for innovative social involvement from Christian believers and emphasizes the importance of envisioning alternatives to the prevailing paradigms in each of these fields. This section prompts readers to reflect on the challenges and opportunities for theological engagement in a post-pandemic world.

MISSION

Chapter 1

THE MISSION OF ALL RELIGIONS FOR HUMANKIND AND NATURE

The world is witnessing a winter of democracy and democratic institutions. The dream of a democratic world seems to be on the wane in a world overshadowed by authoritarianism, religious nationalism and populism. The growing fear, feeling of threat, and insecurity at all levels – political, social, economic, and cultural – have stunted the imagination in quest of alternatives and have led people to acquiesce themselves to the prevailing situation.

The growing social and economic inequality, discrimination, and political marginalization of a large number of people have caused a gross imbalance in inter-human relationships. No wonder our world is plagued by a growing culture of violence. Nations arm themselves more than ever, and simmering and open conflicts forebode a nuclear Armageddon. The market economy fosters these developments by creating a mindset of cut-throat competition. The end result is the growing neglect of the poor and the increasing of their suffering. Regardless of the type of development, it is the poor who bear the brunt of its consequences. An African proverb captures this plain truth: "Elephants fight; the grass is trampled upon; elephants make love; the grass is trampled upon."

There is another scenario we need to take into serious account. The wanton depletion and destruction of nature and the pervasive toxic pollution of air, water, and food have inflicted a heavy toll on life on earth. The alarming impact of drastic climate change and global warming compounds this dire situation. Furthermore, certain technologies, such as advanced information and communication technology, biotechnology, robotics, artificial intelligence, and quantum technology, possess the potential to become formidable entities akin to Frankenstein monsters.

Today the crisis is such that we cannot take for granted the survival and future of us as a human species. Given this grievous situation, it is pertinent to inquire whether other religions, apart from Christianity have a role to play in responding to the pressing challenges facing humanity and nature. Yet, is the mission exclusive to Christianity, or can we envision a shared mission among all religions during this profound crisis? In this chapter, we will explore these questions and delve into the deeper meaning and implications of the mission of all religions, with Christianity serving as a collaborative partner. Moreover, understanding the concept of a shared mission among religions prompts us to critically examine the historical understanding and practice of Christian mission and evangelization. Ultimately, it compels us to raise thought-provoking questions about the prevailing theology of mission and theology of religions.

Tracking the Roots of the Crisis

The crisis that envelops humankind and nature has multiple and interlocking aspects and dimensions. The source of destruction is not only from without but also from within. In nature, human beings are aggressive and fight with each other like wolves - *homo homini lupus* - so said Thomas Hobbes. Violence against each other could have caused the extermination of humanity. However, humankind found a way of survival by organizing themselves into societies with rights and duties. People surrendered part of their freedom to a sovereign authority, which protected them and their property. Without a sovereign authority, there would be chaos and an aggressive situation of nature. The hypothetical "Social Contract" - initially proposed by Thomas Hobbes, John Locke and Jean-Jacques Rousseau[1] is a way out from the primitive state of nature, characterized by selfishness and fear, to that of a civilized human condition. The social contract, especially as proposed by Hobbes, rested on the assumption that people are selfish and always seek their interests. Consequently, they are naturally drawn to what corresponds to their desires and shun from what is not palatable to them.[2] In this dynamic, people are guided by their reason to pursue their advantages and maximise them. The theory of contract became the central organizing principle of human societies and the cornerstone of later political liberalism and market economy.

However, we know that not all human relationships can be subsumed under contract, nor contracts be effective in most critical times. We have realized the limits of contractual thinking more than ever before. For example, how does a social contract work with the threat of nuclear war? Unlike in other conventional wars where despite the loss of precious human lives, re-arrangement of relationships are possible, in a nuclear war, all of humankind is in danger of being obliterated from the earth. The outbreak of Covid-19, which caught like wildfire the entire globe across nations and borders brought to our awareness how humankind could come in no time to the brink of colossal unforeseen disasters.[3] Further, some technologies being developed today can overtake humankind and kill its creator. Such critical predicaments go beyond the parameters of societal life shaped by contractual thinking. Despite unprecedented technological progress and the ability to predict future developments, our world needs to be more secure and balanced to sustain itself and move forward.

Another source of crisis for humanity is the negative consequences of advanced capitalism and free-market - something Pope Francis never ceases to denounce. He has been very forthright in his *Evangelii Gaudium* and *Fratelli Tutti*. The consequences of advanced capitalism and free-market are visible in every part of the world, causing unprecedented wealth on the one hand and income inequality, on the other. The French economist Thomas Piketty in his massive volume titled "*Capital in the Twenty-first Century*" draws our attention to how the concentration of wealth and its unequal distribution produce social unrest and economic imbalance and threaten democratic order and human co-existence.[4]

The disaffection with the market economy seems widespread in the Global North and the South. The exponential growth of economic inequality has left millions of people in disarray, with their dreams trampled upon and their aspirations shattered. Oxfam's 2018 report stated that 82% of the wealth created in the world the previous year had gone to 1% of the human population. The bottom 50% received nothing.[5] When all doors are shut, and a sense of nowhere to go pervades, "saviours" emerge for the folk. Gifted speakers and manipulators of symbols and media systems appear on the scene to exploit popular sentiments of fear and disempowerment and present themselves as alternatives to the prevailing situation. Populism has become the order of the day, seriously imperilling democracy and democratic institutions and sidelining justice and equality issues. Interestingly, in the case of Trump's populism, one could identify a pattern of certain religious sects with their paranoia, self-delusion and occult cult.

No religion can be insensitive to these developments, which derail the human community from the immense challenges of inequality embedded in the economic, social, cultural and political structures of our present times.[6] Hence, the religion of the future must have its ears on the margins to hear the cry of the poor and its hands on the ground to feel the pulse of nature. The quality of religion will be tested by its commitment to shaping a different world of justice and peace and its engagement to critically challenge any economic system and social mores that corrode human solidarity and togetherness. Religions are called upon to play a role of integration and wholeness amid forces of fragmentation - despite globalization - and assist in the birth of a renewed humanity dancing to the rhythm of nature.

From the larger perspective of the universe, humans are reduced to consuming animals that rely on money and the market for anything to happen. Every human relationship is viewed from the viewpoint of the market, and the entire gamut of social life and interactions is judged by market reasoning and logic. There is nothing today that money cannot buy – acquiring citizenship, jumping queues, priority in boarding planes, priority appointment with doctors (concierge doctors), right to emit carbon, recruiting mercenaries for war, buying kidneys, and getting surrogacy to bear children. However, not all human problems can be solved by money, nor can money buy everything.[7] It is an experience of daily life which humanity tends to forget.

The future religion will remind humankind of values beyond commodity and market relations and point to another world of love, compassion, fraternity, friendship, solidarity, and cooperation. It will nurture necessary ethical impulses for the flourishing of humans and nature. The forgetfulness of humans about the essentials will require a perpetual reminder in the form of religions which will point to the best that is forgotten and hidden. There is much to do for religions in terms of a joint mission.

Theological and Anthropological Roots of Friendship and Fraternity

According to Christian belief – which is also shared by many other religious traditions, including the indigenous ones - human beings have the same origin (all of them were created in God's image), and they are brothers, sisters, friends, and partners embarked on a journey of common destination. This basic theological principle laid down in *Nostra Aetate* is deepened further in *Fratelli Tutti* by drawing the consequences of this belief for the life of humankind. As friends, brothers, and sisters, there needs to prevail in human societies equality in dignity and equity in sharing the common mother earth's resources. The conviction of primordial bondedness is the dynamic force for cooperation to create a world of justice and peace in harmony with nature. The indigenous religious traditions, with their integral cosmic vision and consciousness of interdependence, take us deeper into the cord that binds the entire creation.

> The most important aspect of indigenous cosmic visions is the conception of creation as a living process, resulting in a living universe in which a kinship exists between all things. Thus, the Creators are our family, our Grandparents or Parents, and all of their creations are children who, of necessity, are also our relations.[8]

We cannot but be struck by the convergence of Christianity with Islam and indigenous traditions in the belief of a common origin of the entire humankind when we read in Qu'ran:

> O humanity! Indeed, We created you from a male and a female and made you into peoples and tribes so that you may get to know one another. Surely the most noble of you in the sight of Allah is the most righteous among you. Allah is truly All-Knowing, All-Aware.[9]

Friendship and fraternity are noble human realities that go beyond utilitarian calculus and the spirit of consumerism. They take root when we consider other persons as a value in themselves and when our friendship and fraternity are based on truth, goodness, and beauty the others embody. We enjoy such a genuine friendship and fraternity for what it is and not consider what benefits others could bring to us. There is a kind of sacredness to every genuine friendship. Pope Francis seems to apply this principle in inter-religious relationships. We need to look at other religions in what they are in themselves, not what they are in contrast or comparison to one's own religion about which one could feel a sense of superiority. This is what Pope Francis calls "gratuitousness".

> There is always the factor of *gratuitousness*: the ability to do some things simply because they are good in themselves, without concern for personal gain or recompense. Gratuitousness makes it possible for us to welcome the stranger, even though this brings us no immediate tangible benefit… Life without fraternal gratuitousness becomes a form of frenetic commerce, in which we constantly weigh up what we give and what we get back in return[10]

In the Hindu tradition, this is known as *nishkâma karma* (selfless actions without attachment to fruits) and it is well-brought out in the sacred book of *Bhagavad Gita*. The spirit of gratuitousness should animate cooperation among believers of different religions for the common good, the welfare of society, the entire world and creation. Gratuitousness provides interreligious cooperation with a new quality and is not to be likened to cooperation from a modern organizational perspective. Nor can interreligious friendship and dialogue be analogized to modern-day networking and social media. The pope distinguishes such forms of communication from a dialogue based on genuine friendship and appreciation of the other in their otherness. "Dialogue is often confused with something quite different: the feverish exchange of opinions on social networks, frequently based on media information that is not always reliable. These exchanges are merely parallel monologues."[11]

Earth and the Eco-Mission of Religions

For a long time, humankind has been the chief point of reference in forging relationship among religions and the object of common mission. Today, we realize that something more fundamental brings together all religions in common engagement. It is the sharing of a common home – the earth. It is a fact that the religions have been ambiguous vis-à-vis ecological issues. While they treasure deep insights and a positive outlook in their scriptures and traditions, they have also been one of the chief sources of neglect of nature and the earth. Earth and nature need to be viewed from the perspective of justice – Eco-justice.[12]

Though the Stockholm Conference on Environment and Development took place way back in 1972, it took some years for religions to warm up to this important agenda. However, there have been some initial interest on the issue on the part of WCC and many Protestant Churches. Under the influence of the Lutheran theologian Joseph Sittler, WCC founded in 1963 a Faith-Man-Nature group. Thanks to the reflections of many scholars and experiences of ecological movements, WCC came to relate the issue of justice and peace with the integrity of creation.[13] This was set as a priority by the Sixth Assembly of WCC at Vancouver in 1983 and subsequently taken up by the Central Committee, which initiated in 1985 the conciliar process of Justice, Peace and Integrity of Creation (JPIC). Finally, in 1990, a world convocation on the theme brought out the urgency of the ecological issue as reflected in its programmatic document, *"Now is the Time."*

It took more time for the Catholic Church to wake up to environmental issues. Though there are sporadic references in the social teachings relating to nature and ecology, one had to wait until *Laudato Si* of Pope Francis for a very determined stand on the issues affecting nature and the sustainability of the earth and their importance for the flourishing of all life, including the wellbeing of humanity.[14]

Overall, the past couple of decades have been characterized by the various religious traditions digging deep into their tradition and bringing out constructive insights into nature and humankind's relationship to it. This retrieval has been followed by a theological reconfiguration of issues of nature, earth, and environment, leading to crafting an eco-theology.[15] It is not a branch of theology, but, like the theology of liberation, it is a vision, approach and method to mould and practice theology. Eco-theology needs to be developed ecumenically and inter-religiously.

Ecology is a common agenda that all Christian denominations and religions must pursue jointly by pooling together the riches from different religious traditions and fashioning together proposals and programmes that will inspire believers across the religions for an unswerving commitment to the well-being of nature and the earth. It is both an ecumenical and interreligious agenda. As Evelyn Tucker and John Grim observe,

> Although the world's religions have been slow to respond to our current environmental crises, their moral authority and their institutional power may help effect a change in attitudes, practices, and public policies. As key repositories of enduring civilizational values and indispensable motivators in moral transformation, religions have an important role in projecting persuasive visions of a more sustainable future.[16]

Ecology is an area which, unlike many doctrinal issues, could bring together believers of various Churches and religious traditions to face the burning issue of the future of nature and the earth. Hinduism, Buddhism, Islam and other religious traditions have their own unique heritage on the way the interrelationship of humans with the earth, nature, and universe is conceived and practiced.[17] That tells about the richness an inter-religious dialogue and exchange on ecology could bring about.

A shared commitment of religion for the cause of the earth would involve interaction and exchange with many other actors. For example, a sustained dialogue between science and technology needs to be pursued by religions. This is a need of the hour. Besides joint initiatives, religions need to feel a common ethical mandate to contribute to transforming attitudes and values conducive to the flourishing of nature and human life. All this should help, in its turn, to make environmentalism an integral part of the mission of every religion. Even more inter-religious dialogue in this field should help reconsider traditional worldviews, theologies, ethics, wisdom, and spiritualities and reframe them in the light of environmentalism. Religions have great potential to transform humankind's attitude towards nature, and this is a unique contribution we could expect from religions that have decided on an eco-mission.

In particular, the tribal and indigenous religious traditions would be crucial dialogue partners in the shared mission of religions for environmentalism. In fact, the religiosity of these traditions have been very much bound with the earth and nature. Moreover, the cosmology of the tribal and indigenous peoples and the worldview embedded in the culture and day-to-day life starkly contrasts with the prevailing ones.[18] Unfortunately, the tribal and indigenous religious traditions have been for a long period neglected and denigrated as "animism." However, thanks to the resistance of the indigenous people to inroads into their lifeworld, culture, and knowledge system in the name of modernity and development, we still have the benefit of the richness of the local religious traditions.

> The indigenous peoples are among the last cultural groups to teach techniques of dreams and visions and ways to activate an ecological imagination…Yes, studies of indigenous traditions do remind us of alternative visions and possibilities that exist among people who have imagined themselves more intimately into their worlds. Many within mainstream societies feel the allure of this cosmological act of dreaming.[19]

Theological Foundation for Common Mission with Other Religions

Don't the narrations of the fall in the account of Genesis (Gen 3:1-24), the depiction of the times of Noah (Gen 6:11-13), and the construction of the Tower of Babel (Gen 11:3ff.) – all these refer to the shared experience of humankind across nations and races? The question is not what happens to a particular religion but what it has to contribute to the world's salvation and humanity's future. Here the term 'salvation', and its holistic root word *salus* mean good health, wellbeing. This cannot happen without setting right the material basis of life. Religions that care for these material bases of life and their security are doing their mission for the salvation of the world. This cannot be done simply by increasing charity and developmental work. It needs to be done through political processes. In *Fratelli Tutti*, Pope Francis makes us understand it by a simple but revealing analogy. One can help an older person cross the river – this is something we characterize as a work of service, development, and welfare. However, it takes "political love" to have a bridge over the river which serves the common good.[20] It shows the need for religions to set their contribution to salvation in the context of politics and economy.

"The earth is the Lord's and all that is in it" (Ps. 24:1); so, do all religions belong to humankind, under divine dispensation. No religion can claim full ownership of its beliefs and practices. After all, ownership in the Christian tradition is justified only when it is for *autarkia* and *koinonia* (self-governance and communion).[21] Therefore, belonging to a religion does not close the doors; instead, it acquires meaning only as a means for communion.

As for understanding religions, precisely because they and their scriptures belong to humankind, they are open to a broad spectrum of interpretations. For example, the medieval Indian hermeneutical tradition developed by Anandavardhana and Abhinavagupta compared texts to a woman and said that because a father has generated a daughter need not mean that he is also the best judge of her beauty; the best judge could be her admirer, lover or husband.[22] The modern hermeneutical tradition of autonomy of texts could be profitably applied to religious traditions whose interpretation need not necessarily be confined to the group of believers but is open-ended. This is what comparative theology is trying to do.[23]

In the light of our above analysis and reflections, we could state that all religions belong to humankind as a whole and *in a primary sense*. In contrast, a particular religion belongs to the limited community of its believers in a *secondary and derivative sense*. This is similar to what has been said by the Christian tradition on the universal destiny of earthly goods that takes precedence over private property rights. In the latter case, an appeal has been made to the Biblical injunctions for the year of jubilee, according to which hereditary properties are to be restored to all (Lev. 25: 8-55). Several Fathers of the Church, like Basil, Ambrose, Chrysostom, were critical of the rich who amassed wealth at the expense of the poor. In this context, they reminded the rich that the goods of creation are the gifts of God to be shared among God's children equitably. Drawing on the scriptures and the patristic tradition, Catholic social teaching has underlined the social mortgage on private property, which cannot be claimed as an absolute right. This tradition is continued in *Gaudium et Spes,* which spoke about the universal destination of earthly goods (GS no. 69), and the same is to be found in the recent encyclicals of Pope Francis, *Laudato Si* and *Fratelli Tutti.*

Let us embrace this principle and apply it to religions and their missions: Every religion should recognize and acknowledge that its message and teachings are intended for the entire human race. It is crucial for religions to adopt a universal perspective and strive to reach out to all people, irrespective of their background or beliefs.

By doing so, religions can contribute to the well-being and spiritual fulfillment of all individuals.

As a result of this principle, every human being could draw upon the collective wisdom and cultural heritage of humanity in their personal quest for a meaningful life and spiritual growth. People should be encouraged to explore and benefit from the diverse traditions, practices, and insights that have emerged throughout human history since these enhance their own journey of self-discovery and spiritual enrichment.

By embracing these ideas, religions can foster a sense of unity and inclusivity among humanity. They can play a significant role in promoting mutual understanding, respect, and the realization of our shared values and aspirations. Ultimately, this approach encourages individuals to seek wisdom and inspiration from various sources, allowing for a richer and more holistic exploration of the human experience.

Are there other reasons to speak of the mission of all religions? The divine mystery, which envelops all religions, is not the possession of any particular religion. It belongs to the entire human family, which is enveloped by that mystery. Obviously, no religion can claim to exhaust that mystery, much less to possess it. It would be a sin against humankind to claim exclusively for oneself what, in reality, belongs to all.

Moreover, being a believer entails being a witness. Thus, belonging to a religious community does not grant exclusive ownership of that particular religion. Rather, belief is a testament to the personal experience of the divine mystery. As witnesses, believers acknowledge that their encounters with the mystery extend beyond themselves and their religious group, encompassing a broader realm of human experience.

By recognizing these truths, we embrace a perspective that honours the inherent interconnectedness of all religions and the shared spiritual journey of humanity. It encourages us to move beyond the confines of religious boundaries and engage with the profound mystery that unites us all. Through this inclusive approach we can foster greater understanding, harmony, and collective growth as we navigate the depths of the divine together.

Furthermore, the various experiences of religions – creeds, rituals, laws etc., *are not an end in themselves but only a means*. Even scripture is only a means, according to Saint Augustine, who distinguishes between *use* and *enjoyment* (*uti et frui*) – the latter identified with the experience of God.[24] Religion is a penultimate reality and not the ultimate one. It is a means for something greater – and this 'greater' is the mystery surrounding us all. For the mystery unites all religions and confers meaning and sustenance to them. The experience and enjoyment of the ultimate mystery to which the whole human family is called are nourished with a wide variety of spiritual foods offered by the religions, and no one has full control of the spiritual metabolism of the experience and enjoyment the mystery causes.

Finally, a powerful argument for why religions are called to enter into a joint mission is given through a re-conception of what the plurality of religions ultimately signifies. This has come out very forcefully in the document on Human Fraternity from Pope Francis and the Great Imam of Al-Azhar. It answers the question of why there are so many religions. The answer is that they are not merely human inventions but are willed by God. "The pluralism and the diversity of religions, colour, sex, race and language are willed by God in His wisdom, through which He created human beings."[25] This is a radical statement, at least, as for as the Catholic Church is concerned. If the religions in their plurality come from God, it is clear that they also have a joint mission, a mission from God. The Church needs to rise to this truth and draw the conclusion for its theology of religions and mission theology.

The Religion of the Future

Religion continues to retain its place as a source of moral knowledge and as a system which, though not specialized, could nevertheless respond to questions of momentous significance for humanity – questions that are not raised in other societal systems or remain unanswered. One such momentous question is humanity's destiny, future, survival, and unity. This issue needs to be addressed by all religions.

There are heated debates among religions on revelation, absoluteness of truth, moral imperatives, universality, and other such issues. There is, however, little discussion on the *mission* of all religions. The converging point of the mission of various religions should be the future shape of the human community and the flourishing of creation. This recognition of the mission of other religions and the awareness of being on a common journey towards a shared future can help build up the community of humans as one single family. Respect for other religions necessarily includes respect for the *mission* to which people of particular religious groups feel called, especially when this mission has something to contribute to the unity of the human family and well-being.

In the present day, it is crucial to shift our focus away from contemplating *the future of religion* and instead direct our attention towards the *religion of the future*. When we discuss the future of religion, we inadvertently embrace the notion that religion is under threat, thereby necessitating the defence and preservation of its doctrines and moral principles. This was exemplified by Friedrich Schleiermacher in the nineteenth century in his work "*On Religion: Speeches to Its Cultured Despisers*" (1799).

Conversely, the discourse on the future of religion will revolve around the sustenance and prosperity of humanity and the natural world. Consequently, religions will perceive their beliefs, structures, values, morals, laws, practices, and worship as aligned with these objectives. Religions will no longer concern themselves with their own survival as they will view their purpose as a divine call to serve humanity and safeguard the well-being of the environment.

Facing Challenges

Hitherto, religions have served as bricks and mortar to build up identities; hence they (religions) became sources of conflict.[26] Warmed-up versions of nationalism and populism, on their part, invoke religion and religious symbols for political ends and for creating a social and political order that excludes peoples and communities. We know from history that the ideology of nationalism, like religion, pits nations one against the other, killing millions, as happened in the two World Wars. Today numerous armed conflicts are waged by sub-nationalities in different parts of the world against centralizing and oppressive state powers. State violence gets legitimized by invoking the ideology of nationalism. Warmongering and feigned national security take precedence over the people's real issues and their security vis-à-vis the fundamental needs of life. I am appalled at the sight of countries parading their most lethal weapons on national days or republic days. Through these senseless and mad weapons exhibitions, a nation shows how effectively it can kill others, and this spectacle is applauded and celebrated by millions in the name of nationalism. A culture of death becomes a showpiece and a badge of honour.

The perils inherent in the ideology of nationalism were sensed with much prescience by two great thinkers – one from the Global North and the other from the South. The one from the North was Immanuel Kant, who in his work *"Perpetual Peace,"* proposed an arrangement for the life of humanity that goes beyond the division of nations.[27] It was a vision like that of the astronauts who from space can see just one earth and not identify the borders of nations that are zealously but senselessly guarded at the cost of many human lives. The other thinker, from the South, was Rabindranath Tagore, who was very universalistic in his outlook. Even before the outbreak of World War I, in his lectures delivered in the United States and Japan, he warned about the danger of nationalism. He stated that the reality of humans is above the imagined nation.[28] If Kant maintained that "all politics must bend its knees before right [morality],"[29] Tagore taught us that human has primacy over the nation. The contributions of these thinkers from the North and the South are fundamental lessons for today. What they said is equally applicable to religion.

Religion, like nationalism – often intertwined - must be tamed and cured of its instinct for violence. It will have to shed many dead habits and shared prejudices which pass for tradition. What nationalism is to a country, tradition is to religion. However, the deadwood of tradition is so thick, and it has so covered religion that the latter is numbed and unable to sense humanity's burning issues. As a result, it remains narcissistic, preoccupied all the time with itself. It is like nationalism clouding the mind and heart and instilling aggression.

Like the instinct for violence, religions have an innate proclivity to taboos. Taboos about beliefs and rituals are things that defy reason. They are believed and performed with a magical consciousness. The religion of the future will critically interrogate its own belief system, rituals, and practices on what they could really signify for the well-being of humankind and nature. I am not advocating the abolition of all existing religions, instead suggesting that they should die to many things to rise up as future religions with a different focus and orientation. Symbols, worship and rituals of a future religion will not serve only its adherents and followers. However, they will be open-ended to the larger goal of the well-being of the entire human family. In other words, I am advocating that every religion becomes cosmopolitan in its vision, spirit, beliefs, rituals, worship, etc.[30]

The Poor - Converging Point of Religions

There was a time when the approach to religious diversity meant to look for doctrinal commonalities. The attempt was to discover what we all believe in common, regardless of our particular belief system. For example, one thought that theocentrism, namely belief in God in general without naming any deity, would bring together all believers. However, this approach may not take interreligious dialogue far as history and experience amply attest. Therefore, Pope Francis draws our attention to the common issues and questions humanity is grappling with today. This, for him, should be a point of religious convergence which should bring the believers together.

Further, there are some basic values and common convictions which should serve as a point of unity among religions. The pope names some of these: "religious convictions about the sacred meaning of human life permit us to recognize the fundamental values of our common humanity, values in the name of which we can and must cooperate, build and dialogue, pardon, and grow."[31]

As we noted, for Pope Francis, the shared mission of all religions should flow from the true feeling of fraternity and friendship. Therefore, the cooperation among religions for a joint mission should be different from how organizations and institutions work jointly under managerial principles. The common mission of all religions, instead, has deeper roots of fraternity and friendship.

Today a shared mission of all religions is to foster a hospitable world where no one feels like a stranger, abandoned or not cared for. It is easy to be hospitable when there is mutuality. The one who receives hospitality returns it. This seems so natural and easy that it presents no real challenge. Instead, the real challenge is in offering hospitality to those who cannot return it. Today, they are strangers, migrants, the displaced, refugees, abandoned children, women victims of human trafficking, uncared-for aged people, physically and mentally challenged, and all those who find themselves at the margins of society. This kind of "asymmetrical hospitality" qualifies to be called messianic. The last judgment (Mt 25) takes place based on whether one practised hospitality and extended a welcome to those hungry, naked, homeless, or in prison.[32] This kind of practice would find echo in many religious traditions.

By regarding the marginalized and the vulnerable as friends, brothers, sisters, and guests, we affirm their inherent dignity and recognize their unique identities. Initiatives taken jointly by the various religious groups could contribute to a new culture of love and compassion in our societies. This will be a joint counter-cultural move by faith-motivated religious groups and agents vis-à-vis the prevailing ethos of utilitarianism and contract-based approach to inter-human relationships.

We also need to critically interrogate whether social media, which has become a new platform for fostering friendship and sharing one's life and even intimate moments, could also become a means to nurture "asymmetrical" friendship and hospitality aimed at those who are at the fringes of a society and are left out of the network of communication. Especially in the case of migrant workers, and refugees, hospitality should not give room to a creditor-debtor kind of relationship between the host and the guest. It should not be a host-centred relationship but a guest-centred one.[33] In the context of the increasing phenomenon of migrant labourers from very low-income families and marginalized groups, the relationship is characterized by deep prejudice, insult, and often even violence against them.

Could religions come together to respond to the plight of the migrant workers, whose helpless condition we witnessed during the pandemic, and make them feel at home in the places of their work and stay?

Friendship and Hospitality at Places of Worship

The interreligious journey of Pope Francis has taken him to visit places of worship of brothers and sisters of other faiths. For example, he visited a Buddhist temple in Sri Lanka and synagogues, mosques, elsewhere. What the pope has done is a beautiful example of inviting the Christians to visit the places of worship of our neighbours reverently and with a sense of sacredness. Is there anything preventing Christians from visiting with a sense of the sacred – not as tourists – temples, pagodas, mosques, and gurudwaras? Visits to the places of worship of our neighbours are something to be positively promoted. It will also be a wonderful occasion to get to know the faith of our neighbours from within. It is pretty strange that Christians rejoice that Hindus and Muslims visit Vailankanni and other Christian shrines while silent about why they do not do the same vis-à-vis friends of other religious traditions.

During his stay in Sri Lanka, Pope Francis' visit to the Buddhist temple was not planned ahead, following the canons of diplomacy and protocol, but something that happened spontaneously. The head of a Buddhist temple, who was there to receive the pope at the airport, invited him to his temple. So, without further ado, the pope warmly responded to the invitation of a friend and made adjustments to his programme to visit the Buddhist temple. "He called me, so I went." This is how Pope tells so cutely why he visited the Buddhist temple.[34]

It is interesting how the Asian experience of a visit to a Marian shrine in Madhu in Sri Lanka triggered the pope's thoughts and feelings about the Asian way of interreligious relationships. He witnessed first-hand how in a Christian Church – the Marian shrine of Madhu - Hindus, Buddhists and Muslims were on pilgrimage. While this is quite common in Asia, this was a new experience for the pope, who was very much struck and touched by this inter-religious meeting of people of different faiths. The pope asked himself, if these people come to our Churches to pray, why should I not go to their sacred place? This he gives as a further reason for visiting the Buddhist temple.

Francis' approach to interreligious friendship and fraternity goes beyond comparing and contrasting verbal formulation of doctrines. In the Buddhist and Hindu traditions, this is considered *"upaya"* or simply the skilful 'means' deployed, which is not the same thing as seeing the truth or walking on the path of truth, which is *prajna* or wisdom. Francis is not caught in the prison of doctrinal formulations and their orthodoxy, which builds walls rather than bridges. It insulates the Church and prevents it from reaching out to other religious traditions.

One of the boldest pronouncements of Francis goes against established prejudices in the western world. He explicitly challenges the notion that Islam is inseparable from violence and, by implication, from terrorism. Francis uses a refined understanding of Islam and the contemporary socio-political context to address Islamic brethren, reflected in a Vatican News editorial that draws a common thread across his three papal speeches in Baku, Cairo, and Ur.[35]

Pope Francis' contribution of a new dimension to interreligious dialogue derives from his ecclesiology. It is not a church *incurvate in se* – bent on itself. On the contrary, right from the beginning of his pontificate, Pope Francis has projected a centrifugal Church, which is right in the midst of the world, reaching out to the conditions of the society, aspirations, and dreams of the people.[36] The kind of inter-religious dialogue he promotes precisely chimes with his ecclesiological orientation directed to the world and its pastoral situation, very much in the spirit of *Gaudium et Spes*.

In his words and deeds, Pope Francis blends interreligious dialogue with the pastoral practice oriented to the world. To see through the lens of Vatican II, Francis bridges so beautifully *Nostra Aetate* and *Gaudium et Spes*. From a theological point of view, what he does is indeed a public theology. The realization of his vision of universal fraternity entails that religious resources for peace and harmony be brought to bear upon the struggles and conflicts in the world and society. In other words, the pope sees interreligious relationships embedded in the movement and journey towards a world of universal fraternity.

In 2018, when the Vatican's Pontifical Council for Interreligious Dialogue organized a conference on the theme, "Dharma and Logos – Dialogue and Cooperation in a Complex Age," Francis met representatives of Dharmic religions (Buddhism, Hinduism, Jainism, Sikhism). He thanked God that "religious leaders actively foster a culture of encounter by offering examples of fruitful dialogue and by working together effectively in the service of life, human dignity and the care of creation."[37]

Concluding Reflections

In Tamil, the word for brother or sister (*sakotharan/sakothari*) means those from the same womb; so, is the Greek etymology for this word (*a-delphos/adelphe*; in Sanskrit *sa-garba*). The bondedness originating from the same womb goes beyond religious beliefs. It is a primordial reality regardless of one's beliefs and convictions. In his earlier encyclical, "*Laudato Si'*, Pope Francis showed how humans form, along with all other species, the flora and fauna, one family of mother earth. *Fratelli Tutti* deepens this bondedness among humans by focusing on fraternity and friendship.

Religions do not remove human beings' primordial bondedness and shared destiny. However, the crisis humankind faces today has made us all aware of the need to pursue a joint mission by all believers. It is the mission of salvation, namely, making everything whole, integral, and sane. It is a call to a mission to re-establish broken relationships and disharmony within the human community and the relationship of humans with nature. This is done by religions becoming messengers of peace. Peace is another word for salvation today, and that is a joint mission in which all religions are to come together.

The shared mission of all religions also raises critical questions regarding the practice of mission by Christians hitherto and the many theological assumptions behind it. The traditional theology of mission was based on an antithesis between the Christian faith and other religions. When the starting point is fraternity, friendship, hospitality, and cooperation with other religions for a joint mission, it would mean a sea change also for the traditional theology of religions. In sum, there needs to take place today a radical revision of the traditional theology of mission. What I have shared in this chapter are but preliminaries towards such a larger project.

The approach to interreligious dialogue through friendship and fraternity is one which values dialogue in itself and does not view it as a means for evangelization. This is a point that Asian Bishops and theologians have sought to bring out for several decades amidst stiff opposition. *Fratelli Tutti* is a confirmation of the Asian efforts.

As far back as 1987, Asian Bishops and theologians made this point very clear when they said,

> We affirm that dialogue and mission have their own integrity and freedom. They are distinct but not unrelated. Dialogue is not a tool or instrument for mission and evangelization, but it does influence the way the Church perceives and practices mission in a pluralist world…Dialogue offers opportunities for Christian witness…[38]

This needs to be said against some unfortunate developments of the past. There has been suspicion of Asian theology and harassment of Asian theologians who have been trying to develop a mission theology and theology of religions that reflect Asian experience and resources. One would recall here, for example, the contributions of Michael Amaladoss and Jacques Dupuis. They taught in India for several decades, learning simultaneously from the experience of dialogue with peoples of other religions, which they tried to crystallize and articulate in their theologies. Sad and most unfortunate is the fact that the Congregation for the Doctrine of the Faith, under Cardinal Joseph Ratzinger as its Prefect, went to the extent of imposing such a severe punishment as excommunication on an Asian theologian, Tissa Balasuriya and that too at the fag end of the twentieth century for alleged doctrinal errors hardly anyone took note of at that time, and probably no one remembers today![39] I recall these facts to underline the exceptional significance of *Fratelli Tutti*, which can take Asian Christians to new frontiers of encounter with peoples of other faiths and further encourage them to work jointly with brothers and sisters of other faiths for a peaceful and harmonious world and a renewed earth.

NOTES

1   Thomas Hobbes' theory of social contract appeared for the first time in his work *Leviathan* (1651), and it was the period of civil war in Britain.

2   We must, however, point out that in the view of John Locke, nature is not a situation of violence and aggression but rather a situation of peace and, indeed, a state of liberty in as much as each one could pursue their interests unhindered.

3   Cf. Felix Wilfred, ed., "Handle with Care: Fragile Humans," *Jeevadhara* LI, no.301 (January 2021).

4   Cf. Thomas Piketty, *Capital in the Twenty-First Century* (Hoboken, NJ: Wiley, 2014).

5   https://www.oxfam.org/en/press-releases/richest-1-percent-bagged-82-percent-wealth-created-last-year-poorest-half-humanity [accessed on 4 September 2023].

6   Cf. Felix Wilfred, "Asian Perspectives on Global Economic Inequality," in Mari-Anna Auvinen-Pöntinen and Jonas Adelin Jørgensen, eds., *Mission and Money. Christian Mission in the Context of Global Inequalities* (Leiden-Boston: Brill, 2016), 40–62.

7   Cf. Michael Sandel, *What Money Can't Buy. The Moral Limits of Market* (London: Penguin Books, 2012).

8   Jack D. Forbes, "Indigenous Americans: Spirituality and Ecos," *Daedalus* 130, no. 4 (Fall, 2001): 283–300, at 283.

9   *Quran 49:13.*

10   *Fratelli Tutti* 139 & 140.

11   Cf. *Fratelli Tutti* 200.

12   Cf. Abraham, K.C., *Eco Justice: a New Agenda for Church's Mission* (Bombay: BUILD, 1993).

13   Cf. D. Preman Niles, "Justice, Peace and The Integrity of Creation," in *Dictionary of Ecumenical Movements,* edited by Nicholas Lossky (Geneva: WCC Publications, 2002), 630; See also Jerome Edgar Bailey, "Poverty, Wealth and Ecology": A Critical Analysis of a "World Council of Churches Project (2006-2013)," (A thesis submitted in fulfilment of the requirements for the degree of Magister in Theology, University of the Western Cape 2020); David Hallman, "The WCC Climate Change Programme: History, lessons and challenges," in *Climate Change*, edited by Martin Robra (Geneva: WCC Publications, 2005).

14   I have critically commented upon this papal encyclical. See Felix Wilfred, "New Impetus for Integral Ecology. Theological Significance of *Laudato Si,*" in *Theology for an Inclusive World* (Delhi: ISPCK, 2019), Chapter 8: 153–173.

15   The following works are some examples of efforts to deepen the relationship between religion and ecology: Rosemary Radford Ruether and Dieter Hessel, *Christianity and Ecology: Seeking the Wellbeing of Earth and Humans*

(Cambridge, MA: Harvard University Press, 2000); Roger Gottlieb, ed., *The Oxford Handbook of Religion and Ecology* (New York: Oxford University Press, 2006); Bron Taylor, ed., *The Encyclopedia of Religion and Nature* (London: Continuum, 2006); Laurel Kearns and Catherine Keller, *Ecospirit: Religions and Philosophies for the Earth* (New York: Fordham University Press, 2007).

16   Mary Evelyn Tucker and John A. Grim, "Introduction: The Emerging Alliance of World Religions and Ecology," *Daedalus* 130, no. 4 (Fall 2001): 1–22, at 3–4.

17   From a vast amount of literature on each religion, let me highlight only a few: Christopher Key Chapple, and Mary Evelyn Ticker eds., *Hinduism and Ecology* (Harvard MA: Harvard University Press, 2000); Roger S. Gottlieb ed., *The Oxford Handbook of Religion and Ecology* (New York: Oxford University Press, 2006). This volume has chapters dedicated to different religious traditions, giving an overview from different perspectives. For a volume exclusively dedicated to indigenous traditions, see John A. Grim, ed., *Indigenous Traditions and Ecology* (Harvard MA: Harvard University Press, 2001); S. Nomanul Haq, "Islam and Ecology: Toward Retrieval and Reconstruction," *Daedalus* 130, no. 4 (Fall 2001):141–177.

18   See the various chapters in John A, Grim, "Indigenous Traditions and Ecology."

19   A. Grim, "Indigenous Traditions and Ecology…Introduction." lv.

20   *Fratelli Tutti* 186.

21   Cf. Charles Avila, *Ownership: Early Christian Teaching* (New York: Orbis Books, 1983).

22   Cf. Felix Wilfred, "Navigating Cross-Hermeneutical Currents: A Subaltern Perspective," Nishant Alphonse Irudayam, ed., *Musings and Meaning. Hermeneutical Ripples* (Pune: Jnanadeepa Vidyapeeth, 2016), 1–14.

23   See Felix Wilfred, the special comparative theology issue of the *International Journal of Asian Christianity* 3, no.2 (2020): 127–251.

24   Cf. Werner G. Jeanrond, *Theological Hermeneutics* (New York: Crossroad, 1991), 22–23.

25   *Document on Human Fraternity* https://www.vatican.va/content/francesco/en/travels/2019/outside/documents/papa-francesco_20190204_documento-fratellanza-umana.html [accessed on 2 June 2023].

26   Cf. Felix Wilfred, *Religious Identities and the Global South: Porous Borders and Novel Paths* (Cham, Switzerland: Palgrave Macmillan, 2021).

27   Immanuel Kant, *Perpetual Peace and Other Essays.* Translated by Ted Humphrey (Indianapolis and Cambridge: Hackett Publishing Company, 1983). Initially published in 1917.

28   Rabindranath Tagore, *Nationalism* (Calcutta: Rup & Co. 1992).

29   Immanuel Kant, *Perpetual Peace, op.cit.,*135.

30 Cf. Felix Wilfred, *Religious Identities and the Global South, op. cit.* See especially chapter 13. The Duffy Lectures I delivered at the Boston College, USA, on the theme of "Religious Cosmopolitanism: South Asian Experiences, Perspectives, and Practices," will appear soon in print.

31 *Fratelli Tutti* 283.

32 Cf. Luiz Carlos Susin, "A Church Open to All: Hospitality as the Soul of the Church," in *Concilium* 2022/5, 60–66.

33 Cf. Néstor Medina, "Reconsidering Hospitality in Relation to Migration," in *Concilium* 2022/5, 106–115.

34 Cf. Harold Kasimow – Alan Race, eds., *Pope Francis and Interreligious Dialogue* (Cham, Switzerland: Palgrave Macmillan, 2018).

35 See https://www.vaticannews.va/en/church/news/2021-03/pope-francis-islam-iraq-magisterium-cairo-baku-ur.html [accessed on 24 May 2023].

36 This is the spirit of his *Evangelii Gaudium*. See Klaus Krämer and Klaus Vellguth, eds., *Evnagelii Gaudium. Voices of the Universal Church* (Quezon City: Claretian Communications Foundation, 2015). To understand in-depth the "theology of the people" of Pope Francis, it is important to go back to his formation, the people who influenced his thought, and his pastoral experience. For a very perceptive introduction to the intellectual roots of Pope Francis, see Massimo Borghesi, *The Mind of Pope Francis. Jorge Mario Bergoglio's Intellectual Journey* (CollegeVille : Liturgical Press, 2017).

37 https://www.vaticannews.va/en/pope/news/2018-05/pope-francis-hindu-jain-sikh-interreligious-dialogue.html [accessed on 24 May 2023].

38 This statement came out of a joint meeting of the bishops and theologians of FABC and of the Christian Conference of Asia (CCA) in Singapore in 1987, which I had the opportunity to participate in and address. For the text of the final statement, see *Living and Working Together with Sisters and Brothers of Other Faiths in Asia* (Hong Kong: FABC – CCA, 1989). It is striking that this encounter used the terminology of "brothers and sisters" for believers of other religions, and hence *Fratelli Tutti* on the brotherhood and sisterhood of all beyond religious affiliation finds excellent resonance in Asia. On the issue of the intersection between dialogue and mission from the perspective of WCC, see S. Wesley Ariarajah, *Not Without My Neighbour. Issues in Interrefaith Relations* (Geneva: WCC Publications, 2003), chapter 7: "Dialogue or Mission. Can the Tension be Resolved," 100-130.

39 I have been wondering how, under Joseph Ratzinger, this Congregation for the Doctrine of the Faith which was so particular and quick to impose excommunication on an Asian theologian, Tissa Balasuriya, had almost nothing effective to say, nor did it intervene decisively in the sexual abuse case of Cardinal Theodore McCarrick [now deposed and laicized by Pope Francis] of Washington DC, even though this case was well-known to this Congregation, as the lengthy report of Vatican on this issue reveals. How

does one compare the excommunication punishment imposed on Tissa Balasuriya with the handling of the case of McCarrick by this congregation of the Doctrine of the Faith? On the other hand, I have been wondering how come the Congregation for the Doctrine of the Faith took charge, under John Paul II, of the disciplinary issue of sexual abuse by the clergy. One would naturally expect the Congregation for the Clergy to deal with such issues. Things getting worse with the case of McCarrick, the matter was presented "directly to Pope Benedict XVI. The path of a canonical process to resolve factual issues and possibly prescribe canonical penalties was not taken. Instead, the decision was made to appeal to McCarrick's conscience and ecclesial spirit by indicating to him that he should maintain a lower profile and minimize travel for the good of the Church" See https://www.vatican.va/resources/resources_rapporto-card-mccarrick20201110en.pdf [accessed on 30 January 2021]. Now, compare the haste with which Balasuriya was punished, we do not really know for what, with excommunication, and the lethargy towards the case of McCarrick and failure to take canonical action in the face of a scandal of Himalayan proportions.

FURTHER READING

Abraham, K.C. *Eco-Justice: A New Agenda for Church's Mission*. Bombay: Build, 1993.

Ariarajah, Wesley S. *Not Without My Neighbour. Issues in Interfaith Relations*. Geneva: WCC Publications, 2003.

Avila, Charles. *Ownership: Early Christian Teaching*. New York: Orbis Books, 1983.

Bailey, Jerome Edgar. "Poverty, Wealth and Ecology": A Critical Analysis of a "World Council of Churches Project (2006-2013)." A full thesis submitted in fulfilment of the requirements for the degree of Magister in Theology, University of the Western Cape, 2020.

Borghesi, Massimo. *The Mind of Pope Francis. Jorge Mario Bergoglio's Intellectual Journey*. CollegeVille: Liturgical Press, 2017.

Bose, Sugata, and Ira Pande. "Tagorean Universalism and Cosmopolitanism." *India International Centre Quarterly* 38, no. 1 (Summer 2011): 2-17.

Carrithers, Michael. "On Polytropy: Or the Natural Condition of Spiritual Cosmopolitanism in India: The Digambar Jain Case." *Modern Asian Studies* 34, no. 4 (Oct. 2000): 831-861

Chapple, Christopher Key, and Mary Evelyn Ticker eds. *Hinduism and Ecology*. Harvard MA: Harvard University Press, 2000.

Chia, Edmund. "Towards a Theology of Dialogue." Doctoral Dissertation, University of Nijmegen, 2003.

Dermont, Lane A. *Stepping Stones to Other Religions. A Christian Theology of Inter-Religious Dialogue*. Maryknoll: Orbis Books, 2011.

Escobar, Samuel. *The New Global Mission: The Gospel from Everywhere to Everyone*. Westmont: InterVarsity Press, 2003.

FABC, CCA. *Living and Working Together with Sisters and Brothers of Other Faiths in Asia*. Hong Kong: FABC – CCA, 1989.

Forbes, Jack D. "Indigenous Americans: Spirituality and Ecos." *Daedalus* 130, no. 4 (Fall 2001): 283-300.

Gira, Dennis. *Le dialogue à al portée de tous*. (ou prsque). Montrouge: Bayard, 2012.

Gottlieb, Roger S., ed. *The Oxford Handbook of Religion and Ecology*. New York: Oxford University Press, 2006.

Grenham, Thomas G. "Discovering the Universal in the Particular: A Vision for Christian Mission Spirituality." *Missiology* 40, no. 1 (2012): 49-61.

Hallman, David. "The WCC Climate Change Programme: History, Lessons and Challenges." In *Climate Change*, edited by Martin Robra, 5-40. Geneva: WCC Publications, 2005.

Haq, S. Nomanul. "Islam and Ecology: Toward Retrieval and Reconstruction." *Daedalus* 130, no. 4 (Fall 2001): 141–177.

Jeanrond, Werner G. *Theological Hermeneutics*. New York: Crossroad, 1991.

John A. Grim, ed. *Indigenous Traditions and Ecology*. Harvard MA: Harvard University Press, 2001.

Kant, Immanuel. *Perpetual Peace and Other Essays*. Translated by Ted Humphrey. Indianapolis and Cambridge: Hackett Publishing Company, 1983.

Kasimow, Harold, and Alan Race, eds. *Pope Francis and Interreligious Dialogue*. Cham, Switzerland: Palgrave Macmillan, 2018.

Krämer, Klaus, and Klaus Vellguth, eds. *Evnagelii Gaudium. Voices of the Universal Church*. Quezon City: Claretian Communications Foundation, 2015.

Krickwin C. Marak and Atul Y. Aghamkar, eds. *Ecological Challenge and Christian Mission*. New Delhi: ISPCK, 1998.

Langmead, Ross. "Eco-Missiology." *Missiology: An International Review* XXX, no.4 (October 2002): 505.

Medina, Néstor. "Reconsidering Hospitality in Relation to Migration." In *Concilium* 2022/5, 106–115.

Niles, D. Preman. "Justice, Peace and The Integrity of Creation." In *Dictionary of Ecumenical Movements*, edited by Nicholas Lossky et al., 631-633. Geneva: WCC Publications, 2002.

Panikkar, Raimon. *The Cosmotheandric Experience*. Delhi: Motilal Banarsidass, 1998.

Pinto, Simon, Antony Lawrence, and Stany C. Fernandes, eds. *Politics and Mission in Critical Times. Local and Global Perspectives*. Bengaluru: Theological Publications in India, 2020.

Rupp, George. "Religion, Modern Secular Culture, and Ecology." *Daedalus* 130, no. 4 (Fall, 2001): 23–30.

Samartha, Stanley J. *One Christ – Many Religions*. Maryknoll: Orbis Books, 1991.

Sandel, Michael. *What Money Can't Buy. The Moral Limits of Market*. London: Penguin Books, 2012.

Schreiter, Robert J., ed. *Mission in the Third Millennium*. Orbis Books, 2015.

Susin, Luiz Carlos. "A Church Open to All: Hospitality as the Soul of the Church." In *Concilium* 2022/5, 60–66.

Swami Medhananda. *Swami Vivekananda's Vedic Cosmopolitanism*. Delhi: Oxford University Press, 2021.

Tagore, Rabindranath. *Nationalism*. Originally published in 1917. Calcutta: Rup & Co. 1992.

Thangaraj, Thomas. *The Common Task: A Theology of Christian Mission*. Nashville: Abingdon Press, 1999.

Thomas, Joy. "Mission as Dialogue." *Mission Studies* 14, no. 1 (1997): 228-240.

Tucker, Mary Evelyn, and John A. Grim. "The Emerging Alliance of World Religions and Ecology." *Daedalus* 130, no. 4 (Fall, 2001): 1–22.

Wilfred, Felix, ed. "Handle with Care: Fragile Humans." *Jeevadhara* LI, no.301 (January 2021).

Wilfred, Felix. "Asian Perspectives on Global Economic Inequality." In Mari-Anna Auvinen-Pöntinen and Jonas Adelin Jørgensen, eds. *Mission and Money. Christian Mission in the Context of Global Inequality*, 40–62. Leiden-Boston: Brill, 2016.

Wilfred, Felix. "Navigating Cross-Hermeneutical Currents: A Subaltern Perspective." In Nishant Alphonse Irudayam, ed., *Musings and Meaning. Hermeneutical Ripples*, 1–14. Pune: Jnanadeepa Vidyapeeth, 2016.

Wilfred, Felix. "New Impetus for Integral Ecology. Theological Significance of *Laudato Si*." In *Theology for an Inclusive World*, Chapter 8: 153–173. Delhi: ISPCK, 2019.

Chapter 2

NAVIGATING CRITICAL TIMES MISSION AND POLITICAL ENGAGEMENT

Politics is not something we generally associate with mission. However, no socially engaged mission can bypass the political field. On the other hand, despite heated discussions and debates around the ambiguous intersection between religion and politics, the mission has remained, by and large, neutral and a-political.[1] The discussion on politics today is done mainly in the context of Christian ethics and, rarely, as part of fundamental theology. The focus of this chapter is to interrogate the absence of the political in the understanding of mission and to study and reflect on the faith foundations for the political to become an integral part of mission theology and practice.

There is a particular urgency to relate politics and mission by characterizing our present history as *"critical times."* It awakens us to the conflicting realities of today in the country and worldwide. Today, the life and livelihood, survival needs, aspirations, and dreams of the people for the future seem to hinge on the political. Every sector of life has come under the pervading influence of politics. Could mission isolate itself and conduct itself as a private religious activity, unperturbed by what is happening to people and communities in our country and the rest of the world?

Two Mission Approaches to Politics

In the past few decades, there seem to be at work two different streams or axes of thought regarding the mission of the Church. I would name them *descending missiology* and *ascending missiology*. The descending missiology bases itself on an understanding of Jesus Christ from above. It considers the proclamation of Jesus Christ as God and the unique redeemer and saviour of the world as the missionary calling of the Church. The recent Catholic Church documents such as *Ad Gentes, Redemptoris Missio, Christus Dominus, and Ecclesia in Asia* would represent this axis.

The descending missiology has its own method and approach. One notable aspect of it is that, in its fervour to declare Jesus as God and the universal saviour of the world, it often overlooks the historical context of Jesus and his mission, giving little consideration to his actions and purpose within the specific circumstances of his era. In other words, this missiology concerns preaching the kerygmatic Christ dissociating him from the historical Jesus.[2] A document like *Redemptoris Missio* was written against the background of the fear and suspicion that in Asia, and especially in India, some theologians tended to obscure the truth that Jesus is the unique and universal saviour of humanity.[3] Such a preoccupation colours the methodology and orientation of descending missiology. Issues of politics, economy, and culture take a backseat.

There has been a systematic attempt to force upon Asia a descending missiology, which became evident at the Fifth Plenary Assembly of FABC (1990), held in Bandung, Indonesia.[4] However, this attempt has not gone without stiff resistance. Let me illustrate the point with an example. The *Lineamenta* for the Asian Synod of 1998 reflected a descending missiological orientation. Its central idea was to affirm Jesus Christ as the one and only saviour, as the way, the truth and the life. One of the questions the Lineamenta proposed for discussion in local Asian Churches was the following: "In what ways can the Church present Jesus Christ as the one and only Saviour as well as the universality of salvation in Him?" Many Asian local Churches found themselves quite uncomfortable with this approach to evangelization from above, something reflected in their responses to the Lineamenta. Most explicit and vocal have been the Japanese bishops. In their response, they said,

> One finds in the Lineamenta a certain defensiveness and apologetic attitude. This makes its presentation of certain other theological positions clearly unfair and inadequate. This is especially clear in the section on Christology. This does not help the faith of Asian Christians... Jesus Christ is the Way, the Truth and the Life, but in Asia, before stressing that Jesus Christ is the Truth, we must search much more deeply into how he is the Way and the Life.[5]

Further, the descending missiology is inclined to view the people to be evangelized as objects of proclamation and their life context as the stage on which missionary preaching takes place. In short, Jesus gets de-historicized, and so too the people. The descending missiology is genuinely interested in inculturation but is understood as a means for the effectiveness of the mission enterprise. It considers revelation as something closed and embodied in creeds and dogmas of the past. What remains to be done is to announce them.

This type of missiology has its own interest in politics. The political interest goes only so far as the ruling powers are helpful, or at least not a hindrance to the work of evangelization. One may not mind making some compromises with the powers as long as they allow the freedom to preach and do evangelization work unhindered. This approach has a long history and its own theological explanations. Eusebius, the early Church historian and a "court theologian" of

Emperor Constantine thought that the Roman Empire, with its institutions and a wide network of communication connecting every part of the then western world, was willed by God providing a favourable political climate for the propagation of Christianity.[6] Religious freedom is judged in this descending missiology as an essential condition for evangelization, not as a fundamental human right touching the lives of individuals and societies.

The second axis – the ascending missiology – is focused on the historical life of Jesus, his preaching of the Good News of the Reign of God, his teachings, passion, cross, and the hope of resurrection. Similarly, it is concerned deeply with the historical context of the people amidst whom evangelization takes place. The context is made up of the realms of society, politics, economy, culture, and so on, and the developments taking place therein. A genuine missiology will interpret God through the experience of human, social, and ecological realities and interpret these in the light of God. We have the model for both these interpretations in the incarnated humanity of Jesus that tells us, as we can read in the four gospels, who God is and, at the same time, interprets the human realities and experiences in the light of God.

Evangelization becomes meaningful and relevant when it begins from below, from the concrete reality of the context. God's revelation is viewed as continuing in this history, and it gets interpreted by reading the signs of the times. *Gaudium et Spes, Evangelii Nuntiandi,* and *Evangelii Gaudium* – these documents reflect the ascending missiology.[7] This approach to evangelization does not take the context as merely a platform to proclaim the Good News but something to be transformed through encounter and dialogue. The mission bridges the encounter between the world and God in their inextricable interrelationship.

Failure to Relate Mission and Politics

There are deeper roots for the failure of traditional missiology to address the reality of the *polis* – the city. The first is a sharp separation between a history of salvation, which is sacred, and profane history of the world comprising politics, economy, culture, and so on. The history of the world with all its vicissitudes is regarded, at the most, as a foil wrapping the history of salvation; both histories are viewed as moving on parallel lines. The descending missiology tends to dichotomize both these histories, confines itself to the world of salvation history, and gives scant attention to the history of the world and, consequently, the political realm and context.

Almost four decades ago, I indicated the severe limitations of salvation history as the unifying principle to read the Christian scriptures and revelation of God, and consequently, for theological education.[8] To enter into this discussion will take us far afield. The attempt to interpret mission through the scheme of the history of salvation without reference to the concrete context of the history of the world has insulated missiology from the real life-stream of today. It has made missiology unattractive in its method and contents. It is a fact that there are fewer and fewer takers for the study of missiology. Revitalization of missiology will depend on the extent we are prepared to propose Christian faith in its political, social, economic, and cultural implications.

Missiology indeed envisages much interest in inculturation.[9] However, strangely, it is silent on politics and the economy. The reason is not far to seek. Once mission and evangelization are perceived as proclaiming Jesus Christ set in the context of salvation history, all that is needed is to inculturate this message. But, missiology should enter into the field of politics and economy as it does in the field of culture and inculturation. Today's mission theology needs to re-read with fresh eyes the very first proclamation of Jesus himself and his self-understanding of his mission. He speaks of being sent to "preach the Good News to the poor." "He has sent me to proclaim release to the captives and recovering of sight to the blind, to set at liberty those who are oppressed..." (Lk. 418-19). Can inculturation release the captives and free the oppressed?

A De-Politicized Jesus Figure

Another important reason for divorcing mission from social and political engagement is how Jesus has been presented through misreading the New Testament data. Interpreters of a non-political Jesus argue that there was a revolt and opposition to Roman rule in Jesus' time. Jesus, however, did not belong to this kind of group - the so-called zealots - and hence was not political. Political is identified here exclusively with a particular mode of revolutionary action. It is easy to overlook the fact that the present society of Jesus' time, much like the society of the Old Testament prophets, was characterized by a division between two distinct groups. On the one hand there were the impoverished peasants and artisans, and on the other hand, there existed the elites - both political and religious - who held ownership of the land that peasants tilled. These elites not only claimed a significant portion of the agricultural products for themselves but also imposed exorbitant taxes on the already struggling poor. In short, two classes of people with opposing interests and concerns – the rich and the powerful on the one side and the exploited masses, on the other. Like in the case of the prophets, Jesus' message and indictment are about the rich and the religious elite who exploited the poor. By employing incisive social criticism, as apparent in his teachings and parables, he confronted the existing societal structure, adopting a politically audacious stance that posed a radical challenge to the established authorities. The political in Jesus was much larger than the revolt against the Roman authorities. Instead, it touched upon the very roots of the society of his times. Some time ago, I heard a popular and highly acclaimed Indian guru say, "Jesus was not a good man; he was wonderful." A good man, according to him, does not disturb the society and its functioning, which Jesus did. So, he does not deserve to be called a "good man"!

The reason behind the creation of a non-political Jesus image has also to do with an understanding of him as an eschatological figure. As an apocalyptical proponent, speaking of the end times – and not present reality – he was thought to be freed of all political and social concerns. It is argued that, as an eschatological figure, Jesus expected the change of the world to happen through a sudden intervention of God. This is a very partial and truncated reading of the New Testament data. Many scholars espousing such an image of Jesus have contributed to inculcating in the minds of the people a Jesus who is disinterested in history and the transformation of the world through human intervention.

Further, there has been a too pietistic and individualistic interpretation of the Christian faith, which fits into the frame of western liberalism developed in recent centuries. Accordingly, the individual Christians sought the meaning of their creeds and dogmas as they tried to practice their relationship with God and neighbour, insulated from the societal and communitarian situation and the challenges this presents. Privatization of faith under the influence of individualism and pietism can become insensitive to the lives of the poor, whose liberation is intertwined with the social and the political. Historically, the popular religious practices in Catholicism from the medieval times and the development of pietism in Protestantism in later centuries lost sight of the political edge of Jesus of history. Thanks to liberation theology in our times, Jesus is liberated from all these kinds of de-politicized presentations and brought to life as a fascinating prophetic personality engaged politically and socially. This liberative project was assisted by a multidisciplinary study of the context of Jesus in its social, cultural, and political dimensions.

Basic hermeneutics tells us how our perceptions and interests are tied to our caste and class and how our prejudices condition our reading of any text, event, or work. This also applies to the interpretation of the life and message of Jesus. Most scholars and ecclesial authorities try to read Jesus through their experiences, which is different from how the poor understand the story of Jesus. In this latter understanding, Jesus is at the same time a theological and an eminently political figure. His teachings and involvement are directed to the liberation of the poor and the oppressed (Lk 4: 18–19), thanks to his alternative vision of the world proclaimed as the Kingdom of God. A God-centered understanding of the world and society, far from leading to alienation, challenges Christians to pursue a mission of profound social and political involvement.

Why Evangelization Calls for Engagement in the Political Realm

Faith and the Word of God require effective historical mediation and authentic experiences. The practice and communication of faith are inextricably intertwined with what transpires in society, wherein politics forms an inalienable part. This is, of course, different from the mere intellectual and fiducial understanding of faith. These approaches dichotomize faith and praxis and promote a dualism of the other-worldly vis-à-vis the earthly. A genuine experience of faith takes place in the thick of life – personal and societal - and bears the stamp of the historical situation.

Just like faith, the Word of God is also mediated through history. It is not a past to be transmitted. It would not be an exaggeration to say, for example, that the Word of God is mediated today by the cry and groanings of the poor and the challenges posed to their life and dignity. In short, we need historical mediation to practice and communicate faith and interpret God's Word. But what is a mission without mediated faith and the Word of God? Where the mediation fails, it would come across to others as an imposition.

There is a general conception that politics bears something vile and vicious and hence to be studiously shunned. The non-political is projected as the ideal for a good person, communities and institutions. This standard is applied to the Church-community as well. Understandably, how politics is practised gives room for such preconceptions and attitudes. However, politics is inherently related to the common good and its attainment.[10] Politics is a coming together to participate, deliberate, decide and put into practice the common good by creating the necessary means and institutions. Moreover, the good of the individual and the common good, the object of politics, are interdependent. A good life cannot be defined in terms of what brings happiness and fulfilment to oneself. Real good life means to be part of the community and to pursue social relationships with goals and objectives that benefit all. What benefits all would benefit naturally, also individuals.

Given the purpose of the political realm, namely, coming together of individuals to collectively deliberate and work for the attainment of the common good, how could the mission of the Church seclude itself from this process? Further, the Church is defined in *Lumen Gentium* of Vatican II as a sacrament, a sign and an instrument of the unity of the entire human family (LG 1). This ultimate goal of unity may only be achieved with immersing oneself and participating in the arena of politics since, as we noted, it is here that people come together, discuss, interact, and shape the common good. Moreover, both the political realm and the Church contribute to the same human person. Hence, it is proper that the Church does not disengage itself from the political realm in realizing its mission for the wellbeing of human beings, their salvation, and liberation.

The political community or state, its various institutions, and organs must respect the moral order. The Church's prophetic mission calls for involvement in the political realm, especially when the state and its organs increasingly go against moral order, human dignity and rights. Evangelization without prophetism is a body without a soul. The Church could become an echo chamber of its voice and may not become a force of change as the Old Testament prophets were.[11] Rightly then, Pope Francis tells us in his *Evangelii Gaudium* about the importance of involving ourselves in the political realm, which is an expression of Christian charity. "Politics, though often denigrated, remains a lofty vocation and one of the highest forms of charity, in as much as it seeks the common good."[12]

Innumerable historical instances testify to the crucial importance of political engagement for defending human dignity and rights and the consequences of its failure. Let me cite one instance that vigorously challenges a de-politicized mission of the Church. In his autobiography, Ellie Wiesel, a Jewish survivor of the Auschwitz concentration camp during the Holocaust, recounts a deeply disturbing incident. He witnessed the hanging of three individuals on campgrounds. While two of them perished quickly, the third, a youth, struggled on the noose, fighting for his life. Overwhelmed by the shocking brutality of this scene, Wiesel asked himself, "Where is God?" With a heavy heart, he could only conclude that "God is hanging there on the gallows." According to Wiesel, the concentration camp, was a place where everything came to an end – human dignity, rights, life, literature, religion, and even God. It was a terrible night.[13]

In today's world, there are numerous concealed concentration camps and dark nights where all values are destroyed, human dignity is stripped naked, and God seems to be on the gallows. How could one preach about the crucified Christ without referencing the political play of power at the root of the terrible state of societies, nations, and the world? When Peter begins his preaching on the day of the Pentecost, he pointedly refers to "Jesus of Nazareth, a man attested to you by God with mighty works and wonders and signs that God did through him in your midst, as you yourselves know..." (Acts 2:22 – 24). However, this Jesus, he says, was betrayed by men who took the law into their hands and handed it over to be crucified. The just man Jesus, the servant of God, was condemned to the cross through intrigue and politicking. Johann Baptist Metz speaks of the ultimate "authority of those who suffer."[14] This is an important source of the authority of Jesus, and cross is the symbol. Those who suffer for the cause of justice participate genuinely in the authority of Jesus. Incidentally, it is also an invitation to rethink authority in the Church as it is conceived and practised today.

When a political order condemns the innocent to death, imprisons, tortures, and kills those who raise their voice in the name of God and humanity, how could the Church look the other way and preach that Jesus is the unique and universal saviour? This might come across to the listeners as the babbling of worn-out and empty formulae to the preachers' satisfaction. Is not working towards transforming the political order a constitutive part of the mission, just like working for justice?

Both the Church and the political order are there to serve the *common good.* Hence, there is a need for cooperation between them. "For it is her [Church's] task to uncover, cherish, and ennoble all that is true, good, and beautiful in the human community."[15] In doing this, one should distinguish between society and the political order or the state. The goals of the society are more extensive than that of the state. But, when the political order is made to overlap with society, serious problems could arise. State turns authoritarian and coercive, gets centralized, and suppresses civil society and freedom of expression on public issues touching the lives of everyone. In these circumstances, it is critical to defend the rights of human persons and the freedom of society and the citizens.

Mission and the Call to Transform

Evangelization needs to aim at transformation. Its purpose is not self-preservation of the Church, nor is it an attempt to swell its numbers. The better ordering of society is a crucial aspect of the transformative task of evangelization. This is the clear message of *Gaudium et Spes*, which, as I noted, is a forward-looking mission document based on the vision of the Kingdom of God, the central message of Jesus' preaching. The Reign of God is not merely a futuristic eschatological reality to be awaited – the so-called consistent eschatology - but something already here and now taking shape. This is spelt out so clearly by Gaudium et Spes:

> Far from diminishing our concern to develop this earth, the expectancy of a new earth should spur us on, for it is here that the body of a new human family grows, foreshadowing in some way that which is to come. That is why, although we must be careful to distinguish earthly progress clearly from the increase of the Kingdom of Christ, such progress is of vital concern to the Kingdom of God, insofar as it can contribute to the better ordering of human society.[16]

When we speak of the expectancy of a "transformed" world and society, we understand it as a world and society where equality, justice, and peace will rule and be the inspiring force. That this is not anything outside the purview, but the "constitutive part" of the mission was brought out most explicitly by the 1971 Synod on Justice in the World.

> Action on behalf of justice and participation in the transformation of the world fully appears to us as a constitutive dimension of the preaching of the gospel or, in other words, of the Church's mission for the redemption of the human race and its liberation from every oppressive situation.[17]

However, when we look at the global political scenario, we are far from the ideal of politics. The political order, St Augustine remarked, is meant for attaining justice. States or kingdoms are to be guided towards attaining justice; if not, they become "great bands of robbers" sharing the booty among themselves – something we can confirm from the political practices of our own days.[18] It may be pointed out here that there is a difference between the Catholic and Lutheran approach to the state. From a Lutheran perspective state is a response to human sinfulness as it takes care of order in society, failing which there will be chaos. On the other hand, in the Catholic understanding, the state is something positive as it is called to contribute to the common good and enhance the quality of life.

The state, surely, is an important institution for the attainment of the common good.[19] However, it has limits and it should function according to the principle of subsidiarity. This means the state need not and should not replace other initiatives and programmes for peace and justice and the general well being of the society. Involvement in these is also a political process. One should not confine the political involvement only to what relates to the state, election, voting etc. On the other hand, voluntary associations, media, and modern world of digital communication, social movements touch upon the political realm.[20] Participation in these institutions and movements too is a political engagement and a part of evangelization. Further, the state has the power to enact laws, but these laws are to be ethically just and fair. Challenging laws that go contrary to the poor – to whom the Good News is addressed – is also Christian commitment to the political field.

As we noted, today, we are witnessing a global emergence of fascist populism and authoritarianism, which is causing a sense of disorientation and undermining the fundamental objectives of political order. Populism emerges when individuals experience a sense of being adrift, witnessing their aspirations being crushed and their dream fading away.[21] Skilled orators and masters of symbols and media effortlessly exploit the prevailing sentiments of fear and a feeling of disempowerment among the populace. They promise everything the people think they have lost, or have no prospects to attain. Populist leaders present the elites as the enemy, because they are corrupt, or show the outsiders, the migrants as enemies. These leaders present themselves as credible alternatives, but in reality, end up as authoritarian rulers projecting themselves to be the messiahs through their rhetoric, symbolic gestures, and theatric performances. When the positive goals and ideals of a society and political order are corrupted, could the Church simply sit back?

When we speak of politics, in the same breath, we need to speak of economy. Both are inextricably intertwined. The reform of the political order is not possible today without setting the economy on humanizing path. When we have an economic system of capitalism and market, the political realm gets poisoned and vitiated. Pope Francis pointed out most poignantly the "murderous" character of the present-day economy with its consequences for our world. It is worth quoting at length his words in this regard.

Just as the commandment "Thou shalt not kill" sets a clear limit in order to safeguard the value of human life, today we also have to say "thou shalt not" to an economy of exclusion and inequality. Such an economy kills. How can it be that it is not a news item when an elderly homeless person dies of exposure, but it is news when the stock market loses two points? This is a case of exclusion.

> Can we continue to stand by when food is thrown away while people are starving? This is a case of inequality. Today everything comes under the laws of competition and the survival of the fittest, where the powerful feed upon the powerless. As a consequence, masses of people find themselves excluded and marginalized: without work, without possibilities, without any means of escape.[22]

Inequality, competition, exclusion, lopsided priorities, asymmetry of power, callous indifference to the suffering of the poor – all these are issues of the economy as much as of politics. What is evangelization if such fundamental issues of life are not addressed? How does the Good News figure into this calamitous socio-political situation?

Incarnation and Immersion

Our preceding reflections showed the importance of and reason for bringing together mission and politics. In the following, we will briefly recall some of the theological motives and foundations for a politically conscious engagement of mission. We begin with the mystery of the incarnation. The self-manifestation of God takes place in history.

Now, history is dynamic and comprises political processes, economic dealings, social interactions, and cultural creations. God becoming flesh implies God's self-manifestation in politics, economy, society, culture, and so on, all of which constitute human life and history. A reading of the life of Jesus, as we find expressed in the gospels, bears witness to the self-manifestation of God in history. The whole of the Old Testament is a story of God's journeying with the people, and there is no dichotomy of the material realm and the spiritual realm. Exodus was a saving event, no less political than theological. For Israel, proclaiming and praising God meant recalling this central event of its political history.

The involvement with peoples' political and social history calls for focusing on *Jesus of history*. Unfortunately, this has not been so in most instances. As I noted, the mission has been based on an abstract and de-historicized Christology. A metaphysically conceived Christianity with its belief system and precepts will have serious difficulty following Jesus' mission. The self-emptying – *kenosis* of God – is an antidote. At the same time, it is a dissolution of metaphysically conceived Christianity and of a metaphysical God. The incarnate God is one of history, world, politics, culture, economy – all that touches human beings, nature, and the universe. It is this God of history and God in history that Christians are called upon to proclaim. It is a mission situated in the political and historical context of our times.

Kingdom of God

As attested by the gospels, the public life of Jesus was unmistakably marked by the proclamation of the Reign of God. The Kingdom of God represents a disruption of human ways. The rule of God brings with it justice and peace. It reverses human planning and calculation. It is a Reign where the mighty are brought down from their thrones, and the poor and the lowly are raised to the true dignity of sons and daughters of God (cf. Lk 1:46-55). Jesus tells how his teachings, miracles, passion, and death mark the arrival of the Reign of God. He announces that his impending death would coincide with the definite coming of the Kingdom. On the eve of his death at the last supper, he tells the disciples, "I shall not drink again of the fruit of the vine until that day when I drink it new in the Kingdom of God" (Mk 14:25). The arrival of the Reign is not something to be taken for granted. It comes through struggles and temptations, through a continuous process of conquering evil embedded in the various institutions, structures, and realms of the human.

Evangelization is an invitation to participate and commit to the Reign of God that is already taking shape. This participation is intended to mend a broken world and re-order social, political, and economic conditions so that the righteousness of God prevail over the evils that humans, as individuals and as collectives, are capable of. Viewed thus, the Kingdom of God opens up a large vista for mission engagement.[23] But what often happens is a false equation of the Church and the Kingdom of God.[24] As a result, there is a Church-centered mission rather than Kingdom-centered evangelization. As we noted, if the Reign of God is taking shape here and now in human history, then it is highly important that the mission engagement addresses political, social, economic and cultural issues. Pope Francis is emphatic about this when he states,

> The Gospel is about the Kingdom of God (cf. Lk 4:43); it is about loving God, who reigns in our world. To the extent that he reigns within us, the life of society will be a setting for universal fraternity, justice, peace and dignity. Both Christian preaching and life, then, are meant to have an impact on society.[25]

Seen this way, evangelization becomes a dynamic force in the service of the Kingdom of God, here and now in history. It becomes an expression of Christian faith, love, and hope, bearing responsibility for the future shape of the world and for things to come.

Theology of Creation and Evangelization

Theology of creation provides a different Christological orientation for relating mission and politics. Christ, in whom all things were created is also the end-point of creation, for God wants to unite all things in Christ (Eph 1: 9-10). This puts us in a movement, in a process. Our world and universe are radically evolving with great dynamism, something modern science has brought to light. We have the creation motive also in the interpretation of the death of Jesus by Duns Scotus and in more recent times in Teilhard de Chardin and others. Christ is perceived as the one who was at the beginning and the end towards whom we move (Col 1:15-20). Christ is Alpha and Omega. We can identify a tradition of *cosmic Christ* from Origen and the Greek Fathers of the fourth century onward.[26] Evangelization proclaims not only Jesus who came but also the Christ who is to come. A creation-inspired and eschatologically-oriented understanding of Jesus Christ will stir the work of evangelization to involve itself deeply in politics. The FABC document "Theological Perspectives on Church and Politics" inspires us in this direction when it states that "the upholding of the public character of the Christian faith stems from the recognition of Christ's lordship over all creation, including all aspects of human life, among which is the socio-political aspect."[27]

The Cross and Taking Down the Crucified

Creation continues in our resistance to the powers of evil corroding and maiming life. Rightly then, the cross is at the very heart of the Christian gospel. The cross, however, is not an empty symbol. Besides recalling the suffering and death of Jesus, it invites us to respond to human suffering in our present historical moment.

> The key dangers arise when the cross is separated from the crucified in such a way that it appears as an abstract, idealized, or de-historicized symbol of negativity in general…These dangers are real, not merely speculative. They can be encountered in history today, where innocent victims suffer ten thousand versions of "crucifixion" at the hands of historically real and guilty crucifiers.[28]

Closely reading the gospels will tell us that Jesus was not concerned so much about sin: his main concern was human suffering. His deep compassion for and solidarity with those suffering led to his extreme suffering, humiliation, and horrifying violent death.

> By the public display of a naked victim at a prominent place – at a crossroads, in the theatre, on high ground, at the place of his crime – crucifixion also represented his utmost humiliation, which had a numinous dimension to it… Crucifixion was aggravated further by the fact that quite often its victims

were never buried. It was a stereotyped picture that the crucified victim served as food for wild beasts and birds of prey. In this way, his humiliation was made complete.[29]

The death of Christi is not merely a past event, nor is it lived only mystically and sacramentally.[30] Unfortunately, many forms of Catholic theology have led us to believe the continuity of the death of Jesus solely in sacraments and in popular piety. The cross, as the tree of life, signifies flourishing and wellbeing, which is salvation – *salus* meaning hale, healthy and whole. The Cross holds out the promise of active and collective participation in a new creation, however far off that may seem at times. It implies a political process with both feet on the rough grounds of reality. This political process, I suggest, must include the whole created order, and a soteriology for our time must address the ecological crisis.[31]

The struggle against evil needs to continue through our discipleship amidst conflicts and contradictions in the political and economic realms. How will the Christians continue to proclaim Jesus, his teachings, death and resurrection? We get a response from Ignacio Ellacuría when he states, "*A historical sequel* is required which continues realizing what he realized and how he realized it." For as he notes, "the continuity is not purely mystical and sacramental, any more than his activity on earth was purely mystical and sacramental."[32]

The understanding of evangelization imposed on Asia has been so obsessed with proclaiming Jesus as God, and as the unique and universal saviour of the world, that one forgot about the passion of Jesus, his death, the cross, and the political implications of all these historical realities. Focusing on the proclamation of Jesus as God, as Son of God and the unique saviour of the world (as the descending missiology does) may not excite our neighbours. For, in Hindu tradition, there are thirty-three crore gods and goddesses who also have children. Proclaiming Jesus as God or as the Son of God may appear that we are adding to this pantheon. Not so when we speak of the cross. It is arresting, and it simply shatters the conventional understanding of God. Cross invokes the troubled human history, political play of power, human suffering at its extreme, forces of evil and so on – all of which vibrate with people's experience. It becomes an open message of love, sacrifice, and abandonment to God. The erected cross is a permanent interrogation on all our political, social, economic, and cultural systems.

"The ground beneath the cross" is a world of politics. From this rough ground emerge systems, instruments, and forces that cause the crucifixion of the poor of God. The Christian tradition has held that the poor person is the *vicarius Christi* - vicar or representative of Christ.[33] The suffering and negations the poor suffer are the loci from where we can understand more closely the cross of Jesus Christ, which we have failed to proclaim enough. Taking down the poor from the cross involves a politics of resistance, challenge, and prophetism vis-à-vis the powers that cause the crucifixion. Evangelization is about preaching Jesus Christ crucified, "a stumbling block to Jews and folly to Gentiles" (I Cor 1:23); it is also about how to take down from the cross the crucified people with the wisdom and power of God.

Missiology – Shifting from Geographic Space to Public Space

Public theology, which expresses the fusion of mission and politics, should become an integral part of the mission studies of missiology curriculum. Even more, missiology needs to reinvent itself as public theology. This will help make the mission more vibrant and responsive to the signs of the times. Mission is not merely conveying to people what we believe in. Mission is to respond to the concerns and questions which touch upon them and their daily lives. For too long, missiology has been associated with some geographic regions, in practice, with lands colonized by the western powers. These lands were considered prospective fields for an abundant harvest of souls. There was a narrow understanding of soteriology.

Today, we need to shift from this paradigm of physical space to public space. Public space is the arena of mission and evangelization for our times. Moreover, this public space comprises political, social, economic, and cultural sites. These spaces are the new geography of the mission. Here the Church will gain credibility for its message when it is involved in the cause of liberation and justice. In this regard, we may recall the words of the 1971 Synod on Justice here.

> The present situation of the world, seen in the light of faith, calls us back to the very essence of the Christian message, creating in us a deep awareness of its true meaning and its urgent demands. The mission of preaching the Gospel dictates at present that we should dedicate ourselves to the liberation of man even in his present existence in the world. For unless the Christian message of love and justice shows its effectiveness through action in the cause of justice in the world, it will only with difficulty gain credibility with men of our times.[34]

If evangelization is oriented to justice and liberation, it is impossible to achieve them without immersion into the world of politics. For both liberation and justice involve the issue of power in public life, which is the realm of politics.

Theology for Public Life and Public Theology

Public theology is different from another kind of approach which can be characterized as *theology for public life*. This latter kind of theology does not originate from the context, or experiences; rather, it focuses on interpreting the truths of the scriptures and dogmas of belief in their normative and moral implications. It concerns how a believer could be a good citizen and a patriot. The contents of faith provide motivation and inspiration to act in the public realm. Here one follows a one-sided method, namely from the religious sources to the reality without regard for the complexity of the situation on the ground. This approach is accompanied by an effort to regulate public life and its various departments according to the norms of faith.

A variant of this kind of theology for public life is pursued in Protestant neo-orthodoxy by authors like Max Stackhouse and John Milbank.[35] This theology differs from that of *Gaudium et Spes* of Vatican II, which speaks of reading the signs of the times and engaging oneself in the temporal realities. The above authors and their likes remain fixated on an essentialist conception of faith and the Church, and they see the mission of public theology as making the world and society conform to the standards and normativity of the scriptures and Christian doctrines rather than faith reaching out to the world. Theology, according to them, is to be practised in such a manner as to be a critique of modernity. For Milbank, ecclesiology would be the model and normativity for sociology and the "secular" would be a heresy.[36] In short, the public theology of Stackhouse and Milbank aims at shaping through the power of the Christian faith the structures and policies of public life, including economics.

Public Theology – Casting the Net Wider

The kind of public theology we are speaking about is a different one. In this kind of public theology, the faith resources – scripture, tradition etc. – are approached not simply in their claimed normativity, but rather in their potentiality to interact with public life with a view to transformation.[37] The truths of faith thus become not simply dogmas to be proclaimed independently of any correlation to life in public. Truth becomes fluid like flowing water de-freezed from doctrinaire rigidity and rigour. A belief for the sake of belief would make little sense. Even more, it could create a magical consciousness.

Further, the missiology we envisage as public theology presupposes that every article of faith has an a priori public and open character and significance for the life of the world. To use traditional terminology, there is a transcendental or pre-thematic moment in the practice of the proposed public theology. The significance of the articles of faith is to be discovered ever afresh and in new situations and contexts by reaching out. They are not to be embalmed and preserved in the Church as if it were a tomb. In public theology, we are led to feel like participants in a narrative larger than us and whose dynamics and contours surpass our limits.

When we understand missiology in terms of public theology, what happens is that the urgency of the context seizes us. We try to creatively bring out the more profound message of the gospel in every new situation. Evangelization becomes innovative and fresh every moment and in every situation. The Bible itself could be viewed as an open public book for everyone to read as it provides wisdom and insights for the life of society and for shaping the world through its many narration, symbols, values, and ideals.

Instances of Public Theology

The encyclical *Pacem in Terris* of Pope John XXIII is one of the earliest examples of public theology in modern times. Up until then, the teachings of the popes were meant for the Catholic community. The encyclical of John XXIII was revolutionary because it was the first time that the official Church addressed itself to the entire world and to the whole of humankind, and indeed on an issue of vital significance in the context of the time. It was the time of the Cold War between two superpowers, characterized by political and ideological divides threatening war at a global level with all its consequences. As Joseph Gremillion observes, "millions who had never paid the least attention to popes and their jaw-breaker encyclicals suddenly sat up and listened. Here for the first time, a pope was addressing himself 'to all men of goodwill'. And his message responded to a deep longing shared by all."[38]

We could recall here the figure of Martin Luther King Jr – An African-American pastor from the periphery of Montgomery, Alabama who was faced with the stark reality of denial of civil rights, and practice of racial discrimination against African-Americans, including segregation in public transportation. His faith and sense of mission took him to the path of the civil rights movement, of which he became an articulate and most visible spokesperson. His stirring public speech in 1963, addressed to over 250,000 people at the Washington DC march, began with those memorable and historic words, "I have a dream…". It was public theology in action and performance.

Through his public theology, Martin Luther King could galvanize the energies of the public across race and religion in service of the mission of liberation and create a "coalition of conscience." It was a political act. He led the Selma to Montgomery March of 1965 to attain voting rights for the discriminated and oppressed black people. The Jewish Rabbi Joshua Heschel and a great Biblical scholar who participated in the Selma march said of his experience,

> For many of us, the march from Selma to Montgomery was about protest and prayer. Legs are not lips, and walking is not kneeling. And yet our legs uttered songs. Even without words, our march was worship. I felt my legs were praying.[39]

In East and Central Africa, Wangari Maathai, a Christian woman brought up and inspired by the Benedictines, was doing public theology when she created "The Green Belt Movement" - a massive ecological movement.[40] Under her inspiration, thirty million trees were planted by women. She was awarded Nobel Prize in 2004 in recognition of her ecological commitment. However, her ecological mission brought her into conflict with those grabbing common lands that belonged to the people. She dared to speak the truth to power. Her ecological mission became a political conflict. The environmental movement she initiated and sustained became in effect, also a movement empowering women and nurturing their agency. Her local initiative blossomed into a global force for democracy, the defence of human rights, and environmentalism. Her vision for public life was shot through with humanistic and environmental values and her Christian faith.

At this juncture, we need to recall the encyclical of Pope Francis – *Laudato Si*. The encyclical has brought into a beautiful synthetic perspective the ecological issue, the question of poverty, and the political process required to overcome the present environmental crisis. The pope brings the light of the gospel on a vital issue affecting the entire human family and nature. Like the case of peace, environmental issues are a question about salvation – the well-being of human communities and the flourishing of nature. Peace studies and environmental issues, with all their political implications, should become an integral part of the missiological curriculum.

Conclusion: Mission of Other Religions and Politics

We are at a critical juncture in which the Good News and mission of all religions need to converge towards the transformation of the world, and creation of a peaceful and harmonious human coexistence, along with care for nature and the environment. It involves a political process. Inheriting the Kingdom of God is not about whether we hold on to our unique Good News to the exclusion of others but what we do to the little ones (Mt 25: 31-46). What other religions share with us, and what we share with them offer a lot of common ground for jointly moving ahead towards participation in a political process.[41] The defence of human dignity and rights, care for the earth, equality, justice and peace, reflecting the Kingdom of God, will define the common agenda of the mission of all religions and it is intertwined with political involvement.

It makes much sense to speak of the mission of other religious traditions, especially after the joint statement of Pope Francis and the Great Imam of Al-Azhar, 4 February 2019.

> Freedom is a right of every person: each individual enjoys the freedom of belief, thought, expression and action. The pluralism and the diversity of religions, colour, sex, race and language are willed by God in His wisdom, through which He created human beings. This divine wisdom is the source from which the right to freedom of belief and the freedom to be different derives. Therefore, the fact that people are forced to adhere to a certain religion or culture must be rejected, as too the imposition of a cultural way of life that others do not accept.[42]

This is a statement which opens up the mission horizon much wider. If God wills other religions just as colour, sex, race and language, God has indeed given also a mission to them, which we need to discern. Recognition of religions as willed by God is made in the context of a call to work towards peace and fraternity – a political mission. We could profitably read the above text along with the statement in *Redemptoris Missio*, which states,

> The Spirit's presence and activity affect not only the individuals but also society and history, peoples, cultures and religions. Indeed, the Spirit is at the origin of the noble ideals and undertakings which benefit humanity on its journey through history: The Spirit of God, with marvellous foresight, directs the course of the ages and renews the face of the earth.[43]

Given the presence of the Spirit in other religions, we need to listen to the Good News God is giving to the world through them. The Christian Good News does not become less by acknowledging the Good News the other religions have to offer. Good News of other religions need not make us sad. How poor Christian faith would be if it were to fear about the Good News of other religions! But this will happen if we think in merely competitive terms of comparison

and contrast, or in terms of perfect and imperfect, full and not full.
But the thoughts and ways of God are different and inscrutable.

> For my thoughts are not your thoughts,
>
> nor are your ways my ways, declares the LORD.
>
> For just as the heavens are higher than the earth,
>
> so are my ways higher than your ways,
>
> and my thoughts than your thoughts (Is 55: 8-9).

NOTES

1   However, we need to point out that the history of Christianity has been far from being a-political. Kings and emperors patronized Christianity, and Christian theology provided ideological backing to imperial political powers. Besides arguing for the divine right of kings, one saw in kings and emperors the earthly version of the heavenly Christ the King.

2   From a historical point of view, this trend could be traced to the Christological debates and controversies of the early centuries. The Council of Nicaea (C.E. 325) affirmed that the Son is of equal dignity with and consubstantial to the Father. The Council of Chalcedon (C.E. 451) ensured the unity of the divine and human nature in Jesus Christ. The life of Jesus, his teachings, his passion, death and resurrection never figured in the early Christological tradition. On the whole, the Christological orientation of the early centuries remained de-historicized. This trend will express itself in different forms throughout the Christian centuries. Descending missiology of today derives from a partial Christology formulated in a polemical and controversial context.

3   This preoccupation is reflected in the very title formulated for the Asian Synod (1998): "Jesus Christ the Saviour and His Mission of Love and Service in Asia."

4   Cf. Felix Wilfred, "Fifth Plenary Assembly of FABC. An Interpretation of Its Theological Orientation," *Vidyajyoti Journal of Theological Reflection* 54 (1990): 583–592. I have shown in this article the kind of interventions made to force upon Asia a particular de-historicized and de-contextualized understanding of mission. In contrast, Asian bishops tried to underline the importance of the context and Asian historical processes in understanding the mission, as delineated in my keynote to the Assembly.

5   See Peter C. Phan, ed., *The Asian Synod. Texts and Commentaries* (New York: Orbis Books, 2002), 30; see also Felix Wilfred, *From the Dusty Soil* (Chennai: University of Madras, 1995), chapter 8: "Jesus Christ in Today's Asia. An Interpretation of FABC Documents," 161–175.

6   Cf. Michael J. Hollerich, "Religion and Politics in the Writings of Eusebius: Reassessing the First 'Court Theologian,'" *Church History* 59, no. 3 (1990): 309–25.

7   Though *Gaudium et Spes* is not an explicit mission document, however, in its orientation and content appears to be most suited for Asia. Arguably, this is the most inspiring mission document of the twentieth century.

8   Cf. Felix Wilfred, "A Matter of Theological Education - Some Critical Reflections on the Suitability of 'Salvation History' as a Theological Model for India," *Vidyajyoti Journal of Theological Reflection* 48 (1984): 538–556.

9   A simple analysis of the literature on missiology in the last few decades reveals that inculturation has been the theme most studied and discussed.

10   Cf. David Hollenbach, *The Common Good. Christian Ethics* (Cambridge: Cambridge University Press, 2002); Id., *The Global Face of Public Faith* (Washington D.C.: George Town University Press, 2003).

11   Cf. Walter Brueggemann, *The Prophetic Imagination* (Minneapolis: Fortress Press, 2001); Id., *Disruptive Grace. Reflections on God, Scripture and the Church* (Minneapolis: Fortress Press, 2011).

12   *Evangelii Gaudium* 205.

13   Cf. Ellie Wiesel, *Night* (London: Penguin Books, 2008).

14   Johann Baptist Metz, "Die Autorität der Leidendenden," in Leonardo Boff, ed., *Prinzip Mitgefül* (Freiburg: Herder, 1999).

15   *Gaudium et Spes* 76.

16   *Gaudium et Spes* 39.

17   *Synod on Justice in the World* 6.

18   St Augustine, *The City of God*, IV. 4: "Without justice, what are kingdoms but great bands of robbers? And what is a band of robbers but such a kingdom in miniature? It is a band of men under the rule of a leader, bound together by a pact of friendship, and their booty is divided among them by an agreed rule. Such a blot on society, if it grows, assumes for itself the proud name of Kingdom."

19   Cf. Charles E. Curran, *Catholic Social Teaching 1891 – Present. A Historical, Theological, and Ethical Analysis* (Washington: Georgetown University Press, 2002), 137–171.

20   Charles Curran, *Op.cit.*

21   Cristóbal Rovira Karlwasser, et al., *The Oxford Handbook of Populism* (Oxford: Oxford University Press, 2017); see also Cas Mudd and Cristóbal Rovira Karlwasser, *Populism: A Very Short Introduction* (New York: Oxford University Press, 2017).

22   *Evangelii Gaudium* 53.

23   Cf. Antony Lawrence, *Mission in the Third Millennium. Emerging Trends in India* (Bangalore: ATC Publishers, 2019), 65–118.

24 Cf. Felix Wilfred, *From the Dusty Soil* (Chennai: University of Madras, 1995), chapter 7: "Church and Kingdom of God. A Reinterpretation," 137–160.

25 *Evangelii Gaudium* 180.

26 Cf. J. A. Lyons, *The Cosmic Christ in Origen and Teilhard de Chardin* (Oxford: Oxford University Press, 1982); Cf. also John D. Caputo, *Cross and Cosmos. A Theology of Difficult Glory* (Bloomington: Indiana University Press, 2019).

27 Vimal Tirimanna, ed., *Sprouts of Theology from the Asian Soil.* Collection of TAC and OTC Documents [1987 – 2007] (Bangalore: Claretian Publications, 2007), 62.

28 F. Burke, *The Ground Beneath the Cross. The Theology of Ignacio Ellacuría* (Washington D.C.: Georgetown University Press, 2000), 175. See also Leonard Boff, *Passion of Christ, Passion of the World* (New York: Orbis Books, 1987).

29 Martin Hengel, *Crucifixion in the Ancient World and the Folly of the Message of the Cross* (Philadelphia: Fortress Press, 1977), 87.

30 Felix Wilfred, "No Return to the Normal: Church after Covid – 19," in Francis Gonsalves & Vinod Victor eds. *Corona of Thorns? Or Corna of Life? Changing Church in the Covid Context* (Delhi: ISPCK, 2020), 25–32.

31 "Before the tenth or eleventh century, both Eastern and Western depictions typically Refrained from showing Jesus as suffering physical agony and death. Consistent with the earliest known crucifixions, they tended to present Christ as vigorously alive with his eyes wide open and often robed in the purple garments of a king… Gradually, from the ninth to the eleventh century, the depictions of Christ's triumph over death began to shift towards a visual representation of the suffering man-God, or *Christus patiens*". Robin M Jensen, *The Cross: History, Art and Controversy* (Cambridge, Mass: Harvard University Press, 2017), 151.

32 As quoted in Kevin F. Burke, *The Ground Beneath the Cross. The Theology of Ignacio Ellacuría* (Washington D.C.: Georgetown University Press, 2000), 180.

33 Cf. Michel Mollat, *The Poor in the Middle Ages. An Essay in Social History* (New Haven: Yale University Press, 1986).

34 *Synod on Justice in the World 1971*, 35.

35 Max Stackhouse, *Public Theology and Political Economy* (Grand Rapids: Eerdmans, 1987); L. Hainsworth et al., eds., *Public Theology for a Global Society: Essays in Honor of Max L. Stackhouse* (Grand Rapids, Mich.-Edinburgh: William B. Eerdmans, 2010); Max L. Stackhouse - Peter Paris, eds., *God and Globalization* (New York: T & T Clark, 2007); John Milbank, *Theology and Social Theory. Beyond Secular Reason* (Oxford/Cambridge: Blackwell, 1990); Oli Simon Oliver - John Milbank, *The Radical Orthodoxy Reader* (London: Routledge, 2009).

36 Cf. Georges De Schreijver, *Recent Theological Debates in Europe and Their Impact on Interreligious Dialogue* (Bangalore: Dharmaram Publications, 2004), 37ff.

37 Cf. Felix Wilfred, *Asian Public Theology* (Delhi: ISPCK, 2010); ID., *Theology to Go Public* (Delhi: ISPCK 2013); Sebastian Kim, *Theology in the Public Sphere* (London: SCM Press,2011); Gnana Patrick, *Public Theology. Indian Concerns, Perspectives, and Themes* (Minneapolis: Fortress Press, 2020).

38 Joseph Gremillion, *The Gospel of Peace and Justice. Catholic Social Teaching Since Pope John* (New York: Orbis Books, 1976), 68.

39 https://blogs.library.duke.edu/rubenstein/2015/01/14/jewish-voices-selma-montgomery-march/ [accessed on 12 July 2020].

40 https://www.britannica.com/biography/Wangari-Maathai [accessed on 12 July 2020].

41 I have dealt with this question in detail in my work, *Theology for an Inclusive World* (Delhi: ISPCK, 2018), 355–377.

42 http://www.vatican.va/content/francesco/en/travels/2019/outside/documents/papafrancesco_20190204_documento-fratellanza-umana.html[accessed on12 July 2020].

43 *Redemptoris Missio*, no. 28.

FURTHER READING

Araujo, Robert J. "Political Theory and Liberation Theology: The Intersection of Unger and Gutiérrez." *Journal of Law and Religion* 11, no. 1 (1994–1995): 63–81.

Bevans, Stephen. *Models of Contextual Theology*. New York: Orbis Books, 2002.

Beyers, Jaco. "Religion as Political Instrument: The Case of Japan and South Africa." *Journal for the Study of Religion* 28, no. 1 (2015): 142–164.

Bremmer, Jan N. "Prophets, Seers, and Politics in Greece, Israel, and Early Modern Europe." *Numen* 40, no. 2 (May 1993): 150–183.

Cahill, Lisa Sowle. "Theological Ethics, the Churches, and Global Politics." *The Journal of Religious Ethics* 35, no. 3 (Sep 2007): 377–399.

Carvalhaes, Cláudio, and Fábio Py. "Liberation Theology In Brazil." *CrossCurrents* 67, no. 1(Mar 2017): 157–179.

Chinnici, Joseph P. "The Cold War, the Council, and American Catholicism in a Global World." *U.S. Catholic Historian* 30, no. 2, The Second Vatican Council (Spring 2012): 1–24.

Christoyannopoulos, Alexander. *Christian Anarchism: A Political Commentary on the Gospel*. Charlottesville: Imprint Academic, 2011.

Cubas, Ramacciotti, and Ricardo Daniel. *The Politics of Religion and the Rise of Social Catholicism in Peru (1884-1935): Faith, Workers and Race Before Liberation Theology*. Leiden - Boston: Brill, 2017.

Cviic, K. F. "The Politics of the World Council of Churches." *The World Today* 35, no. 9 (Sep. 1979): 369–376.

Daniel H. Levine, "Assessing the Impacts of Liberation Theology in Latin America." *The Review of Politics* 50, no. 2 (Spring, 1988): 241–263.

Djupe, Paul A, and Christopher P Gilbert. "Politics and Church: Byproduct or Central Mission?" *Journal for the Scientific Study of Religion* 47, no. 1 (Mar., 2008): 45–62.

Dodson, Michael. "Liberation Theology and Christian Radicalism in Contemporary Latin America." *Journal of Latin American Studies* 11, no. 1 (May, 1979): 203–222.

Dodson, Michael. "Prophetic Politics & Political Theory in Latin America." *Polity* 12, no. 3 (Spring, 1980): 388–408.

Ellis, Stephen, and Gerrie Ter Haar. "Religion and Politics: Taking African Epistemologies Seriously." *The Journal of Modern African Studies* 45, no. 3 (Sep. 2007): 385–401.

Farazmand, Ali. "Religion and Politics in Contemporary Iran: Shia Radicalism, Revolution, and National Character." *International Journal on Group Rights* 3, no. 3 (1995/96): 227–257.

Ferguson, Everett. "The Kingdom and Jesus." *The Everlasting Kingdom: The Kingdom of God in Scripture and in Our Lives*. Abilene, Texas: Abilene Christian University, 1989, 20-26.

Fiorenza, Elisabeth Schüssler. "Jesus and the Politics of Interpretation." *The Harvard Theological Review* 90, no. 4 (Oct. 1997): 343–358.

Givens, Tommy. "The Election of Israel and the Politics of Jesus: Revisiting John Howard Yoder's 'The Jewish—Christian Schism Revisited.'" *Journal of the Society of Christian Ethics* 31, no. 2 (Winter 2011): 75–92.

Greenberg, Anna. "The Church and the Revitalization of Politics and Community." *Political Science Quarterly* 115, no. 3 (Autumn 2000): 377–394.

Hall, Thomas C. "Christianity and Politics: V. The Modern Church and Politics." *The Biblical World* 41, no. 5 (May. 1913): 298–303.

Hanska, Jan. "Prophetic Politics — Leadership Based on the Stories of a Golden Past and a Glorious Future." *Perspectives* 17, no. 2 (2009): 93–117.

Heltzel, Peter Goodwin. *Jesus and Justice: Evangelicals, Race, and American Politics*. New Haven and London: Yale University Press, 2009.

Hendricks, Jr., Obery M. "Class, Political Conservatism and Jesus." *CrossCurrents* 55, no. 3, (Fall 2005): 304–321.

Hollenbach, Paul W. "Jesus, Demoniacs, and Public Authorities: A Socio-Historical Study." *Journal of the American Academy of Religion* 49, no. 4 (Dec. 1981): 567–588.

Hudson, Darril. "The World Council of Churches and Racism in Southern Africa." *International Journal* 34, no.3, Race and Religion (Summer 1979): 475–500.

Irvine, Stuart A. "Politics and Prophetic Commentary in Hosea 8:8-10." *Journal of Biblical Literature* 114, no. 2 (Summer, 1995): 292–294.

Johnson, Israel Ndu. "The Church and Politics in the Niger Delta." *Journal of the Historical Society of Nigeria* 26 (2017): 92–106.

Judson, Harry Pratt. "The Political Effects of the Teaching of Jesus." *The Biblical World* 11, no. 4 (Apr. 1898): 229–238.

Kelly, Karen, and Elizabeth Hutchison. "Crosscurrents: Liberation Theology." *Harvard International Review* 8, no. 2 (Dec. 1985): 22–24.

Kirylo, James D, and James H Cone. "Paulo Freire, Black Theology of Liberation, and Liberation Theology: A Conversation with James H. Cone." *Counterpoints* 385 (2011): 195–212.

Kirylo, James D. "Liberation Theology and Paulo Freire." *Counterpoint* 385 (2011): 167–193.

Levine, Daniel H, and Alexander W Wilde. "The Catholic Church, 'Politics,' and Violence: The Colombian Case." *The Review of Politics* 39, no. 2 (Apr. 1977): 220–249.

Levine, Daniel H. "From Church and State to Religion and Politics and Back Again." *World Affairs* 150, no. 2 (Fall 1987): 93–108.

Levine, Daniel H. "Religion and Politics, Politics and Religion: An Introduction." *Journal of Interamerican Studies and World Affairs* 21, no. 1 (Feb. 1979): 5–29.

Longman, Timothy. "Church Politics and the Genocide in Rwanda." *Journal of Religion in Africa* 31, no. 2 (May 2001): 163–186.

Martin, Craig. "Jesus' Empire or the Empire's Jesus?" *Method & Theory in the Study of Religion* 26, no. 2 (2014): 211–216.

Michael, Matthew. "African Theology and the Paradox of Missions: Three Intellectual Responses to the Modern Missions Crisis of the African Church." *Transformation* 31, no. 2, (Apr. 2014): 79–98.

Moxnes, Halvor. "Making Jesus Masculine: The Historical Jesus and the Challenges of Nineteenth-Century Politics." *Neotestamentica* 48, no. 1 (2014): 57–74.

Pinto, Simon, Antony Lawrence, and Stany C. Fernandes, eds., *Politics and Mission in Critical Times. Local and Global Perspectives*. Bengaluru: Theological Publications in India, 2020.

Rensberger, David. "The Politics of John: The Trial of Jesus in the Fourth Gospel." *Journal of Biblical Literature* 103, no. 3 (Sep. 1984): 395–411.

Rubenstein, Richard L. "The Political Significance of Latin American Liberation Theology." *World Affairs* 148, no. 3 (Winter 1985–86):159–167.

Spencer, Leon P. "Church and State in Colonial Africa: Influences Governing the Political Activity of Christian Missions in Kenya." *Journal of Church and State* 31, no. 1 (Winter 1989): 115–132.

Stephenson, Lisa P. "Prophetically Political, Politically Prophetic: William Cavanaugh's 'Theopolitical Imagination' as an Example of Walter Brueggemann's 'Prophetic Imagination.'" *Journal of Church and State* 53, no. 4 (Autumn 2011): 567–586.

Yirenkyi, Kwasi. "The Role of Christian Churches in National Politics: Reflections from Laity and Clergy in Ghana." *Sociology of Religion* 61, no. 3 (Autumn, 2000): 325–338.

Zeilstra, Jurjen A. "The Cold War, the Unity of the Church and Eastern Orthodoxy, 1948-1966." In *Visser't Hooft, 1900–1985: Living for the Unity of the Church*. Amsterdam: Amsterdam University Press, 2020.

Chapter 3

THE GOSPEL MISSION IN SOUTH ASIA: TODAY AND BEYOND

Some years ago, I spoke to a group of college students studying arts and science. Although I cannot recall the exact content of my speech, one question from a young student remains vivid. He asked, "Father, why is God so selfish?" This question intrigued me, and I inquired about the reason behind his query. The student explained that in our church prayers, we repeatedly praise God, thank him, and glorify him. If humans were to expect such an adulation, we might consider them selfish. Thus, he concluded, if God desires to be praised, thanked, and glorified, then God must be selfish.

In response to the perplexing question, all I could offer the young man was a gentle reminder of the words spoken by Saint Irenaeus: *Gloria Dei, vivens homo* - the glory of God is the human being fully alive. By praising and glorifying God, we do not augment God's greatness. Instead, something happens to us human beings: we are transformed.

All this echoes with what we profess in the *Credo*- our profession of faith. Speaking about the mystery of incarnation, we confess that it happened *propter nos et propter nostram salutem* (for us and for our salvation). What the one who was in the form of God does (Phil 2: 6- 11) - namely, taking on human flesh – happens for us and for our salvation. By evangelizing, we are not increasing the glory of God, but doing something, following the incarnation, for the cause of human beings whom God loved so much (Jn 3:16). Evangelization is, then, both a story of God and a story of human beings, especially of the poor. An evangelization that speaks of God and neglects the story of the poor and their flourishing cannot be genuine. Jon Sobrino goes to the heart of the matter when he tweaks the words of Iranaeus and says, "The glory of God is the poor man alive."[1] In this sense, the glory of God becomes a call to a programme of life.

When we speak of evangelization in South Asia, we need to be, at the same time, aware that it happens for the benefit of the peoples and nations in this South Asian region. That is precisely also the reason that we constantly correlate the task of evangelization with the socio-political and cultural context of our region.

This chapter consists of three parts: Part I: Some Theological Principles for Evangelization in South Asia; Part II: The Dynamics of Evangelization in South Asia; Part III: South Asian Pedagogy of Evangelization.

Part I: Some Theological Principles for Evangelization in South Asia

Ad Gentes of Vatican II speaks *ex professo* of the mission. It is a well-known document and much studied. We are not going into it in this chapter. I suggest we read *Ad Gentes* with another important document of Vatican II, namely *Gaudium et Spes*, the Pastoral Constitution on the Church in the Modern World. This will help us better understand the mission today and tomorrow in our South Asian region.

If we read the signs of the times in South Asia, we would also realize how relevant and significant Gaudium et Spes is as a mission document for our context.[2] It is a unique document that tried to re-calibrate the Church-world relationship. Here, we would find some important theological principles to pursue evangelization in the broader frame of human and communitarian issues which challenge South Asian societies. This document allows us to begin our reflections on evangelization from below – from our societies' concrete social, political, economic, and cultural situations. Given the diversity in the global situation, this document's reception will also be different. Hence there is legitimate room to speak about the South Asian reception of Gaudium et Spes in the contextual task of evangelization.

Secondly, the document inspires us to pursue evangelization in the spirit of dialogue, aware that Church not only contributes to the flourishing of human beings and the world but that it also *receives*. Gaudium et Spes make this point clear when it states,

> The Church is not unaware of how much it has profited from the history of the development of mankind. It profits from the experience of past ages, from the progress of the sciences, and from the riches hidden in various cultures.[3]

In the vision of Gaudium et Spes, dialogue is one through which "new avenues to truth are opened up". An important task follows for the Church and for all the faithful.

> With the help of the Holy Spirit, it is the task of the whole people of God, particularly of its pastors and theologians, to listen to and distinguish the many voices of our times and to interpret them in the light of the divine Word.[4]

Let me highlight some of the crucial insights of Gaudium et Spes, which will guide us in evangelizing, in the spirit of dialogue with the world of South Asia.[5]

Evangelization Based on Creation and Incarnation

Gaudium et Spes takes us back to the very beginning – to the story of God's *creation*. Creation, as Biblical scholars tell us, is a saving event. This story treasures a fundamental truth, namely the dignity of human beings as the image of God. Through Gaudium et Spes, the Council reminds us of the primordial and unconditional value of human persons, which cannot be compromised. To uphold the dignity of every man and woman and to defend their fundamental right is an integral part of the Church's evangelizing mission. Such a challenging task is rooted in the Christian faith in God's creation of human beings in God's own image. This dignity is also what the mystery of incarnation proclaims. The self-manifestation of God takes place in history "The Word became flesh" (Jn 1:14). The flesh here denotes creatureliness, human history, weakness and the transient character of life. God becoming flesh means that God is part of human history with all its fragility and ambiguities. The continuity of God's presence in history indicated in the prologue of John is echoed in the book of Revelation, which says:

> See, the home of God is among mortals.
> He will dwell with them;
> they will be his peoples,
> and God himself will be with them (Rev. 21:3).

Henceforth, for humans, history becomes the meeting place of God. This history is dynamic and comprises political processes, economic dealings, social interactions, and cultural creations. God becoming flesh means that God is involved in God's self-manifestation in politics, economy, society, culture, and so on, which constitute human existence. A reading of the life of Jesus as expressed in the gospels bears witness to the self-manifestation of God in history.

The positive view about the world in the light of creation adopted by Gaudium et Spes as the platform for dialogue and evangelization found resistance in Vatican II, especially among theologians like Henri de Lubac and Joseph Ratzinger, for whom this most extended document of the Council suffered from optimism. However, the problem was with the Neo-Augustinianism of these scholars which led them to interpret Gaudium et Spes in that way.[6] The ecclesiology behind such a position is opposition between the Church and the world since the Church is defined as a perfect supernatural society (*societas perfecta supernaturalis*) vis-à-vis the sinful world. Obviously, such a dichotomy characterized by pessimism, diffidence and fear that our faith could be surrendered to modernity is not a good starting point for dialogue with the world and the World Religions.[7]

Human Community

Gaudium et Spes dwells on another crucial theological principle, namely God's creation of the *human community*. Humans are not merely individuals; society is not an aggregate of individuals. People are bound together based on their common origin and destiny. The mystery of the Church as a sacrament, explored by Vatican II, means that it is "a sign and instrument both of a very closely-knit union with God and of the unity of the whole human race."[8] In our present-day world, the dominant explanation of human community is given by the ideology of neoliberalism, which bases human interrelationships on a hypothetical *social contract*. Human beings create a society which is enabled by contractual obligations. This is a fragile foundation.

One of the things of contemporary experience is the crisis in the foundation of human co-existence. Many people, especially those who follow the logic of the market, ask, why help the poor? If the poor are poor, they are to blame; they do not know how to compete, so they say.[9] Like the rest of the world, South Asia is in the grip of a serious crisis. Mere contractual thinking cannot save it. The future of South Asia and the world will rest on the *solidarity* we build among human beings. It will depend upon creating authentic communities in true love and communion, in the spirit of cooperation, mutual exchange, and solidarity. Evangelization means to strengthen and help found the society at a deeper level: It is love that binds together; unconditional love accepts the other as he or she is. This should be the cornerstone of every human community and public morality.[10]

Engagement in History

Another important principle which flows from Gaudium et Spes for our task of evangelization is the call to engage ourselves in the history of South Asia comprising social, political, cultural, and economic spheres. The more we interact in faith with this history, the more evangelization occurs. There is no other way than to immerse in this history in order to understand the why and how of evangelization. For, human activity or engagement contributes to the coming of God's Kingdom, which is taking shape already here and now, as Gaudium et Spes tells us, and hence our societal engagement with earthly realities and their transformation is an integral part of evangelization. As noted, it is a perspective on evangelization that removes the dichotomy between the material and the spiritual, this-worldly and the other-worldly. As Gaudium et Spes states,

> Far from diminishing the concern to develop this earth, the expectancy of a new earth should spur us on, for it is here that the body of a new human family grows, foreshadowing in some way the age to come.[11]

The Mystery Dimension of Evangelization

Speaking on some of the principles of evangelization, I want to highlight how important it is to pursue evangelization with a *sense of mystery*. Without this, evangelization will be simply proselytization; it will be like swelling our ranks and files as political parties and other organizations do. Evangelization must be accompanied by a sense of mystery because we humans are those to whom *God comes in search*. More than we seek God and proclaim the Good News, God seeks every human person more intensely and bestows divine knowledge and grace. We need to pay attention to the presence of God and the working of the Spirit in every human person, communities, cultures, and traditions. I am reminded of the words of Augustine in his confessions:

> Lo, you were within,
> but I outside, seeking there for you,…
> You were with me, but I was not with you…[12]

Evangelization imposes on local South Asian Churches the task of bringing the Good News to others and discovering with a sense of awe that even before we reach people with our evangelization, God is with them - working in them and their lives. Evangelization, then, becomes a service to help people discover God in themselves and their lives. If we respect people, we must respect the mystery of God's presence in others.

Further, human beings are images of God and share in the divine mystery. Their encounter with the divine is also a mystery. Our faith tells of the overwhelming grace that shatters human plans and calculations. What happens between the heart of a human being and God is shrouded in mystery, and we have no means of comprehending it. Since the encounter of God and the Spirit in people's hearts is sacred, we should never trivialize it or try to reduce it within our human frames of understanding.

The cross needs to be brought to the centre of Christian evangelization. I do not mean an understanding of the cross, which makes us view ourselves as victims, as the persecuted. This latter understanding of the cross could create a false dichotomy of us standing with the good vis-à-vis those against God. Such an attitude could foster self-righteousness. The cross symbolizes the suffering of the poor – "the crucified people." Across religious divides, the poor of South Asia carry the cross imposed on them by a society that is insensitive to human dignity, to the values of equity and justice.

We need a prophetic theology of the cross in evangelization in the sense that the cross becomes a challenge to all powers that oppress the poor. It will critically question institutions and structures – social, political, economic, and cultural – that go against the freedom and dignity of the poor of God. As a call to self-abnegation and servanthood, the cross is an antidote to the power of evil and the promise of a redeeming future. In this sense, the cross needs to accompany every initiative of evangelization.

From Modernity to the Poor

As we noted, Gaudium et Spes provides us with several principles for evangelization. However, this document and Vatican II in general also have their limits. Some of these were realized and addressed in the immediate post-Conciliar period. To understand the question, we need to refer here to the critique to Gaudium et Spes from two different quarters. The traditional European theologians were generally critical of this document for its lack of doctrinal content and rigour. From this perspective, it contrasted with the document on the Church, Revelation, etc. Another critique of Gaudium et Spes and Vatican II, in general, was that it did not deeply address the issue of poverty and the poor. Preoccupied with the dialogue with the modern world, Gaudium et Spes dealt with several valid questions about the modern world in different areas such as politics, economy, culture, war and peace. Evangelization appeared to be focused on meaningfully interpreting and explaining the gospel message to the modern and adult world.[13]

One of the most significant contributions of liberation theology was the turn it effected from modernity to the life and experience of the poor, thereby reconfiguring the understanding of evangelization. In Latin America, both continental assemblies in Medellin and Puebla viewed the task of evangelization through the prism of the poor, effecting a true reform of the Church.[14] The new question was how to interpret the Good News in a world of "non-persons." The documents of Medellin dealing with justice, peace, and the Church of the poor became a turning point. Puebla re-affirmed the approach of Medellin for evangelization and spoke of "preferential option for the poor."[15] The methodology at Medellin and Puebla was one of reflecting on the actual reality, then recalling theological principles, and finally moving into action. These Latin American assemblies highlighted the importance of conscientization in evangelization, which helps turn the poor into active subjects and to effect social transformation in the light of the gospel.

This approach to evangelization called for a sharp critique of the system, of the powers and principalities that preside over poverty, oppression, and the powerlessness of the poor. A prophetic critique of the prevailing socio-political and socio-cultural order is a guiding principle and an integral part of the work of evangelization. This liberation approach to evangelization and taking sides with the poor contrasts the tradition of going along uncritically with the political establishment.[16] Shifting from modernity to the poor also meant a new turn from the traditional approach to the poor through developmental works and charity to that of liberation, justice, and equality. These developments, shifts and liberation orientation get reflected in the document of Pope Paul VI *Evangelii Nuntiandi.*

Part II: The Dynamics of Evangelization

After recalling some important theological principles which need to accompany and inspire the work of evangelization, we now turn our attention to the second part; namely, the current history of South Asia constituting significant challenges to evangelization.

South Asian Predicament

Let me list, without elaborating, some of the critical issues South Asia is grappling with. Crisis of democracy and democratic institutions; shift to authoritarianism and populism; religious nationalism, fundamentalism and violence; widening the gap between the rich and the poor causing gross inequality; caste-hierarchy and new forms of social oppression; oppression of women; environmental crisis; the problem of migration (internal and external) and refugees; violation of human rights and human trafficking; unemployment of growing number of youth; issues of ethnicity and ethnic conflicts; issues of religious and linguistic minorities; issues connected with survival: food, safe drinking water, medical care, housing; issues of illiteracy and education.

As we can note, many of these issues are physical issues about the materiality of human life. Christian faith, however, is not dualistic but holistic. The body is an integral part of salvation. The mystery of God taking human bodily form, the faith in the resurrection of the body (I Cor. 15: 35-50), the hope in the coming of a new heaven and earth (Rev. 21:1) – these prompt us to weave the physical realities and materiality into our evangelization.

Rice Christians?

Let us continue our reflection, recalling the history of evangelization in South Asia, where mass conversions have taken place at specific periods. Those who listened to the Good News and converted to Christianity in the mass-conversion movements were mostly Dalits and those from the so-called lower castes. These people have often been slighted, derided and disparagingly referred to as "rice Christians" by those who claim to be from higher castes. These latter Christians also claim to possess a superior faith, not concerned about materiality. They contrast their "pure" faith with that of the lower castes, who they think converted for material benefits. But what is wrong with rice/wheat Christians?[17] They are fully living their Christian faith by weaving into it their material and physical needs.

In the prayer Jesus taught the disciples (Mt 6: 9 – 13), the first part speaks about the Father in heaven, about glorifying God's name, about the coming of the Kingdom, and fulfilment of God's will. However, the second part of the prayer blends the material realities of daily life with the petitions of the first part. Here the prayer is for daily bread, forgiveness, reconciliation, prayer not to be led into temptation, and so on. Concern for the physicality of life has to do with issues of equality, justice, freedom, human dignity, and so on. They are all to be woven into the practice of evangelization in South Asia.

South Asia is a region where inequality is at its peak. The gift of God's creation and nature's resources are appropriated by a few in our countries, and the vast masses are left in abysmal poverty. Hence, the importance of the issue of justice in our work of evangelization. We are encouraged by the words of the Synod on Justice, which stated,

> Action on behalf of justice and participation in the transformation of the world fully appears to us as a constitutive dimension of the preaching of the Gospel or, in other words, of the Church's mission for the redemption of the human race and its liberation from every oppressive situation.[18]

Hierarchy of Truths

Further, the dynamics of evangelization will be guided by what Vatican II called the "hierarchy of truths." It means that not all truths of faith are of the same value. There are issues of vital importance on which we need to focus. If the Church loses focus, it will talk about all kinds of things, confusing the people. People will be unable to distinguish the most essential things touching the core of the gospel. To cite an example provided by Pope Francis in his *Evangelii Gaudium*, a parish priest may go on passionately speaking in his sermons all through the year about giving up alcohol and the need for practising temperance. He may hardly talk about charity and justice.[19] Similarly, we may speak about the law. Sure, laws are important. However, if we fail to talk about grace, we will miss something that goes right to the heart of the Good News. In evangelization, Christians should be able to communicate what is most important with due proportion. Otherwise, the communication can be lopsided and distorted.

The Poor as the Subject of Evangelization

It is unmistakably clear that the poor occupy a central place in Jesus' preaching of the Good News of the Kingdom of God. The Good News, as noted, is directed to the poor. In the vision of Jesus, the poor are the beneficiaries of the Kingdom of God. Pope Francis reminds us about it and tells us that the way to approach the poor is to respect and love them, which is different from simple developmental or social work. Pope Francis says,

> Only based on this real and sincere closeness can we properly accompany the poor on their path of liberation. Only this will ensure that "in every Christian community the poor feel at home. Would not this approach be the greatest and most effective presentation of the good news of the Kingdom?" Without the preferential option for the poor, the proclamation of the Gospel, which is the prime form of charity, risks being misunderstood or submerged by the ocean of words that engulf us daily in today's mass communications society.[20]

The Bible, from Genesis to the final Book of Revelation, has one message. It is the fact that God is on the side of the poor, the weak, the victims. Here is the core message of the gospel. Jesus constantly and consistently paid attention to those who are small in the eyes of the world, like the widow in the gospel narrative, who puts all that she had, and Jesus praised her (Lk 21:1–4). If we follow Jesus, the poor should be at the centre of Christian evangelizing mission in South Asia. This is precisely what Pope Francis does in *Evangelii Gaudium* inspiring us to follow this path of Jesus.

Gustavo Gutiérrez concludes his classical work focusing on the agency of the poor:

> In the last instance, we will have an authentic theology of liberation only when the oppressed themselves can freely raise their voices and express themselves directly and creatively in society and in the heart of the people of God. When they themselves 'account for the hope' which they bear. When they themselves are the protagonists of their own liberation.[21]

Evangelization is not a one-way traffic. The poor to whom the Good News is addressed are not passive recipients. Pope Francis highlights the agency of the poor and their active role, which need to be borne in mind.

> The new evangelization is to acknowledge the saving power in their [the poor] lives and to put them at the centre of the Church' pilgrim way. We are called to find Christ in them, to lend our voices to their causes, but also to be their friends, to listen to them, to speak for them and to embrace the mysterious wisdom which God wishes to share with us through them.[22]

Pope Francis likes to use more verbs than nouns. We cannot but be struck by the verbs he uses: *To acknowledge,* to *put* them at the centre, to *find* Christ in them; to *lend* our voices to their cause; to *befriend* them; to *listen; to speak* for them; *to embrace* them.

The use of verbs by Pope Francis speaking of evangelization is striking compared to many Vatican jaw-breaking documents on mission full of abstract terms and nouns. In Pope Francis' understanding of evangelization, we note a dynamism and we feel close to how Jesus evangelized.

Evangelization with Others

The history and context of South Asia invite us to do our mission in cooperation with people of goodwill in our part of the world. Here I mean the importance of cooperating with men and women of goodwill in transforming history. Gaudium et Spes, as I noted, is one of the most beautiful mission documents ever, and its language of mission is understandable to South Asians. It speaks the language of human dignity, issues of politics, economy, and culture which affect people's lives. However, the issues facing humanity in this part of the globe cut across religious, ethnic, national, and linguistic affiliations. Christian collaboration with others to transform every stratum of the society will be part of its evangelizing mission. Here is a challenging arena for Christian commitment and action.

There are certainly problems of religious extremism in several countries of South Asia – Nepal, Bangladesh, Sri Lanka, Pakistan and India. This is a real challenge. On the other hand, we have a bright side in South Asia which has a tremendous civilizational heritage of mutual tolerance. This inherent sense of mutual tolerance and respect for each other's religious universe is what is happening in everyday life. The traditional spirit of tolerance gives a grand opening and opportunity to interact with Muslim, Buddhist, Hindu, Sikh, Jain and Parsi neighbours on day-to-day basis.

Let me here refer to an interview of Cardinal Joseph Couts of Karachi, in which he refers to Sr Ruth Pfau[23]. She was a German missionary who laboured in Pakistan tirelessly for many decades amidst lepers. When she died, Pakistan, which is a Muslim country and often depicted as characterized by Islamic fundamentalism, accorded her a state funeral. When Cardinal Couts received his red hat, Pakistan minister of religious affairs attended the event in Rome.

We all know and have experienced religious fundamentalism in our countries of South Asia. However, we should not forget that for every fundamentalist Hindu, Muslim or Buddhist, thousands of Hindus, Muslims and Buddhists have great regard for Christian involvement in education, medical care, and commitment to the poor and the marginalized. They give great support to the work by Christians, and many of them are interested in a joint involvement for the transformation of society.

There is no denying the fundamentalism and oppression of minorities under which Christians suffer in South Asia. I do not want to undermine the ground realities. Despite the numerous difficulties we experience, there are a lot of conducive spaces and opportunities for joint involvement on the part of Christians and Christian communities for the transformation of our societies. These spaces of dialogue and participation could be infused with the spirit of the gospel to create a new and different world, the mirror image of the Reign of God, the central message of Jesus.

Addressing the Issues Behind Fundamentalism

When addressing religious fundamentalism, whether it be within the Muslim, Buddhist, or Hindu contexts, it is essential to consider not only their attitude and reactions towards Christian minorities but also delve into underlying factors. In the following paragraphs, let me highlight some of these issues which profoundly affect the lives of the people of Asia.

The Past – Golden Age?

Fundamentalism projects the past as the golden age, and hence it proposes the agenda of restoration of the old. This is what I would call the temptation of the golden age. Whatever comes after the golden past, is only decline and disintegration *"Après moi le dèluge"* – after me the floods, so said the French King Louis XV. Evangelization is a call to change and transform the existing order, whereas fundamentalists – including Christians - seek to re-establish the past glory, *the status quo ante*. There were the Zealots and the Sicarii of the Second Temple of Judaism, who, though appeared to be revolutionaries, were in fact, a group intent on restoring the past. The Zealots were the fundamentalists and terrorists of the time. Jesus goes not to restore the old, but creates something new and different in response to the call of God. Thus, we have New Testament, new heaven and earth, new Jerusalem, new man and so on. The Jesus-movement was a forward-looking movement of hope, and in this sense, apocalyptical. We cannot respond to fundamentalism by ourselves becoming fundamentalists. This is a constant temptation when we are faced by provocation from Hindu, Muslim or Buddhist fundamentalists.

The Divide

Every fundamentalism is inherently divisive. It creates "we" vs. "they." It is an attempt to create exclusionary identity. Fundamentalism seeks to demarcate clear religious boundaries. Further, fundamentalist movements aim at *purity* of identity which it believes is safeguarded by erecting borders. Such a view suffers from an essentialist conception of religion that defines who is in and who is out, and establishes criteria for religious belonging.[24] In reality, as a result of encounters and exchanges, fluidity has characterized the life of religions. It represents a challenge to any exclusionary theological conception.

Targeting Women

Further, we know from our South Asian experience that most fundamentalist groups target women, and seek to control their bodies and minds by imposing severe restrictions on their thinking and free expression. These groups flaunt patriarchal values to subjugate women and stunt their free development as human persons. In this regard, there is not much difference among the Islamic, Christian, Buddhist or Hindu fundamentalist movements. We also note how the moral policing and accusation of blasphemy, as in the case of Pakistan, cause serious human rights violation. As for South Asia is concerned, targeting women is actually a backlash against their increasing affirmation, autonomy and freedom vis-à-vis the forms of traditional and modern patriarchy. Their growing employment and other new economic prospects have contributed to the new situation. In short, women in South Asia have begun to resist what is imposed on them in the name of religion and its traditions.

These are very serious issues and go beyond the question of minorities. The problems we have named above affect the entire society and nations, calling for faith-inspired response and intervention in our practice of evangelization.

Responding to Fundamentalism

The best response to religious fundamentalism is to address the issues behind them as I tried to indicate through some examples. This approach will enable a different perspective and attitude rather than attempting to repay them in their own currency or seek retaliation. This kind of Christian attitude is beautifully advocated in a letter of St Ignatius of Antioch addressed to the early Christian community of Ephesians faced with the "fundamentalists" of that time:

> Now for other men "pray unceasingly" for there is in them a hope of repentance,
> that they may find God. Suffer them, therefore, to become your disciples,

at least through your deeds. Be yourselves gentle in answer to their wrath; be humble in mind in answer to their proud speaking; offer prayer for their blasphemy; be steadfast in faith for their error; be gentle for their cruelty, and do not seek to retaliate.[25]

Retaliating and revenge are general problems. They do not bring about justice, as often falsely believed. Rajmohan Gandhi, the grandson of Mahatma Gandhi, in his timely work entitled, *Revenge and Reconciliation* notes how in South Asia there has been a tradition of revenge, honour-killing, and conquest of enemies. He refers to many instances in the epics of Ramayana and Mahabharata.[26] However, the advent of Buddhism in South Asian history effected a revolutionary change by introducing the noble value and practice of *compassion* (*karuna*) towards human beings and all creatures. We need to incorporate the spirit of compassion, of divine mercy in the practice of evangelization, especially when we are confronted with fundamentalism in our countries.

One could easily turn the situation of Christians in South Asia into something like what happened in the early Church and hence start interpreting the suffering and death as "persecution" and "martyrdom." This approach is very ambiguous, to say the least, especially in the present-day context. Traditionally, Judaism, Christianity, Islam, and Sikhism attach great value to martyrdom.[27] The expression "martyrdom" is used also among the fundamentalists and even terrorists whose "heroic" deaths are celebrated. Mark Juergensmeyer has gone into this phenomenon and recorded the results of his field-studies in his work *"Terror in the Mind of God."*[28] Are Christians to die *for* Christ?[29] Or rather, as Jon Sobrino rightly points out, Christians need to die *like* Christ? [30] "I have come that they may have life, and have it in all fullness" (Jn 10:10). However, to give life to others, one could be challenged to sacrifice one's own life. "Greater love has no one than this that he lay down his life for his friends" (Jn 15: 13).

Christian involvement in evangelization needs to be free of "martyrdom-complex".[31] Love for others, especially for the cause of the poor and the marginalized, would qualify today as the right perspective to understand Christian martyrdom. In other words, evangelization must be accompanied by unswerving commitment to the poor and a readiness to bear all the consequences of standing in solidarity with the poor. For, the poor stand in the place of Christ (Mt 25: 31–40). In Latin America, martyrdom as dying like Christ is a theologically very significant theme today and is associated with the life and death of Oscar Romero and Ignacio Ellacuría.[32] In South Asia, we need to acknowledge the many unsung heroes and heroines who have lived like Christ and gave up their lives, also like Jesus, so that others may have life. Most glaring recent example is Fr Stan Lourdusamy who stood with the tribal people in deep solidarity which unfortunately led to his martyrdom. When evangelization is viewed through the prism of these martyrs, it is bound to appear very different from proclaiming Christian doctrines.

Evangelization and Advocacy

Another important dimension in the dynamics of evangelization is *advocacy* which we need to practice in collaboration with all people of goodwill. Engaging in advocacy means taking up activities that can influence public policies and decisions in such fields as economy, politics, institutions etc.[33] It can take the form of deploying media, lobbying with people and groups who could wield public influence. This approach could contribute to change and transformation in South Asian societies.[34] As John Samuel rightly points out, public advocacy needs to be people-centered. For this, one needs to adopt a political perspective and not confine oneself to managerial or technical points of view.

> Advocacy without mobilization is unlikely to achieve much. The credibility and socio-political legitimacy of advocacy efforts largely depend on the means and the ends being consistent and compatible. In the Indian context, grassroots support rather than professional background most determines a lobbyist's credibility. A major challenge is safeguarding and extending the political space to advocate for the cause of the marginalized, resisting the agendas set by others, whether the multinational corporations or various kinds of fundamentalism.[35]

Advocacy resonates with the spirit of the gospel. A tiny minority Christians do not have the necessary human, material resources, and structures to alleviate poverty, or provide welfare measures at a large scale. What Christians do could be viewed as symbolic gestures of succour to the poor and the marginalized. The need of the hour in our South Asian context calls for Christians and Churches to play an advocacy role for promoting human rights and protecting weaker sections – women, children, Dalits, tribals, and other vulnerable sections of our societies. Here is a new prophetic role Christians could play. The media advocacy, especially social media, assumes great importance today. This is also part of evangelization.

The engagement with advocacy will happen when we read the signs of the times. More discussion and debate should take place in the Churches regarding public issues. This is a healthy practice which will accompany Christian involvement for evangelization. Studies show that such a method of discussion of public issues was quite common before the political Independence of our countries from the British rule. In India, for example, Christian journals and weeklies discussed the issues affecting the general public and Christians expressed their views freely.[36] Unfortunately, this tradition of exchange and discussion in the Church about what affects everybody is not to be seen much in present times. This tradition needs to be awakened today.

Part III: South Asian Pedagogy of Evangelization

We may have treasures. Yet we may not reach others if we fail to follow sound pedagogy. I think pedagogy is something forgotten in the practice of evangelization. In this third part of the chapter, we shall focus on this aspect. A good pedagogy will tell us how to approach others, and how we need to take into account the background, perception, and context of those to whom we address the Good News.

A Larger Circle of the Disciples of Jesus

We do not begin to speak about Jesus and the gospel in a vacuum. There is a long tradition of people of other faiths who have understood Christ and incorporated his message into their lives. They have read the gospels and let themselves be inspired by the figure of Jesus. This legacy needs to be considered as it helps present Jesus vibrating with the lives of South Asians across religious boundaries. This is a rich heritage which Christians could draw from and learn from.

Evangelii Gaudium, speaks of three settings of evangelization: Regular pastoral ministry to the faithful; the baptized whose life does not reflect Christian faith; and those who do not know Jesus Christ.[37] Our South Asian experience shows still another category of people we face in our engagement of evangelization. I mean to say that the relationship of many to Christian faith can be characterized as *"believing without belonging."* Perhaps millions in South Asia believe in Jesus Christ, his life and teachings. They are devotees of Jesus. However, they do not want to belong to the Church as an institution through the rite of baptism. In some places, these believers are called *Khristbhaktas* or devotees of Christ.[38] In other places they are referred to as *"Jesus Movement."*

Our work of evangelization will build on what already people know and have experienced of Jesus and the gospel.[39] Besides the Khristbhaktas, we could refer here to other individuals who were attached to the person and teachings of Jesus and greatly influenced large masses. For example, Swami Ramakrishna Paramahamsa, a great mystic of the nineteenth century, claimed to have experienced Jesus and had a mystical encounter with him. We must remember that Paramahamsa was an illiterate but got people to read the gospels to him. He was the most influential religious figures in the history of the Indian subcontinent for the past two centuries. It is striking that millions of Hindus learnt about Jesus through Paramahamsa. Can Christians also learn about Jesus from this mystic?[40]

Likewise, Gandhi held a deep affection for the life and principles of Jesus, particularly his Sermon on the Mount. He greatly respected the love-driven message Jesus conveyed and admired the self giving sacrifice symbolized by the cross. Yet another important South Asian personality who followed Jesus and interpreted his teaching was Raja Ram Mohan Roy, an Indian advocate of secular reform. Two centuries ago, Roy penned a remarkable work, titled, "*The Precepts of Jesus.*" Just recently, the well-known Sri Lankan theologian and Biblical scholar, R.S. Sugirtharajah, commented on the work and its lasting impact.[41]

The knowledge about Jesus and faith in him by our neighbours of other religions is also a work of grace. God was there before us. We could help them deepen their understanding and build further on what they know and have experienced. The pedagogy of South Asian evangelization would imply that we dialogue with people who are already in touch with Jesus and the gospel and help them discover more of the person and message of Jesus.

In all this, we could draw inspiration from the gospels. They seem to allow multiple degrees of following Jesus. Jesus had many circles of people around him – the twelve; among the twelve, one or two were closer to him. He also had the seventy-two disciples. Then, there were a large number of people who listened to him in the villages and small towns where he preached. They did not move around with him but were his sedentary disciples. The gospels tell us about Joseph of Arimathea who awaited the Reign of God, certainly not without influence from the teachings of Jesus. It speaks of Zacchaeus and his reception of Jesus. Lazarus, though a friend of Jesus, was among his sedentary followers; so too Cleophas (Lk 24:18); Barsabbas and Mathias (Acts 1:23). Among women, there were Mary Magdalene, Johanna, the wife of Chuza, Susanna, Mary, the mother of James and Salome (Lk 24:10; Mk 15:40-41). As we could see, there were different circles of Jesus' disciples and followers and different ways in which they admired, loved, and followed him.

In South Asia, as we noted, we do not begin from a tabula rasa. There are disciples of Jesus everywhere who relate with him at different levels, including the taxi driver who has a picture of Mother Mary in his taxi along with the goddess Saraswathi and Lakshmi or a Hindu woman who has the picture of the Sacred Heart of Jesus in her puja room, the most sacred place of the house. Then we have many followers among the poorest of the poor, like the Dalit families who may not have undergone baptism but for whom the Bible remains the most prized possession within their modest huts and tenements. Any discourse on evangelization needs to relate to this kind of wider acclaim for Jesus and his message that we find all over South Asia.

New Pedagogy

Christian evangelization is not to make others accept Jesus; instead create the conditions for them *to wish to receive Jesus* and the gospel.

Making others accept Jesus is an imposition, proselytization, coercion. Making others *to wish to accept* Jesus is real evangelization. Real pedagogy is when we make others wish to do or accept our proposal. Evangelization means sharing one's faith with others, knowing that the others are not tabula rasa. In this way, we respect the dignity and freedom of those to whom we propose the Good News. Through evangelization, we create an environment that would evoke in our neighbours a deeper interest in the person and message of Jesus. Their interest is evoked foremost when they see concrete witnesses whose lives have been transformed by their faith in Jesus Christ.

Dialogue and Proclamation

The preceding reflections will also throw light on the relationship between dialogue and proclamation - a very hotly debated question till a decade ago. A significant contribution from south Asia to global Christianity has been to help the Church not to make dialogue a means for evangelization. To do so would be in total dissonance with the experiences in South Asia. One of the best formulation relating dialogue and proclamation was done at the first ever joint meeting of Christian Conference of Asia (CCA) and Federation of Asian Bishops' Conferences (FABC) in Singapore in 1987.[42]

The local Churches of South Asia will learn to harmoniously blend evangelization and dialogue. This dialogue will be with other religious traditions and the larger world of South Asia. We need to apply to South Asia what Pope Paul VI said about dialogue with the world in general. In his celebrated encyclical *Eccclesiam Suam*, speaking of its purpose, he stated:

> The aim of this encyclical will be to demonstrate with increasing clarity how vital it is for the world, and how greatly desired by the Catholic Church, that the two should meet together, and get to know and love one another.[43]

The more we get to know the world of South Asia, the more we encounter it, the more we love it, the more profound the impact of our evangelization.

Conclusion

Let me conclude with the words of Pope Francis "A Person who thinks of only building walls, wherever they may be, and not building bridges is not Christian."[44] This could be said of evangelization. If evangelization builds walls and not bridges, it is not Christian; it is not according to the spirit of the gospel. What Pope Francis tells us goes along with the Christian mystical tradition. There is an aphorism attributed to Dionysius, the Aeropagite, which states, "God is a circle whose centre is everywhere, but his circumference is nowhere."[45] What we need in Asia is a polycentric evangelization that allows Christians and Christian communities a lot of freedom and a wider range of choices to infuse the life of the people, society and nations with the spirit of the gospel. Limiting evangelization to a pre-planned narrow scheme of thinking and planning will not help the cause of the gospel. The strength of Church's mission, as it is only the symbol and servant of the Kingdom, is to be gauged not based on its institutions, but on the values and ideals of the Reign of God it stands for and proclaims.

To build bridges through evangelization we need internal reform in our South Asian local Churches. It also includes constant renewal of the structures of the Church through a broader view of evangelization.[46] The mission of the local Churches of South Asia will be most effective when it becomes a model for the Kingdom values and the observance of human dignity and rights. Triumphalism and exceptionalism are to be avoided. These could be highly damaging for the mission of the Church in our societies structured around caste and hierarchy.

The thesis that what applies to the society does not apply to the Church could be dangerous and counter-witnessing. We saw the weakness and fallacy of such an argument in the case of sexual abuse by the clergy. We know the extent of damage and embarrassment this kind of thinking has caused. There is no exception to the Church in this matter. It is an issue which calls for owning responsibility. This is only an example. If any of the "interests" of the Church is above upholding the values of the Kingdom or human dignity and rights, this cannot be the true interest of the Church. We must remember that human dignity and unity of the whole human family are the inter-related core principles of the Church's social teachings.

A new vision of evangelization also requires a new type of leadership at all levels (episcopal, priestly, religious, and lay), a leadership capable and sensitive to the situation in our societies. Pessimism regarding the world and other traditions and the fear of making mistakes in our openness to them can prevent our local South Asian Churches from acting wisely. We need leadership that takes risks. As Pope Francis tells us in Evangelii Gaudium, "The Lord does not disappoint those who take [this] risk."[47]

NOTES

1   Jon Sobrino, *Karl Rahner and Liberation Theology*, https://www.theway.org.uk/back/434sobrino.pdf [accessed on 1 June 2023].

2   For a perceptive commentary on Gaudium et Spes, see Herbert Vorgrimler ed., *Commentary on the Documents of Vatican II*, vol V (New York: Herder and Herder, 1969); See also Norman P Tanner, *The Church and the World: Gaudium et spes, Inter mirifica*, vol. 2 (New York: Paulist Press, 2005); See also the chapter on *Gaudium et Spes* in Catherine E. Clifford and Massimo Faggioli eds., *The Oxford Handbook of Vatican II* (New York: Oxford University Press, 2023); Michael G. Lawler, Todd A. Salzman, and Eileen Burke-Sullivan, *The Church in the Modern World: Gaudium et Spes Then and Now* (Collegeville, Minnesota: Liturgical Press, 2014).

3   *Gaudium et Spes* 44.

4   *Ibid*

5   On the continuing relevance of Gaudium et Spes, see Joseph Joblin, "L'Église
        Dans Le Monde: Actualité de La Constitution Pastorale 'Gaudium et Spes',"
        Gregorianum 87, no. 3 (2006): 580–96; William Brownsberger, "Hope and
        the Hopeless: The Contemporary Addressee of 'Gaudium et Spes'," *New
        Blackfriars* 89, no. 1019 (2008): 60–76.

6   For the debates during the formulation of the document at Vatican II and in
        the Post-Vatican period, see Massimo Faggioli, "The Battle over *Gaudium et
        Spes*. Then and Now Dialogue with the Modern World after Vatican II," *A
        Council for the Global Church: Receiving Vatican II in History* (Minneapolis:
        Fortress Press, 2015), 143-164.

7   See Joseph Ratzinger, *Dogma und Verkündigung* (München: Erich Wewel
        Verlag, 1973), 183–204.

8   *Lumen Gentium* 1

9   On the connection between competition and exclusion, see Chapter 4.

10   Rebecca Todd Peters, "Theories of Solidarity," *Solidarity Ethics:
        Transformation in a Globalized World* (Minneapolis: Fortress Press,
        2014), 17–32; see also Paul de Beer, and Ferry Koster, *Sticking Together or
        Falling Apart? Solidarity in an Era of Individualization and Globalization*
        (Amsterdam: Amsterdam University Press, 2009).

11   *Gaudium et Spes* 39.

12   *Confessions* Book 10: chapter XXVII.

13   The new question that needs to be faced in the West is how to relate faith and
        postmodernity, Church and the postmodern world. On the need to reflect
        on the significance of Gaudium et Spes for postmodernity, see Lieven Boeve,
        "Gaudium et Spes and the Crisis of Modernity. The End of the Dialogue with
        the World?" (2002): 83–94.

14   David Abalos, "The Medellin Conference," *Cross Currents* 19, no. 2 (spring
        1969):113–132; see also Thomas John Scheuring, *'Evangelii nuntiandi' and the
        Puebla 'Final Document': Their Effects on the Mission of Evangelization with
        the Poor* (New York: Fordham University, 1990); Segundo Galilea, "Between
        Medellín and Puebla," *CrossCurrents* 28, no. 1 (1978): 71–78; Jon Sobrino,
        "The Lessons of Puebla," in https://www.theway.org.uk/back/20Sobrino.pdf.
        [accessed on 15 May 2023].

15   See Renato Poblete, "From Medellin to Puebla: Notes for Reflection," *Journal
        of Interamerican Studies and World Affairs* 21, no. 1[special Issue: The
        Church and Politics in Latin America] (Feb 1979): 31–44.

16   Cf. Anthony Gill, *Rendering unto Caesar: The Catholic Church and the State
        in Latin America* (Chicago: University of Chicago Press, 1998).

17   Cf. Felix Wilfred, *The Sling of Utopia* (Delhi: ISPCK, 2005), chapter 12, 307–
        325.

18   Document of the Roman Synod on Justice in the World: Introduction. For
        the text and comments on the document, see Joseph Gremillion, "Justice in

the World: Synod of Bishops Second General Assembly," in *The Gospel of Peace and Justice. Catholic Social Teaching Since Pope John* (New York: Orbis Books, 1975), 513–530.

19 See *Evangelii Gaudium* 38.

20 *Evangelii Gaudium* 199.

21 Gustavo Gutierrez, *A Theology of Liberation: History, Politics and Salvation* (New York: Orbis books, 1973).

22 *Evangelii Gaudium* 198.

23 *L'Osservatore Romano* -English Edition, 14 September 2018.

24 Cf. Felix Wilfred, *Religious Identities and the Global South: Porous Borders and Novel Paths* (Cham, Switzerland: Palgrave Macmillan, 2021).

25 Letter of St Ignatius to the Ephesians 10:1–2.

26 Rajmohan Gandhi, *Revenge and Reconciliation* (Delhi: Penguin India, 2000).

27 Cf. Margaret Cormkack, *Sacrificing the Self. Perspectives on Martyrdom and Religion* (Oxford: Oxford University Press, 2002); see also Louis E. Fenech, *Martyrdom in the Sikh Tradition* (Delhi: Oxford University Press, 2005).

28 Cf. Mark Juergensmeyer, *Terror in the Mind of God. The Global Rise of Religious Violence* (Berkley, London, Los Angeles: University of California Press, 2000).

29 We know from Christian history of mission, that many, even saints, desired a martyr's death, and going into mission allowed being martyred by the heathens "for Christ."

30 Thomas Fornet-Ponse, "Für Christus oder Wie Jesus Sterben? Zu Jon Sobrinos Verständnis Des Martyriums," *Zeitschrift Für Katholische Theologie* 135, no. 1 (2013): 73–90.

31 Teresa Okure, Jon Sobrino, and Felix Wilfred, eds., "Rethinking Martyrdom," *Concilium 2003/1*.

32 Cf. Kevin F. Burke, *The Ground Beneath the Cross. The Theology of Igancio Ellacuría* (Washington DC: Georgetown University Press, 2000).

33 For a general overview, see, Richard Hoefer, *Advocacy Practice* (New York: Oxford University Press, 2019, fourth edition). See also Rinku Sen, *Stir It Up. Lessons in Community Organizing Advocacy* (San Francisco, CA: John Wiley & Sons, 2003).

34 Cf. Felix Wilfred and D. John Romus, *Local Churches in South Asia and Evangelization* (Chennai: Claretian Communications, 2020). There is a whole section in the volume on Evangelization and Advocacy, 454–517.

35 John Samuel, "Public Advocacy and People-Centred Advocacy: Mobilising for Social Change," *Development in Practice* 17, no. 4/5 (Aug 2007): 615–621, at 617.

36 Cf. Mary John, *Indian Catholic Christians and Nationalism* (Delhi: ISPCK 2011).

37 *Evangelii Gaudium* 15.

38 On the phenomenona of Khristbhaktas, Jerome Sylvester presented a pioneering research as doctoral dissertation, which I had the privilege of guiding, at the University of Madras. It is available in print now. Jerome Sylvester, *Khristbhakta Movement. Hermeneutics of a Religio-Cultural Phenomenon* (Delhi: ISPCK, 2013), especially chapter 6, "The Signficance of the Khristbhakta Movement," 130–138.

39 Cf. M. M. Thomas, *The Acknowledged Christ of the Indian Renaissance* (Madras: C.L.S., 1970).

40 Francis Clooney, "What Christians Can Learn from the Hindu Mystic Ramakrishna" https://www.americamagazine.org/faith/2023/05/09vantage-point-clooney-ramakrishna245245?cx_testId=7&cx_testVariant=cx_1&cx_artPos=0&cx_experienceId=EXX1Z6PTUNON#cxrecs_s [accessed on 11 May, 2022].

41 R. Sugirtharajah, *The Brahmin and His Bible. Rammohun Roy's Precepts of Jesus 200 Years On* (London and New York: T&T Clark, 2019).

42 I had the privilege of presenting the keynote address following the inaugural speech of Msgr. Michael Fitzgerald, then Secretary of the Pontifical Council for Interreligious Dialogue, now cardinal. Stanley Samartha actively participated in the event and contributed significantly to drafting the final document.

43 *Ecclesiam Suam* 3

44 The pope made this comment in response to a journalist's question on Donald Trump, during a flight from Mexico to Rome, on 18 February, 2016. https://www.ncregister.com/news/pope-on-trump-person-who-thinks-only-about-building-walls-not-building-bridges-is-not-christian [accessed on 5 September 2023].

45 Similar statements are found also in several writers among some medieval Christian thinkers.

46 See *Evangelii Gaudium* 27.

47 *Evangelii Gaudium* 3. His example of signing a historic accord with Chinese State on 22 September 2018 is an example. Maybe it will be remembered as the greatest achievement of Pope Francis, or it could become in due course the most disastrous decision in his pontificate. The risk was there. And yet a decision was found under given circumstances. The pope has taken a bold step. It is a model for Church leaders to be brave and courageous in evangelization.

FURTHER READING

Abalos, David. "The Medellin Conference." *CrossCurrents* 19, no. 2 (spring 1969): 113-132.

Boeve, Lieven. "*Gaudium et Spes* and the Crisis of Modernity. The End of the Dialogue with the World?" (2002): 83-94.

Brondos, David A. *Introduction to Salvation and the Cross.* Minneapolis: Fortress Press, 2007.

Brownsberger, William. "Hope and the Hopeless: The Contemporary Addressee of 'Gaudium et Spes'." *New Blackfriars* 89, no. 1019 (2008): 60-76.

Burke, Kevin F. *The Ground Beneath the Cross. The Theology of Igancio Ellacuría.* Washington DC: Georgetown University Press, 2000.

Clifford, Catherine E, and Massimo Faggioli, eds. *The Oxford Handbook of Vatican II.* New York: Oxford University Press, 2023.

Clooney, Francis. "What Christians Can Learn from the Hindu Mystic Ramakrishna." https://www.americamagazine.org/faith/2023/05/09/vantage-point-clooney-ramakrishna 245245?cx_testId=7&cx_testVariant=cx_1&cx_artPos=0&cx_experienceId=EXX1Z6PTUNON#cxrecs_s [accessed on 11 May 2022].

Cormack, Margaret. *Sacrificing the Self. Perspectives on Martyrdom and Religion.* Oxford: Oxford University Press, 2002.

De Beer, Paul, and Ferry Koster. *Sticking Together or Falling Apart? Solidarity in an Era of Individualization and Globalization.* Amsterdam: Amsterdam University Press, 2009.

Faggioli, Massimo. *A Council for the Global Church: Receiving Vatican II in History.* Augsburg Fortress Publishers, 2015.

Fenech, Louis E. *Martyrdom in the Sikh Tradition.* Delhi: Oxford University Press, 2005.

Fornet-Ponse, Thomas. "Für Christus oder Wie Jesus Sterben? Zu Jon Sobrinos Verständnis Des Martyriums." *Zeitschrift Für Katholische Theologie* 135, no. 1 (2013): 73–90.

Galilea, Segundo. "Between Medellín and Puebla." *CrossCurrents* 28, no. 1 (1978): 71–78.

Gandhi, Rajmohan. *Revenge and Reconciliation.* Delhi: Penguin India, 2000.

Gill, Anthony. *Rendering unto Caesar: The Catholic Church and the State in Latin America.* Chicago: University of Chicago Press, 1998.

Gremillion, Joseph. "Justice in the World: Synod of Bishops Second General Assembly." *The Gospel of Peace and Justice. Catholic Social Teaching Since Pope John,* 513–530. New York: Orbis Books, 1975.

Gutiérrez, Gustavo. *A Theology of Liberation: History, Politics and Salvation.* Mary Knoll, New York: Orbis books, 1973.

Hoefer, Richard. *Advocacy Practice.* New York: Oxford University Press, 2019.

Joblin, Joseph. "L'Église dans le Monde: Actualité de la Constitution Pastorale 'Gaudium et Spes'." *Gregorianum* 87, no. 3 (2006): 580–96.

Juergensmeyer, Mark. *Terror in the Mind of God. The Global Rise of Religious Violence.* Berkley: University of California Press, 2000.

Lawler, Michael G, Todd A. Salzman, and Eileen Burke-Sullivan. *The Church in the Modern World: Gaudium et Spes Then and Now.* Collegeville, Liturgical Press, 2014.

Okure, Teresa, John Sobrino, and Felix Wilfred, eds. "Rethinking Martyrdom." *Concilium 2003/1.*

Peters, Rebecca Todd. "Theories of Solidarity." *Solidarity Ethics: Transformation in a Globalized World,* 17–32. Minneapolis: Fortress Press, 2014.

Poblete, Renato. "From Medellin to Puebla: Notes for Reflection." *Journal of Interamerican Studies and World Affairs* 21, no. 1 (1979): 31–44.

Ratzinger, Joseph. *Dogma und Verkündigung.* München: Erich Wewel Verlag, 1973.

Samuel, John. "Public Advocacy and People-Centred Advocacy: Mobilising for Social Change." *Development in Practice* 17, no. 4/5 (Aug. 2007): 615-621, at 617.

Scheuring, Thomas John. *'Evangelii Nuntiandi' and the Puebla 'Final Document': Their Effects on the Mission of Evangelization with the Poor.* New York: Fordham University, 1990.

Sen, Rinku. *Stir it Up. Lessons in Community Organizing Advocacy.* San Francisco: John Wiley & Sons, 2003.

Sobrino, Jon. "The Lessons of Puebla." In https://www.theway.org.uk/back/20Sobrino.pdf. [accessed on 15 May 2023].

Sugirtharajah, R. *The Brahmin and His Bible. Rammohun Roy's Precepts of Jesus 200 Years On.* London: T&T Clark, 2019.

Sylvester, Jerome. *Khristbhakta Movement. Hermeneutics of a Religio-Cultural Phenomenon.* Delhi: ISPCK, 2013.

Tanner, Norman P. *The Church and the World: Gaudium et Spes, Inter Mirifica,* vol. 2. New York: Paulist Press, 2005.

Thomas, M. M. *The Acknowledged Christ of the Indian Renaissance*. Madras: C.L.S., 1970.

Vorgrimler, Herbert, ed. *Commentary on the Documents of Vatican II*, vol V. New York: Herder and Herder, 1969.

Wilfred, Felix, and D. John Romus, eds. *Local Churches in South Asia and Evangelization*. Chennai: Claretian Communications, 2020.

Wilfred, Felix. *Religious Identities and the Global South: Porous Borders and Novel Paths*. Cham, Switzerland: Palgrave Macmillan, 2021.

Wilfred, Felix. *The Sling of Utopia*. Chapter 12, 307–325. Delhi: ISPCK, 2005.

LIBERATION

Chapter 4

ADDRESSING SOCIAL EXCLUSION IN SOUTH ASIA: GUIDING PRINCIPLES AND STRATEGIES FOR INCLUSION

Discrimination and exclusion have a long history in the life of humanity. They are pervasive in everyday social life and differ from society to society. However, the expression "social exclusion" is relatively new and is widely employed today in development studies and other disciplines.[1] In modern times, René Lenoir first used it in France in his work titled "*Les Exclus*" (1974) – The Excluded. He used it to refer to the physically and mentally challenged, the prisoners, migrants, substance abusers, delinquents, widows, the unemployed and so on. The idea was to expand the economic and social benefits to the excluded – one out of ten among the French population. However, over time, social exclusion came to be defined in conjunction with such phenomena as inequality, discrimination, and marginalization.

Grounds for and Forms of Exclusion

Ascriptive identities like ethnicity, caste, race; linguistic and regional identities; religious identities are some of the apparent grounds for exclusion. A universal form of discrimination is that of gender – women in all societies are discriminated against and excluded. The intersection between caste and patriarchy makes the exclusion of women highly oppressive. As a result, they experience discrimination in marriage, inheritance, land tenure, workplace, differential wages, political representation, and, most glaringly, in numerous religiously sanctified practices of exclusion. Then there are forms of social exclusion based on sexual orientation, age, disability, etc.

The spaces particular groups occupy in cities or rural areas are an important factor in exclusion. It reminds us of the word "ghetto." Its origin goes back to the segregation of Jews in a bounded space in the Republic of Venice in the early modern period. They were a community insulated from the rest of society. Gated neighbourhoods in modern cities resemble ghettos wherein the powerful of today lock themselves in. They create modern forts with high walls, barbed wires, and highly controlled entrances. A friend in Dallas, Texas, told me, "We do not allow black families to move into our neighbourhood because the property value will go down".

Marginality is a concept closely related to the idea of exclusion. It often refers to vulnerable segments of people left behind in the modernization process and prone to exploitation. Their life is often characterised by poverty, unemployment, low access to public services, loss of land, illiteracy, social stigmatization, and lack of political voice.

What we experience in South Asia is more than marginality as our history is weighed by the practice of untouchability. Caste has been the central organising principle of South Asian societies. Untouchability is one of the worst forms of social exclusion, which excludes and shuns contact with the Dalit people based on the ideology of purity and pollution. People are stigmatized and excluded as impure and hence prevented from entering into temples, into the settlements of caste people. They cannot even conduct such elementary commercial activities as selling food or milk for fear of letting the caste people getting polluted. Even more, Dalits are confined to the so-called "colonies" or "*cheris*" (Tamil) outside the village. In cities, their habitat is often close to drainage, railway tracks, pavements, under bridges and near garbage mounts. Dalit children internalise this exclusionary situation right from the days of their schooling. For example, Dalit children are assigned to sweep the classroom, while caste children are sent to fetch food for the teacher.[2] Basic statistics regarding the scheduled caste and scheduled tribes' situation of poverty is also, at the same time, a picture of exclusion from development.

> The poverty level among Scheduled Castes (SCs) and Scheduled Tribes (STs) is relatively much higher. In rural areas, 32 % SCs and 45 % STs were found living below the poverty line during the year 2011-12. The state-wise poverty level in rural areas shows the miserable conditions of these two social groups because in several states, more than 50% of the STs and more than 40 % of the SCs are living below the poverty line.[3]

Various Dimensions of Exclusion

Social exclusion is multi-layered and requires to be studied from different angles and disciplines since it is intertwined with economic, social, political, and cultural conditions.[4]

Social exclusion is not simply an economic issue of shortage of income. Hence it cannot be solved by increasing revenue. Instead, the absence of income, poverty and deprivation from basic life needs are bound up with marginalization, discrimination, and exclusion. Poverty is often the *consequence* of social, political, and cultural marginalization. Hence, any poverty reduction or alleviation needs to address the root of it, namely the harsh and complex reality of social exclusion.

In its most profound roots, poverty resulting from social exclusion has to do with denying freedom to individuals and groups in exercising their capabilities and conducting a life of dignity, or as Adam Smith said, the conditions for "being able to appear in public without shame." It sounds to me so familiar. In my childhood, I saw many people in my village unable to attend church in public because they were ashamed to appear in rags. In other words, when we deal with social exclusion, we are dealing with the quality of life; it has to do with "impoverished lives and not just depleted wallets."[5] People can be impoverished if they are prevented from exercising their fundamental human rights and shamed publicly for their social identity – gender, ethnicity, language, region, minority status etc.

At its core, social exclusion has to do with the deprivation of inter-human relations. To say a person is to say a relational being quintessentially. Martin Buber, the Jewish philosopher, expressed this in his work "*I and Thou*" (1923).[6] Relations so define a person that they are also at the root of what one could choose to become through exercising one's freedom. Such being the case, a person must not be excluded from social relationships that enable a qualitative human life which comprises the fulfilment of material and survival needs and the availing of opportunities in life. As Amartya Sen rightly points out,

> Being excluded from social relations can also lead to other deprivation, further limiting our living opportunities. For example, being excluded from the opportunity to be employed or receive credit may lead to economic impoverishment that may, in turn, lead to other deprivations (such as undernourishment or homelessness). Social exclusion can, thus, be constitutively a part of capability deprivation as well as instrumentally a cause of diverse capability failures.[7]

Some Areas of Social Exclusion

Dalits makeup 15% of the Indian population and, cumulatively, could be more extensive than many countries worldwide. Social exclusion is most glaring in the polluting occupations the Dalits are forced to take up, like scavenging, sweeping, and rag-picking, evoking a sense of filth and wretchedness. They also form a significant chunk of the marginalized coolies, the workforce of South Asia.

Being constitutively and structurally excluded, as in the case of Dalits, has consequences in all realms of life – social, political, economic, and cultural. Moreover, this basic deprivation has its effects in all these fields where the excluded are prevented from access to freely fashion for themselves a life of dignity.[8] Thus, for example, landlessness and inability to conduct productive economic activity are instrumental deprivation resulting from social exclusion. The same exclusion causes deprivation from availing credit for undertaking gainful economic activity or exclusion from the labour market and employment avenues.[9]

The excluded and the minorities are often prevented from political participation and governance. They are made invisible in the political field. How could the excluded tribal and Dalit women and transgender people participate in the political process when they undergo multiple forms of social exclusion?[10]

There are psychological consequences resulting from social exclusion.[11] It can easily lead to violence. In addition, the sense of rejection could be a demotivating factor, undermining agency and self-confidence and causing poor performance.[12] All this could stunt the growth into a fuller person. For children of the excluded, rejection could be a traumatic experience.

Towards Overcoming Social Exclusion – An Important Distinction

The difference between equality and equity is crucial. Equality is the principle that everyone should be treated the same way without fear or favour. Everyone is entitled to their rights in the same way without discrimination. Equity is a principle which grounds justice in the actual situation. The state of individuals and societies is intricately woven from the threads of history social structures, circumstances and more. Equity happens when goods, resources, and opportunities are distributed, considering a person's or group's historical and social location. Some may need more attention and resources than others to conduct a decent life.

Where apportioning goods and resources takes historical situatedness into account, equity follows. Let me illustrate the point with a simple example. Imagine Rs.100/ to be distributed for ten individuals for local transportation, among whom there is a physically challenged person. If I distribute ten Rupees each, what I have done is an equal distribution. Now, the physically challenged person cannot take public transportation. To reach the same destination, she needs to take an auto rickshaw. Hence, I give Rs.50/ for the physically challenged person to engage an auto and the rest is divided among the nine. Here what happens is equitable distribution. Equity is pivotal for justice to the excluded.

Consequences of Social Exclusion

Studies show that inclusive and equitable societies where no one is left behind are also the most cohesive ones enjoying peace and harmony.[13] There is a close nexus between social exclusion and inequality. Inequality, injustice and social exclusion are the principal causes of violence and ethnic conflicts in our contemporary world.[14] On the other hand, where there is inclusion, there is social cohesion and solidarity in a nation or community. Social exclusion is a challenge to the stability of social order. It is a fact that a highly significant number of the world's poor live in conditions of conflict. Unless the imbalance and injustice are redressed, we may not expect a harmonious social order.

Social exclusion is not only a forfeiture of the group involved. It is also a loss to the broader community. By depriving a group of people such as women, Dalits, Adivasis, and minorities, the community deprives itself of the talents of these groups and what they could contribute to the common good. Moreover, social exclusion restrains the effort of poverty reduction and the overall economic growth of the community.

Some Principles to Overcome Social Exclusion

The change needs to begin from the mind. A paradigm shift and new mindset are called for to understand the principles to overcome social exclusion and put into practice inclusion. Commitment to social equity and overcoming religious and cultural essentialism, too, are important in this endeavour.

Acceptance of Pluralism and Diversity

Forced centralization and unity are bound to leave behind many people, especially the most vulnerable. An inclusive society is one in which there is more than tolerance. In the western classical sense of tolerance, as expressed by John Locke, tolerance is some unpleasant thing I experience and undergo, but I let it be. True tolerance positively appreciates the difference the other represents and respects the other. There is mutual listening, learning, and the will to fashion together a shared future.

Genuine pluralism is also different from what is known as inclusivism. Inclusivism is counterproductive when it does not respect the identity and the difference the others represent. An ambiguous inclusivism absorbs, co-opts, and assimilates the other within oneself and, in this way, contributes to the loss of the identity of the other. We could call this adverse or unfavourable, or forced inclusion. The caste structure provides an example of systemic integration in a hierarchically ordered society in which each caste has its role to play. It is a well-integrated system but inequitable and unjust.

As we noted, authentic pluralism is based on recognising others in their difference and uniqueness. However, historically, there has taken place the co-optation of what anthropologists call "little traditions" by the "great tradition," resulting in the elimination of the true identity of the former.[15] This did not go without contestation. We can refer here to the rejection of an inclusivist Sanskritization process by India's excluded Dalits and tribals.

Universal Destiny of Natural Resources and Limits to Private Property

The avaricious accumulation creates exclusion and severe social and economic imbalance. Gandhi famously said, "The world has enough for everyone's needs, but not everyone's greed." Natural resources are for the entire human family; some cannot hijack them. Appalled by the opulent way of life of the rich of his times, St Ambrose reminded them how their horses are fitted with golden teeth and how they toy with their diamond rings even while the poor cry for food, and how the rich cover their floors with marble while the poor go naked.

Early Christian Fathers underlined the commonality of the earth and its resources to serve everyone. They denounced the way the rich stole and appropriated for themselves what was common and meant to serve the need of all. Work is the means of sustenance and wealth creation. The Fathers wondered how one could accumulate so much wealth through one's labour in one lifetime. They concluded that the rich man must be a thief; if not, his father![16]

> You rich, how far will you push your frenzied greed …When giving to the poor, you are not giving him what is yours; rather, you are paying him back what is his. Indeed, what is common to all and has been given to all to make use of, you have usurped for yourself alone. The earth belongs to all and not only to the rich…You are paying back, therefore, your debt; you are not giving gratuitously what you do not own….[17]

Creation of Opportunities at All Levels

Education, employment, and leadership are critical areas where opportunities must be available to the excluded and disadvantaged. The refusal to create opportunities is tantamount to wasting talents. Nelson Mandela, in his autobiography, recalling his childhood experience at school, says that Africans do not lack talents; they lack opportunities.[18] The opportunities offer the means for the excluded to shape their own lives with self-respect and dignity, something which any amount of welfare measures in their favour cannot do. As Hugh Collins observes in a law review,

> A job provides the opportunity to acquire knowledge and skills to participate in the workplace community, achieve meaningful goals, acquire status or identity in the community, and form friendships. The social inclusion policy wishes to distribute these non-material goods to all members of society. Work is not regarded as a means to the end of material wealth but an end in itself because it is a vital ingredient of 'well-being'. And the achievement of 'well-being' for all groups is an essential element in constructing a civil and safe community.[19]

Nurturing Social Solidarity – A Corrective to the Social Contract

In liberal theory, society is supposed to be based on a social contract. However, relying on a social contract alone could make the community legalistic and leave some sections of the people out of the benefits of the contract. Hence, the importance of human solidarity, which is, indeed, a principle of inclusion. It expresses social bonding, reciprocity, compassion, and mutual responsibility beyond contractual obligations. The principle of solidarity attends to especially the least privileged and vulnerable people by making them an integral part of the community. We all share a common humanity in a universe and a world of interdependence. To recall the poetic words of John Donne,

> *No man is an island...*
> *Each man's death diminishes me,*
> *For I am involved in mankind.*
> *Therefore, send not to know*
> *For whom the bell tolls,*
> *It tolls for thee* [20]

Instead of promoting common humanity and the spirit of cosmopolitanism, we find that the poor are blamed in the modern market economy for their poverty. It is their mistake if they are lacking, and so goes the capitalist argument. This compares with the traditional attitude of *karma* in South Asia. The poor and excluded need to suffer their condition since they are paying for their sins in their previous birth. This traditional fatalistic attitude prevalent in South Asia has found new applications in the capitalist economy. All this shows the challenging task of building deep human solidarity against the traditional and modern forces and ideologies trying to reinforce exclusion.

Overcoming the Mindset of Competition

Competition is one of the tools of exclusion in the sense that, intentionally and unintentionally, it effects exclusion. It follows the jungle law of the survival of the fittest. Those unable to compete must lose their right to an equitable share in natural and national resources.

Competition has entered every sphere of human life today. Capitalism and market ideology have created a situation wherein competition appears as the only way of social participation and the means for success. We see how in a capitalist economy, only the winner gets attention and the right to resources. The loser, who is already disabled and powerless, disappears silently. Religions and cultures should not follow the capitalist way of competition. For each religion and culture is unique, and all of them have a contribution to make for the common good. A hierarchization of religions and cultures and competition among them will perpetuate conflicts and exclusion.

The most disastrous effect happens when children are indoctrinated through an educational system to compete. Right from their early childhood, unfortunately, they are trained by their own parents to be competitive. In other words, parents teach their children to defeat others and be the number one. Alfie Kohn calls this the 'number one obsession.'[21] The children's knowledge, artistic skills, sports abilities, etc., are evaluated through the lens of competition. Only the winners come to the limelight, and the others get lost, unable to attract public attention.

The all-pervasive mindset of competition has caused a kind of disinterest in education in children, especially from the marginal Dalit and Adivasi communities. It has become the root cause of many dropouts among primary school and middle school children. The same seems to happen at the tertiary education level as an increasing number of suicides in the IITs and other premier educational institutions too function with a "gatekeeping" mindset. How sad that students from a humble background suffer stigmatization, taunt and humiliation and are led to take extreme steps. Referring to a recent incident of this kind in Mumbai, an editorial of *The Times of India* had this to say:

> An IIT Bombay Dalit student, Darshan Solanki, died by suicide last month …Other bright and promising Dalit and Adivasi students have been driven to depression and suicide in India's best educational institutions. Many institutions define 'meritorious' and deserving at the point of the entrance test alone. But many of these students fight immense odds; schooling disadvantages, poor resources, subpar teaching assistance and low English or tech skills. Unfortunately, our elite institutions have downplayed these difficulties when students drop out or even die by suicide. They claim these students do not meet exacting academic standards instead of making a genuine effort for those who have made it this far into their care.[22]

Fostering a spirit of cooperation in young minds can help promote inclusion instead of competition. Critics of competition hold that it should be replaced by cooperation in order to have everyone included with no one losing.

Some Strategic Shifts and Policy Orientations

The entire society needs to be educated on what social exclusion means and how it should be overcome with the cooperation of all citizens. A widespread informal educational practice will bring to the awareness of society the plight of the excluded and the marginalized. The media and communication also have a crucial responsibility in this respect.

Political Participation

The excluded are not the object of charity and welfare. On the contrary, they should have opportunities to be agents in the community and contribute to the goal of the common good. As an illustration, let me refer here to the policy difference between the migrants in the UK with multicultural citizenship vis-à-vis the migrants in France and Germany. In the former case, with political participation and voting right, the migrants get integrated into society and are empowered. In contrast, in the case of France and Germany, the migrants suffer greater vulnerability by a lack of citizenship, voting right, and absence of political participation. As a result, they feel politically excluded, with many practical consequences.

As Gopal Guru rightly points out, the exclusionary situation of the Dalits, tribals, and women rarely figures in election manifestos. Instead, Dalit and women legislatures are mostly entrusted with marginal ministries as if they could not handle important portfolios.[23] In response, the Dalits and tribals today, far from being passive, are increasingly using the democratic process to acquire political power and to come out of their forced exclusion by deploying their own agency. What Kanshi Ram did in Uttar Pradesh in the 1990s was an attempt to break loose of exclusion through the democratic acquisition of power. This political process of liberation from exclusion is accompanied by growing literature by the marginalized (Dalits, tribals and women) and by their autobiographic narratives. These provide a vital cultural force to come out of forced exclusion.

Exclusion also relates to religious minorities. For example, Muslims form about 13% of the Indian population. Because of multiple forms of exclusion and a general situation of backwardness and low literacy level, the community experiences exclusion in economic, civic, cultural, and political fields – as many empirical studies have shown.[24] They are unable to play a political role proportionate to their number. Their representation in different areas of life still needs to catch up to their numbers. To overcome the sense of alienation among the Muslims and as a practical measure of inclusion, the Justice Ranganatha Mishra Commission suggested a 15% reservation in education and employment. Zoya Hasan has argued the importance of strategies for including the disadvantaged Islamic community suffering from discriminatory practices. Structurally minority-inclusive policies are crucial because instead of the state fulfilling its role as the grantor of civil and political rights, there is the danger that it could act at the behest of dominant castes and classes and thus become a source of discrimination against minority and vulnerable groups. The state can undermine the equality of opportunity instead of upholding it.

At bottom, the remedy for political and other forms of exclusion is a transition from procedural to inclusive and substantive democratic practice.[25] The framers of the Indian Constitution envisioned, in fact, an inclusive democratic approach in which a wide variety of groups with linguistic, religious, and cultural differences would be represented and would be active participants, and none would be left behind. Inclusive democratic practice calls for respect for minority rights. As one of the leading political scientists of today, Will Kymlicka of Canada, observes,

> I believe it is legitimate, and indeed unavoidable, to supplement traditional human rights with minority rights. A comprehensive theory of justice in a multicultural state will include both universal rights, assigned to individuals regardless of group membership, and certain group-differentiated rights or 'special status' for minority cultures.[26]

It is indeed intriguing to note that the Universal Declaration of Human Rights (1948) does not explicitly address minority rights. This omission appears to stem from the historical contexts such as the Nazi regime of Hitler which used the pretext of protecting German minorities in Czechoslovakia to justify its invasion.[27] It became *causa belli* – the reason for war. However, later developments in Universal Human Rights came out forcefully on minority rights.

Anti-discrimination Laws and Implementation

Conscious of the historical disabilities suffered by the excluded people of India, the Indian Constitution declared that no person should be discriminated against based on religion, race, caste, sex, and place of birth (art. 15). Though the Indian Penal Code 1860 (section 153a), reflecting the spirit of the Constitution and the Prevention of Atrocities Act of 1989, aims at the protection of Scheduled Castes and Scheduled tribes in particular, we need a more comprehensive legal framework to be able to come to grips with the innumerable expressions of social exclusion. The Sachar Committee expressed its necessity in 2006. The states could take the lead to pass such laws in the context of specific exclusions and make them punishable offences. Though laws are not the ultimate means to eradicate the deep-rooted prejudices and practices of discrimination, appropriate legal measures could serve as essential means in protecting the marginalized, for example, in workplaces and educational institutions.

Creating Social and Cultural Capital

Robert Putnam, James Coleman, and Pierre Bourdieu have elaborated the useful analytical category of "social capital" which can help interpret the movement from exclusion to inclusion.[28] Social and cultural capital refers to the ensemble of networks and interconnections, resources, strategic alliances, reciprocity, membership in associations etc., that facilitate as a ladder to raise one's capabilities or, to use an organic metaphor, make one's talents and resources flower and bring forth fruits. Social and cultural assets are no less important than physical and human capital.

Groups and communities with significant social and cultural capital achieve remarkable results in the economy, education, employment, and other areas of significance. On the other hand, the excluded and marginalized communities, for example, in South Asia, woefully lack social capital. That explains why women, Dalits, tribals, Adivasis and other marginal groups cannot compete despite possessing the best talents. For example, imagine the plight of an

Adivasi girl aspiring for higher education whose parents are illiterate daily wage earners with no money, influence, connections, or capacity to provide career guidance.[29] How does this compare with a child whose parents and relatives are highly educated, wealthy and occupy important positions and wield tremendous influence? Given such situations, it is crucial to build up social and cultural capital among the excluded and marginalized innovatively. Social capital is generated by "bonding" within the community to which one belongs and by "bridging" namely by reaching out to other groups and communities.[30]

Education and Health Care Focused on the Marginalized

Emphasizing the education of marginalized groups including the girl child, tribals, and Dalits across primary, secondary, and tertiary levels is essential. This approach harmonizes the pursuit of academic excellence with the imperative of fostering social inclusion within the education system.[31] As it is, Dalit and tribal children generally end up with courses in arts and social sciences, traditional science subjects, or language courses. Circumstances of life offer no bright prospects. Specialized, job-oriented streams of study are neither accessible to them nor affordable. Moreover, the exponential growth of private education and the progressive withdrawal of the state from the educational sector have a disastrous effect on those from the lower and excluded strata of society.[32] All of these factors pose a challenge in the formulation of novel criteria for evaluating educational institutions, where the principle of inclusion ought to constitute a substantial and integral element. We must pay special attention to the inclusive education of the physically challenged in policies and practices.[33] In the educational policy, we speak of accessibility, affordability, quality, and accountability. There is a need to proactively ensure that children and students are offered opportunities and accompanied with empathy in their educational journey. Even more, the structural basis of inequality in education, employment, and economic activities needs to be addressed urgently.

Like education – healthcare also should become inclusive to cover the well-being of the marginalized. It also calls for policy orientation and instruments aimed at inclusion so that nobody is left behind. Lack of health and undernutrition can prevent opportunities. An increase in public spending is indispensable for the inclusion and social security of the marginalized.

Reservation – Affirmative Action

Another crucial strategy is further strengthening the policies and programmes that help overcome social exclusion, such as reservation or affirmative action. Recently, there has been an acrimonious debate over reservation issues in India and about affirmative action for Afro-Americans in the USA. Reservation policies and legal provisions known as "compensatory discrimination" (Marc Galanter) are meant to make good, to some extent, the disabilities suffered by particular groups by long-standing discrimination and atrocities against them. These stunt their growth and full flowering of their potentialities.[34]

As of now, reservation is practised in the public sector. However, it must also be extended to the private sector, which remains a formidable challenge. The empirical data provided by the researches of Sukhadeo Thorat, Katherine Newman, and others clearly show, contrary to the general impression, the economic discrimination practised by Indian companies and the business world towards the Dalits. Speaking of market discrimination, Thorat and Newman observe:

> We can fairly speak of discrimination when two persons with the same education, training, work experience, and hence identical human capital, differing only in personal characteristics that have no implications for productivity, are treated unequally, with the minority group member denied

jobs, given lower wages, or unfavourable working conditions and the majority
(or higher status) individual favoured in these domains.[35]

The banner of revolt is raised against reservation by the upper castes
and classes. The argument is based on the ideology of meritocracy
while ignoring the importance of social equity. The Mandal
Commission responded to this argument with a telling analogy. In
race, you cannot put the able-bodied and physically challenged and
decide who comes first. The arguments against reservation are often
accompanied by deep prejudices and stigma about the capability and
competence of those excluded. This applies as well in the case of
gender, whenever women's performance is rather hastily or mindlessly
called into question.

Change of Language and Vocabulary

The change from the untouchables to Harijans and then to Dalits is
symbolic and highly significant. "Illegal migrants" is an expression
of an indictment which can set aside and exclude those who most
often are from the poorest segments of society.[36] We remove the
stigma and exclusion when we refer to them as *undocumented
persons*. Another example would be the change of vocabulary from
'handicapped' through 'physically challenged' and 'otherwise-abled'
to 'specially abled'.[37] These are languages of inclusion and recognition.
But, as for women, much of our language about them, unfortunately,
is still conditioned by patriarchy and male domination.

Concluding Reflections

The goal of ending all forms of exclusion and creating a community
of equals calls for challenging the current socio-political order.
We are faced with structural and systemic disadvantages suffered
by its victims. It implies a new set of principles which I tried to
outline. Implementing these principles and strategies will ensure

that no one is left behind. More basically, the dignity and rights of everyone, especially the marginal groups and communities, need to be guaranteed for the advent of a cohesive society.

A crucial issue that needs to be addressed is the power relationship. For, asymmetry in power is what breeds practices of exclusion. We may expect an inclusive society only if there is a transformation in the current power relationship. Asymmetry cannot be changed by welfare measures for the excluded or strategies to include them in the development process. One crucial way to lead to inclusion is to practice human rights as laid down in the Universal Declaration of Human Rights and to follow the UN Convention on economic, social, cultural, civil and political rights. However, we require more than that.

Critical to change of power-relationship is to welcome the agency of the excluded. This agency is often expressed through social movements focusing on women, Dalits, tribals, unorganized labourers, migrants, domestic workers, displaced people, etc. The various excluded groups in South Asia have been engaged in freeing themselves from unjust discrimination and exclusion. In the process, they have done much theorising and adopted innovative strategies. The agency of the excluded is crucial, failing which they will be treated simply as objects of a project of inclusion pursued by others. Every responsible citizen needs to support the agency of the excluded and their social movements of liberation for a just, peaceful, and harmonious society, free of all forms of exclusion. It is they who seem to have the most potential to effect social transformation in South Asia.

The challenge of an inclusive society remains a dream which we need to pursue relentlessly, along with the excluded themselves, in the spirit of the following words of poet Robert Frost:

The woods are lovely, dark and deep
But I have promises to keep
And miles to go before I sleep, and miles to go before I sleep ...[38]

NOTES

1   Cf. Dominic Abrams and Julie Christian, eds., *Multidisciplinary Handbook of Social Exclusion Research* (Chichester: John Wiley & Sons Ltd, 2007).

2   For a general reflection on how social and group exclusion affect children's development, see Melanie Killen, Kelly Lynn Mulvey, and Aline Hitti, "Social Exclusion in Childhood: A Developmental Intergroup Perspective," *Child Development* 84, no.3 (May/June 2013): 772–790.

3   Ehsanul Haq, "Cultural Construction of Poverty in India," *Indian Anthropologist* 49, no.2 (July – Dec 2019): 23–40, at 24.

4   Paramjit S. Judge, ed., *Mapping Social Exclusion in India: Caste, Religion and Borderlands* (Delhi: Cambridge University Press, 2015).

5   Amartya Sen, *Social Exclusion: Concept, Application, and Scrutiny* (Social Development Papers No. 1). Asian Development Bank. http://www.adb.org/sites/default/files/publication/29778/social-exclusion.pdf [accessed on 17 March 2023].

6   Martin Buber, *I and Thou* (London: Bloomsbury Academic, 2013).

7   Amartya Sen, *Social Exclusion*, 5.

8   For statistical details on excluding the Dalits from different fields, see Sukhadeo Thorat, *Dalits in India: Search for a Common Destiny* (New Delhi: Sage Publications, 2009).

9   S. Mahendra Dev, "Financial Inclusion: Issues and Challenges," *Economic and Political Weekly* 41, no.41 (2006): 4310–4313; see also Rajalaxmi Kamath, "Financial Inclusion vis-à-vis Social Banking," *Economic and Political Weekly* 42, no.15 (2007): 1334–1335.

10   Cf. Praveen Rai, "Electoral Participation of Women in India: Key Determinants and Barriers," *Economic and Political Weekly* 46, no.3 (2011): 47–55. On the experience of discrimination and exclusion of transgender see Gee Imaan Semmalar, "Unpacking Solidarities of the Oppressed: Notes on Trans Struggles in India," *Women's Studies Quarterly* 42, no. 3/4 (2014): 286–291.

11   Cf. Dominic Abrams et al., eds., *The Social Psychology of Inclusion and Exclusion* (New York: Psychology Press, 2005).

12   Vani K Borooah, "Social Exclusion and Jobs Reservation in India," *Economic and Political Weekly* 45, no.52 (2010): 31–35. The author shows how the loss of self-confidence is caused by social exclusion.

13   Cf. Richard Wilkinson and Kate Pickett, *The Spirit Level. Why Greater Equality Makes Societies Stronger* (New York: Bloomsbury Press, 2010).

14   Ted Robert Gurr, *Minorities at Risk: A Global View of Ethnopolitical Conflict* (Washington, DC: US Institute of Peace Press, 1993); See also Mark Gradstein and Maurice Schiff, "The Political Economy of Social Exclusion, with Implications for Immigration Policy," *Journal of Population Economics* 19, no.2 (Jun 2006): 327–344; see also Richard Wilkinson and Kate Pickett, *The Spirit Level. op. cit.*

15   Cf. McKim Marriott, *India through Hindu Categories* (Delhi: Sage Publications, 1989).

16   Cf. Charles Avila, *Ownership: Early Christian Teaching* (Eugene, Oregon: Wipf & Stock Publisher, 1983); see also Julio de Santa Ana, *Good News to the Poor. The Challenge of the Poor in the History of the Church* (Geneva: World Council of Churches, 1977).

17   https://sixtogarcia.wordpress.com/2016/12/07/st-ambrose-of-milan-your-wealth-belongs-to-the-poor [accessed on 16 March 2023].

18   Nelson Mandela, *A Long Walk to Freedom. The Autobiography of Nelson Mandela* (Boston, New York, London: Little, Brown and Company, 1994).

19   Hugh Collins, "Discrimination, Equality and Social Inclusion," in *The Modern Law Review* 66, no.1 (Jan. 2003): 25.

20   https://www.yourdailypoem.com/listpoem.jsp?poem_id=2118 [accessed on 17 March 2023].

21   Alfie Kohn, *No Contest. The Case Against Competition* (Boston, New York: Houghton Mifflin Company, 1992), 72–75.

22   *The Times of India*, 10 March 2023.

23   Cf. Gopal Guru, "Marginalised," *India International Centre Quarterly* 27, no. 2 (2000):111–116; see also Id., "Liberal Democracy in India and Dalit Critique," *Social Research* 78, no. 1 (2011): 99–122.

24   Rajeev Singh, "Citizenship, Exclusion & Indian Muslims," *The Indian Journal of Political Science* 71, no. 2 (2010): 497–510.

25   See Sashikant Pandey and Siddhartha Mukerji, "Indian Democracy: Inclusive in Theory Exclusionary in Practice," *The Indian Journal of Political Science* 74, no. 3 (2013): 557–570.

26   Will Kymlicka, *Multicultural Citizenship. A Liberal Theory of Minority Rights* (Oxford: Clarendon Press, 1996), 6.

27   Cf. Neera Chandhoke, *Beyond Secularism: The Rights of Religious Minorities* (Delhi: Oxford University Press, 2002).

28   For an overview of the concept of social capital and the debates around it, see Frans J. Schuurman, "The Politico-Emancipatory Potential of a Disputed Concept," *Third World Quarterly* 24, no. 6 (2003): 991–1010; see also Ben Fine, "Social Capital versus Social History," *Social History* 33, no. 4 (2008): 442–467; Christos J. Paraskevopoulos, "Social Capital: Summing up the Debate on a Conceptual Tool of Comparative Politics and Public Policy," *Comparative Politics* 42, no. 4 (2010): 475–494; Sara Ferlander, "The

Importance of Different Forms of Social Capital for Health," *Acta Sociologica* 50, no. 2 (2007): 115–128. On the interconnection between social exclusion and social capital, see Mary Daly and Hilary Silver, "Social Exclusion and Social Capital: A Comparison and Critique," *Theory and Society* 37, no. 6 (2008): 537–566; Irene van Staveren and Peter Knorringa, "Unpacking Social Capital in Economic Development: How Social Relations Matter," *Review of Social Economy* 65, no.1 (2007): 107–135.

29   See Dev Nathan and Virginius Xaxa, eds., *Social Exclusion and Adverse Inclusion: Development and Deprivation of Adivasis in India* (New Delhi: Oxford University Press, 2012); see also Biswamoy Pati, *Tribals and Dalits in Orissa: Towards a Social History of Exclusion, c. 1800–1950* (New Delhi: Oxford University Press, 2019), 221.

30   See R.D. Putnam, *Bowling Alone* (New York: Simon and Schuster, 2000).

31   Rohini Sahni and V. Kalyan Shankar, "Girls' Higher Education in India on the Road to Inclusiveness: On Track but Heading Where?" *Higher Education* 63, no.2 (2012): 237–256.

32   N Ajith Kumar and K. K George present critically the case of education in Kerala, apparently moving in the reverse direction – from inclusion to exclusion. See N Ajith Kumar, and K K George, "Kerala's Education System: From Inclusion to Exclusion?" *Economic and Political Weekly* 44, no. 41/42 (2009): 55–61.

33   Cf. Ritika Gulyani, "Educational Policies in India with Special Reference to Children with Disabilities," *Indian Anthropologist* 47, no. 2 (2017): 35–51.

34   Durga P Chhetri, "Politics of Social Inclusion and Affirmative Action: Case of India," *The Indian Journal of Political Science* 73, no. 4 (2012): 587–600.

35   Sukhadeo Thorat and Katherine S. Newman, "The Legacy of Social Exclusion. A Correspondence Study of Job Discrimination in India," in *Economic and Political Weekly* 42, no. 41(2007): 4121–4124, at 4122.

36   In this connection, let me refer to how in the European Union, one uses the expression "expatriate" to refer to refugees and migrants of the same race. In contrast, people of other races are called "simply migrants." It was striking how the migrants and refugees from Ukraine were received in the countries of the European Union with open arms and the callous attitudes to the refugees and migrants from Africa, many of whom were let to perish in the Mediterranean Sea.

37   For an enlightening study on the development of disability in India, see C. Raghava Reddy, "From Impairment to Disability and Beyond," *Sociological Bulletin* 60, no. 2 (2011): 287–306. For a similar reflection on disability in the context of the U.K., see Colin Barnes and Geof Mercer, "Disability, Work, and Welfare: Challenging the Social Exclusion of Disabled People," *Work, Employment & Society* 19, no.3 (2005): 527–545.

38   https://www.poetryfoundation.org/poems/42891/stopping-by-woods-on-a-snowy-evening [accessed on 17 March 2023].

FURTHER READING

Abrams, Dominic et al., eds. *The Social Psychology of Inclusion and Exclusion.* New York: Psychology Press, 2005.

Abrams, Dominic, and Julie Christian, eds. *Multidisciplinary Handbook of Social Exclusion Research.* Chichester: John Wiley & Sons Ltd, 2007.

Amster, Randall. "Patterns of Exclusion: Sanitizing Space, Criminalizing Homelessness." *Social Justice* 30, no.1 (91), Race, Security & Social Movements (2003): 195–221.

Ana, Julio de Santa. *Good News to the Poor. The Challenge of the Poor in the History of the Church.* Geneva: World Council of Churches, 1977.

Avila, Charles. *Ownership: Early Christian Teaching.* Eugene, Oregon: Wipf & Stock Publisher, 1983.

Barnes, Colin, and Geof Mercer. "Disability, Work, and Welfare: Challenging the Social Exclusion of Disabled People." *Work, Employment & Society* 19, no. 3 (2005): 527–545.

Borooah, Vani K. "Social Exclusion and Jobs Reservation in India." *Economic and Political Weekly* 45, no. 52 (2010): 31–35.

Bossert, Walter, Conchita D'Ambrosio, and Vito Peragine. "Deprivation and Social Exclusion." *Economica* 74, no. 296 (2007): 777–803.

Buber, Martin. *I and Thou.* London: Bloomsbury Academic, 2013.

Chandhoke, Neera. *Beyond Secularism: The Rights of Religious Minorities.* Delhi: Oxford University Press, 2002.

Chhetri, Durga P. "Politics of Social Inclusion and Affirmative Action: Case of India." *The Indian Journal of Political Science* 73, no. 4 (2012): 587–600.

Collins, Hugh. "Discrimination, Equality and Social Inclusion." *The Modern Law Review* 66, no.1 (2003): 16–43.

Currie, Graham, ed. *New Perspectives and Methods in Transport and Social Exclusion Research.* Bingley, UK: Emerald Publishing Limited, 2011.

Daly, Mary, and Hilary Silver. "Social Exclusion and Social Capital: A Comparison and Critique." *Theory and Society* 37, no. 6 (2008): 537–566.

Das, Nava Kishor. "Identity Politics and Social Exclusion in India's Northeast. A Critique of Nation-Building and Redistributive Justice." *Anthropos* 104, H. 2. (2009): 549–558.

Dev, S. Mahendra. "Financial Inclusion: Issues and Challenges." *Economic and Political Weekly* 41, no. 41 (2006): 4310–4313.

Ferlander, Sara. "The Importance of Different Forms of Social Capital for Health." *Acta Sociologica* 50, no. 2 (2007): 115–128.

Fine, Ben. "Social Capital versus Social History." *Social History* 33, no. 4 (2008): 442–467.

Geiser, Alexandra. *Social Exclusion and Conflict Transformation in Nepal: Women, Dalit and Ethnic Groups: FAST Country Risk Profile Nepal* (Bern: Swisspeace, 2005).

Gradstein, Mark, and Maurice Schiff. "The Political Economy of Social Exclusion, with Implications for Immigration Policy." *Journal of Population Economics* 19, no. 2 (2006): 327–344.

Gulyani, Ritika. "Educational Policies in India with Special Reference to Children with Disabilities." *Indian Anthropologist* 47, no. 2 (2017): 35–51.

Gurr, Ted Robert. *Minorities at Risk: A Global View of Ethnopolitical Conflict.* Washington, DC: US Institute of Peace Press, 1993.

Guru, Gopal. "Marginalised." *India International Centre Quarterly* 27, no. 2 (2000):111–116.

Guru, Gopal. "Liberal Democracy in India and Dalit Critique." *Social Research* 78, no. 1 (2011): 99–122.

Haq, Ehsanul. "Cultural Construction of Poverty in India." *Indian Anthropologist* 49, no. 2 (2019): 23–40.

Hiroshi, Fukurai, and Richard Krooth, eds. *Race in the Jury Box: Affirmative Action in Jury Selection Racially Mixed Juries and Affirmative Action.* New York: State University of New York Press, 2003.

Judge, Paramjit S, ed. *Mapping Social Exclusion in India: Caste, Religion and Borderlands.* Delhi: Cambridge University Press, 2015.

Kadun, Pradeep, and Gadkar Ravindra. "Social Exclusion – Its Types and Impact on Dalits in India." *Journal of Humanities and Social Science* 19, no. 4 (2014): 81–85.

Kamath, Rajalaxmi. "Financial Inclusion vis-à-vis Social Banking." *Economic and Political Weekly* 42, no. 15 (2007): 1334–1335.

Killen, Melanie, Kelly Lynn Mulvey, and Aline Hitti. "Social Exclusion in Childhood: A Developmental Intergroup Perspective." *Child Development* 84, no. 3 (2013): 772 – 790.

Kohn, Alfie. *No Contest. The Case Against Competition.* Boston, New York: Houghton Mifflin Company, 1992.

Kumar, N Ajith, and K. K. George. "Kerala's Education System: From Inclusion to Exclusion?" *Economic and Political Weekly* 44, no. 41/42 (2009): 55–61.

Kymlicka, Will. *Multicultural Citizenship. A Liberal Theory of Minority Rights.* Oxford: Clarendon Press, 1996.

Mallick, Nirakar, and Bibuthi Bhushan Malik. "Sociology of Exclusion: Dalits in East Uttar Pradesh." *Social Change* 46, no. 2 (2016): 214–37.

Mandela, Nelson. *A Long Walk to Freedom. The Autobiography of Nelson Mandela.* Boston, New York, London: Little, Brown and Company, 1994.

Marriott, McKim. *India through Hindu Categories.* Delhi: Sage Publications, 1989.

Nathan, Dev, and Virginius Xaxa, eds. *Social Exclusion and Adverse Inclusion: Development and Deprivation of Adivasis in India.* New Delhi: Oxford University Press, 2012.

Nevile, Ann. "Amartya K. Sen and Social Exclusion." *Development in Practice* 17, no.2 (2007): 249–255.

Pandey, Sashikant, and Siddhartha Mukerji. "Indian Democracy: Inclusive in Theory Exclusionary in Practice." *The Indian Journal of Political Science* 74, no. 3 (2013): 557–570.

Paraskevopoulos, Christos J. "Social Capital: Summing up the Debate on a Conceptual Tool of Comparative Politics and Public Policy." *Comparative Politics* 42, no. 4 (2010): 475–494.

Pati, Biswamoy. *Tribals and Dalits in Orissa: Towards a Social History of Exclusion, c. 1800–1950.* New Delhi: Oxford University Press, 2019.

Porter, Fenella. "Social Exclusion: What's in a Name?" *Development in Practice* 10, no.1 (2000): 76–81.

Putnam, R.D. *Bowling Alone.* New York: Simon and Schuster, 2000.

Rai, Praveen. "Electoral Participation of Women in India: Key Determinants and Barriers." *Economic and Political Weekly* 46, no. 3 (2011): 47–55.

Reddy, C. Raghava. "From Impairment to Disability and Beyond." *Sociological Bulletin* 60, no. 2 (2011): 287–306.

Sahni, Rohini, and V. Kalyan Shankar. "Girls' Higher Education in India on the Road to Inclusiveness: On Track but Heading Where?" *Higher Education* 63, no. 2 (2012): 237–256.

Schuurman, Frans J. "The Politico-Emancipatory Potential of a Disputed Concept." *Third World Quarterly* 24, no. 6 (2003): 991–1010.

Semmalar, Gee Imaan. "Unpacking Solidarities of the Oppressed: Notes on Trans Struggles in India." *Women's Studies Quarterly* 42, no. 3/4 (2014): 286--291.

Sen, Amartya. *Social Exclusion: Concept, Application, and Scrutiny.* The Philippines: Asian Development Bank, 2000.

Singh, Rajeev Kumar. "Manual Scavenging as Social Exclusion: A Case Study." *Economic and Political Weekly* 44, no. 26/27 (2009): 521–523.

Singh, Rajeev. "Citizenship, Exclusion & Indian Muslims." *The Indian Journal of Political Science* 71, no. 2 (2010): 497–510.

Spicker, Paul. "Cohesion, Exclusion and Social Quality." *The International Journal of Social Quality* 4, no.1 (2014): 95–107.

Staveren, Irene van, and Peter Knorringa. "Unpacking Social Capital in Economic Development: How Social Relations Matter." *Review of Social Economy* 65, no.1 (2007): 107–135.

Thorat, Sukhadeo, and Katherine S Newman. "The Legacy of Social Exclusion. A Correspondence Study of Job Discrimination in India." *Economic and Political Weekly* 42, no. 41(2007): 4121–4124.

Thorat, Sukhadeo, and Paul Attewell. "Caste and Economic Discrimination: Causes, Consequences and Remedies." *Economic and Political Weekly* 42, no.41 (2007): 4141–4145.

Thorat, Sukhadeo. *Dalits in India: Search for a Common Destiny.* New Delhi: Sage Publications, 2009.

Thorat, Sukhadeo, and Katherine S Newman. *Blocked by Caste. Economic Discrimination in Modern India.* Delhi: Oxford University Press, 2013.

Verma, Vidhu. "Conceptualising Social Exclusion: New Rhetoric or Transformative Politics?" *Economic and Political Weekly* 46, no.50 (2011): 89–97.

Wilkinson, Richard, and Kate Pickett. *The Spirit Level. Why Greater Equality Makes Societies Stronger.* New York: Bloomsbury Press, 2010.

Chapter 5

WOMEN'S LIBERATION
INTER-TEXTUAL READING OF ŚAKUNTALĀ AND BIBLICAL NARRATIVES

In this chapter, I attempt to read Kālidāsa's classic *Abhijñānaśākuntalam*[1] through some Biblical narratives. The objective is to bring out through this method the beauty of both the Indian classical as well as the Biblical narratives as they grapple with human realities and experiences, especially touching upon the liberation of women. What is expected is mutual enrichment of both the texts - Śakuntalā and Biblical texts - as bearers of ever-new impulses and meanings for the cause of women. This attempt is based upon certain premises and assumptions about the art and method of interpretation as well as understanding about literature and poetics.

Prelude to Hermeneutics and Inter-textuality

Traditional Indian hermeneutics[2] and contemporary western theories of interpretation[3] are at one in acknowledging the open-endedness of texts, which allows them to be understood in infinite ways.[4] It means that the text is not bound to the author's meaning and his or her intentionality. The *dhvani* interpretation in Indian tradition is based on the assumption that a text is autonomous and need not be bound by the author's meaning. In Biblical studies and researches, when there was the danger of limiting oneself to the literal sense of the texts, the search for the socio-cultural context of their origin came to assume great importance as a means to overcome the danger of biblical fundamentalism. Hence, from the nineteenth century onwards, the historic-critical method gained momentum and helped situate the text in context, thus challenging Biblical fundamentalism.[5] From another angle, realizing that literal sense does not bring out the depth of the texts, early Christian writers, following some Jewish interpreters, laid stress on the allegorical meaning.[6] The allegorical method of interpretation broke the limits of literal interpretation, pointing to truths beyond the text.

The developments in the study of Biblical texts go along with the new insights provided by contemporary philosophical hermeneutics and the contribution of modern linguistics. These have created a theoretical space to read one particular text through another. This is not totally new in Indian tradition. For, in the tradition of writing *bhāshyas* – commentaries - one of the strategies was to illumine one text through another. This is a step further to reader-centred interpretation, namely reading a text from the existential situation in which the reader finds herself. Further, in the classical *dhvani* interpretation in India, the text says different things to different persons depending on their situatedness. It led to the creation of even different variants of the same story with suitable omissions and additions that bespoke the experiences and concerns of the interpreters and interpreting communities. Thus, we have different recensions/versions/translations of *Rāmāyaṇa* and *Mahabharata*, not to mention many diverse interpretations, including postcolonial and feminist ones.[7] Every version places a different accent on the narrative. This is also true of the story of Śakuntalā of which there exist more than one version.

It is interesting to note the reception of Śakuntalā in different periods and social and cultural milieux. The history of the reception of this classic can be very revealing.[8] The different representations of the same story of Śakuntalā indicate how the past becomes "a reconstruction drawing on the needs of the present."[9] In other words, the different renditions of the same story have to do with the changes in the history of a society, its culture, its system of values and its world-view. The difference in the story of Śakuntalā is not only due to historically different cultural and social conditions but also to a different *literary genre*. Epic is the literary form of the original story of Śakuntalā in *Mahābhārata*. The story in *kāvya* is turned into the genre of *nātaka* drama (under the broader category of *rūpaka*) - a play by Kālidāsa. In this contribution, my point of reference will be the story as recounted by Kālidāsa in *Abhijñānaśākuntalam*.[10]

Prelude to Literature and Poetics

Literary criticism takes us into studying various aspects and dimensions of literature. There are many schools of thought, some accentuating the analysis of the content of the literary texts, while others on their forms. Literature leads us through its rich and imaginative language, symbols and metaphors into real life and its complexities, into the understanding of numerous human characters with their different personal and psychological traits. It unfolds before us inter-human relationships, moods, motivations, emotions, etc. Classical and modern poetics study how these are woven into the literary text. Kālidāsa's masterpiece Śakuntalā could be studied closely through Sanskrit poetics, modern poetics, and literary criticism.

In the context of Biblical narrations, scholars have explored the extent to which Biblical narratives come under the category of literature and therefore viable objects of study under literary criticism and poetics.[11] This is an important but complex question. For, Christians believe the Bible to be a sacred book that expounds God's revelation, eliciting readers' faith in response to it. It is not a piece of poetry or play about which we could speak of *rasa*, as we use it in the classical Indian literary tradition. One may argue that biblical narratives are to be responded to in faith and not by *rasa*. Such a view of the Bible as an inspired book set apart from other human writings is widespread, which would make it difficult for us to make any inter-textual reading of it with a literary text like Śakuntalā.

However, another stream of thought allows us to look at the Bible as literature without diminishing its sacred value. Studying the Bible and its narratives as a piece of literature, far from secularizing the sacred texts, in fact, enlivens the text and allows the emergence of new layers of meaning closer to the experiences of life. If we look at the Bible from the point of view of its origins, it is far from being a book coming from God at one stroke, in one dictation, as it were. What we call Bible is in fact an amalgamation of writings that span about three thousand years of history with many writers involved. These writings do not belong to a single literary genre but to several. So, then, we have in the Bible history, myths, fairy tales, fables, sagas, legends, hymns, lamentations, legislative texts, and narratives of apocalyptic imagination.

In the New Testament, the four gospels narrating the story of Jesus represent a new literary genre in which faith and history are fused with teachings of wisdom, moral injunctions, and paraenetic passages. Paul and others use another literary genre namely letter writing. All this has led some scholars in more recent times to explore the various writings of the Bible from a literary point of view. This was not done for a long time for the reasons cited above. In the present chapter, we will view the Bible as literature and cull out texts and passages through which we will attempt to read the classical literary work of Śakuntalā and women's liberation.

Inter-textuality in Dialogue with Contemporary Experiences

Our preceding reflections have opened up the possibility of an inter-textual reading of *Abhijñānaśākuntalam* and *the Bible*. The justification for this approach lies in the open-endedness of the text and in the legitimacy of viewing the Bible as a treasure of many literary works. Even though this approach may help us discover new springs of meaning in both texts, however, they will be limited to the world of texts themselves. What we need to do is to bring another dialogue partner to this reading, and this partner is none other than our contemporary experiences. Reading the Bible and *Abhijñānaśākuntalam* through the prism of today's realities and life experiences will not only be a new source of meaning as far as the texts are concerned but also a way to enlighten our present-day experiences. In the concluding reflections, we will enter into a hermeneutical process to connect all the three from a synoptic view.

Śakuntalā and Hagar

We begin the inter-textual reading of Śakuntalā, starting with the Biblical narrative of Hagar in the first book of the Bible, the Genesis (Gen. 16 & 21). In many respects, there is a close resemblance between the life-story of Śakuntalā and Hagar. Hagar is a slave woman from Egypt in the service of Abraham (a patriarch whom all the three Semitic traditions – Jewish, Christian and Islamic venerate) and of his wife Sarai. Her name was changed from Sarai (meaning "princely") into Sarah through God's intervention (Gen. 17:15). In a society in which male children were privileged to carry on the ancestral heritage, the couple did not have any heir, and they were advanced in age. The personal and social compulsion of having an heir was such that Sarai realizing that she cannot bear any child, lets Abraham unite with her slave maid Hagar to generate an heir. However, when this slave woman conceives a child, she becomes the object of jealousy of her mistress and is sent away into the wilderness and suffers exceedingly. At this point, there is a divine intervention in the form of an angel who tells the fleeing maid to return to the house of her mistress, where she gives birth to Ishmael. However, when Sarai, in her old age, miraculously conceives and brings forth a child – Isaac - she does not want Hagar and her child anymore to stay in their house. They are driven out into the desert where the child is on the verge of dying for want of water. Shown a spring by an angel in the desert, the child revives and becomes, as per divine promise, the father of a great nation.[12] Let us now look at some common threads between the two narratives.

The Theme of Rejection and Exploitation

The main characters in both narratives are women – Śakuntalā and Hagar. There are many similarities in the narratives. In the case of Śakuntalā, though her parentage is traced to Viśvāmitra and Menakā (a nymph), her plight is that of an abandoned child without the experience of love and care of her father and mother. She is brought up as an adopted child by the ascetic *Kaṇva* in a hermitage in the forest, far away from the world. Though she is surrounded by friends and enjoys their company, her social status is that of an orphan, an unwanted and abandoned child. The case of Hagar is a similar one. She is a slave from Egypt (Gen 16:1), and slaves were bought and sold in the ancient world. It is the free people, the nobility, who have genealogy and ancestry, which a slave girl like Hagar does not have. No one would know who are her father and mother, and that is unimportant in the case of an enslaved person whose duty it is to serve faithfully the masters and scrupulously follow their dictates.

A slave is not supposed to have an identity of her own; instead, she is an object of possession, like any other object of a master. Like things, she could be used and discarded. That is precisely what happens to Hagar. A similar thing happens to Śakuntalā, an abandoned child without identity. She is also rejected by the king, who married her but disowned her. She thus experiences a double rejection by her own parents and then by a man who marries her with many promises. The slave girl Hagar is exploited not only in terms of labour but also in a very personal way. She is, in a way, made use of so that Abraham may beget an heir,[13] with no hope of one from his wife of advanced age. Hagar bears a son who she imagines will inherit the patrimony of Abraham, but experiences rejection and exploitation when Abraham and Sarai miraculously beget a son. Hagar, who was wanted, now feels rejected; so too is his son as the heir. Even more, she is cast out into the wilderness along with her son Ishmael, heir apparent until Isaac was born to Sarai (Gen 21:9-21).

Assertion and Agency

Śakuntalā and Hagar, both experiencing rejection and exploitation, do not resign themselves to their fate. Instead, they rise to assert themselves and create their destiny by bringing their unique agency into play. This agency is seen first in the fact that Śakuntalā does not wait for her adopted father and other elders to decide on her marriage. She decides independently; follows her heart, falls in love with the king, and enters freely into *gāndharva* marriage. There is yet another clear instance where her agency comes out forcefully. She goes to the king's palace carrying the ring he gave her with his name etched on it. She is brimming with hope and dreams of herself as the queen and her son as heir to the throne. But King Dushyanta disowns her and rejects her. It was undoubtedly, for her once again an experience of dejection and a shattering of her dreams. It was also an experience of humiliation.[14] A simple woman was humiliated in the court of the powerful. Like a guileless rustic girl, she believed the king's words, and she got pregnant. As the ascetic Gautamī from the hermitage of Śakuntalā would argue in the king's court later, she was brought up in a hermitage and did not know deceit.

Śakuntalā does not give up but stands up to the king and vindicates her case passionately to the dismay of the courtiers who were not used to any such assertion by a simple woman, and that too challenging none other than the king himself. We can hear the echo of Kannagi in the Tamil classic *Cilappatikāram*, who challenged the Pandya king when her innocent husband was detained by guards of the palace and killed for a theft which he did not commit.

When Śakuntalā, the pregnant lady, feels cheated by King Dushyanta, her piercing words resound in the court of the king. Śakuntalā reasons out her case when she addresses the king "O descendant of Puru, it is indeed, becoming in you, having at first in that manner deceived this person, naturally simple-minded, after a formal agreement in the hermitage, thus to disown her now!" (Act V). When Gautamī is tired of arguing the case of Śakuntalā with the king and tries to walk out, Śakuntalā comes out most eloquently, characterizing the king himself as a "rogue." "How now! I have been deceived by this rogue, and you too abandon me?" (Act V). The king's response to the challenging words of Śakuntalā is a diversionary tactic. He evades the central issue of justice and fairness demanded by her. The king digresses and speaks very mean words about women and womanhood. Women are for him, those who speak "honeyed words, full of falsehood...seeking to encompass their own object" (Act V). His anger is such that he goes to the point of humiliating the entire female gender.

> Intuitive cunning of the womankind is seen to exist even in females other than human. What then in the case of those that posses power of understanding

(or, knowledge)? Then female cuckoos, indeed, cause their offspring to be reared by other birds, before flying into the sky (Act V).

The humiliating words of the king do not dishearten Śakuntalā who rebukes him wrathfully as "wicked" and as a hypocrite who covers up his evil by donning a garb of virtue, like a well-covered with grass.

In the narrative on Hagar, we do not have anything about the confrontation of Hagar with Abraham and Sarai by whom she feels defrauded. Like Śakuntalā, a simple woman from the hermitage, so too is the slave girl Hagar cheated. However, Hagar does not take it lying down. We can imagine the way she would have argued with Abraham and Sarai. There are specific, clear indications of her assertion and agency vis-à-vis her master and mistress. For, after conceiving, Hagar, who until then had no identity of her own, becomes conscious of her new dignity and consequently becomes assertive.[15] She can stand up to Sarai who has been persecuting the poor slave girl, humiliating her and extracting work out of her. Her relationship with Sarai changes with her newly gained identity as carrying the heir to Abraham in her womb. Hagar feels emboldened. "And when she (Hagar) saw that she had conceived, she looked with contempt on her mistress" (Gen. 16:4). The reaction to the self-assertion of Hagar was fierce. "Then Sarai dealt harshly with her (Hagar), and she fled from her" (Gen 16: 6).

Reading Śakuntalā through Biblical Song of Songs

Kālidāsa's Śakuntalā is also a story of deep love between a man and a woman. It is a story of King Dushyanta and Śakuntalā falling in love. Kālidāsa very romantically describes this with many imageries characteristic of his poetics. An inter-textual reading of this aspect of the narrative through the Song of Songs in the Bible could be very illuminating. It is a unique book in the Bible, enigmatic and, at the same time, an embarrassment to many. For, the Song of Songs is a book of lyrics in which the love of a man and a woman and their longing for each other is celebrated – something exceptional in the Bible, which speaks mostly of the love of God and the love of neighbour.[16] Human love with mutual fascination and enchantment of a man and woman (*śṛṅgāra rasa*), we will not find it in the New Testament either. While the Greek tradition spoke highly both of *éros*– sensuous love between husband and wife or between lovers - and of *agape* (loving God and neighbour selflessly), the former did not become the object of any serious consideration in the biblical tradition.

In early Christianity, under the influence of Manichean dualism, whatever belonged to the human body, sensuality, sexuality and intersexual relationships, were looked down upon. Whereas Song of Songs speaks of the real and concrete carnal love of a man and a woman, most commentators, unable to accept this, tried to spiritualize the songs and give allegorical interpretations to them.[17] They saw the bride as the human soul and the bridegroom as God and interpreted the entire Song of Songs as a book of mutual relationship of the human soul's longing for God and God's love for the soul.

A similar line of interpretation was one which saw in this love poem the relationship of the Old Testament God Yahweh with Israel, viewed as a bride. Later in the light of the New Testament, it was read as imagery portraying the love of Christ for his bride, the Church, something St Paul would elaborate on in his letters, especially in the Letter to the Ephesians (5:21-33). It is only in recent theological interpretations that sensuous and sexual human love is viewed as a value in itself and even as mirroring the beauty of divine love.[18]

There was another reason why the presence of such a book in the heart of the Bible came across to many even "scandalous." For, in a patriarchal society, the relationship of man to woman was not on an equal basis. The woman is to be subjected to her husband

and do according to his bidding. In complete contravention to the patriarchal culture of the time, here in this book, we have the affirmation of equality of man and woman, bride and bridegroom whose love and emotions move on the same plane and in the spirit of mutuality. There is no room for any subjugation of the bride to the bridegroom. The Bible, both the OT and the NT, discusses marriage as a social institution. So, only the social implications of this institution are dealt with. Song of Songs is the only book in the Bible that deals with the mutual love of partners or lovers.

In India, love and sexuality have been part of its spiritual tradition ("sacred sexuality").[19] The body and its beauty are very important aspects in inter-sexual relationships. In Indian Classical literature, whether in Sanskrit or Tamil, luscious descriptions of various parts of the body become a trigger for love. In doing so, the writers of classical literature draw amply from images of nature and compare human parts of the body to what we observe in nature.

In describing the beauty of the human body, Kālidāsa's poetic genius gets expressed in images and metaphors. The description of the beauty of the human body is exceptional in the Bible for the reasons cited above. But the Song of Songs enters into such a poetic description, and it is close to Śakuntalā and other Indian classical literature. It also describes the physical beauty of the beloved with images drawn from nature:

Behold, you are beautiful, my love
Behold you are beautiful!
Your eyes are doves behind your veil
Your hair is like a flock of goats,
Moving down the slopes of Gilead
Your teeth are like a flock of shorn ewes...
Your lips are like a scarlet thread
And your mouth is lovely
Your cheeks are like halves of a pomegranate...

Your breasts are like two fawns
Twins of a gazelle that feed among the lilies... (Song of Songs 4:1 ff).

The description is not only about the female body, but about the male body as well. This is how the bride perceives her handsome bridegroom:

My beloved is all radiant and ruddy ...
His eyes are like doves beside springs of water bathed in milk, fitly set...
His lips are lilies, distilling liquid myrrh
His arms are rounded gold set with jewels
His body is ivory work encrusted with sapphires
His legs are alabaster columns set upon bases of gold (Song of Songs 5:10-15).

Love for one's beloved can affect a person deeply with its effects on the body too. Śakuntalā is so overwhelmed by her love for the king from the first sight of him that she feels tormented in mind and body. It is a condition of a queer mix of love-ecstasy with pain and torment. The effects on the body of Śakuntalā are described by Kālidāsa as follows:

Her face has its cheeks excessively emaciated; her bosom has its breasts destitute of hardness; her waist is even more slender; her shoulders are exceedingly sunken; and her complexion is pale; she (thus) tormented with love, appears both lovely and deplorable, like Mādhavi creeper shaken (*lit.* touched) by the wind causing its leaves to wither (Act III).

We can glean this kind of affliction by love-sickness through the words of the bride and bridegroom in Song of Songs. Every line of this little work overflows with love and affection for the beloved. Here we can see a close resemblance to how Kālidāsa describes the love between Śakuntalā and King Dushyanta. When Śakuntalā expresses her feelings and emotions through a love letter to Dushyanta, she conveys her sentiments thus: "I know not your mind, O cruel one, but, day and night, Cupid causes acute pain to the limbs of me whose affection is centered in you" (Act III). Dushyanta responds that he is "slain by the shafts of love" (Act III).

In this play, we can identify three moments of the love story – a union of the beloved, separation, and reunion. So, we have Śakuntalā and Dushyanta falling in love and united with each other, and Śakuntalā conceiving; then there is the separation when the King leaves Śakuntalā behind, and finally, after many mishaps, a happy reunion with each other takes place. We do not have any such clear storyline in the Song of Songs. However, the Song of Songs alludes to the experience of union, separation, and reunion of the beloved. Particularly the frenzied quest and delirious search for the loved one stands out as the following verses show:

> Upon my bed by night
> I sought him whom my soul loves;
> I sought him, but found him not;
> I called him, but he gave no answer.
> I will rise now and go about the city
> In the streets and in the squares;
> I will seek him whom my soul loves...
> The watchmen found me,
> As they went about the city.
> Have you seen him whom my soul loves (Song of Songs 3:1-3)

What is remarkable in the Song of Songs is the fact that erotic love, sexual desire, and pleasure are presented here as mutual, not only of man but as well of woman. David McLain Carr observes how the agency of women in sexuality gets highlighted in the Song of Songs.

> Where men are the primary initiators of sexual activity in the Torah and Prophets, the woman is every bit in the Song – at least in words, calling on her man to join her in "the garden". Where the man...had terrorizing power over his woman in the Torah and Prophets, it is the woman of the Song, if anything, who dominates speech and gains power throughout the book.[20]

The Bond with Nature

The bond of humans with nature is powerful in Śakuntalā. This can be sensed right through the narrative.[21] Living in the hermitage surrounded by trees, plants, birds and animals, Śakuntalā cultivated a deep affection for them. Nay, when she was lying as a hapless and abandoned child in the forest, vultures stood on guard to protect her until *Kaṇva*, the sage, found her, took her to the hermitage, and brought her up as his daughter. Since she was protected by the birds (*śakuntās*), they became part of her very name – Śakuntalā. She could commune with the trees and her favourite creepers. They are personified, and Śakuntalā can enter into a conversation with them. Ansūyā, the friend of Śakuntalā, tells her, "Friend Śakuntalā, here is the *Jasmine* creeper, the self-selecting bride of the mango tree to which you have given the name of *Vanajyostnā*. You have forgotten it" (Act I).

Besides trees and plants, there is talk of a fawn which Śakuntalā took care of as her own son and affectionately reared it. As she departs to the king's palace, she takes leave not only from her foster father, her companions, and other inmates of the hermitage but also from the trees, creepers, and animals she nurtured. A moving passage describes in the words of her foster-father *Kaṇva*, the bond of Śakuntalā with nature as she prepares to leave the hermitage:

> Ye neighbouring trees of the penance-grove! She who never attempts (proceeds) to drink water first, when you have not drunk (i.e., before you are watered), she who though fond of ornaments, never plucks (*lit.* takes) your leaves through affection for you, she to whom it is a festivity when you first put forth your blossoms, that same Śakuntalā now departs to her husband's house; let her (or this) be permitted by you all (Act IV).

When we read the biblical Song of Songs with Śakuntalā, we cannot but be struck by how this obscure book of the Bible situates the mutual yearning of the bride and the bridegroom and their amorous incantation interspersing them with the language of nature – flowers and fruits, gardens and vineyards, ointment and fragrance, wind and water, mountains and fields.

Lynn White holds the view that the Judeo-Christian tradition was responsible for the current ecological crisis.[22] According to him, this is because of its anthropocentrism, which led to view nature as subjugated to humans and to be used for their needs. The view of Lynn White has been contested. Be that as it may, a striking fact is that we do not find any romantic description of nature and its processes in the Bible. The reason could be geographical. West Asian soil from where the books of the Bible sprung consists mostly of deserts and wilderness with sparse vegetation confined to a few pockets. This geographical fact did not give room to any particular attention to nature as we have it in Śakuntalā and Indian literature at large. The desert is the experience of the people of West Asia, to which the Bible is replete with references. Desert (read nature) is where humans encounter God and discover themselves.

In the Hagar narrative, too, as we noted, she flees to the desert. Dessert motive goes along with that of water and spring.[23] In the desert of Sinai, when Moses leads the people of Israel, they suffer from extreme thirst and then comes the response of God with a command to Moses to strike the ground from where gushed forth life-giving waters (Ex 17:1-7). In the Hagar story too, when the child is on the verge of death for want of water, the angel of God leads her to a spring of water which revives the child (Gen 21:15-21). Nature as trees, plants, creepers, birds and animals, is a rarity in the Bible. However, we have an exceptional passage on the beauty of nature in the Song of Songs. The following verses describe the arrival of spring-time.

> Arise, my love my fair one
> And come away;
> For lo, the winter is past, the rain is over and gone
> The flowers appear on the earth
> The time of singing has come
> And the voice of the turtledove is heard in our land

> The fig tree puts forth its figs
> And the vines are in blossom; they give forth fragrance
> Arise, my love my fair one, and come away (Song of Songs 2:10-13).

This announcement of the arrival of springtime is, perhaps, the most beautiful poetic passage in the entire Bible on the enchanting beauty of nature. In the Song of Songs, we have the depiction of nature flourishing with vegetation, and nature seems to be a participant in the love and mutual desire of the bride and bridegroom.

The supreme beauty of nature as it comes out in Kālidāsa's Śakuntalā reminds us also of St Francis of Assisi (1181/1182-1226), who in the Christian history is viewed as a universal saint, precisely for his integral vision of reality and the way he was able to relate himself to nature.[24] In his famous Canticle of Creatures, he calls the Sun brother and the moon sister. He could converse with fishes, preach to birds, and instruct a threatening wolf not to harm anyone. For Śakuntalā, nature is a companion she loves and cares for, and it is personalized with names. The spirits of Śakuntalā and St Francis seem to meet.

Remorse and Repentance

Sin is a major category in the biblical tradition and a significant element in Christian history. Many Biblical narratives and lives of Christian saints and sages through the centuries centre on sorrow, grief, and anguish about sin and punishment and on the process of repentance and reconciliation leading to peace. These are very central concepts in the biblical and Christian understanding because they are inextricably bound up with the Christian understanding of salvation. Significantly, the play Śakuntalā also has a distinct place for remorse and repentance. King Dushyanta experiences deep remorse for repudiating a poor lass as Śakuntalā.[25] There is a beautiful passage on the King falling at Śakuntalā's feet and asking pardon for having repudiated her. He wants to be "free from remorse" (Act VII).

> O fair-bodied one, let the unpleasant feeling caused by my repudiation (of you) pass from your heart; somehow, great was the infatuation of my mind then; such for the most part are the modes of action towards auspicious things of those seized by a powerful delusion (*lit.* Darkness); a blind man shakes off even a garland of flowers thrown on his head, mistaking it for a serpent (Act VII).

Disowning a woman who was lawfully married is not only a sin of injustice committed against her but also her family, kith and kin. Aware of the broader social repercussion of his sin, King Dushyanta confesses to *Prajāpati* for causing pain to her foster father and all those close to Śakuntalā. This is something moving as it expresses the utter sincerity of the king. So goes the confession of the king:

> Divine Sir, having married this (lady) your servant, by the *gāndharva* form of marriage, I offended (*lit.* made myself guilty towards) his reverence *Kaṇva*, your kinsman (descendant), by disavowing her through weakness of memory, when brought (to me) sometime after by her relatives (Act VII).

This text could be read inter-textually with the biblical episode of the sin of King David. In the case of David, it was a sin against a woman and her husband. To briefly recall the biblical narrative, King David, while walking on the roof of his palace one afternoon, caught sight of an exceedingly beautiful woman, Bathsheba, bathing. She was the wife of Uriah. Lured by her irresistible charm, he plots to do away with Uriah. He arranged through his army general Joab that Uriah be placed in the hardest battlefront. Thus, David killed Uriah and took full possession of his wife Bathsheba (cf. 2Sam 11). The sins of adultery and murder of an innocent man became the object of God's punishment for King David. He felt remorse and repented for his sins throughout his life (cf. 2Sam 12). In the Book of Psalms in the Bible, seven Psalms (6, 32, 38, 51, 102, 130 & 143) are attributed to King David as expressive of his deep emotion of repentance.

In the case of Śakuntalā, the ascetics and friends who accompanied her to the palace challenged the king and argued about how he could disown whom he had married, according to *the gāndharva* form. Though King Dushyanta did not recognize what was spoken to him, he realized the truth when freed from his delusion, ignorance, and loss of memory. In the case of King David, we have the prophet Nathan who becomes the spokesperson for the innocent who was murdered and whose wife was taken away. Nathan provokes pangs of conscience in the king through a telling parable. It is the parable of a poor man in a city with only one little lamb. A rich man had many flocks and herds. To treat a guest, the rich man does not want to take any sheep of his own, but steals the only lamb that was so dear to the poor man. Hearing this, King David is outraged at the injustice and wants to punish the rich man who stole the only sheep from a poor fellow. At this point, Prophet Nathan tells him, "You are the man" (2 Sam. 12:7). He refers to the case of Uriah with his only wife, whereas the rich man was King David with his harem of women. However, he covets and steals the wife of the poor man Uriah. The response of a penitent king was, "I have sinned against the Lord" (2 Sam.12:13).

The words of repentance of King David seem to echo the experience of King Dushyanta, who, out of deep remorse for his sin, "passes the night sleepless rolling about in the bed; ...then for a long time he remains confused with shame" (Act V). The mood of the sorrow of King Dushyanta is expressed in that he interdicts the joyous spring festivities and abstains from the enjoyment it brings. As a sign of his repentance, he also discards the decoration of his body, "bearing but one bracelet of gold" (Act VI). The king confesses, "This accursed heart (of mine) has now awakened to experience the anguish of remorse" (Act VI). We can hear the echo of the penitential psalm of King David: "Have mercy on me o God...

wash me from my iniquity. For I know my transgressions and my sin is ever before me" (Psalm 51: 1-3). The New Testament is full of calls for repentance. In fact, the words "repent" and "repentance" occur fifty-eight times, indicating their importance. Repentance is not simply feeling sorry about one's evil doing. It signifies a change to a new mindset (*metanoia* in Greek). Seen from this perspective, the repentance of Dushyanta consists in that *change of mind* which led him from disowning Śakuntalā as his wife to warm acceptance of her as his wife and queen along with their son.

Curse, Boon and Blessings

A key element of plot in the drama of Śakuntalā is the curse by the sage Durvāsas. Curse and boon are common themes in many Indian traditional stories and *purāṇas*. Though there is not much emphasis on boon in the Bible, we have numerous Biblical narrations which speak of curses and blessings. Śakuntalā, before her departure to the palace of her husband, is blessed by her father, companions and even by nature.

Curse in the Bible takes the form of imprecations about one's enemies, and they derive from the experience of deep pain and anger. We have so many such imprecations in the biblical book of Psalms. These curses and imprecations are often uttered as prayers addressed to God, whose punishment is invoked on the enemies. The Bible speaks a lot about the love of enemies. How could it then allow such curses against enemies? Bible scholars offer various explanations, into which we need not go here.[26] What we can safely state is that, as a work of literature, Bible lets the aggrieved express their deep feelings and sentiments, which God need not endorse. It is the way the victims feel. We also have several examples of curses by God in the first book itself of the Bible – Genesis. The story of Adam and

Eve's temptation concludes with God's curse on man, woman and the serpent. For example, the curse on Adam reads as follows:

> Cursed is the ground because of you; in toil you shall eat of it all the days of your life; thorns and thistles it shall bring forth to you; ...in the sweat of your face you shall eat bread till you return to the ground for out of it you were taken; you are dust, and to dust you shall return (Gen. 3:17-19).

Cain, who killed his brother, Abel, the just, incurred the curse of God (Gen 4:10-12). Many biblical prophets use the genre of curses for their foretelling, and they claim to speak in the name of God.

This biblical background enables us to interpret, in another way, the curse pronounced by the sage Durvāsas upon Śakuntalā. We do not have the words of the ascetic reported in the play. Like the biblical prophets, the ascetics were symbols of extraordinary power acquired through their *tapas*, austerities and penances. Even gods feared the *tapas* of the ascetics, eremites, and sages. Their curse creates a disastrous situation for those against whom it is pronounced.

In ancient times, the ascetics, like the biblical prophets, stood out from the rest of the people and were greatly admired but also feared for their powers. No one would like to incur their wrath. However, in our story, this happens to the heroine – Śakuntalā. Her social standing as an orphaned child in a hermitage is very marginal. Consumed by love for the king, Śakuntalā turned "absent-minded" and fails to offer the distinguished visiting guest the kind of hospitality expected of her. Her negligence in offering hospitality and treating the visiting sage reverently provokes his rage. This was not wilful or deliberate but the result of her intoxication by love. Even the request for pardon by her companions does not soothe the ascetic. This is how Kālidāsa narrates the circumstance of the curse of Durvāsas:

> The absent-minded Śakuntalā has offended some person worthy of adoration. And indeed, not an ordinary person! Here is the great sage Durvāsas who is easily irritated. Having cursed (Śakuntalā) in that way, he has turned away with a gait brisk (quick) with impetuosity and difficult to be checked (Act IV).

The Christian scriptural tradition offers means of expiation when sin is committed. This is not the case with curses in the Bible. On the other hand, in the Indian stories and *purāṇas,* the curses are mostly accompanied by a proposal or means to overcome them or circumvent their effects. This is also the case with the curse of Durvāsas. When will the curse on Śakuntalā cease? Answers the sage saying, "My curse shall cease by showing (or, at the sight of) some ornament of recognition" (Act IV).

Celestial Interventions at Critical Moments

In ancient Indian tradition, there is no barrier between the world of gods and of humans, between heaven and earth. The deities constantly commute between their world and the world of humans and intervene in human vicissitudes. In the biblical tradition, too, there is the intervention of divinity in human affairs, but it is done through the mediation of celestial powers or angels who speak and act in God's name. It is interesting to observe that both in the story of Hagar and in the play of Śakuntalā, we have narrations of divine interventions. Śakuntalā breaks down and weeps when the king fails to recognize her and turns her away. Of this, the priest reports to the king:

> The girl [Śakuntalā] reproaching her stars began to cry aloud, tossing up her hand...And immediately, in the vicinity of Apsarastirtha, a flash of light in female form lifted her up and vanished (Act V).

In the Hagar narrative, when she chooses to flee to the desert due to the painful experience as an enslaved person in the house of Abraham and Sarai, an angel of God intervenes, assuring her the birth of a son, Ishmael, and a multitude of descendants (Gen. 16: 7ff). When Hagar was driven out this time and found herself in the wilderness of Beersheba, and the child was dying for want of water, again, a new divine intervention rescues Hagar from such a situation. An angel directs her to a well in the desert with which Hagar revives and refreshes the child (cf. Gen 21:17-19). In both cases – Śakuntalā and Hagar – the hand of God is stretched out to protect the weak and the marginalized. The gospel of Luke reports that when Jesus was in great agony on the eve of his cruel death by crucifixion and found himself in the garden of Gethsemane outside Jerusalem, an angel appeared to him and consoled him (cf. Lk 22:43). Bible is replete with instances of divine interventions at crucial moments.

In Śakuntalā, the play's climax is constituted by the sudden realization of King Dushyanta of the truth his muddled mind had failed to acknowledge. The new realization comes about through celestial intervention. He is transported into heaven by the chariot of Indra, and when he returns to the hermitage of *Kaṇva* after conquering the demons, he recognizes the brave young boy to be his own heir, and Śakuntalā as his wife and queen. The transportation to heaven can be taken as a metaphor for self-realization in the life of humans, which lifts them to another level of consciousness and helps them overcome ignorance and reach the splendour of truth.

Concluding Reflections

We often look at texts as objects of our interpretation. The ways the text, the author, and the reader correlated also signify different hermeneutical orientations. In the hermeneutical framework in which *the author's meaning* is central, one would employ the historic-critical method, which helps locate the author in her context and understand the text in that light. When we focus on *the reader*, we will follow reader-response criticism. *Dhvani* interpretation goes beyond these frameworks and lets the text address the present with its suggestive meaning. A second hermeneutical intuition is what Gadamer calls *"fusion of horizons."*[27] The world of the text – in our case, Śakuntalā and biblical narratives – and the context of the reader fuse to yield new meanings relevant to the present conditions.

Further, to relate the two traditions – Śakuntalā and biblical narratives – to the present, we base ourselves also on the hermeneutical principle that it is not always we who interpret the text. The text can also interpret us, our life and our existential experiences. In other words, we submit ourselves to the text and allow it to shed light on our situation.[28] So then, in what ways could narratives on women like Śakuntalā and biblical narratives like Hagar address our situation today and interpret it? Among the number of issues both of them could address, let me highlight a few by way of example.

Both traditions challenge us to direct our attention to the present-day situation of women who are marginalized, orphaned, abused, subjected to moral and physical violence, and exploited to the loss of their identity and agency – like Śakuntalā and Hagar. The two narratives also give much hope to women caught up in the system of patriarchy. Śakuntalā and Hagar are not cowed down by their situation of powerlessness as a fate to be borne meekly, but take it as a challenge to be proactive, exercising their agency and asserting their rightful claims. Both narratives could be an inspiration to the continued struggles of women to find their legitimate place in the family and society at large.

Genuine love between man and woman is trivialized today by caste and honour-killings and several other social forces. Not a day passes in this country without some or other case wherein young people – boys and girls in deep love with each other – are forcefully separated and even brutally killed. There is a refusal to accept the nobility of the *éros*. It is sacrificed on the altar of caste and false family-pride. Śakuntalā and King Dushyanta are icons of deep human love, bolstered by free choice to give fully to each other in marriage – the *gāndharva* form of marriage. Here a woman decides freely to choose her partner in the absence of her foster-father *Kaṇva*. When he returns, this father is not in a rage that his daughter did not take his counsel; rather he respects the free decision of his daughter, approves it, and accepts her unconditionally in her freely chosen life of love and marriage. This narrative, interpreted against the background of today, cannot but be critical of all the ostracization and violence that are taking place in our society against a woman's freedom for her life of love. When the child is born to Śakuntalā from her union with Dushyanta, *Kaṇva* happily performs all the rites for the newborn child. Seen in this light, Śakuntalā is a play that critically interprets our present-day practices that might be keen on obstructing the agency, identity, and freedom of women.

The Song of Songs too interprets critically anything that stands in the way of genuine human love and mutuality. Today, we speak about the safety of women. The bride of Song of Songs feels emboldened to express her intimate feelings of love without inhibition. She wakes up at night and desperately looks for her lover in the city at the dead of night and enquires from the watchmen whether they have seen him (Song of Songs 3:1-3). Is anything like this possible today? Śakuntalā and Song of Songs is a judgement on our society of today and all the violence to which women are subjected when they dare to be free and be themselves.

Śakuntalā, Hagar, and the bride in the Song of Songs have much to say on the gender relationships of today. They subvert the conventional frames and mores of man-woman relationships and challenge patriarchal dominance. Śakuntalā and the bride in Song of Songs reflect an equal partnership between man and woman. There is much mutuality in gender relationships. There is no indication of women being subjected to patriarchal power. The woman Śakuntalā and the bride in Song of Songs are also liberated women from patriarchy-induced inhibitions. They feel empowered by the unhindered power of love. Love lived in partnership becomes joy and fulfilment of life. In these times when women's desire and sexuality continue to be suppressed through moral and physical violence, the Song of Songs and Śakuntalā present a different picture of women's agency in erotic love. The desire of woman and her sexual initiative is portrayed when at the very outset of the Song of Song, the bride says, "O that you would kiss me with the kisses of your mouth! For your love is better than wine; your anointing oils are fragrant" (Song of Songs 1:2).

In the prevailing situation of deeply-entrenched corruption in high places among leaders, we are saddened that there is hardly any compunction or remorse in them for amassing public money and goods for private interests. If to err is human, humans get out of that situation and avoid repeating the same by feeling sorry about the wrongdoing. On the contrary, we are given spirited justification of what is manifest injustice by the rulers. In this context, King Dushyanta and King David present a counter-cultural instance.[29] They are deeply affected by the evil they committed and seek forgiveness. In this respect, both narratives are a judgment on our present-day unrepentant leaders who continue to commit evil with impunity against women and persist in their misdeeds.

In these times of wanton destruction of nature through human greed and false model of development, it is salutary to allow these classical texts to interpret our situation of ecological crisis. Śakuntalā is a superb play that lets us savour the beauty of nature, which comes alive through the poetic genius of Kālidāsa. We can sense the unity of all life in this play and the harmonious relationship between humans and nature. The drama of human life is played out in the womb of mother nature, whose depiction by Kālidāsa can be exhilarating and soothing for modern men and women getting progressively alienated from it.

NOTES

1   This classical work has several translations in English and other languages. The quotes in this chapter are from the translation of M.R. Kale, *The Abhijñānaśākuntalam of* Kālidāsa, 10th edition (Delhi: Motilala Banarsidass Publishers, 1969). Reprint of 2005.

2   Cf. K. Kunjunni Raja, *Indian Theories of Meaning* (Chennai: Adyar Library and Research Centre, 2000); K. Satchidananda Murty, *Vedic Hermeneutics* (New Delhi: Shri Lal Bahadur Shastri Rashtriya Sanskrit Vidyapeetha, 1993); P.C. Muraleemahadevan, ed., *Indian Theories of Hermeneutics* (Delhi: New Bharatiya Book Corporation, 2002); See also, M. Leelavathy, "Evolution of Indian Theories of Hermeneutics," in P.C. Muraleemahadevan, *Indian Theories of Hermeneutics, op. cit.* 129–144; T. Vasudevan, "Hermeneutics and the Dhvani Theory of Interpretation," *op. cit.* 343–348; Anand Amaladass, *Indian Exegesis: Hindu-Buddhist Hermeneutics* (Chennai: Satya Nilayam Publications, 2003).

3   Cf. Richard E. Palmer, *Hermeneutics: Interpretation Theory in Schleiermacher, Dilthey, Heidegger, and George Gadamer* (Evanston: Northwestern University Press, 1969); Paul Ricœur, *Interpretation Theory: Discourse and the Surplus of Meaning* (Fort Worth: Texas Christian University Press, 1976): 87f; ID., *Hermeneutics and the Human Sciences* edited and translated by John B. Thompson (Cambridge: Cambridge University Press, 1981); Don Ihde, ed., *The Conflict of Interpretations: Essays in Hermeneutics,* (Evanston: Northwestern University Press, 1974); John Sturrock, ed., *Structuralism and Since: From Levi-Strauss to Derrida* (Oxford: Oxford University Press, 1979); ID., *Structuralism,* 2nd ed. (London: Fontana Press, 1993); Wolfgang Iser, *The Act of Reading: A Theory of Aesthetic Response* (Baltimore: Johns Hopkins University Press, 1978); Josef Bleicher, *Contemporary Hermeneutics: Hermeneutics as Method, Philosophy and Critic* (London, New York: Routledge, 1980)

4   Cf. Felix Wilfred, "Navigating Cross-Hermeneutical Currents: A Subaltern Perspective," in Nishant Alphonse Irudayadason, ed., *Musings and Meanings: Essays on Eastern and Western Hermeneutical Traditions* (New Delhi: Christian World Imprints, 2016), 1–14.

5   Cf. Robert M. Grant and David Tracy, *A Short History of the Interpretation of the Bible,* (London: SCM, 2012); see also Werner Jeanrond, *Theological Hermeneutics* (New York: Crossroad, 1991).

6   Allegorical interpretation developed drawing inspiration from Plato and it flourished especially in the ancient school of Alexandria.

7   Cf. Paula Richman, ed., *Many Rāmāyaṇas: The Diversity of a Narrative Tradition in South Asia* (Berkeley: University of California Press, 1991); Nell Shapiro Hawley, and Sohini Pillai, eds., *Many Mahābhāratas,* (New York: New York University Press, 2021); Ankita Sharma, "Memory and the 'Many

Mahabharatas': A Reading of Mahabharata, The End of an Epoch and The Palace of Illusions," in *Gnosis* 7, no.2 (2021): 32–44; A Deconstruction of Mahabharata: When Draupadi Writes Back," in *Miscelánea: a Journal of English and American Studies* 55 (2017): 13–29; Si. En. Śrīkaṇthannāyar, and Sārā Jōsaph, *Retelling the Ramayana: Voices from Kerala* (Delhi, Oxford: Oxford University Press, 2005).

8   See, for example, Romila Thapar, *Sakuntalā, Texts, Readings, Histories* (New York: Columbia University Press, 2010).

9   Romila Tapar, *Sakuntalā*, 2.

10   As is well-known, the story of Śakuntalā is recounted in *Mahābhārata*. The poetic genius of Kālidāsa turned this story into an elegant drama with some twists and turns to the original story. Particularly significant change is the motif of a ring, its loss and recovery.

11   Cf. Jeanie C. Crain, *Reading the Bible as Literature: An Introduction* (Cambridge: Polity Press, 2010); Meir Sternberg, *The Poetics of Biblical Narrative: Ideological Literature and the Drama of Reading* (Bloomington: Indiana University Press, 1987); Robert W. Funk, *The Poetics of Biblical Narrative* (Sonoma, California: Polebridge Press, 1988); Herman Northrop Frye, *The Great Code: The Bible and Literature* (New York: Harcourt Brace Jovanovich, 1982); Tremper Longman, *Literary Approaches to Biblical Interpretation* (Grand Rapids: Zondervan, 1987).

12   Recently, some very original studies have tried to read Hagar from the perspective of the marginalized African-American women and from the perspective of Dalit women. Delores S. Williams, *Sisters in the Wilderness: The Challenge of Womanist God-Talk* (New York: Orbis Books, 1993); Antony John Baptist, *Together as Sisters: Hagar and Dalit Women* (Delhi: ISPCK, 2012). For other studies on Hagar from a feminist perspective, See Savina J. Teubal, *Hagar the Egyptian: The Lost Tradition of the Matriarchs* (New York: Harper & Row Publishers, 1990); Renit J. Weems, *Just a Sister Away* (San Diego: Lura Media, 1988); P. Trible, and Letty M. Russell, eds., *Hagar, Sarah and Their Children: Jewish Christian and Muslim Perspectives* (Louisville: John Knox Press, 2006).

13   For a detailed exegetical study of the verses on Hagar, see Antony John Baptist, *Together as Sisters*, 95–117.

14   "Humiliation" has become today a key concept in interpreting the situation of Dalits, African-Americans and other marginalized groups. See Gopal Guru, ed., *Humiliation: Claims and Context* (New Delhi: Oxford University Press, 2009).

15   See Antony John Baptist, "Hagar and Dalit Women in Exercising their Agency," in *Jeevadhara* 41, no. 241 (Jan 2011): 56–65.

16   Out of the vast literature on this book of the Bible, the following articles will be helpful for inter-textual reading. J. Paul Tanner, "The History of

Interpretation of Song of songs," in *Bibliotheca Sacra* 154 (January – March, 1997): 23–46; David Carr, "Gender and the Shaping of Desire in the Song of Songs and Its Interpretation," in *Journal of Biblical Literature* 119, no.2 (2000): 233–248.

17   See Ann W. Astell, *The Song of Songs in the Middle Ages* (Ithaca & London: Cornell University Press 1995); Roland E Murphy, and S. Dean McBride, *The Song of Songs: A Commentary on the Book of Canticles or the Song of Songs* (Minneapolis: Fortress Press, 1990); J. P. Tanner, "The History of Interpretation of the Song of Songs," *The Bibliotheca Sacra* 154, no. 613 (1997): 23–46.

18   A text has a life in a community with which it grows in meaning. In this case, the Song of Songs originated and developed in the Jewish community of the Old Testament. Over time, it is possible that this community began to see not simply a literal meaning in the text referring to human sexual love but began to view this reality as an allegory for the love of God for his bride, the people. This is very different from reading Song of Songs only as allegoric in meaning, for fear of the sexual love its literal meaning clearly indicates. What we have here is an anagogical (*anagōgé* in Greek means "leading upward") interpretation, namely a transposition from sexual love (without denying its human reality and value) on a human level to another plane of seeing in it the relation of God, the bridegroom with the bride, the human soul. Interestingly, the homilies of St Gregory of Nyssa on Song of Songs made an anagogical interpretation. It was occasioned by the request of deaconess Olympias of Constantinople, a very young widow, given to ascetic life and deeply involved in community service, for whom such an anagogical interpretation seems to have made much sense. In Medieval Europe, such an interpretation was called *sensus plenior* - fuller meaning of the text. See Hans Boersma, "Saving Bodies: Anagogical Transposition in St Gregory of Nyssa's Commentary on the Song of Songs," in *Ex Auditu* 26 (2010): 168–200.

19   Cf. Hugh B. Urban, *The Power of Tantra: Religion, Sexuality and the Politics of South Asian Studies* (London: I. B. Tauris & Co Ltd., 2011); José Ignacio Cabezón, ed., *Buddhism, Sexuality, and Gender* (Delhi: Sri Satguru Publications, 1992). See also Joseph Runzo and Nancy M. Martin, eds., *Love, Sex and Gender in the world Religions* (Oxford: Oneworld Publication, 2000); Georg Feuerstein, *Sacred Sexuality: The Erotic Spirit in the World's Great Religions* (New York: Jermy P. Tarcher, 1992).

20   David McLain Carr, "Ancient Sexuality and Divine Eros: Rereading the Bible through the Lens of Song of Songs," in *Union Seminary Quarterly Review* 54, no.3-4 (2000): 12; See also Denys Turner, *Eros of Allegory: Medieval Exegesis of the Song of Songs* (Collegeville: Cistercian Publication, 1995); Stephen D. Moore, "The Song of Songs in the History of Sexuality," in *Church History: Studies in Christianity and Culture* 69, no. 2 (June 2000): 328–349.

21   No wonder that Kālidāsa's Śakuntalā found enthusiastic reception in the
     European Romantic movement. In the nature romanticism extolling rustic
     life, Śakuntalā was viewed as a rustic girl and a "child of nature."

22   Lynn White, "The Historical Roots of Our Ecological Crisis," in *Science*
     (March 10, 1967): 1203–1207.

23   In the creation account, especially in the second account (Gen 2:4–25),
     the garden theme is spoken of. It emerges from a geographical setting of
     Palestine with deserts and sporadic oases. The humans are to "till it and keep
     it." (Gen 2:15)

24   Cf. Roger D. Sorell, *St Francis of Assisi and Nature: Tradition and Innovation
     in Western Christian Attitudes towards the Environment* (New York: Oxford
     University Press, 1988); Edward Armstrong, *Saint Francis: Nature Mysticism*
     (Berkeley: University of California Press, 1973).

25   As is well known, in the original story of Śakuntalā in *Mahābhārata*, the
     episode of the ring and the non-recognition of Śakuntalā because of a curse
     does not appear. This is the imaginative addition and plot by Kālidāsa.

26   For example, in Biblical history, there was no idea of an afterlife where one
     would have reward or punishment. This life being the only one, the aggrieved
     wanted to see retribution and punishment of the unjust and evildoers here
     and now. That would explain the tone of curses and imprecations on one's
     oppressors.

27   Cf. Hans-Georg Gadamer, *Truth and Method,* trans. William Glen-Doepel,
     edited by John Cumming and Garrett Barden, 2nd ed. (London: Sheed and
     Ward, 1979).

28   For Heidegger, the manifestation of being itself is a hermeneutical act.
     It is in interpretation that being comes to be and reveals itself (*aletheia*
     – truth as manifestation of being), for which, of course, language is
     very important, as the second Heideggerian efforts will show. However,
     interpretation is not so much about bringing out the meaning of a text
     (*Auslegung*), as bringing to manifestation the being. It is not so much about
     meaning (*Bedeutung*) as about *significance* (*Bedeutsamkeit*). Heideggerian
     hermeneutics is about the significance and meaning of human existence,
     an interpretation of *Dasein* – being-in-the-world. Ultimately, for Heidegger,
     human understanding of existence is hermeneutics. Rudolf Bultman, one of
     the most celebrated twentieth-century interpreters of the New Testament,
     built on the hermeneutics of Heidegger, his programme of de-mythologized
     interpretation of the Bible. He saw an interpretation of human existence
     in the Bible, freed from myths. See Roger Johnson, ed., *Rudolf Bultmann:
     Interpreting Faith for the Modern Era* (London: Collins, 1987).

29   In *Cilappatikāram*, one of the five great epics in Tamil, the Pandiya king
     collapses once Kannagi proves her husband's innocence and challenges the
     king for unjustly executing her husband, accusing him of theft.

FURTHER READING

Amaladass, Anand. *Indian Exegesis: Hindu-Buddhist Hermeneutics.* Chennai: Satya Nilayam Publications, 2003.

Armstrong, Edward. *Saint Francis: Nature Mysticism.* Berkeley: University of California Press, 1973.

Astell, Ann W. *The Song of Songs in the Middle Ages.* Ithaca & London: Cornell University Press 1995.

Baptist, Antony John. "Hagar and Dalit Women in Exercising their Agency." *Jeevadhara* 41, no. 241 (Jan 2011): 56–65.

Baptist, Antony John. *Together as Sisters: Hagar and Dalit Women.* Delhi: ISPCK, 2012.

Bleicher, Josef. *Contemporary Hermeneutics: Hermeneutics as Method, Philosophy and Critic.* London, New York: Routledge, 1980.

Boersma, Hans. "Saving Bodies: Anagogical Transposition in St Gregory of Nyssa's Commentary on the Song of Songs." *Ex Auditu* 26 (2010): 168–200.

Cabezón, José Ignacio, ed. *Buddhism, Sexuality, and Gender.* Delhi: Sri Satguru Publications, 1992.

Carr, David McLain. "Ancient Sexuality and Divine Éros: Rereading the Bible through the Lens of Song of Songs." *Union Seminary Quarterly Review* 54, no.3–4 (2000): 12.

Carr, David McLain. "Gender and the Shaping of Desire in the Song of Songs and Its Interpretation." *Journal of Biblical Literature* 119, no.2 (2000): 233–248.

Crain, Jeanie C. *Reading the Bible as Literature: An introduction.* Cambridge: Polity Press, 2010.

Feuerstein, Georg. *Sacred Sexuality: The Erotic Spirit in the World's Great Religions.* New York: Jermy P. Tarcher, 1992.

Frye, Herman Northrop. *The Great Code: The Bible and Literature.* New York: Harcourt Brace Jovanovich, 1982.

Funk, Robert W. *The Poetics of Biblical Narrative.* Sonoma, California: Polebridge Press, 1988.

Gadamer, Hans-Georg. *Truth and Method,* trans. William Glen-Doepel, edited by John Cumming and Garrett Barden, 2nd ed. London: Sheed and Ward, 1979.

García-Arroyo, Ana. "Deconstruction of Mahabharata: When Draupadi Writes Back." *Miscelánea: A Journal of English and American Studies* 55 (2018): 13–29.

Grant, Robert M, and David Tracy. *A Short History of the Interpretation of the Bible,* 2nd ed. Philadelphia: Fortress Press, 1984.

Guru, Gopal, ed. *Humiliation: Claims and Context.* New Delhi: Oxford University Press, 2009.

Hawley, Nell Shapiro, and Sohini Pillai, eds. *Many Mahābhāratas.* New York: State University of New York Press, 2021.

Iser, Wolfgang. *The Act of Reading: A Theory of Aesthetic Response.* Baltimore: Johns Hopkins University Press, 1978.

Jeanrond, Werner. *Theological Hermeneutics.* New York: Crossroad, 1991.

Johnson, Roger, ed. *Rudolf Bultmann: Interpreting Faith for the Modern Era.* London: Collins, 1987.

Kale, M.R. *The Abijnnasakuntalam of* Kālidāsa. 10th ed. Delhi: Motilala Banarsidass Publishers, 1969. Reprint of 2005.

Longman, Tremper. *Literary Approaches to Biblical Interpretation.* Grand Rapids: Zondervan, 1987.

Moore, Stephen D. "The Song of Songs in the History of Sexuality." *Church History: Studies in Christianity and Culture* 69, no.2 (June 2000): 328–349.

Muraleemahadevan, P.C, ed. *Indian Theories of Hermeneutics.* Delhi: New Bharatiya Book Corporation, 2002.

Leelavathy, M. "Evolution of Indian Theories of Hermeneutics." In P.C. Muraleemahadevan, ed., *Indian Theories of Hermeneutics,* 129-144. Delhi: New Bharatiya Book Corporation, 2002.

Murphy, Roland E, and S. Dean McBride. *The Song of Songs: A Commentary on the Book of Canticles or the Song of Songs.* Minneapolis: Fortress Press, 1990.

Murty, K. Satchidananda. *Vedic Hermeneutics.* New Delhi: Shri Lal Bahadur Shastri Rashtriya Sanskrit Vidyapeetha, 1993.

Palmer, Richard E. *Hermeneutics: Interpretation Theory in Schleiermacher, Dilthey, Heidegger, and* George Gadamer. Evanston: Northwestern University Press, 1969.

Raja, K. Kunjunni. *Indian Theories of Meaning.* Chennai: Adyar Library and Research Centre, 2000.

Richman, Paula, ed. *Many Rāmāyaṇas: The Diversity of a Narrative Tradition in South Asia.* Berkeley: University of California Press, 1991.

Ricœur, Paul. *Hermeneutics and the Human Sciences.* Edited and translated by John B. Thompson. Cambridge: Cambridge University Press, 1981.

Ricœur, Paul. *Interpretation Theory: Discourse and the Surplus of Meaning.* Fort Worth: Texas Christian University Press, 1976.

Ricœur, Paul. *The Conflict of Interpretations: Essays in Hermeneutics.* Edited by Don Ihde. Evanston: Northwestern University Press, 1974.

Runzo, Joseph, and Nancy M, Martin, eds. *Love, Sex and Gender in the World Religions.* Oxford: Oneworld Publication, 2000.

Sharma, Ankita. "Memory and the 'Many Mahabharatas': A Reading of Mahabharata, The End of an Epoch and The Palace of Illusions." *Gnosis* 7, no.2 (January 2021): 32–44.

Sorell, Roger D. *St Francis of Assisi and Nature: Tradition and Innovation in Western Christian Attitudes towards the Environment.* New York: Oxford University Press, 1988.

Śrīkaṇthannāyar, Si. En, and Sārā Jōsaph. *Retelling the Ramayana: Voices from Kerala.* Delhi: Oxford University Press, 2005.

Sternberg, Meir. *The Poetics of Biblical Narrative: Ideological Literature and the Drama of Reading.* Bloomington: Indiana University Press, 1987.

Sturrock, John. *Structuralism and Since: From Levi-Strauss to Derrida.* Oxford: Oxford University Press, 1979.

Sturrock, John. ed. *Structuralism*, 2nd ed. London: Fontana Press, 1993.

Tanner, J. P. "The History of Interpretation of the Song of Songs." *The Bibliotheca Sacra* 154, no. 613 (1997): 23–46.

Teubal, Savina J. *Hagar the Egyptian: The Lost Tradition of the Matriarchs.* New York: Harper & Row Publishers, 1990.

Thapar, Romila. *Śakuntalā, Texts, Readings, Histories.* New York: Columbia University Press, 2010.

T, Vasudevan. "Hermeneutics and the Dhvani Theory of Interpretation." In P.C. MuraleeMahadevan, ed., *Indian Theories of Hermeneutics,* 343–348. Delhi: New Bharatiya Book Corporation, 2002.

Trible, P, and Letty M. Russell, eds. *Hagar, Sarah and Their Children: Jewish Christian and Muslim Perspectives.* Louisville: John Knox Press, 2006.

Turner, Denys. *Eros of Allegory: Medieval Exegesis of the Song of Songs.* Collegeville Cistercian Publication, 1995.

Urban, Hugh B. *The Power of Tantra: Religion, Sexuality and the Politics of South Asian Studies.* London: I. B. Tauris & Co Ltd., 2011.

Weems, Renit J. *Just a Sister Away.* San Diego: Lura Media, 1988.

White, Lynn. "The Historical Roots of Our Ecological Crisis." *Science* (1967): 1203–1207.

Wilfred, Felix. "Navigating Cross-Hermeneutical Currents: A Subaltern Perspective." In Nishant Alphonse Irudayadason, ed. *Musings and Meanings: Essays on Eastern and Western Hermeneutical Traditions,* 1–14. New Delhi: Christian World Imprints, 2016.

Williams, Delores S. *Sisters in the Wilderness: The Challenge of Womanist God-Talk.* New York: Orbis Books, 1993.

Chapter 6

SMART CITY vs. CARING CITY
REFLECTIONS ON URBANIZATION
WITH FOCUS ON THE POOR

With rapid globalization, use of Information and Communication Technology (ICT), creation of infrastructures and fast urban transport systems, the Indian cities have been going through a sea-change. The state-sponsored project of creating five hundred "smart cities" have added momentum to the transformations underway. However, it is crucial to critically evaluate the state of Indian cities and emphasize the need for compassionate urban environments that prioritize the well-being of the underprivileged, migrants, and other vulnerable groups. Such cities should ensure the fulfillment of basic needs and respond to the aspirations of the marginalized people. In this context, it is essential to question the meaning of smart city in an urban landscape that is divided by caste, class, and religion, and where people and their housing patterns are distinct.

In June 2015, the mission of creating hundred smart cities in different states of India was launched by the prime minister.[1] This project follows close on the heels of the model of European Union and other developed countries where the concept was introduced.

The primary objective in adopting this western model of smart cities and promoting them is to create state-of-the art, infrastructure, technology-driven communication and governance so as to attract foreign investments and multinational business enterprises. In essence, small cities are envisioned as catalysts of economic growth driven by the concept of leapfrog development. Institutional, physical, social and economic infrastructures are created to achieve the objectives of market and business. Life is made comfortable with the introduction of internet of things.[2]

The government and urban planners want to make Indian cities "world-class." All this fuels the aspirations of the Indian nouveau riche and the middle class who reside in India but dream to experience the life-style of world-class cities like New York, Paris, London, Tokyo, and Singapore.

Though there is a wide variety of definitions, what smart city is,[3] it is undeniable that the prevailing understanding of smart city aligns with urbanization with fast economic growth through private actors, competition, efficiency, and techno-management. According to one technical definition, "a smart city is one in which the physical infrastructure of the city itself becomes accessible and represented in the digital infrastructure of that city. Case in point: If it's smart, there's intelligence."[4]

Smart city is a top-down approach which tends to standardize city-life imagining one size fits all. Ironically, those who shout themselves hoarse in the name of nationalism, national pride and culture, fail to anchor themselves in the traditional city-life. Totally unrelated to real life conditions in the city and failing to reflect transformation from bottom up, smart city project cannot but appear as a utopian experiment chasing a chimera. However, it has given us an opportunity to reflect deeply on the issue of urbanization and the plight of the poor.

In the first part of this chapter, after some brief general remarks on what cities represent in the life of the people, we shall focus on analyzing some aspects of the city through the lens of the urban poor and the marginalized. In the second part, we shall enter into some theological reflections on urban life to show why the plight of the poor and the marginalized calls for a compassionate and caring city rather than a smart city.

Part I: Urban Landscape and the Cry of the Poor

The Fascination of City

Many are the reasons and motives for people to move into the cities. For some, city is a place of wealth, comfort and high quality of living; for others, it offers facilities and opportunities for their skills and talents to flourish. Aristotle characterized city as a self-sufficient association, and that it exists by nature. It is an indispensable place for "living well" by which he meant a place for leading a life of happiness and for pursuing "virtues" or talents.[5] In fact, unlike the hinterlands, cities with dense human proximity and concentration of talents create an ambience for the maximization of human capacities and for innovation. It creates opportunities to practice justice and serve common good. Moreover, city is a place of freedom providing a milieu to cultivate individual self, free from social pressures, oppressive traditions, and conventions.

Besides such ideals, in many developing countries, and increasingly also in the developed countries, city is the shelter to many victims of our world today – the impoverished, the landless, the abandoned, the displaced, the refugees, asylum-seekers, victims of ecological disasters, floating population from the countryside in search of labour and so on. City is some hope of survival amidst many deprivations the poor suffer. Chinese cities offer labour opportunities and draw people from hinterland, and Indian cities offer for many Dalits a sense of anonymity sparing them the humiliation of their oppressive caste-identity.

Gandhian Village vs Bourgeoning Indian Cities

Though Gandhi readily admitted the pathetic state of Indian villages, for him India, by and large, is a rural civilization.[6] He had more negative view of cities. To cite just an example, when his attention was drawn to the decline of wildlife in jungles, his satirical reply was that wildlife was in towns and cities, and that it is flourishing there![7] For Gandhi, India truly lives in the villages - 700, 000 in his time. How true is this today? Is not the heart of India beating today in the cities? Cities have caught the imagination of Indians, and villages have lost their romantic and idyllic touch.

The urban population of India is spread out in about 4000 towns and cities of which 40 are cities with more than one million inhabitants.[8] These cities and towns, as elsewhere, are the engines of growth and development in the country, and they seem to hold the key for lifting the millions of poor out of their poverty. In fact, it is projected that by 2030 (just seven years away) 75% of GDP in the country will be from the cities. As per UN statistics, today about 55% population of the world live in cities. With phenomenal growth of cities in Asia, Africa, and Latin America, it is going to be 68% in the coming decades. The growth of Indian cities is part of the global phenomenon of surging urbanization. The city of Tokyo, the largest city in the world has today about 37 million people, and Delhi, probably the second largest, has a population of 29 million. However, Delhi is moving to become the largest city overtaking the population of Tokyo, by 2028.[9]

Once popularly looked at as a breeding ground of vice and immorality, city has transformed in recent decades the consciousness of the people. Villages are no more the repositories of culture counterposed to urban life, as the anthropologists used to do in yesteryears. Rather, it is the cities that seem to set the parameters for culture and good life in the villages. The turning point for a radical transformation of Indian cities was the introduction of neo-liberal economy in 1990s. The investment by the state and by private entrepreneurs have led to the creation of vast infrastructures in cities and towns. The transformations in the city and the new level and quality of life call for its reappraisal.

What is most striking is the transformation of consciousness regarding city and village. Whereas village was extolled and seen as building blocks of the nation, this has given place today to a new image of the city as the basis for the nation and its growth. To the peasants losing confidence about their future prospects in cultivation of lands and burdened with debts, city offers an attractive alternative to explore. In fact, the agrarian crisis and the hopeless situation of farmers are one of the root-causes for massive migration into cities. In the absence of skills and social capital, the migrants in the cities fail to find any employment in formal sector, and end up in discreet odd jobs to make a living.

The Urban Life on the Margins

India has today an urban population of 377 million – larger than the entire population of the USA. Of these, several millions live in slums like Dharavi in Mumbai, the largest slum in Asia. They cook, eat, sleep and copulate in crammed spaces and pavements, and defecate in the open. Slums are "unintended cities."[10] Does the project of smart city really address the abysmal condition of the poor in cities?

> Urban poverty in the country is quite evident with 26.4 per cent earning
> less than 1 dollar a day …A million-plus cities are home to 40 per cent of
> the slum population, while 80 per cent of the urban poor live in cities with
> a population of less than 1 million. The extent of informality observed in
> urban employment is quite high (around 70 per cent), with a considerably low
> wage structure, adverse service conditions and location outside the purview
> of the social safety net. The largest category of urban employment is non-
> trade services, which includes large-scale informal employment comprised
> primarily of domestic workers and rag-pickers.[11]

Moreover, the urban poor also become victims of human trafficking, sexual abuse, dangerous medical experiments, drug peddling and so on. One speaks of quality of life today. Where is the quality of life in our cities if we exclude people and deny a modicum of space for them to conduct a dignified human life? With lack of open spaces and social isolation and no common spaces to meet and socialize – as the case in the villages – the poor opting to live in the city suffer immensely. There is an inextricable connection between poverty and environmental degradation. Poverty is the greatest pollutant, something one could experience palpably in our Indian cities. It is also what forces children instead of attending schools to go on rag-picking. A recent study among rag-picking children in the city of Allahabad showed that at least one child in each household in the slum was engaged in rag-picking to support the family.[12]

In the top ten cities of India, 95–98% of the urban land is in the hands of 20% at the helm of the society, whereas the poor just have about 1% of the city space. Public spaces are aggressively encroached upon by rapacious real estate business. With inequality of space starts a host of exploitation among the urban poor. As we noted, 26.4% of India's urban population lives on less than a dollar per day.[13] How could they afford spaces that are marketed at astronomical rates? Ironically, the labour and services of the new urban poor have become indispensable for the middle- and upper-class life in the cities. From the toil of the slums come gems of products for the consumption of the affluent and the middle-class.

The state and elite city-planners want to create world-class cities replicating modern metropolis elsewhere. Modern urban aesthetics and false pretensions drive them to demolish the slums of the poor and beautify the cities. These planners seem to have ignored the processes through which Indian cities and towns have developed and unaware of how the cities embody the precolonial, colonial, and postcolonial legacies. To illustrate the point more concretely, the present cities and towns are a mélange of planned approach by administration as well as local ad hoc and unplanned developments by the poor and the middle-class according to their needs and exigencies.[14] The demolition drives simply forget these latter unplanned developments as integral part of the creation of Indian cities. Doing away with the hybrid nature of Indian cities will hurt the poor and the marginalized terribly, because it has serious implications for the informal economy on which the livelihood of the poorest sections of the city is dependent. As Annapurna Shaw observes,

> Several global experts have repeatedly advised that informal ways of city expansion must be recognized and facilitated, as far as possible, rather than abruptly destroyed. A balance between formal and informal growth should be the basis of an urbanism of the future.[15]

Here is another reason why we need to be apprehensive about the smart city project. It could be a city of exclusion, namely a city for the well-to-do with the exclusion of the poor and without consideration to the needs of the different weaker economic classes and segments. At this juncture, it is important to recall the 74th Constitutional Amendment Act of 1992 which provided for the creation of self-governing local urban bodies with elected representatives. These bodies are entrusted with eighteen new functions at the economic, development and social levels, to be carried out at the local level and responding to local exigencies. However, in practice, the vision and ideals behind such decentralization of governance unfortunately are far from being achieved.

To realize the political and administrative objectives, the local bodies will be attentive to differences in terms of occupation of city spaces by different groups and identities – in terms of caste, religion etc. In most cases poverty is connected with the minority status. For example, though India has 18% of Muslim population and is a country with third largest Muslim population in the world, it is a fact that Muslims have been progressively marginalized in our cities in every realm – social, economic, political and cultural.[16] This marginalization is reflected also in the poor representation in fields of power such as bureaucracy, politics, and police force. Further, the literacy rate among the Muslims is very low and almost the same as the Dalits. The percentage of Muslims living in cities below poverty line too is higher.

To highlight a data of the Sachar Committee going into the plight of the Muslim minority in Indian cities, only 8% of Muslims are part of the formal sector in Indian cities, against the national average of 21%.[17] Such factors need to be taken into account by the local urban self-governing bodies in building the future of Indian cities. These bodies, to be effective, will need the support of non-state actors who have their pulse on the ground with the concrete experiences of daily lives of the city-dwellers, especially the marginalized.

Indigenous Urban Ethos

Does smart city project reflect in any way the ground reality at the urban periphery? It does not seem to be so. There are cultural reasons why the smart city may not find echo among the urban poor and the migrants. For example, one of the important characteristics in the community-living in India – be it in the city or in slums of the city – is the self-organization. Whether it is irrigation in the field of agriculture or regulating life in business in bazaars or occupying home-spaces, there are certain internal community rules and norms. The community sees to it that everyone abides by these internal norms for the purpose of attaining common good. In such a cultural environment, norms flowing from technology and communication-based organization from above do not simply work. More importantly, the issues that matter most for the people at the periphery are not taken into account or simply sidelined and neglected. These are, for example, housing closer to their places of work or small manufacturing or trade, clean drinking water, electricity, sanitation, schooling for their children and educational opportunities at affordable cost etc. In the project of smart city these substantial issues get submerged in the pursuit of ICT–based planning and governance. Amidst the anonymity of the city and its scaring isolation, the solidarity of the community is the real security.[18] This can be observed clearly in city-slums.

The project of smart city does not seem to have any place for community and its agency, as its planning and management are in the hands of technocrats. In sum, the smart cities which could enthuse the upper and middle classes spell something quite different for the poor masses of city-dwellers. It means further aggravating of inequality. The new infrastructure and facilities planned for the smart cities will only increase the potential of these classes to profit and accumulate wealth, thus widening the gap between the rich and the poor.

Yet another reason why we need to raise critical questions regarding smart city is that it overlooks substantial issues like opportunities and employment for the teeming millions of our youth who flock to the city with a lot of aspirations and hopes. This is such a major issue that we cannot think of the future of Indian cities without addressing it. As Jaideep Gupte rightly observes,

> If India's experiment with "smart" urbanisation is to succeed, there is a critical need for investing in the priorities of youth, creation of jobs they aspire to have, spaces they can engage with and thereby connecting them with the city. Rather than an undue emphasis on "harnessing technology" for the betterment of citizens, the focus should be on inclusive urbanisation, where no one is left behind.[19]

Sustainable City Environment amidst Hutments and Hovels

Nothing goes wasted in India. How true is this of our cities! Unlike in village, in cities the poor do makeshift arrangements to lay their heads using waste materials like plastic, broken bricks, asbestos, canvas, shreds from broken billboards. Such housing becomes for the elites and city-planners, "pimples and scars" on the face of the city. The beautification is achieved by continuous drive of demolition of the hutments of the already marginalized and those at the periphery of city-life. Low-cost housing is what the planners propose as solution to replace slums. But as Ashis Nandy notes, that it only contributes to make slums invisible. He notes,

> The urge to make slums invisible is there in almost every unthinking Indian – not just in the powerful, the foolish and the heartless. The desire to secure services from slums and yet not see them is one of the diseases of our times that is taking an epidemic form.[20]

If as it is said, poverty is the greatest pollutant, the agenda for a healthy environment needs to begin where the poor are. This is very different from a bourgeois romantic approach to city environments, heir to industrial revolution. With increased pollution resulting from the advent of industry, there started in the West the movement to protect individual households and the public by such measures as creating public parks, providing open spaces etc. It sets in motion the so-called "green-agenda." Later on, we saw the spreading of the "Green City" movement. Today, we are in a different situation in this country where we need to treat the issue of poverty and environmental sustainability as one major issue with two manifestations. Public parks and green-preserves and even open spaces are interdicted to the poor from where they continue to be evicted. When survival needs are topmost priority, the question of clean environment takes a back seat among the poor. Hence eradication of poverty (not to be equated with economic growth)[21] is the basis on which new environmental and ecological agenda are to be set. Natural resource conservation and sustainability interventions could be carried out when along with green agenda, a "brown agenda" is also set in motion. The latter is an agenda that makes the poor have access to basic needs and just share in the resources of nature. The brown agenda will include also initiatives for clean environment and waste management in slums and shanties. Sustainable environmental agenda will include as well a well-integrated and affordable public transport system.

Contested City Spaces and Conflict of Symbols

In the city of Chennai where I live, I need to be careful to check before hiring an auto whether there has been any change of name of the road where I am heading to! It is not uncommon that names of roads keep changing according to the political party in power and it could happen overnight. Naming roads has become a political event in the country, not to speak of erection of statues at busy thoroughfares and lanes where people struggle for spaces for their daily life. The cult of renaming roads and erecting statues is perhaps the best example of how power is exercised through symbols. Power-conflicts and political and social confrontation take on a symbolic dimension.

If it is true that space is never neutral but is constructed through discourses, and is socially mediated, namely by human encounter and interaction, this is surely the case of Indian cities.[22] Here we realize that city space is more than its materiality; it is a construct. The process of social, economic and political construction of city-streets and spaces turns them into arena for play of power. City spaces are today contested through a process of politicization in which conflict of classes and castes take place through symbolic affirmation. The religious affirmation takes place by sprinkling town and city-spaces with innumerable temples, dargahs, shrines etc. – some of them just in the middle of the road and junctions. There is hardly any town or city in the country that does not experience such conflicts in assertion of their respective symbols.

Indian city streets besides being a space for passage, plays an important social, cultural, political and economic role. Streets and byways and lanes are where people gather for socializing, for trade. Petty shops, vendors and hawkers of all hues and colours dot the city space. It is here the agency of the poor and the marginalized often come to expression.[23] Streets function as places of spectacle and public entertainment of many sorts. Indian city streets are the best example against the questionable public-private dichotomy. Streets are also where political and religious assertion takes place through all kinds of gatherings and processions – big and small. Streets are where our politicians erect stages to gather and address the public. They, then cease to be a space of passage but a theatre of political intervention.

In short, town and city streets are where power-assertion takes place in daily lives of the people and no wonder that they are hotbeds of riots and violence. The conflict between classes and castes take place by unleashing violence against inimical caste, religious, ethnic or linguistic groups. Political and religious processions have to go through the streets and lanes where one's enemies have their habitation or commercial or religious activities.

Divided by Caste and Religion and United by the Digital?

The project of smart city in India runs into another contradiction. It raises the question of deep-rooted division and discrimination in the occupation of city-spaces by different groups. Are we to think of the digital world and technological means without regard to caste and religious division? To imagine that the digital and the technological can unite without addressing social and religious contradictions would be an illusion.

US Fair Housing Policy Act of 1968 was the culmination of civil rights movements of the period with stalwarts like Martin Luther King leading. It was aimed at abolishing the discrimination of a buyer or seller of land, house etc., on the basis of his or her race, class, religion, gender and so on. In spite of legal measures taken, the practice of discrimination, unfortunately, still persists. The advantage however is that there is a legal measure in place to which one could have recourse in cases of violation. But any such legal provision is wanting in Indian cities. What is embarrassing is the Supreme Court Judgement of 2015 - Zoroastrian Housing Cooperative Society Ltd v District Registrar, Coop. Societies (Urban) in which the court upheld the right of a particular housing society based on religion to allow or not allow housing to others outside its religious fold.

The Brahmin and high-caste settlements in the city would see to it that no Dalit is anywhere around to 'defile' them and their traditions. Houses are rented out and sold only to one's own caste people. This sacrosanct tradition is transmitted from generation to generation. No matter what happens with the digital world, nothing changes when it comes to access to housing in caste-dominated areas.[24] It is a taboo protected by a lot of euphemisms. For example, areas or housing localities with no "non-vegetarians" means Dalits and Muslims need not think of settling anywhere around even if they have the economic means. There are many such codes of exclusion in different areas of the cities and towns. Housing system seems to be similar to endogamous marriage system – one's own caste only. Even the most sophisticated networking and digital means prove impossible to penetrate such deeply entrenched and ossified caste segregations in the cities. Indian cities carry in their bellies this contradiction between caste-based life and the modern digital and technological world.

What has the 'smart city' project to say to this discriminatory and caste-based urban housing pattern? The state which is so very keen on creating 500 smart cities in India, why is not forthcoming with a housing-policy that will challenge ghettoization and discriminatory housing practices? The state needs to uphold the right of the individuals to choose freely their housing without being incumbered by "protected" areas (protected not for national defence but for caste and religious defence!). That would be a critical reflection of the humanistic thrust of modernity. But what we have is a selective modernity with the smart city while traditional discrimination in urban housing goes on with impunity. What results could we expect from the 'smart city' project when it does not attend to some of the radical issues plaguing our cities and towns?

Part II: Humanistic Theological Reflections on Life in the City

The dominant city-projects of today are but contemporary application of the European Enlightenment paradigm of linear or dialectical human progress, development, and evolution. This paradigm has exercised such a great influence through history that even the Christian scriptures were so interpreted as if God, like a city-planner and manager, had God's own map and *plan of salvation*!

Captivating as it may sound, the project of smart city hides behind it a multitude of human social, economic, and political issues. A humane city cannot be created and sustained without putting people above technology, which has only a service role to play. All human problems cannot be solved by money; nor by technology and management. Policies and practices are to be evolved after interaction and dialogue with the people and ascertaining their needs and aspirations. We succumb to the dangerous Enlightenment idea of progress and development when we place plans above dialogue. In short, the project of a city is a continuous process of dialogue and human intercourse in harmony with the local environment and climate. This process will create cities from below. As Annapurna Shaw notes,

> In the haste to fill costly urban land with iconic towers, Indian cities should not lose their 'horizontality' or their links to the ground and its social and climatic exigencies. Keeping a sense of horizontality will make for more comfortable living spaces...No amount of steel and glass can compensate for natural shade, sunshine and cross-ventilation in the tropics.

Humanism and Compassion

A crucial problem with smart city is that it is a totally *de-politicized* project acting on presumed neutrality and impartiality vis-à-vis the inequality among the citizens, their contrasting socio-economic positions, and their conflicting interests. What is often forgotten is that there is a whole political process involved in the construction of the city where one has to come to terms with opposing classes and castes, different ethnicities, migrants, refugees, displaced people, and divergent economic interests.

As it is, city-planning is heavily influenced by the capital and the demands of the market with lip-service paid to the poor and those pushed to the margins of city-life. The city of the future, on the other hand, requires badly the spirit of human solidarity, radical care and infinite compassion which are really in shorty-supply today. We cannot expect these where human relationships are mediated by money and market. In fact, Friedrich Hayek was candid when he said love has no place in economics.[25] One of the most important contribution faith and theology could make for the future of our cities is to instil a new and alternative humanistic vision and orientation inspired by the spirit of love, care, and compassion.

We build on a very weak foundation if we were to ground our contemporary social life and political institutions on the theory of an imaginary *social contract* (Jacques Rousseau), or to rely on justice to happen on a hypothetical "*original position*" (John Rawls). We are seeing the serious limits and weakness of such a basis which also explains the crisis of liberalism, capitalism, and market.[26] If we go by social contract and the logic of the market, there is no convincing answer for solidarity with the poor and the marginalized. The poor are to blame themselves for their lot, so goes the argument. Such being the situation, we are in need of an alternative vision and new perspectives that will illumine our common humanity, define our social life and interhuman relationships beyond the frame of self-interest and competition. This needs to get reflected in the way we construct and reconstruct cities with different priorities and values, other than the ones dictated by the market and consumerism.

In this connection, we may recall here that United Nations adopted in July 2011 a resolution *Happiness: Towards a Holistic Definition of Development*. UN brings out since then every year a World Happiness Index (WHI). The parameters used for development are very different from GDP calculations. As it is often said, "some people are so poor; all they have is money."[27] There are several humanistic dimensions to a happy life, such as societal harmony, psychological wellbeing, sense of security, care for the weaker ones, etc. Development of cities then are to be measured not by the economic success or the grandeur of skyscrapers and infrastructures but by the quality of humanistic relationships and peace in society and harmony with nature. In the latest World Happiness Index of 2018, India ranks as low as 133 out of 156 countries, whereas our neigbours China is in 86th place and Bhutan occupies 97th place.[28] Other neighbours – Pakistan, Nepal, Sri Lanka and Bangladesh are far ahead of India. Compassionate city is one where we seek to follow the measures of happiness and care for one's neighbours, for the marginalized and excluded. Indian rulers obsessed with crony capitalism have brought down the people of the country to a low ebb for whom things are, unfortunately, getting worse. With brutal violence escalating day by day, and instinct of revenge taking upper hand, compassion and happiness look like pipe-dreams in our cities.

Seeing the City with New Eyes

No amount of technology and managerial mantras can supplant human solidarity, care and compassion which will be the heart-beat of the cities of the future. Compassionate eyes see more and far than the most advanced technological means and projects. Like in the gospel narrative, whereas the eyes of the elites are turned on the grandeur of the temple and its beauty, the compassionate eyes of Jesus were turned to the poor widow. The quite offer of her mite in the temple invites praise from Jesus (Mk 12:41-44, Lk 21:1-4). The very people who contribute the lion's share in the creation of city through their hard labour – the poor, the migrants, the refugees, the discriminated – are ignored and sidelined, with no voice in shaping their habitat. This is diametrically opposed to the vision of a new Jerusalem Isaiah projected.

> I will rejoice in Jerusalem,
>   and be glad in my people;
> no more shall be heard in it the sound of weeping
>   and the cry of distress.
>
> No more shall there be in it
>   an infant that lives but a few days,

> or an old man who does not fill out his days,
> for the child shall die a hundred years old,
>   and the sinner a hundred years old shall be accursed.
>
> They shall build houses and inhabit them;
>   they shall plant vineyards and eat their fruit.
> They shall not build and another inhabit"
> they shall not plant and another eat (Is 65:19, 21-22).

In our Indian cities, the poor build gorgeous mansions, but they sleep under the bridges, on the pavements of roads and by railway tracks. The transformation of the city Isiah projects is one in which those who build the houses will also inhabit them. It is a revolution. He means that the poor will not be alienated from the fruits of their hard labour. In the city yet to come there will be housing for everyone. There will not be in this vision of the city any child mortality which happens today among the poor because of dismal sanitary and nutritional conditions that affect children's health and compromise their lives. Here is a city where the cry of the poor finds hearing and action. In the city of Pharaoh, on the other hand, the cry of the poor was not heard.

Besides sound economy, infrastructure creation, environmental safety, recycling of waste, and governance, city requires *a human face* or as Emmanuel Levinas would put it, *"humanist urbanism."*[29] Here faith and theology could contribute to create a human face to the city by addressing those issues and concerns of the people which economic, political, and cultural actors leave out of their purview.

For many, city pastoral work means how best we could bring faith to the people who are being secularized and save them from becoming materialists and consumerists. But we must begin with a fundamental question: Where do we encounter God in the city? I think it is in the cry of the urban poor we hear the voice of God today. There may be for historical reasons some cities designated as "holy." But every city can be holy as long as we experience the presence of God in the suffering of its urban poor. Every city can be renewed by transforming the life condition of its poor and victims, and could become new like "New Jerusalem." The gospel option for the poor will translate into a city-planning that will start from bottom up, listening to the cry of the poor, attending to their conditions, responding to their needs and aspirations.

Today, we need to interpret faith and pastoral involvement in the light of *Gaudium et Spes*. The term 'pastoral' here refers to the holistic nature of the presence of the Church in the world. It means how Church, faith, and theology could address the larger issues of the city affecting the people, especially the poor, across religion, geography, race, and culture. In the condition of our country and in many parts of the developing world, the challenging question for the believers is not unbelief resulting through secularization, as the case in the West may be, but the encounter with non-persons. They are to be the interlocutors for believers today.

The city is not simply a place, but a *milieu*. It is a milieu of community where peoples and groups can flourish by bonding together and living in solidarity. As a theoretical premise to this humanistic and faith-inspired approach to city as a community (and not simply a network of systems), we need to be aware that identity of city space, like other identities, are constructed relationally, and is not to be viewed in terms of a priori essentialist conceptions. Spaces are ascribed meanings, and they become places, through interhuman encounters and relationality. What technocratic approach does is to take city space in its materiality leaving out the constructive aspect that makes space a humanly endowed reality which is an important presupposition for understanding the poor in city spaces.

The complexity of life in the city has made difficult what were once taken for granted. Loving one's neighbor, for example, was relatively easy as long as the neighbor was of one's own, caste, race, colour, religion, culture and language. It could become a serious issue when we do not share any of these, and yet called to love and forge relationships. Further, neighbour is not simply a matter of physical proximity but a matter of negotiation and communication. This is important as our cities are pluricultural and multireligious with migrants from other states, speaking other languages. Often these are people who migrate just for their survival. With little education and exposure, they cannot be expected to speak our language and follow our customs and traditions in the way we would want them to do. Recently we have had example of people from the North Eastern states fleeing from the city of Bangalore, and workers from Bihar and Uttar Pradesh fleeing the violence in Gujarat.

The strangeness of the neighbour creates *xenophobia*. In Assam, the issue of "foreigners" has become a serious political issue, and a lot of poor people below poverty line have been excluded and denied citizenship. Assam's National Register of Citizenship has aggravated the situation with about two million people nowhere to go. Now how does one move from the situation of xenophobia to *xenophilia* – that is the love for the stranger? Most migrant workers are coolies, watchmen, housemaids and who are engaged in informal sector with meagre earnings and with no real security. Further, the situation of their being minorities makes them vulnerable. City-life could be vitiated if there is mistrust among peoples and groups. How could we transform the growing mistrust that cuts off the vital human communication, by creating greater sense of confidence and solidarity among city-dwellers? That leads us to the next point.

The Body of the City

In ancient times, cities were markers of identity and people were recognized in terms of their association with one or other city. Early Christianity not only spread first in cities; its own shape and progress in history were impacted by the urban environment.[30] It found in the city both acceptance and rejection – ambivalence. Theology too was developed in engagement with people of cities. It is significant that almost all the letters of Paul were written to inhabitants of the cities of the time (Rome, Corinth, Philippi, Galatia, Colossae etc.), addressing the problem of the communities there.[31] Using a rare expression, Paul enjoins the Philippians "to conduct themselves as good citizens (*politeuesthe*)" (Phil. 1:27).[32] For Paul, city is a place of community, mutuality, relationships, completely different from today's image of city as a concentrated space of traders and consumers; different from the understanding of citizenship today connected with paying taxes, voting etc. He exhorts the citizens of Colossae to clothe themselves with compassion (Col. 3:12) which should characterize their responsibility in the community of the city. The image of Church as "body" which Paul frequently uses, is probably taken from the experience and discourse of city itself functioning like a body – a kind of civic *ekklesia* - resulting in social harmony.

Justice in Cities

We have in India cities that are in continuous existence with a history of over two thousand years. We need to only think of the city of Madurai in the South and Varanasi in the North. Few cities in the world could claim such uninterrupted city-life for millennia as in these cases. The Tamil epic *Cilappatikāram* - almost two thousand years old - is a story of the life of a trader couple (Kōvalan and Kaṇṇaki) hailing from the ancient city of Poompuhar.[33] When Kōvalan was violently killed in the city of Madurai by the king's guards, suspecting him to have stolen the anklets of the queen from the palace, the enraged Kaṇṇaki at this great injustice done by the power, takes the king to task and challenges him to prove that her husband is guilty. She on the other hand proves the innocence of her husband in a dramatic and audacious act in the court, causing the king's collapse from the throne and death out of shock. Could such a story from an ancient Indian city inspire all those "small" people on the margins of our Indian cities seeking justice, and claiming their rights for a dignified human life with security?

This story is particularly significant since the one who fights for justice is a wronged woman in a city and the one who she challenges is none other than the highest power – the king. It is not so much theories of justice as narratives of justice that could encourage the marginalized in their struggles for justice in our cities. The victims of bride-burning (an Indian city phenomenon), victims of rape and sexual violence, ill-treated and wronged domestic helpers have become today the Kaṇṇakis of Indian cities who will not take injustice, gender-discrimination and sexual harassment lying down. The recent # Me Too movement that has brought about an avalanche of shocking revelations has become a new path to gender-justice in the cities and a warning to machismo and patriarchy. However, # Me too movement itself, to have wider impact on the entire society, it should not remain a phenomenon most visible among the middle and upper classes, and an issue of entertainment and media industry, but should focus attention as well on what is happening at the periphery to the women on the margins who lack media sensation and social capital to make their woes known to the world.

Where will the marginalized turn to when they experience spiral of injustice and callousness in every sphere of city-life? In city slums like Dharavi in Mumbai, it is the activists and NGOs who assist the marginalized to exercise their agency, seek justice, and protect themselves when their small hutments and shovels are threatened with demolition.[34] The slum-dwellers live in perpetual anxiety of the little spaces they occupy being taken over by rapacious real estate business in collusion with the civic authorities and police force.

City and Ecology

The planning of the city should be such that it chimes not only with canons of aesthetics but most importantly that it contributes *to the quality of life* and facilitates human interconnectedness, solidarity and sense of belonging. Pope Francis dreams of another model of city. To quote his words,

> How beautiful those cities which overcome paralyzing mistrust, integrate those who are different and make this very integration a new factor of development! How attractive are those cities which, even in their architectural design, are full of spaces which connect, relate and favor the recognition of others![35]

Laudato Si invites planners to consider the environmental impact of city projects and integrate the human and the social with the natural environment.

Alternative vision concerns also development of environmentally sustainable city landscapes. The environmental decline and climate change may not be responded to only with technocratic solutions or change in urban planning. It calls for a new mindset and a way of life that is respectful of nature and responsible in the use of its resources, something to which faith and theology could richly contribute. In keeping to the rhythm of nature, we could draw from the immense resources of the Indic religious traditions, which includes primeval religions.[36]

City for and by All and a Church without Walls

City as a community is a creation by all. Unsustainable city is the one where there is no community participation. Refusing to accept the participation of the poor, the migrants, and refugees will only add further to their vulnerability.[37] The poor are not "guests" in the city but citizens whose claim go beyond right to the city.

> The right to the city means more than just access to its resources. It suggests
> that people, particularly the marginalized, not only have the right to inhabit
> a city, but also the right to design, reshape and transform it.[38]

In large cities, especially in developing countries, we note how the rich insulate themselves in the so-called "gated-communities" by erecting walls and fences and barring access to the poor. The wealthy also ensure for themselves the best lands and greeneries, privatizing public spaces.[39]

If the Church wants to be a witnessing body in such situations, one of the best ways is to make available Church buildings, premises, infrastructure and other facilities for the common purposes of the citizens, especially the vulnerable ones. This would mean, learning to be a Church without walls. In this way, the Church will be entering into genuine communication with the local community, and the people will begin to feel that the Church is there for them. These are the ways to create solidarity and community. All this will help also to allay the fears and suspicion by "secularists" and by peoples of other religious traditions about the motive of the Church in its city-involvement.

In the Church, the properties are not what they are in terms of market-value, but what these properties really could mean to the community and the service they could render to it. If the commercial value and title of possession were to be the guiding principles, then, there is no difference from capitalist and feudal ownership of land with their value-system. In the early Fathers of the Church, we see a vigorous defence of the property as means of service (*diakonia*), and resistance to the use of it as a source of power, which goes against the spirit of the gospel.

Indian Cities and a New Pastoral Praxis

We do not have a pastoral praxis that is corresponding to the challenges presented by cities. What we do have is rather an extension of village pastoral practice into cities. There is little study and research on the dynamics of cities and the different transformative pastoral methods to be adopted.

Further, the ministers and Church-establishment are happy to deal with the middle class whose religious needs they seek to fulfil, and are happy with the increasing remuneration and donations they get. As the middle-class people nurture great dreams and are very competitive in achieving their material goals, they seek divine assistance and no wonder that they flock to all kinds of services, devotions and novenas the Church establishment offers. The clergy in the cities are happy to support them with their blessings and by increasing all sorts of devotional practices as per the needs of the devotees. In short, the pastorale in the Indian cities has become bourgeois and without challenges.

In this context, we need to also critically reflect upon a pastoral praxis centered on the territorially-based parish structure. The mobility in the city and the networking among the people have become so pervasive that distance and territory are no bars for interaction and creation of groups and communities. While the territorially-based parish structure may have certain advantages, we need to think of a pastorale that allows the believers to benefit spiritually from other sources and structures that are not conditioned by the parish structure. Young people in a parish, for example, may feel closer to youth in other parts of the city than the local parish community. Similarly, socially engaged believers may feel close, in terms of their commitment, with others doing the same kind of work in other parts of the city.

Our towns and cities today require adult faith.[40] It is a faith that reads the signs of the times, reflects on the experiences of the city in the light of the gospel and engages itself with the life of the people in the urban milieu, especially the poor and the marginalized. What it implies is that the Church needs to move beyond being provider of religious services to devotee-consumers. The Roman Synod of Bishops for the youth (a synod of the old for the young?) was very much focused on the digital world and the experience and culture that it produces among the youth.[41] But that alone is quite insufficient. A lot of young people are concerned about very substantial issues like justice, participation, respect for dignity and human rights, environment, the participation of women, etc. City-youth and others who are concerned about such vital questions would expect pastoral praxis and approach in the cities be deeply attuned to their sensitivities.

A significant document of the Anglican Church titled "*Faithful Cities*" reminds us what faith-sources could represent vis-à-vis the cities of today. It notes,

> Despite its ambivalent history, and its capacity to incite hatred and conflict, religious faith is still one of the richest, most enduring and most dynamic sources of energy and hope for cities. Faith is a vital— and often essential— resource in the building of relationships and communities. In the values they promote, in the service they inspire, and in the resources, they command, faith-based organizations make a decisive contribution to their communities.[42]

I wonder whether and to what extent the several Roman Catholic episcopal bodies in the country – each with its own distinct ritual, regional interests etc. - have taken time to reflect on the implications of faith in the city and what orientations and directions they have set forth for a city pastorale. All the three rites have busied to establish themselves in the cities and institutionalize – a power agenda – and there has been unfortunately little common engagement among themselves beyond the comfort zones of rites. Have the financial and sexual scandals which have exposed the Roman Catholic Church in recent times in the country anything to do with the rites? Which one of them is in a position of assuming "holier than thou" attitude? Has something gone wrong with "apostolic experience" which the Oriental Rights claim for themselves? Maybe it is a wake-up call for all of them to busy themselves deeply with the issues of the people most glaringly reflected in the life of cities, rather than convert these cities into bastions of ecclesial power.

Challenge to Theology

The dominant theological question today is not about our traditions or development of doctrines. Drawing from the rich faith-resources, theology, anchored in life, will address life-issues of poverty, material deprivation, justice, issues of human dignity, human rights, community and social cohesion. This has implications for theological method and orientation. To be able to respond to the life of the city, for example, theology needs to increasingly take on an enlightened narrative form embedded in life-experience of the people. For lack of this kind of approach, the institutions pursuing theology today, unfortunately, have very little public influence. The challenges our cities offer is an opportunity for theology to break loose of its self-isolation and enter into conversation with wider issues and questions taken up by non-state actors (NGOs) today, so vital for coexistence and harmony.

Further, theology could widen its scope and contribute to create *public intellectuals* who would advocate the cause of an equitable and environmentally sustainable cities. Public advocacy of the issues touching the life of the city, especially its poor, can be a support to the formulation of economic and environmental policies to redress the persisting woes. The Church, and theology could accomplish all these hand in hand with non-state actors.

Out of these experiences we need to think of new areas of study and research on the part of theologians as public intellectuals with the future of their cities as the focus. Though cities across the world share many things in common, yet, there are undeniable differences deriving from past history, and the social, political conditions in each case. Theologians could look into some of the most pressing issues and concerns and identify areas of reflection, study and research in context. This would support the formulation of urban public policies bearing upon the promotion of social justice and cohesion, and protection of the environment. This can be done meaningfully when theology and theological researches are shaped by other disciplines, and theology itself takes on the character of public theology.[43]

Conclusion

Eradication of poverty, fulfilment of basic needs of the urban poor and those at the periphery, upholding justice and rights of the victims, facilitation of their active participation in the life of the city, the quality of social relationships, harmony and cohesion among the diverse cultural, linguistic, ethnic groups of the people in the city, care and compassion – these should become new parameters and criteria for evaluating the cities of the future. When these fail, city becomes a theatre of violence. Far from providing security as in classical times, cities today could turn out to be just the opposite – a place of insecurity of the worst kind. As Zygmunt Bauman points out with reference to urban situation at the global level,

> Today, in a curious reversal of their historical role and in defiance of the original intentions of city builders and the expectations of city dwellers, our cities are turning swiftly from shelters against dangers into dangers' principal source. Dicken and Laustsen go as far as to suggest that the millennia-old link between civilization and barbarism is reversed. City life turns into a state of nature characterized by the rule of terror, accompanied by omnipresent fear.[44]

On the contrary, cities are to become spaces filled with *community obligations* the fulfilling of which expresses a sense of solidarity and interdependence. Promoting the participation and cooperation of all in building the city could help overcome the opposition between residents and strangers. Exercise of adult faith in the city calls the believers to assist in the process of making everyone in the city feel at home.

The language of "hospitality" often employed today appears to me as an ambiguous concept. It does not express the much-needed *sense of belonging*. Here is the crux of the question. The migrants, the refugees, the asylum seekers, undocumented persons, and displaced people need to feel at home in the cities and have a sense of belonging there. Such humanistic criteria will override the assessment of cities on the basis of their physical structure and technocratic management on which the agenda of smart city is focused.

An utopian vision of harmonious urban existence beyond conflicts of all kinds - national, cultural, religious, social and ethnic – led to the imaging of a city of the future which took concrete shape in the Auroville near Pondicherry. Inspired by Sri Aurobindo and the French mystic Mira Alfassa ("The Mother"), Auroville embodies another vision of the city.[45] As the charter of this city states, "Auroville will be a place of unending education, of constant progress and a youth that never ages."[46] Could our Indian cities one day reflect this grand vision?

NOTES

1   India is to spend a very large amount for the project of smart cities. See Sharma, R.T., "Union Cabinet to Spend Rs. 1 Lakh Crore in 5 Years on Smart Cities, AMRUT," *The Economic Times*, 30 April 2015, available at http://articles. economictimes.indi atimes.eom/2015-04-30/news/61689564_l_lakh-crore-100-crore-new-cities [accessed on 18 May, 2023]. The principles and policies have been worked out by Centre for Study of Science, Technology and Policy (CSTEP), and endorsed by the Government of India. For the document of

CSTEP, see, "Reconceptualizing Smart Cities: A Reference Framework for India," www.cstep.in [accessed on 29 October, 2018]. See also Amitabh Satyam and Igor Calzada, *The Smart City Transformations: The Revolution of the 21st Century* (Delhi: Bloomsbury, 2017); Sameer Sharma, *Smart Cities Unbundled. Ideas and Practice of Smart Cities in India* (Delhi: Bloomsbury, 2018). Space does not permit me to provide detailed references to many works. I have confined myself in this chapter to minimum references.

2   Cf. Nicole A. Drepaul, "Sustainable Cities and the Internet of Things (IOT)," *Technology Consilience* no. 22 (July 6, 2020): 39–47.

3   This is recognized also by the Ministry of Urban Development, Government of India, in its "Smart City Mission Statement and Guidelines." New Delhi, India: Ministry of Urban Development, Govt. of India, 2015. https://smartnet.niua.org/content/2dae72ca-e25b-4575-8302-93e8f93b6bf6 [accessed on 3 Aug 2023].

4   Jem Pagan, "Smart Cities: The Next Frontier," in *US Black Engineer and Information Technology* 42, no. 1 (2018): 78–80.

5   Cf. Wayne H. Ambler, "Aristotle's Understanding of the Naturalness of the City," *The Review of Politics* 47, no. 2 (1985): 163–85.

6   Cf. Ramachandra Guha, *Gandhi: The Years that Changed the World 1914-148* (Delhi: Penguin Random House, 2018), *passim*.

7   See Vinay Lal, ed., *The Oxford Anthology of the Modern Indian City. The City in Its Plenitude* (Delhi: Oxford University Press, 2013), Introduction, xxiv.

8   On various aspects of Indian Urbanization, see Renu Desai, and Romola Sanyal, *Urbanizing Citizenship: Contested Spaces in Indian Cities* (Thousand Oaks: SAGE, 2012); Annapurna Shaw, *Indian Cities* (Delhi: Oxford University Press, 2012).

9   Progressive urbanization has taken place already in Europe with 74% of the population living in cities; so too in North America (82%) and South America (81%). Asian/Indian cities started growing fast in recent decades with neo-liberal economic growth. As per projection, cities in Asia and Africa will show very rapid urbanization in the coming decades. See https://www.un.org/development/desa/en/news/population/2018-revision [accessed on 30 October, 2018]. See also http://www.theguardian.com/cities/2015/nov/23/cities [accessed on 30 October, 2018].

10   Cf. Jai Sen, "The Unintended City," in Vinay Lal, ed., *The Oxford Anthology of the Modern Indian City. Making and Unmaking the City* (Delhi: Oxford University Press, 2013), 145–154.

11   Souvanic Roy, "The Smart City Paradigm in India: Issues and Challenges of Sustainability and Inclusiveness," *Social Scientist* 44, no. 5/6 (May–June 2016): 29–48, at 39.

12   Cf. Bhaskar Majumder and G. Rajvanshi, "Child Rag Pickers in the City of Allahabad, Uttar Pradesh: Some Facts," *Man and Development* XL, no.

3 (2018): 53–68; see also V.K. Shankar and Rohini Sahni, "Waste-Pickers and the Right to Waste in an Indian City," *Economic and Political Weekly* 53, no.48 (December 8, 2018): 54–62.

13   Cf. Souvanic Roy, "The Smart City Paradigm in India," 29–48.

14   Cf. Shaw, *Indian Cities*, 172.

15   Shaw, *Indian Cities*, 178.

16   On the marginalization of Muslims in the city of Ahmadabad, see the contribution of Francis Gonsalves, "Shrinking Spaces of Ahmedabad's Muslim Minority," *Jeevadhara* XLIX, no. 289 (2018): 39-53.

17   See Laurent Gayer and Christopher Jaffrelot, eds., *Muslims in Indian Cities. Trajectories of Marginalisation* (Delhi: HarperCollins Publishers, 2012), 3–4.

18   See the special issue Michael Becka, Felix Wilfred and Mile Babic, eds., "Human Security," *Concilium* 2018/2 (London: SCM Press, 2018).

19   Jaideep Gupte, "Not just about Jobs and 'Smart' Cities," *Economic and Political Weekly* 51, no.41 (8 October 2016): 21; see also D. Kundu, and D. Samanta, "Redefining the Inclusive Urban Agenda in India," *Economic and Political Weekly* 46, no. 5 (2011): 55–63.

20   Vinay Lal, ed., *The Oxford Anthology of the Modern Indian City*, 237.

21   Cf. Amartya Sen and Jean Drèze, *An Uncertain Glory: India and its Contradictions* (Princeton, NJ.: Princeton University Press, 2013).

22   On this point see the classical work of Henri Lefebvre, *The Production of Space* (Oxford: Basil Blackwell, 1991); see also Edward W. Soja, *Postmodern Geographies: The Reassertion of Space in Critical Social Theory* (London: Verso, 1988); Doreen B. Massey, *Space, Place and Gender* (Cambridge: Polity, 1994); Seth Schindler, "Urban Transformation, Inequality, and the Future of Indian Cities," *Georgetown Journal of International Affairs* 16, no. 1 (2015): 7–15. see also Ajay Gandhi and Lotte Hoek, "Introduction to Crowds and Conviviality: Ethnographies of the South Asian City," *Ethnography* 13, no.1 (2012): 3–11.

23   This is important to note, since agency is most often attributed to external forces and the city-poor depicted as victims without agency. If we widen the discourse, it is but an expression of the contrast made between the global and the local. What Escobar notes regarding this polarity is very much applicable to city-life at the margins: "The global is associated with space, capital, history and agency, while, the local conversely, is linked to place, labour and tradition – as well as with women, minorities, the poor and, one might add, local cultures." Arturo Escobar, "Culture Sits in Places: Reflections on Globalism and Subaltern Strategies of Localization," *Political Geography* 20, no. 2 (2001): 139–174, at 155–156.

24   Recently, there was a row at the IIT-Madras which I think is an expression of this mindset. The students eating in non-vegetarian canteens were prohibited from entering the vegetarian canteen! Posters were put up to this effect.

Moreover, separate wash-basins for vegetarian students and non-vegetarian students were marked. Is it not modern extension of untouchability, and ironically in a premier institution of science and modernity? How true it is that caste is like the proverbial cat which has nine lives – it appears and re-appears in myriad forms.

25   Cf. Friedrich A. von Hayek, *The Constitution of Liberty* (Chicago: Chicago University Press, 1960).

26   See *The Economist* (September 15 – 21, 2018), dealing with the crisis of liberalism.

27   This saying is attributed to Patrick Meagher, but similar statements have been expressed by many others, so much so it has become common currency.

28   See http://s3.amazonaws.com/happiness-report/2018/WHR [accessed on 3 November 2018].

29   Cf. Michael L. Morgen, *Levinas's Ethical Politics* (Bloomington: Indiana University Press, 2016), 179.

30   On this point, see the article of A. John Baptist, "Urban Space in the Pauline Ministry and Writings: Lessons for Today's Urbanized Church," *Jeevadhara* XLIX, no. 289 (2018): 54-67.

31   Cf. Steve Walton et al. eds., *The Urban World and the First Christians* (Grand Rapids: William B. Eerdmans, 2017); see also Rodney Stark, *Cities of God: The Real Story of How Christianity Became an Urban Movement and Conquered Rome* (New York: HarperCollins, 2009).

32   Cf. Dennis R. Edwards, "Good Citizenship: A Study of Philippians 1:27 and Its Implications for Contemporary Urban Ministry," *Ex Auditu* 29 (2013): 74–93.

33   R. Parthasarathy, trans., *The Tale of an Anklet: An Epic of South India: The Cilappatikāram of Iḷaṅkō Aṭikaḷ* (Columbia: Columbia University Press, 1992).

34   Cf. Jeremy Seabrock, "Dharavi," in Vinay Lal, ed., *The Oxford Anthology of the Modern Indian City. Making and Unmaking the City* (Delhi: Oxford University Press, 2013), 196–208.

35   *Evangelii Gaudium* no. 210.

36   See for example Christopher Key Chapple and Mary Evelyn Tucker, eds., *Hinduism and Ecology: The Intersection of Earth, Sky, and Water* (Cambridge, MA: Harvard University Centre for the Study of World Religions, 2000); John A. Grim, ed., *Indigenous Traditions and Ecology* (Cambridge, Mass.; London: Harvard University Press, 2001).

37   For the role migration plays in development, see R. B. Bhagat, "Development Impacts of Migration and Urbanization," *Economic and Political Weekly* 53, no. 48 (8 Dec. 2018): 15–19.

38   Anil Kumar Vadiraju, "Urban Governance and Right to the City," *Economic and Political Weekly* 51, No.32 (6 August 2016), 21.

39   Seth Schindler, "Urban Transformation, Inequality, and the Future of Indian Cities," *Georgetown Journal of International Affairs* 16, no. 1 (2015): 7–15. Such segregations go back to the colonial times when residential area of the British and their administrative and military (cantonment area) were marked off from the residential area of the local people. It would be interesting to research the pattern of residence-clustering in cities on caste-basis. There are for example, undeclared "*agraharams*" of Brahmin residential areas in cities closely protected from other caste people trying to migrate. Then there is the case of minorities, especially Muslims from low economic background who have their own settlement areas in cities, for security and for mutual help. On this latter point, Laurent Gayer and Christophe Jaffrelot, eds., *Muslims in Indian Cities. Trajectories of Marginalisation* (London: Hurst & Company, 2012).

40   See Felix Wilfred, *Theology for an Inclusive World* (Delhi: ISPCK, 2019), 201–224.

41   See, *La Croix*, October 12 & 25, 2018.

42   The quotation is from *Faithful Cities* – a document of the Anglican Church, as quoted in *International Journal of Public Theology* 1 (2008): 17. This document from the Anglican Church was preceded by *Faith in the City* (1985), different in tone, approach, and orientation.

43   See Felix Wilfred, *Theology for an Inclusive World* (Delhi: ISPCK, 2019); ID., *Asian Public Theology* (Delhi: ISPCK, 2010); ID., ed., *Theology to Go Public* (Delhi: ISPCK, 2013).

44   Zygmunt Bauman, *Does Ethics Have a Chance?* (Cambridge MA: Harvard University Press, 2008): 65.

45   In 1954, The Mother depicted her dream city of the future. See http://wiki.auroville.org.in/wiki/22 [accessed on 3 November 2018].

46   https://www.auroville.org/contents/1 [accessed on 30 September 2018]; see also Anu Majumdar, *Auroville. A City for the Future* (Noida: HarperCollins, 2017). Even if this is a distant dream, there seem to be, amidst the dismal situation in our cities, some signs of hope. Isher Judge Ahluwalia illustrates the innovation that is taking place in some of the cities in India. See Isher Judge Ahluwalia, *Transforming Our Cities* (Noida: HarperCollins, 2014).

FURTHER READING

Ahluwalia, Isher Judge. *Transforming Our Cities*. Noida: HarperCollins, 2014.

Aristotle. *Politics*. London: Penguin Books, 1992.

Bauman, Zygmunt. *Does Ethics Have a Chance?* Cambridge MA: Harvard University Press, 2008.

Becka, Michael, Felix Wilfred and Mile Babic, eds. "Human Security." *Concilium* 2018/2. London: SCM Press, 2018.

Bhagat, R. B. "Development Impacts of Migration and Urbanization." *Economic and Political Weekly* 53, no. 48 (8 Dec. 2018): 15–19.

Chapple, Christopher Key, and Mary Evelyn Tucker, eds. "Hinduism and Ecology: The Intersection of Earth, Sky, and Water." *Religions of the World and Ecology.* Cambridge, MA: Harvard University Centre for the Study of World Religions, 2000.

Desai, Renu, and Romola Sanyal. *Urbanizing Citizenship: Contested Spaces in Indian Cities.* Thousand Oaks: SAGE, 2012.

Drepaul, Nicole A. "Sustainable Cities and the Internet of Things (IOT)." *Technology Consilience* no. 22 (July 6, 2020): 39–47.

Edwards, Dennis R. "Good Citizenship: A Study of Philippians 1:27 and Its Implications for Contemporary Urban Ministry." *Ex Auditu* 29 (2013): 74–93.

Escobar, Arturo. "Culture Sits in Places: Reflections on Globalism and Subaltern Strategies of Localization." *Political Geography* 20, no. 2 (2001): 139–174.

Gandhi, Ajay, and Lotte Hoek. "Introduction to Crowds and Conviviality: Ethnographies of the South Asian City." *Ethnography* 13, no.1 (2012): 3–11.

Gayer, Laurent, and Christopher Jaffrelot, eds. *Muslims in Indian Cities. Trajectories of Marginalisation,* Delhi: HarperCollins Publishers, 2012.

Grim, John A. ed. *Indigenous Traditions and Ecology.* Cambridge, Mass.; London: Harvard University Press, 2001.

Guha, Ramachandra. *Gandhi: The Years that Changed the World 1914-148.* Delhi: Penguin Random House, 2018.

Gupte, Jaideep. "Not just about Jobs and 'Smart' Cities." *Economic and Political Weekly* 51, no.41 (8 October 2016): 21-23.

Hayek, Friedrich A. von. *The Constitution of Liberty.* Chicago: Chicago University Press, 1960.

Kundu, D, and D. Samanta. "Redefining the Inclusive Urban Agenda in India." *Economic and Political Weekly* 46, no. 5 (2011): 55–63.

Lal, Vinay, ed. *The Oxford Anthology of the Modern Indian City. The City in Its Plenitude.* Delhi: Oxford University Press, 2013.

Lefebvre, Henri. *The Production of Space.* Oxford: Basil Blackwell, 1991.

Majumdar, Anu. *Auroville. A City for the Future.* Noida: HarperCollins, 2017.

Majumder, Bhaskar, and G. Rajvanshi. "Child Rag Pickers in the City of Allahabad, Uttar Pradesh: Some Facts." *Man and Development* XL, no. 3 (Dec. 8, 2018): 53–68.

Majumder, Bhaskar, and G. Rajvanshi. "Waste-Pickers and the Right to Waste in an Indian City." *Economic and Political Weekly* XL, no. 3 (Dec. 8, 2018): 54–62.

Massey, Doreen B. *Space, Place and Gender.* Cambridge: Polity, 1994.

Morgen, Michael L. *Levinas's Ethical Politics.* Bloomington: Indiana University Press, 2016.

Pagan, Jem. "Smart Cities: The Next Frontier." *US Black Engineer and Information Technology* 42, no. 1 (2018): 78–80.

Parthasarathy, R. trans. *The Tale of an Anklet: An Epic of South India: The Cilappatikāram of Iḷaṇkō Aṭikaḷ.* Columbia: Columbia University Press, 1992.

Roy, Souvanic. "The Smart City Paradigm in India: Issues and Challenges of Sustainability and Inclusiveness." *Social Scientist* 44, no. 5/6 (May–June 2016): 29–48.

Satyam, Amitabh, and Igor Calzada. *The Smart City Transformations: The Revolution of the 21st Century.* Delhi: Bloomsbury, 2017.

Schindler, Seth. "Urban Transformation, Inequality, and the Future of Indian Cities." *Georgetown Journal of International Affairs* 16, no. 1 (2015): 7–15.

Seabrook, Jeremy. "Dharavi." In Vinay Lal, ed., *The Oxford Anthology of the Modern Indian City. Making and Unmaking the City*, 196-208. Delhi: Oxford University Press, 2013.

Sen, Amartya, and Jean Drèze. *An Uncertain Glory: India and its Contradictions.* Princeton, NJ.: Princeton University Press, 2013.

Sen, Jai. "The Unintended City." In Vinay Lal, ed., *The Oxford Anthology of the Modern Indian City. Making and Unmaking the City*, 145-154. Delhi: Oxford University Press, 2013.

Sharma, Sameer. *Smart Cities Unbundled. Ideas and Practice of Smart Cities in India.* Delhi: Bloomsbury, 2018.

Shaw, Annapurana. *Indian Cities.* Delhi: Oxford University Press, 2012.

Soja, Edward W. *Postmodern Geographies: The Reassertion of Space in Critical Social Theory.* London: Verso, 1988.

Stark, Rodney. *Cities of God: The Real Story of How Christianity Became an Urban Movement and Conquered Rome.* New York: HarperCollins, 2009.

Vadiraju, Anil Kumar. "Urban Governance and Right to the City." *Economic and Political Weekly* 51, No.32 (6 August 2016): 21-23.

Walton, Steve, et al. eds. *The Urban World and the First Christians.* Grand Rapids: William B. Eerdmans, 2017.

Wilfred, Felix. *Asian Public Theology.* Delhi: ISPCK, 2010.

Wilfred, Felix. *Theology for an Inclusive World*. Delhi: ISPCK, 2019.

Wilfred, Felix. *Theology to Go Public*. Delhi: ISPCK, 2013.

DEMOCRACY
AND
HUMAN RIGHTS

Chapter 7

EVOLVING HUMAN RIGHTS AND ENGAGING CHRISTIAN FAITH
WHERE HAVE ALL THE PROPHETS GONE?

Human rights is a vibrant area for socially conscious religions and religious agents who are called to engage in. Close attention to this area could contribute to the practice of human rights as well as to sharpen and expand its conception. In present-day circumstances, the ethical and legal implications enshrined in human rights require more than a rational foundation and justification. For these rights to attain their ultimate goal, it is indispensable that they are undergirded by other motivational and energizing forces such as religious beliefs. Like literature, religion could evoke the necessary empathy for the suffering of the other, which needs to accompany any effective practice of human rights.

Further, these rights ought to touch the moral chords of persons and hence not to be viewed as a mere legal means for enforcement. This chapter takes up the case of Christianity, particularly Catholicism, and shows how the evolving new dimensions of human rights are appropriated by it, adding its own accent for their practice and conception. The chapter also explores how Christianity could contribute to further enlarge the interpretation of the human rights regime and become increasingly an important moral force for its upholding, practice, and defence.

Commonality

Historically, religious believers in God and secular non-believers have something in common: Both of them have been violators of human dignity and rights. The violence created by religion is well-known. Less discoursed and debated are the human rights violation, torture, genocide and crimes against humanity perpetrated by secular states, ideologies and institutions. The most notable instances are the brutalities of the national socialism of Hitler, the Great Purge (Gulag) of Stalin, the killing spree by Mao Zedong of China in the name of peasant revolution, the genocide in Bosnian – Herzegovina (Srebrenica), Rwanda and Darfur – all of them involving the death of no less than two hundred million people, according to one estimate.[1]

Who has violated more – the religious or the secular forces – is a matter of odious comparison – reminding one of the kettles calling the pot black. Our purpose is not to go into this question. Rather, this chapter intends to enquire in the vast changed circumstances of today, whether religions could play the role of promoters of human rights setting aside the history of violations.[2] It would appear, given the great motivating force of religion and its practice everywhere in the world, that it (religion) could and should play a very engaging and positive role to uphold the dignity and rights of human persons and support the letter and spirit of the Universal Declaration of Human Rights (1948) – a declaration that was brought to existence following the horrible experiences of brutality inflicted on human beings in the two World Wars.[3]

Similar reflections could be made from the perspective of other religious traditions. The human rights regime keeps evolving and acquires new layers of meaning with the change of context and circumstances. Historically what started as civil and political rights expanded to include social and economic rights – so-called second-generation rights – and evolved further to include cultural, minority, and gender rights – third generation rights. Today we see how the human rights of the poor are inextricably bound up with the protection of the environment. A new generation of human rights focus on the dignity and rights of the physically and mentally disabled, the prisoners, refugees, migrants, and many such others. Religions could play a creative and constructive role in the evolution of these rights to become more and more inclusive.

Tracing the WCC Historiography of Human Rights

In this chapter, we limit our considerations to the relationship of Christian faith and human rights, and probe how a faith that is supportive of human rights could contribute to a world of justice and peace. There is a new found commitment to human rights in ecumenical movement.[4] As for the World Council of Churches is concerned, its earliest phase of human rights engagement of 1940's goes back to the times of suppression of them in the communist regimes and especially in Soviet Union.[5] The engagement was there throughout the Cold War period. Similarly, there was a critical commitment to the defence of human rights in some Islamic countries such as Indonesia and Nigeria.

Ironically, WCC and the Protestant Churches had to fight for their human right of religious freedom in the Catholic Spain as they felt oppressed.[6] From 1960's, WCC was engaged with the issue of civil rights and from 1970s with struggle against racism and apartheid.[7] In more recent times the concern of WCC was directed to Latin America in the face of dictatorship and militarization with gross violation of human rights. Studies show how some ecumenically oriented Christian leaders impacted the formulation of Universal Declaration of Human Rights.[8]

Human Freedom with Solidarity

It is well-known that in the nineteenth century, the Catholic Church rejected human freedom, democracy, human rights etc. as belonging to modernist heresy.[9] There has taken place, since then, a dramatic turn-around so much so that the Catholic Church projects itself as a force in the world today for the defence of human rights. This highly significant shift was visible in the encyclical of Pope John XXIII, *Pacem in Terris,* which was also the first papal document to address the entire humanity – people of goodwill. Some interpret this change as a surrender of Catholicism to liberal thought. The orientation set by *Pacem in Terris* was further reinforced by two important Vatican II documents – Document on Religious Freedom (*Dignitiatis Humanae*) and The Church in the Modern World (*Gaudium et Spes*). The Catholic Church did accept the freedom of human beings but with a significant modification, and tried to widen this concept in such a way that the canvas of human rights could expand further. As Calo notes,

> While the Church opened itself to modern political ideas, the process did not entail granting an unqualified imprimatur to the whole of liberalism. The development of Catholic liberalism instead involved cultivating a unique understanding of rights theory that incorporated aspects of liberalism while advancing a fundamental reconceptualization of its meaning and foundations.[10]

Whereas in the liberal tradition, individual freedom is viewed as absolute, Catholic Social Teaching saw it not as something that insulates a person in his or her own autonomous world. Freedom is inherently related to others. It is freedom exercised in solidarity and oriented to the achievement of the common good and moral ends. This is because, just as human beings enjoy freedom because of their inherent dignity, so also human beings are inextricably social beings, inserted in the life of a community. Therefore, freedom should serve the common good and the cause of solidarity with others. This wider basis of freedom is important to situate social, economic, gender, and minority rights beyond the civil rights realm of freedom for free speech, movement, etc. Rightly then, the African Charter (1981) speaks not only of Human Rights but also Peoples' Rights wherein equality is not a matter of individual human beings alone; people are also viewed as equal.[11] Ethnic and racial equality has become today a central issue at local and global levels.

Liberation Theology and Human Rights

It has been often pointed out that in the classical work of Gustavo Gutiérrez, there are not many references to human rights.[12] There is reason for the lack of warming up to human rights in the initial stages of liberation theology. For, the universal declaration of human rights appeared to be a liberal and bourgeois project lacking in concreteness and reference to the poor. Human rights appeared to be in defence of the rich and powerful about their civil rights and their individual property rights. The suspicion about the language of human rights grew even more when the United States under President Carter made human rights an important component in its international policy. It was in stark contrast with the American complicity with authoritarian rulers and the situation of oppression and hunger in different parts of the world.

Moreover, the discourse on human rights sounded too abstract and conceptual whereas liberation theology was deeply concerned not so much about clarification of concepts and their meaning as praxis and transformation. However, the experience of militarization and totalitarian regimes which trampled upon the poor and their rights, led to the realization of the importance of the regime of universal human rights. The liberation theologians in that continent accepted human rights discourse somewhat reluctantly as a useful instrument in their struggles against dictatorial regimes and the situation of repression by national security states. Saving human lives became a crucial concern.

In more recent phases of the development of liberation theology, there has taken place a critical appropriation of the regime of human rights.[13] In this latest phase, human rights are read, interpreted, and practiced through the lens of the option for the poor, and the rights of the poor.[14] Liberation theology does not speak of the individual endowed with basic human rights. Rather it speaks of the poor as "non-persons," and sees human right as an effort to bring dignity and rights to the non-persons. The non-persons are those "who are not considered to be human beings with full rights, beginning with the right to life and to freedom in various spheres."[15] In this project, liberation theology has not treated human rights in one single monolithic and universalist framework – a view from nowhere - but rather has grappled with different generations of human rights, and indeed with reference to concrete contexts and social, economic, and cultural rights.

Liberal Approach vis-à-vis Theological Understanding

Moreover, in the frame of liberal individualism, there is no room for any consideration of ultimate ends of human life or societal, communitarian life – a reason it wants to keep off religion from any political process. In the theologically infused approach to human rights, the inherent dignity of human persons derives precisely from human destiny and moral ends, something different from viewing the individual as pursuing self-centered goals with rational means. Also, the mere fact of belonging to the human species can only be a loose rational foundation for human dignity and rights. For, rights of individuals can be easily demolished for ideological and presumed collective goals. Moreover, this freedom is also not libertarian but carries with it the responsibility to search for truth; it is not to be viewed as a general license for choice according to one's whims.

Bringing solidarity and the common good into the purview of human rights has been another corrective to the understanding of freedom. In effect, what the Catholic Church has been contributing to human rights since Vatican II is to widen the scope of human rights and bolster it up with themes such as option for the poor and the equitable sharing of the goods of the earth. In this way, there is a shift from the understanding and interpretation of human rights as an instrument to defend individual freedom and property and view them as a legal regime to defend the rights of the poor and the marginalized. This also needs to be considered an integral part of developing the concept of human rights, which, as we noted, is constantly evolving. As Pope Francis rightly observed,

> Sometimes it is a matter of hearing the cry of entire peoples, the poorest peoples of the earth since peace is founded not only on respect for human rights but also on respect for peoples' rights. But, sadly, even human rights can be used as a justification for an inordinate defence of individual rights or the rights of the more affluent peoples.... To speak properly of our own rights, we need to broaden our perspective and to hear the plea of other peoples and other regions than those of our own country.[16]

Any human rights approach without reference to the poor can end up simply as bourgeois liberal rights.[17] Human rights viewed from the perspective of the poor acquires new depth, range and power. In the last few decades, different popes have not only spoken at international fora on human rights but have also made them an integral part of the continuing social teachings of the Church. Liberation theology and political theology that have emerged since Vatican II have contributed further to deepening the understanding of human rights and their practice. It is not the abstract, rational, and procedural approach to human rights but a theologically reworked one that has proved more effective in practice.

Lest all this should sound theory, let me refer here to the religiously inspired "Truth and Reconciliation Commission" and its work in South Africa in the face of human rights violation. If it relied only on a rationally founded justification for human rights, this commission could not have gone ahead with the dispensation of justice. It is not an exception. There are similar instances where religiously inspired upholding of human rights has yielded rich practical dividends. I am not trying to drive any wedge between secular and religious human rights tradition. Instead, there is enough reason for both the traditions to converge and enrich mutually. The dominant trend to dismiss religiously inspired human rights discourse will only weaken the secular tradition. The argument that the secular approach to human rights is neutral, unlike the religious approach, is difficult to sustain since there is no single secular approach, and none of them is free from ideology.

On the other hand, the secular tradition of human rights points out the deficit in the Catholic approach to human rights regarding women's rights and reproductive rights, gay rights - enough reason to continue the dialogue between these two traditions.[18] In fact, the Catholic Social Teaching, far from deviating from the Universal Declaration of Human Rights (1948) have tried to adopt its religious language to the secular one. The popes and the Catholic social Teachings have repeatedly referred to this watershed document of human rights. Reciprocity from the secular approach to human rights would be to accept the legitimacy of cementing human rights with religious motives, narratives, tropes and symbols.

Transcendent Reference

The developments in the Catholic Church have contributed to re-found human rights in theological anthropology that invokes the dignity of a human person deriving from his or her creation as the "image of God" - a conviction also shared by other Abrahamic religions. This theologically founded dignity is further bolstered in the Christian tradition through its belief in the incarnation – God becoming a human being. All this needs to be stressed over and against any misrepresentation that sees Catholic human rights tradition as rooted only in natural law. The concept of natural law derives from Stoic heritage and the medieval scholastic philosophy of St. Thomas Aquinas and others. Jacques Maritain and John Courtney Murray count among modern proponents of human rights deriving from natural law.[19]

We could sense the transcendent foundation of human right also in the eighteenth-century American Declaration of Independence. It not only shaped the United States' quest for freedom but also played a vital role in inspiring the universal ideals of human rights embraced by the United Nations. While drawing inspiration from its Christian roots and recognizing the influence of "the Laws of Nature and of Nature's God," the declaration prominently emphasized the concept of equal human rights. By proclaiming that "all men are created equal" and acknowledging that individuals are endowed by their *creator* certain unalienable rights, the declaration established a foundation for constructive reform.[20]

The reference to human dignity deriving from a transcendent foundation appears to be important increasingly since human dignity is the moral foundation for the legal regime of universal human rights. It unites both the moral dimension of human duties (once seen as residing in individual conscience) and the modern subjective claims of legal rights. We are in the face of dignity that belongs to everyone as human persons, regardless of the social position they occupy in any hierarchically ordered societies such as caste or feudal societies, and regardless of ethnicity, nation, and religion. In new situations and contexts in which human beings are humiliated, exploited, trafficked etc., new legal provisions would be required in terms of human rights. Human dignity, derived from a transcendent source will serve as an immanent and permanent source for deriving new human duties and rights according to ever new and changing situations and contexts.

The claim of secular humanism to be the guardian of human rights based on an assumed abstract human being cannot but meet with serious theoretical difficulties. Moreover, how history of secularism and humanism have played out with no relation to any transcendental foundation to human dignity and rights presents another set of challenges to any such claim. The basic question is what is the foundation of human dignity and what is the basis for every person for his or her human rights? Why should we love another person? Are other people hell, as Jean-Paul Sartre remarked in one of his novels – *No Exit*?[21] Michael J. Perry and many other scholars have shown that the dignity of human person is based on his on her *sacredness* from where derive inalienable and unconditional rights. Hence, human rights are inevitably spiritual in nature. A secular person may argue that he or she believes in the sacredness of human person without having to espouse a religious worldview. So, the question is, how does an anti-religious or non-religious person base his or her belief in the sacredness of human persons?

The sacredness derives in Abrahamic traditions from the story of the creation of human beings in God's image. Further, the relationship within human community is that of brothers and sisters having God as the parent. Hinduism may find the sacredness of human beings since the spark of the divine dwells in each one; and Buddhism may find sacredness in the fact that every person, without any distinction, is capable of Enlightenment. The religious vision also tells us that the concern for brothers and sisters in the human community is an integral part of one's own self-constitution and well-being. That is, we are inherently wired to care for others.

> One need not count oneself religious in order to wonder whether much secular moral-philosophizing hasn't been, for a very long time now, a kind of whistling in the dark…Jeffrie Murphy, for example, insists that it is, for him, "very difficult – perhaps impossible – to embrace religious convictions," but he nonetheless claims that "the liberal theory of rights requires a doctrine of human dignity, preciousness and sacredness that cannot be utterly detached from a belief in god or at least from world view that would be properly called religious in some metaphysically profound sense."[22]

It should be made clear that the transcendent reference to the sacred in a religious world view does not ignore the historical fact that religions have been in numerous instances violators of human dignity and rights. One cannot sweep under the carpet the dark pages of this ambiguous history of the World Religions. Our reflections for a transcendent reference are limited to the bedrock of sacredness that religious views provide, thus leading to a deeper understanding of human beings and the inter-related nature of their social existence.

Historical Roots

Several scholars have argued, the regime of human rights is not something that Christianity has learned from the Enlightenment or liberalism, but something for the birth of which it has contributed decisively. In fact, as historians tell us, several medieval decretalists and theologians had argued, though in a seminal way, for the cause of human rights.[23] In that sense, modernity and liberalism have served as occasions for the Church to recapture some of the forgotten pages of its own history.[24] The recoup of human rights tradition by the Church, thanks to modernity, goes along with the impregnation of it with new insights and experiences.[25] Amidst the harsh experience of totalitarianism and dictatorship, Pope Pius XII underlined the importance of a transcendent reference to defend human dignity and rights.

> Where the dependence of human right upon the Divine is denied, where appeal is made only to some insecure idea of merely human authority, and autonomy is claimed which rests only upon a utilitarian morality, there human law itself justly forfeits in its weightier application the moral force which is the essential condition for its acknowledgement and also for its demand for self-transcendence and sacrifices.[26]

We could observe that the different papal backgrounds have shaped a shift in accent in the approach to human rights. Pope John Paul II is known as an internationally outspoken crusader of human rights, and his concerns are expressed in his speeches to international bodies such as United Nations and in his discourses and documents. As someone coming from the Cold War background and from a country under Soviet communist influence, he relentlessly fought for political and civil rights and pointed out human rights violations in the atheist communist Eastern Bloc.

On the other hand, we find in Pope Francis, coming from poverty-stricken Latin America, the accent shifting strongly towards social and economic rights, something evident in his stringent critique of capitalism and the market.[27] In this, the pope is very much along the biblical and prophetic tradition wherein the dignity of the human person found in the creation account is concretized historically in that the dignity of the poor, the widows, the orphans, and the last and the least are acknowledged and respected.[28] Pope Francis places himself in this tradition of interpreting human dignity and rights from the periphery. Further, Pope Francis takes human rights to the frontiers of the environment and sees the interconnection between human rights and integral ecology, precisely because the defence of the poor, their survival, and livelihood are today inextricably bound up with a healthy and hale environment.

Pope Francis has further widened the scope of human rights by incorporating them within the structural problems of society. The defence of human rights could effectively happen only if simultaneously there takes place changes in the social, political, and economic structures.[29] This is a new perspective that has emerged robustly in the Catholic Social Teaching, thanks to Pope Francis, although some traces of it could also be found in his predecessors' teachings. In Pope Francis' vision, human rights are to serve not only as claims and ethical restraint on the freedom of others but also should become an important means to achieve the goal of social justice, and more broadly, the common good. This will bring out more clearly the Christian core in the larger discourse of human rights.

> When it comes to human rights advocacy, Francis sticks to a different view than his predecessors. His reference to social justice, structural problems, the periphery, and collective solutions, which individual rights do not solve, best captures this difference. Francis consistently emphasizes these issues rather than only referring to individual human rights.[30]

In other words, one may not be content by pointing out individual transgression of human rights and "shaming" the violators. Instead, human rights are set in the overall situation of justice in the world, the collective issues humanity faces, its structural roots, and the international order. This happens because Pope Francis looks at the socio-political situation from the periphery, and indeed through the eyes of the victims.

Implications of the Shift

The shift Francis has made is indeed something remarkable within the Catholic tradition. However, it is not altogether new to social movements, voluntary organizations, and institutions that have availed human rights as a legal means to ensure a dignified life for every human person. It is important to note this, lest there be any triumphalism on the part of the Church in this matter. I do not want to enter into the development of this shift in the secular realm. Let me just cite a couple of examples. The Indian Constitution speaks of right to life (art. 21). It has always been interpreted as a civil right as it should be in any constitutional democracy. However, the illustrious supreme court justice Krishna Iyer, widened this interpretation to include the social and economic realm. He meant that the *right to life* needs to be also interpreted as *right to livelihood*.[31] Jürgen Habermas formulates the same in a theoretical manner when he states,

> In fact, however, the citizens have equal opportunities to make use of these rights [civil rights] only when they simultaneously enjoy guarantees of a sufficient level of independence in their private and economic lives and when they are able to form their personal identities in the cultural environment of their choice.[32]

Recently, ruling on the plight of migrant workers in the critical time of pandemic and the obligations of the state to provide them the necessary means for their survival, the Supreme Court of India invoked art. 21 of the Constitution on right to life. It stated,

> The Constitution of India does not have any explicit provision regarding right to food. The fundamental right to life enshrined in Article 21 of the Constitution may be interpreted to include right to live with human dignity, which may include the right to food and other basic necessities.[33]

The more profound implications of Francis' position are this: Whereas in general, the Church lags behind the secular developments on many social and public issues, in the matter of widening the scope of human rights, the Church keeps abreast with many secular developments, which is important in translating human rights in practice, in everyday life. The accent of Pope Francis on securing in practice the socio-cultural rights of the poor and the excluded (option for the poor) adds moral strength to the human rights regime. Moreover, in the face of the crisis of immigrants and refugees, the pontiff has unambiguously upheld the basic rights of these victims over democratic sovereignty claimed by nation-states.[34] Also, he has never let this be a religiously-tinted stand taking a strident posture even against the so-called Christian nations that have shown little Christian attitude and practice in embracing immigrants and refugees. Amidst the backdrop of escalating political strife that seeks to capitalize on anti-immigration sentiment, Pope Francis' unwavering and resonant voice stands out as both powerful and challenging. He has backed his public stand with private actions that are symbolically powerful and prophetic – taking in refugee families at the Vatican and having the Vatican sponsor refugees into Italy.[35]

"Where Have All the Prophets Gone?"[36]

In a highly interesting study on South African Churches and human rights, Simanga Kumalo surveys the situation since abolishing the apartheid regime and installing a democratic government with a new Constitution. The role of the Churches in the struggle against apartheid is well-known, and it won universal acclaim. However, the situation since then has been one in which the Churches have bent on themselves, retreated to internal issues, and cultivated quite alien interests from the actual situation in which violation of human rights continues to happen at a large scale. The absence of the Churches to intervene in this critical situation makes the author wonder, "Where have the prophets gone?"[37]

The Churches functioned as a force from below and challenged the communist regimes of the East Bloc in Europe, but then it petered out after a brief spell. It is quite interesting to observe how the Catholic Church in the Philippines and its leadership which was chiefly responsible to galvanize democratic forces against the totalitarian regime of Marcos and its brutal human rights violation, has turned itself more and more to a Church of the charismatic movement and is unfortunately not able to stand up to the gross violation of human rights and extra-judicial killings in the country witnessed under the presidentship of Rodrigo Duterte.

As for India, in the 1970s and 1980s, there was a groundswell of energy in the Catholic Church, which could be seen in the commitment to human rights and defence of the poor against oppressive forces. The Indian institutional Catholic Church today has allowed itself to be marginalized as it is no more a force to stand up to the erosion of democracy, democratic institutions, and gross violation of human rights all over the country. We are led to ask the same question: Where have the prophets of yesteryears gone? Of course, many of them are very old and many others no more. We need more prophets who can speak truth to power because they are not beholden to the forces in power.

Unfortunately, the institutional Church in India is so fearful of the price of conviction and in many ways too beholden to politicians and the rich to have the detachment it takes to stand with and for the poor and oppressed. Fr Stan Lourdusamy S.J. and his ilk are exceptions rather than the rule. The people of this kind and stature we find at the grassroots – the true unsung heroes and heroines weathering the storm without support and encouragement from the official Church. In other parts of Asia, too, we find such valiant human rights activists inspired by faith. Most glaring is the example of Cardinal Joseph Zen of Hong Kong who has continued to challenge the Communist Party of China, its policies and human rights violation – a great example for Indian Church leaders. Then there are the young men and women all over Asia, like the ones associated with the Umbrella Movement in Hong Kong. Some them continue to languish in prison for their bold stand for human rights and freedom.

Rising up to the Situation

What conclusions do we want to draw from these experiences? The Church becomes active in certain situations and turns itself into a champion of human rights. But then it disappears and is not seen when new situations arise, making Church's human rights intervention sporadic, haphazard, and even volatile. The Indian Church has fallen into the same pattern as Churches elsewhere, lacking consistency in its response to human rights issues. Without relentless struggles, political process, and courageous resistance in today's circumstances, the defence of human dignity and protection of human rights is not possible. The earnestness of Catholicism's involvement for the cause of human rights will necessarily depend upon the extent of its entering into political activism and struggles.

For many secular groups, the Church is no reliable ally in the struggle to uphold and sustain human rights. The widening the scope of human rights and their theoretical deepening we noted in the Catholic Social Teachings will become effective if only they are translated into practice.[38] The whole global and local situation presents a significant challenge for Catholic Christianity to struggle and uphold civil rights, socio-economic rights, gender and minority rights, and environmental rights. The field is so vast, and the challenges are many. In India and worldwide, the voluntary and non-governmental agencies have suffered a setback under undemocratic and totalitarian regimes. It is precisely in such a situation that the engagement of the Catholic Church and other faith-based voluntary groups are urgently required. Human rights engagement can no more be a convenient option. It is a necessity that springs from the heart of the Christian faith since human beings' dignity and rights are deeply embedded in the substance of the Christian faith.

Conclusion

There has been a religious tradition of human rights; so too a secular one. The one cannot simply dismiss the other. We traced some critical moments in the development of the Christian thought on human rights, and indeed from outright denial to their espousal through re-appropriating the core of the biblical message and the early Christian tradition. The coming together of both the religious and secular traditions in an "overlapping consensus" is the need of the hour to make this moral and legal instrument effective. One needs to move ahead "keeping faith with human rights."[39] Although liberals and secularists dispute the claims of Christianity on human rights' religious origin, they see practical value in both traditions coming together.[40]

As a matter of fact, there is ample room for mutual enrichment, correction, and overcoming of limitations. Human rights are "Janus-faced" – one facing the legal side and the other moral.[41] For effective implementation, both these dimensions are indispensable. The religious tradition, in general, enriches the human rights regime with moral content, often with the accent on duties, whereas without the legal weight of human rights as something enforceable, they would lack teeth. Human dignity is the bridge that connects both these traditions. We saw how deeply the Christian, especially the Catholic human rights tradition is rooted in human dignity, enlightened by reason, and theological tropes and motives. But religious traditions could become myopic. They could forget the larger picture and get bogged down in specific moral issues, as, for example, the right to life could become a question of opposition to abortion and euthanasia. For some Catholics and Church leaders, human rights end there. Moreover, there are many dark areas in the religious tradition that stubbornly resist the application of human rights and refuse to submit themselves to universal human rights justifying such a posture in the name of arcane and obscurantist beliefs and traditions.[42] A reason-based and critical approach becomes indispensable to rid religion of its shibboleth.

There are also dangers of human rights being cast in the liberal political mould. These rights could be so manipulated that they become a defence of the powerful instead of being an instrument to protect the weak. It could provide the smokescreen for the "humanitarian intervention" by imperial forces. At its core, the liberal approach to rights was meant to protect the individual in his or her exercise of commerce and in the choice of religion by keeping off any intrusion of the state. The crass liberal approach to human rights is open to distortions and abuse. It is here then the input and inspiration of religions are important to maintain the intimate connection between human rights and the defence of the weak. When drawn from one's religious community's tradition, beliefs, symbols and narratives, engagement with human rights become durable.

If this orientation is lost, human rights could become simply something procedural and not substantive. Faith-inspiration could provide the necessary empathy for the victims in putting human rights into practice.[43] These rights could be used as a political tool, as for example, when aid is attached to compliance to basic human rights. They could become a new instrument of colonialism or imperialism. These are some of the aporias from which the regime of human rights needs to be protected.

For Christians, and indeed for any religious group, it is crucial to observe the signs of the times in every sphere of human life – political, economic, social and cultural – to make its courageous contribution to the defence of human dignity and rights. Once again, welcoming it simply as a religiously inspired motivational force or reinforcement of its foundation through religious resources is still inadequate unless actual struggles against and resistance to violations of rights become part of Church's life and mission.

NOTES

1   Cf. Alette Smeulers, and Fred Grünfeld, *International Crimes and Other Gross Human Rights Violations: A Multi- and Interdisciplinary Textbook* (Leiden: BRILL, 2011).

2   Michael J. Perry in one of the chapters of his work examines whether and to what extent the idea of human rights is connected to religion. *The Idea of Human Rights. Four Inquiries* (New York: Oxford University Press, 1998), 11 – 41.

3   This foundational document of 1948 got expanded and became legally enforceable through International Covenant on Civil and Political Rights (1976), and International Covenant on Economic, Social, and Cultural Rights (1976), Convention on the Elimination of All Forms of Discrimination against Women (1981), Convention on the Rights of Child (1990), and many other similar documents. See Henry J. Steiner and Philip Alston, eds., *International Human Rights in Context. Law, Politics, Morals* (Oxford: Clarendon Press, 1996).

4   Cf. Clement John, ed., "Human Rights and the Churches: New Challenges: Reports and Papers of the Global Review of Ecumenical Policies and Practices on Human Rights," *CCIA Background Information* no. 1998/1 (Geneva: WCC, 1998); Otto Frederick Nolde, and Charles Habib Malik, *Free and Equal: Human Rights in Ecumenical Perspective* (Geneva: WCC, 1968); Erich Weingärtner, *Human Rights on the Ecumenical Agenda: Report and Assessment* (Geneva: WCC, 1983).

5   J. A. Hebly, Michael Bourdeaux, and Eugen Voss, eds., *Religious Liberty in the Soviet Union: WCC and USSR: A Post-Nairobi Documentation* (West Wickham: Keston College, 1976); Bastiaan Bouwman, "From Religious Freedom to Social Justice: The Human Rights Engagement of the Ecumenical Movement from the 1940s to the 1970s," *Journal of Global History* 13, no. 2 (2018): 252–273; Edward Duff, *The Social Thought of the World Council of Churches* London:Longmans, Green and Co, 1956); Jacques Nicole, and Jean Nicolas Bitter, "The WCC and the Question of Human Rights in Eastern Europe," *Religion, State and Society: The Keston Journal* 21, no. 3-4 (1993): 257–262.

6   Jacques Delpech, *The Oppression of Protestants in Spain,* trans. Tom and Dolores Johnson (London: Lutterworth Press, 1956); see also Carmen Irizarry, *The Thirty Thousand: Modern Spain and Protestantism* (New York: Harcourt, Brace & World, 1966).

7   WCC, *Racism in Theology and Theology against Racism: Report of a Consultation Organized by the Commission on Faith and Order and the Programme to Combat Racism* (Geneva: WCC, 1975).

8   Cf. John Nurser, *For All Peoples and All Nations: Christian Churches and Human Rights* (Geneva: WCC, 2005).

9   This history is well-documented and researched. See for example, Zachary C. Calo, "Catholic Social Thought and Human Rights," *The American Journal of Economics and Sociology* 74, no. 1 (2015): 93–112. On various current Catholic views on human rights, see Keith Soko, *Mounting East-West Tension: Buddhist-Christian Dialogue on Human Rights, Social Justice and a Global Ethic* (Milwaukee: Marquette University Press, 2009), chapter 3, 111–161.

10 Zachary C. Calo, "Catholic Social Thought …", *art. cit.*, 94.

11 https://www.achpr.org/legalinstruments/detail?id=49 [accessed on 24 June 2021].

12 Gustavo Gutiérrez, *A Theology of Liberation. History, Politics, and Salvation* (New York: Orbis Books, 1973). However, Gutierrez gives greater prominence to human rights in his other volume, *The Power of the Poor in History* (Eugene, Oregon: Wipf & Stock Publisher, 2004).

13 For the various phases of the relationship of liberation theology to human rights, see Mark Engler, "Toward the 'Rights of the Poor': Human Rights in Liberation Theology," *The Journal of Religious Ethics* 28, no. 3 (2000): 339–65; Ethna Regan, "Liberation Theology and Human Rights: In Interruptive Realism to the Centrality of La Realidad," *Theology and the Boundary Discourse of Human Rights* (Washington DC: Georgetown University, 2010), Chapter 4, 143–177.

14 A few decades ago, I wrote an article on the need of making human rights into rights of the poor. See Felix Wilfred, "Human Rights or Rights of the Poor?: Redeeming the Human Rights from Contemporary Inversions," *Vidyajyoti Journal of Theological Reflections* 62, no. 10 (Oct. 1998): 734-752.

15 Gustavo Gutierrez, *A Theology of Liberation*, xxix.

16 *Evangelii Gaudium* 190.

17 Cf. Felix Wilfred, "Human Rights or the Rights of the Poor? Redeeming the Human Rights from Contemporary Inversions," *Vidyajyoti Journal of Theological Reflections* 62, no. 10 (Oct. 1998): 734-752.

18 Cf. Jodok Troy, "The Papal Human Rights Discourse: The Difference Pope Francis Makes," *Human Rights Quarterly* 41 (2019): 66–90, at 68.

19 Cf. On the concept of natural law regarding human rights, see Brian Tierney, *The Idea of Natural Rights: Studies on Natural Rights, Natural Law and Church Law 1150 – 1625* (Grand Rapids: William Eerdmans Publishing Co 1997); Keith Soko, *Mounting East-West Tension*, 111–161.

20   https://www.archives.gov/founding-docs/declaration-transcript   [accessed on 25 May 2023].

21   Jean-Paul Sartre, *No Exit* (Paris: Theatre du Vieux-Colombier, 1944).

22   Michael J. Perry, *The Idea of Human Rights*, 40–41.

23   Cf. John Witte Jr., and Justin J. Latterell, "Christianity and Human Rights: Past Contributions and Future Challenges," *Journal of Law and Religion* 30, no. 3 (2015): 353–385.

24   On the Christian roots of human rights, see Charles Villa-Vicencio, "Christianity and Human Rights," *Journal of Law and Religion* 14 (1999-2000): 579–600. On critical approach to the historical nexus of Christianity and Human Rights, see the special issue: *Journal of the History of Ideas* 79, no. 3 (2018).

25   Historically, a more explicit reference to human rights was made by Pope Pius XI in his encyclical *Mit Brennender Sorge* (1937), and later Pope Pius XII called for a transcendent foundation to human rights. Finally, *Pacem in Terris* of John XXIII made explicit Church's engagement at the international arena for issues of human rights and just world order.

26   Pius XII, Encyclical *Summi Pontificatus* 55.

27   See Pope Francis' encyclicals, *Evangelii Gaudium* and *Fratelli Tutti*.

28   The Christian understanding of love for the neighbours, especially for the last and the least, implies an unambiguous recognition of human dignity; so too the history of works of charity favouring the poor – hospitals, orphanages, schools, etc. These services have been further inspired by the thought on the dignity of the poor as they represent no less than Christ himself. – V*icarius Christi*. Cf. Michael Mollat, *The Poor in the Middle Ages. An Essay in Social History* (New Haven and London: Yale University Press, 1986).

29   Cf. https://www.washingtonpost.com/posteverything/wp/2015/09/17/pope -francis-has-given-up-on-human-rights-thats-a-good-thing/[accessed   on 30 June 2021].

30   Jodok Troy, "The Papal Human Rights Discourse," *art. cit.*, 74.

31   Cf. Shailja Chander, *Justice V.R. Krishna Iyer on Fundamental Rights and Directive Principles* (Delhi: Deep and Deep Publications,1992).

32   Jürgen Habermas, "The Concept of Human Dignity and the Realistic Utopia of Human Rights," *Metaphilosophy* 41, no. 4 (July 2010): 464–480, at 468.

33   https://economictimes.indiatimes.com/news/india/sc-orders-implementation-of-one-nation-one-ration-card-scheme-by-july-31/articleshow/83945695.cms [accessed on 30 June 2021].

34   This is striking over against the position of liberals like Michael Walzer, David Miller and others who argue for the priority of sovereign states in deciding who will be let in and who will not in their territories. See John Exdell, "Immigration, Nationalism, and Human Rights," *Metaphilosophy* 40, no. 1 (January 2009): 131–146. This liberal nationalist position is challenged

by Jürgen Habermas and Carol Goud, who argue for open borders, which according to them, need not be utopian.

35 https://www.theguardian.com/world/2015/sep/06/pope-francis-calls-on-catholics-to-take-in-refugee-families> [accessed on 30 June, 2021]; https://www.ncronline.org/news/vatican/pope-francis-welcomes-refugees-new-life-italy [accessed on 30 June 2021].

36 This is the title of a very engaging book by Mervin A. McMickel, *Where Have All the Prophets Gone?: Reclaiming Prophetic Preaching in America* (Cleveland, Ohio: Pilgrim Press, 2006).

37 Cf. Simango Kumalo, "The Role of the Church in Human Rights in a Democratic South Africa," in Wilhelm Gräb, and Lars Charbonnier, eds., *Religion and Human Rights: Global Challenges from Intercultural Perspectives* (Berlin; Boston: De Gruyter, 2015), 175–186.

38 The nexus between religion (especially Christianity) and social movements for creating peace and reconciliation is explored in a Korean case study. See Youngseop Lim & Dong Jin Kim, "Mobilising Social Movement for Peace: A Case Study on Christian Ecumenical Organisations in the Context of the Korean Conflict," *International Journal of Asian Christianity* 4, no.2 (2021): 248–260.

39 Linda Hogan, *Keeping Faith with Human Rights* (Washington DC: Georgetown University, 2015). See also Linda Hogan, "A Different Mode of Encounter: Egalitarian Liberalism and Christian Tradition," *Political Theolog* 7, no. 1 (2016): 59–73. Interestingly, the need for this dialogue with the secular reason in human rights is also advocated by the Russian Orthodox Church representatives. See Kristina Stoeckl, "The Moral Argument in the Human Rights Debate of the Russian Orthodox Church," in George E. Demacoupoulos and Aristotle Papanikolaou, eds., *Christianity, Democracy, and the Shadow of Constantine* (New York: Fordham University Press, 2016), 11–30.

40 Cf. Louis Henkin, "Religion, Religions, and Human Rights," *The Journal of Religious Ethics* 26, no. 2 (1998): 229–239.

41 Cf. Jürgen Habermas, "The Concept of Human Dignity," *art. cit.*, 470.

42 It is here that critically thinking canonists call for a *Lex fundamentalis* in the Church which will conform to the requirements of universal human rights. See Adrian Loretan and Felix Wilfred, eds., *Revision of the Codes. An Indian-European Dialogue* (Zürich: LIT Verlag, 2018). See also Rik Torf, "Human Rights in the History of the Roman Catholic Church," in Hans-Georg Ziebert and Johannes A. van der Ven, eds., *Human Rights and the Impact of Religion* (Leiden: Brill, 2013), 55–74.

43 Cf. Frederik von Harbou, "A Remedy Called Empathy: The Neglected Elements of Human Rights Theory," *Archives for Philosophy of Law and Social Philosophy* 99 (2013): 133–151.

FURTHER READING

Bourdeaux, Michael. *Religious Ferment in Russia: Protestant Opposition to Soviet Religious Policy*. London: Macmillan, and St. Martin's Press, 1968.

Bouwman, Bastiaan. "From Religious Freedom to Social Justice: The Human Rights Engagement of the Ecumenical Movement from the 1940s to the 1970s." *Journal of Global History* 13, 2 (2018): 252–273.

Calo, Zachary C. "Catholic Social Thought and Human Rights." *The American Journal of Economics and Sociology* 74, no. 1 (2015): 93–112.

Carr, Burgess. "Biblical and Theological Basis for the Struggle for Human Rights." *The Ecumenical Review* 27, no.2 (1975): 117–123.

Chander, Shailja. *Justice V.R. Krishna Iyer on Fundamental Rights and Directive Principles*. Delhi: Deep and Deep Publications,1992.

Delpech, Jacques. *The Oppression of Protestants in Spain*. London: Lutterworth Press, 1956.

Irizarry, Carmen. *The Thirty Thousand: Modern Spain and Protestantism*. New York: Harcourt, Brace & World, 1966.

Duff, Edward. *The Social Thought of the World Council of Churches*. London, New York, and Toronto: Longmans, Green and Co., 1956.

Engler, Mark. "Toward the 'Rights of the Poor': Human Rights in Liberation Theology." *The Journal of Religious Ethics* 28, no. 3 (2000): 339–65.

Exdell, John. "Immigration, Nationalism, and Human Rights." *Metaphilosophy* 40, no. 1 (January 2009): 131–146.

Gräb, Wilhelm, and Lars Charbonnier, eds. *Religion and Human Rights: Global Challenges from Intercultural Perspectives*, 175–186. Berlin; Boston: De Gruyter, 2015.

Greenberg, Udi, and Daniel Steinmetz-Jenkins. "Introduction: Special Forum on Christianity and Human Rights." *Journal of the History of Ideas* 79, no. 3 (2018): 407–409.

Gutiérrez, Gustavo. *A Theology of Liberation. History, Politics, and Salvation*. Maryknoll, New York: Orbis Books, 1973.

Gutiérrez, Gustavo. *The Power of the Poor in History*. Eugene, Oregon: Wipf & Stock Publisher, 2004.

Habermas, Jürgen. "The Concept of Human Dignity and the Realistic Utopia of Human Rights." *Metaphilosophy* 41, no. 4 (July 2010): 464–480.

Harbou, Frederik von. "A Remedy Called Empathy: The Neglected Elements of Human Rights Theory." *Archives for Philosophy of Law and Social Philosophy* 99 (2013): 133–151.

Hebly, J.A, Michael Bourdeaux, and Eugen Voss, eds. *Religious Liberty in the Soviet Union: WCC and USSR: A Post-Nairobi Documentation*. West Wickham: Keston College, 1976.

Henkin, Louis. "Religion, Religions, and Human Rights." *The Journal of Religious Ethics* 26, no. 2 (1998): 229–239.

Hogan, Linda. "A Different Mode of Encounter: Egalitarian Liberalism and Christian Tradition." *Political Theology* 7, no. 1 (2016): 59–73.

Hogan, Linda. *Keeping Faith with Human Rights*. Washington DC: Georgetown University, 2015.

John, Clement, ed. "Human Rights and the Churches: New Challenges: Reports and Papers of the Global Review of Ecumenical Policies and Practices on Human Rights." *CCIA Background Information*, no. 1998/1. Geneva: WCC, 1998.

Kumalo, Simango. "The Role of the Church in Human Rights in a Democratic South Africa." In Wilhelm Gräb, and Lars Charbonnier, eds., *Religion and Human Rights: Global Challenges from Intercultural Perspectives*, 175–186. Berlin; Boston: De Gruyter, 2015.

Lim, Youngseop, and Dong Jin Kim. "Mobilising Social Movement for Peace: A Case Study on Christian Ecumenical Organisations in the Context of the Korean Conflict." *International Journal of Asian Christianity* 4, no.2 (2021): 248–260.

Loretan, Adrian, and Felix Wilfred, eds. *Revision of the Codes. An Indian-European Dialogue*. Zürich: LIT Verlag, 2018.

McMickel, Mervin A. *Where Have All the Prophets Gone?: Reclaiming Prophetic Preaching in America*. Cleveland, Ohio: Pilgrim Press, 2006.

Mollat, Michael. *The Poor in the Middle Ages. An Essay in Social History*. New Haven and London: Yale University Press, 1986.

Nicole, Jacques, and Jean-Nicolas Bitter. "The WCC and the Question of Human Rights in Eastern Europe." *Religion, State and Society: The Keston Journal* 21, no. 3-4 (1993): 257–262.

Nolde, O. Frederick. *Free and Equal: Human Rights in Ecumenical Perspective*. Geneva: WCC, 1968.

Nurser, John. *For All Peoples and All Nations: Christian Churches and Human Rights*. Geneva: WCC, 2005.

Perry, Michael J. *The Idea of Human Rights. Four Inquiries.* New York: Oxford University Press, 1998.

Regan, Ethna. "Liberation Theology and Human Rights: in Interruptive Realism to the Centrality of *La Realidad.*" *Theology and the Boundary Discourse of Human Rights,* 143–177. Washington DC: Georgetown University, 2010.

Sartre, Jean-Paul. *No Exit.* Paris: Theatre du Vieux-Colombier, 1944.

Seko, Keith. *Mounting East-West Tension: Buddhist-Christian Dialogue on Human Rights, Social Justice and a Global Ethic,* Chapter 3, 111–161. Milwaukee: Marquette University Press, 2009.

Smeulers, Alette, and Fred Grünfeld. *International Crimes and Other Gross Human Rights Violations: A Multi- and Interdisciplinary Textbook.* Leiden: BRILL, 2011.

Steiner, Henry J, and Philip Alston, eds. *International Human Rights in Context. Law, Politics, Morals.* Oxford: Clarendon Press, 1996.

Stoeckl, Kristina. "The Moral Argument in the Human Rights Debate of the Russian Orthodox Church." In George E. Demacoupoulos and Aristotle Papanikolaou, eds., *Christianity, Democracy, and the Shadow of Constantine,* 11–30. New York: Fordham University Press, 2016.

Tierney, Brian. *The Idea of Natural Rights: Studies on Natural Rights, Natural Law and Church Law 1150 – 1625.* Grand Rapids: William Eerdmans Publishing Co., 1997.

Torf, Rik. "Human Rights in the History of the Roman Catholic Church." In Hans-Georg Ziebert and Johannes A. van der Ven, eds., *Human Rights and the Impact of Religion,* 55–74. Leiden: Brill, 2013.

Troy, Jodok. "The Papal Human Rights Discourse: The Difference Pope Francis Makes." *Human Rights Quarterly* 41 (2019): 66–90.

Villa-Vicencio, Charles. "Christianity and Human Rights." *Journal of Law and Religion* 14 (1999–2000): 579–600.

WCC. *Racism in Theology and Theology against Racism: Report of a Consultation Organized by the Commission on Faith and Order and the Programme to Combat Racism.* Geneva: WCC, 1975.

Weingärtner, Erich. *Human Rights on the Ecumenical Agenda: Report and Assessment.* Geneva: WCC, 1983.

Wilfred, Felix. "Human Rights or the Rights of the Poor? Redeeming the Human Rights from Contemporary Inversions." *Vidyajyoti Journal of Theological Reflections* 62, no. 10 (Oct. 1998): 734-752.

Witte, John Jr, and Justin J Latterell. "Christianity and Human Rights: Past Contributions and Future Challenges." *Journal of Law and Religion* 30, no. 3 (2015): 353–385.

Chapter 8

CHRISTIAN CHURCHES AND DEMOCRATIC CHALLENGES
THE CASE OF INDIAN CATHOLICISM

The translation of Christian faith in everyday language brings us face to face with the issue of democracy in Christian communities. It is approached differently by the numerous Churches in South Asia – the Protestant, the Oriental Churches, the Pentecostals, the Evangelicals and so on. The issue is extensive and cannot be treated adequately in the space of one chapter. Hence, we limit our reflection to Indian Catholicism, which can help us compare and contrast the developments taking place in other ecclesial traditions and enter into a fruitful ecumenical relationship.[1] Speaking of different Church traditions, we need to acknowledge a far greater affinity of Protestantism to democracy than the Catholic tradition. Commenting on the issue, the well-known sociologist Peter Berger observes,

> The Protestant Reformers of the sixteenth century were certainly not interested in political democracy. Yet certain key features of Protestantism inadvertently laid the cultural foundations for what, under favourable conditions, could become a democracy. These features were: 1) the emphasis on individual conscience guided by the scriptures (classically expressed by the image of Luther refusing to recant before the Imperial Diet); 2) the doctrine of the universal priesthood of all believers (which, as Max Weber showed, led to a

secular concept of vocation); and 3) the importance ascribed to literacy and lay education, which naturally followed from the other two.[2]

To what extent has the Catholic Church in India become a participatory and democratic Church? This is the question the present chapter grapples with. It seeks to analyze the deeply embedded legacy of a hierarchical worldview and practice, anti-democratic doctrinal tradition, and clericalist mode of governance. The hierarchy inherited from ecclesial tradition is further reinforced by the central principle of social organization in India – the caste hierarchy. The present chapter will probe into the interplay between these two hierarchies and their expressions. It also presents the struggles of Indian Catholicism to imbibe the spirit of the Vatican II Council and to avail, at the pastoral level, its democratic vision and openings. Indian Catholicism is weighed down by the above-mentioned two hierarchical legacies – something clearly seen in the absence of any significant representation of Dalit Catholics in the governance of the Church. The final section of the chapter explores whether and to what extent Indian Catholicism has contributed to the democratization of Indian society and polity.

Any Catholic honestly looking at the actual state of democracy in India would be the last one to wish for a democratic Church. Could Indian Catholicism be something else than a democracy? However, demeaned in practice and trivialized in conception, the question of democracy cannot be avoided as it has become an integral part of the culture of our modern times and the quest for freedom and equality.

It is important, right at the beginning of our reflections to take stock of a basic distinction. One thing is democracy as a form of governance with its procedures, such as the will of the majority in the decision-making process, formal voting, and election. We could characterize it as *low-intensity democracy*. People who oppose any talk of democracy in the Church mostly refer to low-intensity democracy, for example, when they say that the truths of faith and principles of morality cannot be decided by the majority. However, there is another crucial aspect to democracy which we could characterize as *high-intensity democracy*. It represents an egalitarian vision of human society and stands for a set of values, ideals, and ethos. These have not only affinity with faith but are also deeply rooted in the Christian scriptures and tradition. Hence, the absence of democratization in the Catholic Church is more than a failure to keep abreast of political modernity; at bottom, it is a failure to be faithful to the core of the Christian message.

We shall not enter into the formal and procedural aspects of democracy but reflect on the vision and core values the ideal democracy embodies. Some of these values are human dignity, equality, freedom, representation, agency, due process, and restraint on power. Those who want to silence any discussion on democracy in the Church resort to a short-cut and categorical argument: Church is not a democracy. What they mean is that the Church is not an organization governed by elected representatives through a process of party politics. However, the same people fail to say that Church is not a monarchy. Once democracy is reduced to an electoral system, it is easy to counter it as not applicable to the Church. However, no one can deny that the form of governance in the Church should respect the core values of the gospel, which are democratic in nature.

Viewed from this perspective, indeed, democratic forms are more prone to respect and defend the dignity and rights of persons created in the image of God than monarchical, feudal, and oligarchic forms of governance. These latter forms, as history shows, infringe upon the dignity and rights of the individuals and their freedom and lead them into a dependent and subservient relationship. The negative attitude to democratic values reminds us of how freedom of conscience was once viewed by the Catholic Church – Pius IX – as "absurd and foolish."[3]

An investigation into whether and to what degree there is democratization in the Indian Catholic Church will lead us to discover whether discrimination is still practised, whether there is the agency of the people, and whether there is a restraint on power and widening of participation and inclusion of everyone. All these elements are very much based on faith and the central message of Christianity, as we will see later in this chapter. We shall concentrate on the democratization process within the Indian Catholic Church in the larger framework of contemporary discussion on Church and democracy.[4] We shall conclude with some reflections on democratization as a mission of the Catholic Church in Indian society and the larger community of the nation.

This contextual study of democracy is, indeed, needed and could hopefully contribute to the global discussion. A report on the *State of Democracy in South Asia* has pointed out how the conception of democracy is reworked differently in each context, and its practice is reshaped by adopting "innovative institutional strategies to handle diversities in society."[5] This applies as well to the correlation between the Church and democratization in Indian Catholicism.

Exacerbating Legacies

When discussing about democracy and the democratization of the Catholic Church, one mostly tends to see it as an issue of absence of liberal values – freedom of expression, the constraint on free thought, absence of election to offices, and so on. The issue of democracy in India does indeed include such a liberal agenda,[6] but it is much more complex, involving the caste structure of Indian society. As no one could really analyze the Indian democratic process without studying its interplay with caste, the same is true of democracy and democratization in the Catholic Church.[7] Caste is a hierarchical order of society based on the principle of purity and pollution and the major source of inequality, discrimination, and oppression in India. It has been operative in the Catholic Church as much as in the wider society, the most glaring example being the way the Dalits have been treated in the society and in the Catholic Church.

Historically, the Catholic missionaries hailing from the Mediterranean region, and accustomed to the feudal system, accommodated themselves to the caste system and its hierarchy. This is in marked contrast to the Protestant missionaries from the northern countries of Europe who were inspired by the spirit of the Reformation and the Enlightenment. They mostly hailed from lower ranks of society and were imbued with a keen sense of justice and equality.[8] They were, in general, highly critical of the caste against which they protested and brought a greater sense of equality and freedom within the Protestant Churches and in their governance.[9]

As for the Catholic missionaries, besides the feudal cultural background, we need to consider the fact that they came from a Catholic environment in Europe that was resistant to the French Revolution and supportive of royalty and nobility. The idea of democracy was viewed as a modern heresy and even thought of as "absurd." Resistance to democracy in the official position of the Church lasted till the middle of the twentieth century.[10] A change in the position of the Church in support of democracy came about quite late, when confronted by communist, Fascist and Nazi totalitarianism in mid-twentieth century.

Catholic missionaries carried with them a culture that emphasized hierarchy, obedience, and loyalty and were averse to individual freedom of thought and expression. Democracy and democratization were far from their thought and mode of conduct with the local converts. So, then, we have asymmetry between the traditional Indian hierarchical system of caste and the Catholic legacy of anti-democratic posture. Present-day Indian Catholicism is the confluence of these two hierarchies and the attitude and values attendant on them. In many respects, the caste system resonated with the imported hierarchical thinking of the Catholic Church. Converting to Catholicism while holding onto the shackles of the caste system presented no contradiction to the Indian Catholic clergy and laity. Vatican II and its new vision of the Church as the communion of the people of God, though enthusiastically received in India, has been going through a complex process of translation into everyday life.

When Pope John XXIII took the initiative of convoking the Council Vatican II, one of the goals he had in mind was what he called "*aggiornamento*," namely updating and renewing the Church vis-à-vis the conditions of contemporary life.[11] *Pacem in Terris* was the first encyclical that a pope addressed to "all men of goodwill," rather than only to Catholics – a paradigm shift from a pope, challenging the Church to think anew. Greater participatory, dialogical, and democratic practice in the life and governance of the Church was part of the realization of "aggiornamento."

It was followed up by Pope Paul VI, who dwelt in his encyclical "*Ecclesiam Suam*" on dialogue within the Church and with the world. The democratic openings of Vatican II by understanding the Church primarily as *People of God* (*Lumen Gentium*), by recognizing Religious Freedom (*Dignitatis Humanae*), and by creating participatory structures set in motion the core values of democracy.[12]

The pursuit of increased democratization within the Church does not diminish its core essence; rather, it signifies a deeper embrace of gospel principles. The Christian communities of the earliest centuries, in fact, bear witness to a way of life that incorporated the best of democratic values – active participation, recognition of a plurality of cultures and ministries, freedom of the Spirit, equitable sharing of goods, and a non-hierarchical model of governance. As historians tell us, in the course of centuries, the Church adopted different forms of governance, of which the monarchical model became the dominant and standard one for a long time.

Divine Hierarchy

Augustine's theory of two cities introduced a dichotomy and a hierarchy of submission of the City of Man to the City of God. The hierarchical order, inspired by Neo-Platonism, was endowed with a mystical aura in that it was claimed that the hierarchy in the Church is the reflection of the divine hierarchy, something which got entrenched in the Christian tradition, thanks to the work of an anonymous early Christian writer – Pseudo-Dionysius - through his work on celestial hierarchy ("*De hierarchia divina*"). As Jean Leclercq notes, "What is deemed to be the case with the celestial hierarchy is considered to have a counterpart in the structure of the Church."[13]

This kind of hierarchical conception of the Church in the medieval period gave birth to strong centralization and authoritarianism, with little space for fostering the gospel values that the ideal of democracy embodies.

In the modern period, a de-historicized conception of truth divorced from any reference to the subjectivity of human beings undergirded the hierarchical hold of the Church. When the divine right of kings was challenged in Europe and the temporal powers of the Church were threatened through revolutionary movements like the French Revolution and Italian nationalism, a full-blooded anti-revolutionary ideology was forged, accompanied by tough disciplining against any liberal and democratic thought.

Harking back to Scripture and Tradition

Denial of democratization in the Church ignores the spirit and teachings of Christian scriptures and tradition. In the Old Testament, there is a tension between the royal trajectory of accumulating wealth and centralizing power on the one hand and the prophets' egalitarian and people-centred trajectory on the other.[14] The prophetic message was a check on the unrestrained and irresponsible exercise of power. Absolutist and totalitarian power structure is dehumanizing, and Christianity could never, in principle, go with any such mode of governance, though we know from history this was not always the case. There is the need to constantly hark back to the prophetic source to sustain the democratic spirit.

Inclusion, especially of the marginalized, is a crucial democratic value that is reflected in the life and teachings of Jesus, the founder of Christianity. Diversity is yet another important component of democracy that could draw inspiration from the Christian conception of God, which is neither monotheistic nor monarchical but Trinitarian - three persons with equal dignity and in communion with one another. There is the individuality of persons and commonality of life. The identity of a person should not be at the expense of communion and the common good.

The New Testament times witnessed a "discipleship of equals" in the community of Jesus with different functions according to different charisms, as Paul would later elaborate.[15] This was counter-cultural in a period conditioned by a hierarchical approach to the world and human relationships. According to Aristotle, some are born free and others as slaves. This is an extreme and paralyzing determination with no possibility for change. There is no room for nurturing dreams, developing freedom, and constructing any new self-identity.

Equality also means equal opportunity for everyone to express his or her talents in service of the common good. No one is excluded. Equal discipleship and the common priesthood of all the faithful imply fostering an inclusive community. The birth of monasteries signified a new model of communities whose members decided through mutual consultation everyday matters – spiritual or material. The Christian community was conceived by its founder as a "contrast society," that renounces domination also in its governance.[16]

Further, the innovative theological and canonical approach in the medieval period was inspired by democratic spirit. The maxim "*quod omnes tangit, ab omnibus tractari et approbari debet*" (what concerns all, needs to be deliberated and approved by all) summarizes the spirit that needs to inspire the governance of Christian communities.[17] In fact, far from democratic thought flowing from the secular world to the Church, it was the other way around. The medieval canonists provided the theoretical backing for parliamentary and constitutional democracy in their efforts to give a juridical articulation to governance in the Church.[18]

Democratic values in the Church could be theologically derived also from the reality of baptism, which gives equal dignity and right to every believer and equal opportunity for participation in the life and mission of the Church. "But you are a chosen race, a royal priesthood, a holy nation, God's own people, that you may declare the wonderful deeds of him who called you out of darkness into his marvellous light" (1 Pt 2:9). This truth has been re-articulated in the conception of the Church in Vatican II. We spoke of a hierarchical legacy of Indian Catholicism from the colonial mission period. On the other hand, the biblical and historical data are a challenge to it in today's circumstances.

An Issue of Credibility

Apart from other reasons, democratization remains a very crucial matter because it touches upon the credibility of the Church. To be able to function as a credible institution today and bear witness to the gospel, Indian Catholics may not neglect the importance of the democratic ethos which men and women of our times value greatly. The absence of democratic values could lead the Church to a crisis of legitimation.[19] When a Church neglects accountability and participation in deliberations for its common good and fails to enlist the cooperation of all the faithful, how could one expect it to become a credible Church?

As Charles Curran rightly notes, Catholic ecclesiology has a lot to learn from its social teachings.[20] The Catholic Social Teachings directed to the world speak of human dignity, rights, freedom, participation, the principle of subsidiarity, and a democratic form of life. These need to find application within the Church. The Synod on Justice in the World was aware of how what the Church preaches to the world needs to be realized within its own life. It stated, "While the Church is bound to give witness to justice, she recognizes that anyone who ventures to speak to people about justice must first be just in their eyes. Hence, we must undertake an examination of the modes of acting and of the possessions and lifestyle found within the Church itself."[21] The same would also apply to the issue of democracy and democratic practices.

Innovative Structures and Inherent Obstacles

Vatican II created seven different participatory structures so that the conception of the Church as people of God could be translated into practice. These are: Diocesan Synod, Diocesan Finance Council, Presbyteral Council, College of Consultors, Diocesan Pastoral Council,

Parish Pastoral Council and Parish Finance Council. According to Vatican II, these participative bodies are to function, reflecting the collegial and synodal nature of the Church.[22] The teaching on the collegiality of bishops dismantled a monarchical conception of the papacy and saw governance in the Church as done by the college of bishops presided over by the bishop of Rome, the pope. Vatican II brought about a shift from the prevalent monarchical approach to an understanding of Church governance closer to democracy and inspired by democratic vision and values. The new participatory structures introduced by Vatican II are to be understood in light of the above democratic shift.

In implementing the democratic openings of Vatican II, however, Indian Catholicism experienced some inherent difficulties, some of which are common in other parts of the world too; and others more specific to the Indian situation. The practising of core democratic values stumbles upon a structural and legal problem, pervasive in the governance of the Catholic Church worldwide. It is the lack of division of power. For, the legislative, executive, and judiciary functions are vested with the same person of the bishop, resembling a monarchical model of governance. Further, by and large, the participatory structures proposed by Vatican II are *consultative* in nature and do not have decision-making powers that are reserved to the clergy.[23] Further, the new democratic openings of equality and co-responsibility of the entire faithful for the Church and its mission are undermined for want of institutional safeguards and legal provisions.[24]

This inherent weakness in the participatory structures is felt by the Indian laity, who are struggling against clericalism and clerical control of every aspect in the life of the Church. Clerical control and resistance to democratic values are most evident where the Churches have rich material sources of money, assets, large swathes of land and property, institutions, and political clout. In most parts of North India, where Christians are a minuscule minority and widely dispersed, and the Church itself has much fewer material means and properties, it has been observed that bishops and priests have a close rapport with the people, and the leaders are quite informal in their dealings. This has facilitated a relatively stronger practice of the values of democracy spontaneously. There is better consultation, dialogue and interaction among the various segments of the Church – the clergy, the religious, and the lay people. The same could also be said of North-East Indian Catholicism among the tribal people who are culturally at home with an egalitarian way of life, quite different from the fossilized caste structure in the rest of the country.

The South presents a different scenario. In states like Keralam, Tamilnadu, and Andhra Pradesh, where there are a relatively high number of Catholics, and the Churches are endowed with a lot more material resources and property, there is much less of democratic culture and more clericalism and monarchical model of governance.

The laity have tried to use some of the traditional structures to restrain the clerical hold of power. In many parishes of the South, for a long time, there has been a system of what is called parish or village committees composed of lay persons who own and manage the property and material resources of the parish, including the maintenance and salary of the parish priest. It is something like the trustee system in the Catholic parishes of nineteenth-century America, except for the fact that the Indian system bears the mark of caste. Members of upper castes making up the committee exclude other castes and the Dalits. Moreover, the Indian village committee does not allow the membership of women. This system has come into clash with the clergy, who would like to control by themselves the parish, including its assets. This village committee system has been challenged to some extent by the introduction of parish councils, as per the directives of Vatican II.

Documents and resolutions at all levels have been produced, and sincere efforts were made to introduce the participatory structures. All this notwithstanding, Indian Catholicism, by and large, is far from embodying democratic spirit and values. We could go into a deeper analysis of the contradiction between the proclaimed ideals and actual practice.

One important reason is the quality of leadership and the process through which they and the members of the consultative bodies are chosen both in the dioceses as well as in the numerous religious orders. Quality of leadership mostly determines whether democratization will happen or not. It has been observed that a leader who is incompetent, not open and ready to listen, makes sure only those espousing his interests and views are elected. As a result, the participatory bodies at the diocesan level become the echo chamber of the bishop, who wishes to hear his own views and opinions. Similarly, parish participatory bodies simply echo the views and preferences of the parish priest. The body of consultors in religious congregations is so chosen that they simply toe the line of their major superiors.[25]

What happens in these participatory and consultative bodies is, so to say, a "gaming" of the system and, ultimately, a subversion of them. Often there is a lack of honest communication and mutual challenge in these bodies, in contrast to what was found in the Council of Jerusalem, where there was honest discussion and resolution of issues among Judaizers and those working for the gentiles (Acts 15). It may be recalled here how bishops in early centuries paid serious attention to consulting the clergy and the faithful with an open spirit – something that is reflected in the words of St Cyprian.

> I have made it a rule, ever since the beginning of my episcopate, to make

no decision merely on the strength of my own personal opinion without
consulting you (the priests and the deacons) and without the approbation
of the people.[26]

The present circumstances are significantly impeding the smooth
operation of participatory institutions, making it imperative that
the faithful, particularly the clergy, receive a comprehensive training
that fosters an understanding of democratic principles and values.
Moreover, they should acquire the essential skills required for active
participation in the affairs and mission of the Church.

Checks and Balances

The trustee system I referred to earlier tried to restrain clerical power
and facilitated the participation of the laity. Understandably, such
a trustee system was a source of conflict between the laity and the
clergy, the latter claiming ultimate authority and power over the
management of the parish. The trustee system also had its weaknesses
and limitations. In a society structured around caste, it was common
that the trustees hailed from the upper castes and classes, with no
power and participation for the lower castes and Dalits. Though the
trustee system may appear democratic, it was, in fact, non-inclusive
and elitist and oligarchic in spirit rather than democratic.

As for the Catholic Oriental Churches – the Syro-Malabar and
Syro-Malankara – a kind of democratic system called *Palliyogam* was
in vogue for centuries. *Palliyogam*, or the Church assembly consisted of
one member from each family, and this representative body managed
the Church affairs. It held in check clericalism. On the other hand,
the *Palliyogam* was an assembly of *male* members, and women could
not represent the family in the assembly. The introduction of the
parish council since Vatican II appeared to remedy the limits of the
traditional systems in that this participatory body is expected to be
representative across gender, caste and class.

The various consultative bodies, if they function with an open and inclusive spirit, could become institutions that maintain checks and balances, which is very important for practising democratization. There is no reason why, what the social teachings of the Church say about the principle of subsidiarity and justice, which reflect the spirit of democracy, cannot be applied to the Church and its governance.

If a Church leader is threatened by democratic practice, it is not so much because it is against any truth of revelation, but rather because he is afraid that his exercise of power will be checked and restrained. Checks and balances of power in the Church ensure two things: First, that there is no abuse of power; second, power is directed to the achievement of the common good, for which it is meant. As is well-known, the restraint on the power of ecclesiastical authorities is a global problem. As I noted earlier, the present code of canon law lets the bishop be the holder of legislative, executive, and judiciary powers all in one. All three powers are vested with the same person, making it almost impossible to hold a Church authority accountable for wrong decisions and misdeeds. For the Church to be truly democratic, it is in need of correcting this anomaly. An essential component in a democratic form of governance is a legal system that sets limits to the power of governance. This could be achieved through reform of the present canon law so that it becomes really human rights-based.[27]

Philip Berryman, reflecting on the situation of democratization in Latin America, observes that contrary perhaps to the general expectation, democracy has not been a significant theme in the Church on that continent. The reason he adduces is quite revealing. "The relative lack of personnel, real estate, and money often reduces the distance between the hierarchy and ordinary people."[28] The growing power, money and influence among the leaders of the Church and the clergy makes democratization a theme of concern in Indian

Catholicism. Hence, addressing the democratization of the Church means, at the same time, facing the issue of money and power. The material assets and resources keep the people at bay and let the leaders take arbitrary decisions and follow a very authoritarian and undemocratic course. The bishops of South India, Keralam and Tamilnadu, for example, are among the influential public persons in their states. They command over vast estates and money and enjoy political clout since the Christians represent a sizable population (in Keralam – about 20%), and hence they are sought after by politicians for electoral gains. The power and influence the clergy enjoy in southern states of the country have made them less sensitive to consultation and participatory governance.

Co-Responsible Partners – The Dalits and Subalterns

The litmus test of democratization in the Church is whether those marginalized and excluded, like women and children, are included and their voices are listened to. More specific to India would be the case of the Dalits.

"The lives of the Dalits are historically and contemporarily a saga of denial."[29] Besides experiencing the negation of human dignity, material resources for survival, education, and employment, they were even denied entry into the Church. It may be recalled here, for example, that the upper caste Syrian Christians of Keralam were opposed to the conversion of the outcaste Dalits who were detained as slaves. They also stoutly opposed missionary efforts to free the Dalits and provide them with education. A recent study has brought out this Syrian-Christian resistance to any effort towards freedom and empowerment of the Dalits.

> Syrian Christians were major slaveholders and agents of the Portuguese and Dutch in Kerala, and recent studies show how slaves in Cochin were mostly

> sold by Syrian Christians as part of their alignment with Dutch East India
> Company officer.[30]

Even today, Dalits are mostly viewed as beneficiaries of what the Church doles out. The arrogance of the upper castes and Church leaders expect the Dalits to be grateful and show obeisance. The relationship between the leadership and the Dalits is characterized by paternalism and condescendence, which is bereft of any adult relationship, a presupposition for the democratic spirit to prevail. A recent research in Keralam analyses the ways upper-caste Syrian Christians discriminate against the Dalits. It notes,

> The public sphere created in the Church is almost like a bourgeoisie public sphere where Dalit Catholics and the marginalized have little chance to be part of because the dominant caste Christians monopolize it… The contribution of the common people, especially the Dalits, is considered trivial and not enriching enough in the administration and organization of the Church and its ministry. The hierarchical setup of the Church tends to consider Dalits, who are the last and least as mere clients and recipients of charity and benevolence devoid of dignity and rights of their own. The mood of several Catholics and clergy is imbued with parochialism when sharing the Church's resources with Dalit Catholics.[31]

The point is that Church is not primarily a developmental organization; it is a communion. It is supposed to be a witness to the equality of all sons and daughters of God. The baptismal equality calls for the removal of all walls of separation and renunciation of caste or ethnic discrimination (cf. Gal 3:27-28). The Church happens only when there is the practice of true communion. The community grows through dialogue. As it is, the upper castes do not consider the Dalits as equal partners in dialogue within the Church.

On the other hand, the Dalits teach the grammar of dialogue and democratization by their fundamental and legitimate claim to be equal partners in the deliberations and decisions that concern everyone in the community. They bring a democratic impulse increasingly within the Church and its management. Acceptance of others as equal partners is the condition for every genuine dialogue and a democratic mode of governance.[32]

A Call for Inclusion and Representation

India's future will not be decided by the growth in GDP, but by the degree of inclusion. Hence, in a way, the future of India as a nation depends on the expansion of freedom, agency, and representation of the Dalits. The Catholic Church's commitment to democratic principle of inclusion would be incomplete if it does not address and rectify any forms of discrimination against Dalits, within its own ranks. Such marginalization exacerbates the already existing social and political exclusion experienced by the Dalit communities.

It may be recalled here that politically the Dalits were marginalized while the mainstream was dominated by the high-caste people all along. If there is, to some extent, political participation and agency of the Dalits in the Indian democracy, this is due to the policy of affirmative action or what is called the policy of "reservation," for which Dr Ambedkar and other Dalit leaders fought. Thanks to their representation, it enabled at least a small section of Dalits to enter mainstream democracy.

Nothing prevents the Dalits from claiming a similar policy of "reservation" which will ensure their representation and active participation in the life, leadership and governance of the Catholic Church. The importance of their claim stands out against the stark contrast between the number of Catholic faithful in the country and their inadequate representation in present-day Church leadership. Though the Dalit Catholics are 12 million out of 19 million Catholics of India – that is about 60% - of the Catholic population, as recognized officially by the Catholic Bishops' Conference of India,[33] they have been suppressed by the upper caste Catholics who garner the leadership position as bishops, major superiors, and heads of large and powerful institutions.

When the missionaries departed, they left the reins of the Church in the hands of the upper castes; as a result of which, there was not a single bishop appointed in India from the Dalit community until the 1980s. Even today, there is a tiny number of bishops and others in leadership positions from the Dalit community, totally disproportionate to the Dalit faithful. In order to redress the situation, and as a result of the continuous struggles of the Dalit people, the Catholic Bishop's Conference of India (CBCI) came out with a policy document in 2016.[34] It wants to ensure Dalit agency and representation in the life of the Church. The good intention behind the document notwithstanding, it remains a pious wish list for lack of will and absence of a mechanism for implementing the laudable policies declared. There is no auditing and accountability either. Earnestly implementing these policies will bring a greater sense of democracy, inclusion, and participation into the Catholic Church.

Experience and history show that the Dalits continue to be excluded in open and subtle ways in the Indian Catholic Church within the existing frame and structures. Their continued struggles for representation and inclusion have not borne any significant results. In such a case, a separate identity affirmation within the communion of the Catholic Church could open up the possibility of attaining the values of democracy, such as freedom, equality, inclusion, agency and so on. In this context, some Dalit Catholic thinkers such as Cosmon Arokiaraj, S. Lourdusamy, Devasagaya Raj, and Antony John Baptist propose creating a "Dalit Rite."[35]

The above proposal needs to be understood against the background of the development of Catholicism since the1980s. The two Catholic Oriental rites – Syro-Malabar and Syro-Malankara were resentful of how Catholic Church leadership was dominated by the Latin rite Goans and the Mangalorians of the western coast, from among whom bishops were appointed in many dioceses of North and North-East India. The Catholic Orientals, traditionally confined to the state of Keralam, felt that they were discriminated against by the Church-leadership dominated by Latin rite Catholic bishops. Hence, since the 1980s, they have used their rite identity as a strategic means for power-sharing in the governance of the Church by claiming equal rights as the Latin rite. They succeeded in expanding their presence far and wide in the whole country, and today they are assured of good representation in all matters of the life and mission of the Catholic Church.[36]

From a theological perspective, Vatican II gives due recognition to the various local Churches endowed with their own culture, tradition and history. The difference in culture and context and other circumstances can motivate the plurality of Churches within the Catholic communion. The Dalit Catholic thinkers seem to believe that there is enough reason to claim a separate cultural, ritual, and historical identity for a rite of their own within the Catholic communion.[37] It is their hope such a path will ensure, as it happened with the other two Oriental Rites, a greater opening for attaining the core values of democracy, which, in turn, will empower them to be active agents in the world and society.

Democratization as a Mission

The Catholic Church in modern times passed through several stages vis-à-vis democracy - from opposition to reluctant concession and, finally, support. Samuel Huntington is widely known for his thesis on the "Clash of Civilizations." Less known, however, is his observation on how Catholicism has caused a "Third Wave" of democratization in the latter part of the twentieth century. He notes,

> The third wave of the 1970s and 1980s was overwhelmingly Catholic. Two
> (Portugal and Spain) of the first three third-wave countries to democratize
> were Catholic … Overall, roughly three-quarter of the countries that transited
> to democracy between 1974 and 1989 were Catholic countries.[38]

The recent history of several nations of Latin America, The Philippines, and Korea in Asia attest to the role played by institutions and movements inspired by Catholicism in the creation of democratic societies. In this context, it is a valid question to inquire to what extent, in history and present times, Indian Catholicism has contributed to the democratization of society and polity.

Suspicion of Indian Democracy – A Look at the Past

If the Catholic missionaries, as we saw, were imbued with an anti-democratic spirit in the context of the threat experienced by the Church in Europe, this was further reinforced by a certain colonial argument. As Mary John notes after researching the Catholic literature of the nineteenth century and early twentieth century, "Most of the Christians and Catholic missionaries supported the British Raj based on the assumption that the British rule was ultimately good for India and that India was not ready for democracy."[39]

Such a view is corroborated by the official views of the Vatican on Gandhi and his struggle for freedom and democracy. Gandhi's method of non-cooperation and civil disobedience was anathema to the Vatican.[40] Not only did Pius XI deny an audience to Gandhi, but also the struggle for sovereignty and democracy in India was looked at with suspicion by the Vatican.[41] All this notwithstanding, there has been a group of lay Indian Catholics who believed democracy was something important for the future of India.[42] This view was entertained and spread by a journal edited by the Catholic laity "*The Week*" (1927-1932), whereas the anti-democratic missionary view was circulated through the weekly *The Examiner*.

Catholicism and Democratic Challenges of Today

History and experience bear out that the Catholic Church leaders, in general, tend to espouse the view that one should cooperate with civil authorities. The critical point arrives when the civil authority turns out to be totalitarian with anti-people policies and becomes a violator of human rights. The most glaring example is the attitude and practice of bishops during National Socialism in Germany. There are also Church leaders shifting their position when pressure mounts from the people from the bottom up. A case in point is the democratization of the Philippines, where the Church leaders from the doctrine of cooperation with Marcos' dictatorial regime turned against it galvanizing the swell of democratic forces from the bottom.[43] There are other examples and similar experiences from the continent of Latin America.

Though India is a democratic country, it also experienced a short spell of dictatorship, known as the "Emergency" during the prime-ministership of Indira Gandhi when the Constitution was set aside, human rights were trampled upon, and freedom of speech was suppressed. The Catholic bishops of India, unfortunately, did not speak up for democracy and the rule of law.[44] They were seized by fear that any challenge to the dictatorial regime would mean jeopardizing the institutions run by the Church, the cancellation of licenses to receive foreign funds, and carry on missionary work. One of the Catholic bishops confessed this failure to uphold democracy at a critical time.

> Personally, I feel very guilty that we bishops did not speak out strongly against the injustice of the Emergency... There was at the time, the difficulty with the government over the appointment of Bishops. Maybe we were afraid to make that problem worse. We have always avoided clashing with the government. The Church is a minority and acts as one. We protested more about the anti-conversion laws that would limit our proselytizing than we did about the jailing, tortures and forced sterilization of our people.[45]

It is said time and again that India is experiencing politically a tempestuous period. When a religious-nationalist party with rugged totalitarian tendencies is in power and Indian democracy is generally perceived to be in deep crisis today, it is legitimate to ask what could be the contribution of Catholicism in these critical times. The overwhelmingly Catholic context of the Philippines or that of Timor-Leste is not the situation of India, where Catholics are a minuscule minority. Catholic contribution to democratization cannot but be different in a widely different context. The Archbishop of Delhi, Anil Couto, wrote a letter to the Christian faithful on 8 May 2018, before the national elections, referring to the situation of concern in the country. He said, "We are witnessing a turbulent political atmosphere which poses a threat to the democratic principles enshrined in our Constitution and the secular fabric of our nation," and exhorted the people to do a prayer campaign for the country. He also formulated a prayer to be said in the churches.

> May the ethos of true democracy envelop our elections with dignity and the flames of honest patriotism enkindle our political leaders. This is our cry, Heavenly Father, in these troubled times as we see the clouds eclipsing the light of truth, justice, and freedom.[46]

This comment on the country's situation and call for prayer was deeply resented by the ruling party. The letter became a matter of public controversy. Despite being a minority, such a stance on the part of Catholic leadership regarding public issues affecting the people, their dignity and rights certainly made an impact, as could be witnessed from the media coverage and discussion.

One would find a convergence of the moral foundations of the Indian Constitution and the gospel on human dignity and democratic values.[47] But, regrettably, the Indian Catholic leadership is timid and lacks the courage to speak truth to power. The leaders do not want to rock the boat. Gripped by a siege mentality, the Indian Catholic leadership isolates itself by digging moats all around the citadel of the

Church. Further, the division of the bishops into ritual conferences has sapped the energies of the Indian Catholic Church and has broken its unity to stand together for the cause of the people, for justice and human rights. Ironically, ever since the ritual division, the Oriental Catholic Churches are embroiled in scandalous internal strife on the rubrics and modality of celebrating the eucharist, leaving little time, energy and dedication to the cause of the central values of the gospel.

Be that as it may, it is at the periphery that priests, religious, and laypeople courageously struggle for democratization of the country in the remotest villages of India in the most trying conditions. They have a model in the eighteenth century St Devasahayam from Kanyakumari district, the first lay person from India to be canonized recently. He was courageous enough to speak up for equality and against the caste system although he himself hailed from upper caste Hindu Nairs and suffered criticism from his own community on account of his being Christian.[48]

Priests, men and women religious, and many laypeople and young students have been involved since the late 1970s in various human rights movements and have created at the grassroots level consciousness about human dignity and rights, equality, and justice and have promoted the agency of ordinary people and their participation. Joining various grassroots movements and what was known as "action groups," they focused on specific issues – the unorganized labourers, domestic workers, displaced people, refugees, migrants, victims of human trafficking, etc. Slowly, networks were built by which individual initiatives of groups were mutually strengthened. The Catholic Social Teaching inspired them.[49]

The contribution of Indian Catholicism to democratic life in the broader society can take on different forms. It could be in the form of participation by the faithful in democratic and civil society movements focused on specific issues. It could instil a democratic spirit through advocacy programmes and through media. Most Indian Catholic media are oriented to promote piety and devotion and cover ecclesiastical news about Vatican, bishops, and the religious.[50] Another important way the Catholic Church can nurture democratization is by using the reach and influence it has in education. Do the students passing through Catholic schools and colleges imbibe the democratic spirit and are they trained in democratic values? Have these educational institutions observed democratic values in practice? Do the students and staff in Catholic educational institutions have the freedom to speak out their minds without fear? Another important way the Indian Catholic Church could contribute to democratization is by including women in leadership positions rather than paying mere lip service to them. This would automatically accelerate democratization.

Unlike in pre-Independent India when, thanks to the active involvement of the laity, a serious discussion took place among Catholics about public issues, including democracy; today, this is almost totally absent.[51] However, *Indian Currents*, a weekly journal brought out under the patronage of the Capuchins of North India, has been making a very critical and constructive contribution to the promotion of democracy, justice, peace, and human rights.[52] It carries analysis and comments by many intellectuals across religious boundaries bearing upon current social and political events in the country. It is also creating political consciousness among educated Indian Catholics, priests, and bishops.

To trace back history, a Catholic Indian Association was formed in 1889 to bring to the public realm and to the authorities of the state the grievances and demands of the Catholic community.[53] The All India Catholic Union (AIUC) was created in 1919. Among its declared objectives are: "To spread the influence of Catholic ideals and principles in Indian public life through any medium of communication and promote unity and solidarity among the people of India through Christian endeavour. To be the exponent of Catholic opinion and to make representations to authorities and public bodies in all matters affecting Catholics."[54] The bishops of the country are so very concerned about their control also of the public realm that even bodies like AIUC cannot function effectively, with their freedom curtailed. This shows a certain pattern at work from the early twentieth century on when "social and political activity could only be allowed to occur under the firm grip of ecclesiastical authority."[55] The Indian Catholic Church appears to be immersed, especially in the last couple of decades, in the issue of minority rights and anything connected with their infringement. It has yet to demonstrate its serious engagement with larger political issues like democracy, inclusion, and participation.

To take on the mission of democratization in the broader society, the Indian Catholic Church needs to create an ethos of democracy within its own life. The associational life within the Church could become the nursery for the development of skills that support and sustain democratic life in the society and country. Basic Christian Communities or Basic Ecclesial Communities, wherever they are vibrant, have the potential to contribute to a culture of equality, dialogue, sharing, and democratic spirit.[56] With all their limitations, they seem to have helped the better functioning of the participatory structures introduced by Vatican II.

Concluding Reflections

Regarding the Indian Catholic community, it is unlikely that it will experience a similar phenomenon of *'Church exodus'* seen in the western world, primarily driven by secularization, clerical sexual abuse, Church-tax and so on. In India, the Churches continue to thrive making it difficulty to foresee such a scenario in the near future.

However, a noticeable trend is the gradual decline of the Catholic community's public influence and impact within the national sphere, particularly in relation to its extensive involvement in educational, charitable, and healthcare institutions. In contrast to its historical role as a benefactor, the Catholic Church is currently perceived as a competitor in various fields where it previously excelled. In fact, a competitive and commercial mindset has infiltrated Indian Catholicism. Many Church-run educational institutions have become profit-oriented. The revitalization of Indian Catholicism hinges on its ability to act as a catalyst for democratization within the broader society, instilling the values and principles it embodies across all aspects of life. This necessitates increased political engagement by the Catholic Church.

In order to fulfil this broader mission of democratization, it is necessary to nurture a democratic spirit and uphold democratic values within the Church, both in its practices and organizational framework. By fostering these democratic principles, the Indian Catholic Church can overcome the dual challenges posed by the hierarchical understanding inherited from the missionary era and the hierarchical structure associated with caste-based discrimination and inequality. It is evident that democratization extends beyond a mere liberal agenda and holds deeper implications for the transformation of both the Church and the larger society. The litmus test for gauging the progress of democratization within Indian Catholicism lies in the inclusion and equal participation of Dalits, tribals, and women, letting them have full access to leadership roles.

The traditional avenues for the Catholic Church to make an impact on society continue to shrink. Against this background, the case of Dalit Catholics offers a bright prospect. Their involvement in the Church and in society will make a difference in Indian society in terms of justice, equality, inclusion, and representation. These belong to the very core of Christianity. The Dalit Catholics could become the heralds of these values in a hierarchical Church and a caste-ridden society. It is by activating the agency of the Dalit community that the prospects of the future of the Catholic Church could be ensured. For they know what the absence of value of freedom, participation, and agency means, and hence could be a formidable force to infuse the spirit and values of democracy into public life.

Moreover, a reform centered on democracy would necessitate a radical undertaking to extirpate the deeply ingrained casteism within the Church. This issue exists not only among the laity but, more significantly, among the clergy and religious congregations. The clergy and religious reflect the caste-based reality within the Catholic community, and, due to their positions of power, perpetuate it further. Considering the ongoing economic advancement and demographic shifts such as declining family size among Catholics, it is highly probable that a crisis could emerge in less than two decades, leading to a significant decline in vocations to priesthood and religious life. The early indications of this trend are already evident. Hopefully, this circumstance will awaken a heightened sense of pragmatism, paving the way for the eradication of power struggles within the Church's structures. Subsequently, attention can be directed towards the most essential aspects of the Christian faith, which will promote equality and foster greater communion within the Church community.

NOTES

1   There are two interconnected questions at play here. The first pertains to the conception and practice of democracy within the Church, where the second question revolves around the vision and attitude of the Church towards democracy in the wider world and society. Often, these two issues cannot be disentangled. In this chapter, we will address both aspects, placing particular emphasis on the ongoing struggle for participatory governance within the Catholic Church in alignment with democratic principles.

2   Peter Berger, "Christianity and Democracy. The Global Picture," in *Journal of Democracy* 15, no. 2 (April 2004): 76–80.

3   Cf. Edward Schillebeeckx, *Church. The Human Story of God* (London: SCM Press, 1990), 204; see also Bernt T. Oftestad, *The Catholic Church and the Liberal Democracy* (Oxford: Routledge, 2019).

4   On the global discussion on democracy and Catholicism, see Eugene C. Bianchi and Rosemary Radford Ruether, eds., *A Democratic Catholic Church. The Reconstruction of Roman Catholicism* (New York: Crossroad, 1992). Emile Perreau-Saussine, *Catholicsim and Democracy: An Essay in the History of Political Thought* (Princeton: Princeton University Press, 2012); Michael J. Schuck and John Crowley-Buck, eds., *Democracy, Culture, Catholicism: Voices from Four Continents,* (New York: Fordham University Press, 2016); Grasso, Kenneth L, Bradley, Gerard V, and Robert Hunt P, eds., *Catholicism, Liberalism, and Communitarianism: The Catholic Intellectual Tradition and the Moral Foundations of Democracy* (London: Rowman & Littlefield, 1995); George Weigel, *Catholicism and the Renewal of American Democracy* (New York: Paulist Press, 1989); Elizabeth A. Fenton, *Religious Liberties: Anti-Catholicism and Liberal Democracy in Nineteenth-century U.S. Literature and Culture* (New York: Oxford University Press, 2011); Frances Hagopian, ed., *Religious Pluralism, Democracy, and the Catholic Church in Latin America* (Notre Dame: Notre Dame University Press, 2009); Jay P Corrin, *Catholic Intellectuals and the Challenge of Democracy* (Notre Dame: Notre Dame University Press 2002). Thomas Bokenkotter, *Church and Revolution: Catholics in the Struggle for Democracy and Social Justice* (New York: Image, 1998).

5   *State of Democracy in South Asia. A Report* by the SDSA Team (Delhi: Oxford University Press, 2008), 31.

6   Cf. R. Bruce Douglass and David Hollenbach, *Catholicism and Liberalism. Contributions to American Public Philosophy* (Cambridge: Cambridge University Press, 1994); Daniel Philpott and Ryan T. Anderson, eds., *A Liberalism Safe for Catholicism? Perspectives from the Review of Politics* (Notre Dame: Notre Dame University Press, 2017).

7   Sebasti L, Raj and G.F. Xavier Raj, eds., *Caste Culture in Indian Church: The Response of Church to the Problem of Caste within the Christian Community* (New Delhi: Indian Social Institute, 1993); George Koilparampil, *Caste in the Catholic Community in Kerala: A Study of Caste Elements in the Inter Rite Relationships of Syrians and Latins* (Cochin: St Teresa's College, 1982); Ninan Koshy, *Caste in the Kerala Churches* (Bangalore: The Christian Institute for the Study of Religion and Society, 1968); Chandra Mallampalli, *Christians and Public Life in Colonial South India, 1863-1937: Contending with Marginality* (London: Routledge Curzon, 2004).

8   Cf. Ducan B. Forrester, *Caste and Christianity. Attitudes and Policies on Caste of Anglo-Saxon Protestant Missions in India* (London: University of London, 1979).

9 Cf. Robert Eric Frykenberg and Alaine M. Low, eds., *Christians and Missionaries in India: Cross-cultural Communication since 1500, with Special Reference to Caste, Conversion, and Colonialism* (Grand Rapids, Mich.: W.B. Eerdmans Pub., 2003).

10 The first indication of the Church's openness to democracy came with the Christmas Message of Pope Pius XII in 1944.

11 Cf. John W. O'Malley, *What Happened at Vatican II* (Cambridge MS: Harvard University Press, 2008), 36–43.

12 Cf. J. Bryan Hehir, "Roman Catholicism and Democracy: The Post Conciliar Era," in George E. Demacapoulos and Aristotle Papanikolau, eds., *Christianity, Democracy, and the Shadow of Constantine* (New York: Fordham University Press, 2016).

13 Jean Leclercq, "Introduction," in *Pseudo-Dionysius. The Complete Works* (New York: Paulist Press, 1987), 31.

14 Cf. Walter Brueggemann, *The Prophetic Imagination* (Minneapolis: Fortress Press, 2001).

15 Cf. Hans Küng, *The Church* (London: Search Press, 1968); see also Hans von Campenhausen, *Ecclesiastical Authority and Spiritual Power in the Church of the First Three Centuries* (London: Adam & Charles Black, 1969).

16 Cf. Gerhard Lohfink, *Jesus and Community. The Social Dimension of Christian Faith* (London: SPCK, 1985),115–132.

17 Cf. Yves Congar, "Quod omnes tangit, ab omnibus tractari et approbari debet," *Revue historique de droit français et étranger* 35 (1958): 210–259.

18 Cf. John Beal, "Toward a Democratic Church: The Canonical Heritage," in Eugene C. Bianchi and Rosemary Radford Ruether, eds., *A Democratic Catholic Chuch* (New York: Crossroad, 1992), 52–79.

19 Cf. John Coleman, "Not Democracy but Democratization," in Eugene C. Bianchi and Rosemary Radford Ruether, eds., *A Democratic Catholic Church*, 229.

20 Cf. Charles Curran, "What Catholic Ecclesiology Can Learn from Official Catholic Social Teaching," in Eugene C. Bianchi and Rosemary Radford Ruether, eds., *A Democratic Catholic Church, op. cit.,* 94–112; ID., *Catholic Social Teaching 1891 – Present* (Georgetown: Georgetown University Press, 2002).

21 *Justice in the World*, 40.

22 Cf. "Synodalities," special issue of *Concilium* 2021/2.

23 Cf. Sabine Demel, "From Junior Helpers to Valued Collaborators: Giving the Laity Their Rightful Place in the Clergy-Centred Church," in *Concilium* 2016/5, 78–89.

24 What was expected of the Latin Code of Canon Law (1983), namely to reflect the Vatican II understanding of the Church and translate it into legal provisions, unfortunately, did not materialize. The power of governance, for

example, is reserved only for the clergy and not the lay faithful. It means that one could exercise the power of governance if only he (no she) is ordained. According to CIC canon 129, the laity do not have any power of governance by themselves but can only cooperate (*ad normam iuris cooperari possunt*) in the exercise of the clerical power of governance. Cf. Felix Wilfred, "Theology and Canon Law: Journeying Together," in *Concilium* 2016/5, 41–52.

25   Cf. Sebastian S. Karambai, "Consultative Bodies in the Particular Churches Revisited in the Light of *Evangelii Gaudium*," in Adrian Loretan and Felix Wilfred, eds., *Revision of the Codes. An Indian-European Dialogue* (Zürich: LIT Verlag, 2018), 283–292.

26   As quoted in Yves Congar, *Power and Poverty in the Church* (London: Geoffrey Chapman, 1964), 43.

27   Cf. Adrian Loretan and Felix Wilfred, eds., *Revision of the Codes. An Indian-European Dialogue* (Zürich: LIT Verlag, 2018).

28   Cf. Philip Berryman, "Other Experiences, Other Concerns: Latin America and the Democratization of the Church," in Eugene C. Bianchi and Rosemary Radford Ruether, eds., *A Democratic Catholic Church, op. cit.,*128–138, at 138.

29   Prakash Louis, "A Prophetic Evangelization for Dalit Salvation," in Felix Wilfred and John Romus, eds., *Local Churches in South Asia and Evangelization* (Kolkata: Morning Star Regional Seminary), 388.

30   Cf. Vinil Baby Paul, "Onesimus to Philemon: Runaway Slaves and Religious Conversion in Colonial Kerala, India, 1816–1855, in *International Journal of Asian Christianity* 4. no.1 (2021): 50–71, at 53. See also C.J. Mathew, "Empowerment and Agency of Dalit Catholics of Kottayam District, Kerala" (Unpublished PhD dissertation written under my supervision and submitted to the University of Madras, 2012).

31   C. J. Mathew, "Empowerment and Agency of Dalit Catholics of Kottayam District, Kerala," 197.

32   Cf. Felix Wilfred, "Dalit Future: Future of the Nation," in *Vidyajyoti Journal of Theological Reflection* 73 (2009): 325–336. ID., *Christians for a Better India* (Delhi: ISPCK, 2014).

33   https://www.cbci.in/DownloadMat/dalit-policy.pdf [accessed on 22 April 2023].

34   For the text of the policy, see the reference above, footnote no. 33.

35   In a personal conversation with the author on 21 May 2021. S. Lourdusamy, Cosmon Arockiaraj, and Devsagaya Raj have served as secretaries of the Scheduled Caste [Dalit]/Scheduled Tribe Commission of the Catholic Bishops Conference of India (CBCI). See also Felix Wilfred and Cosmon Arockiaraj, "Towards an Indo-Dalit Individual Church and Rite: A Proposal," *Journal of Indian Theology* xiv, no. 2 (2021): 8–30.

36   Cf. Felix Wilfred, "Catholics," in Kenneth R. Ross et al., eds., *Christianity in South and Central Asia* (Edinburgh: Edinburgh University Press, 2019), 211–22.

37   According to the Eastern Code of Canon Law, "a rite is a liturgical, theological, spiritual, and disciplinary heritage, differentiated by the culture and the circumstances of the history of peoples, which is expressed by each Church *sui iuris* in its own manner of living the faith" (Canon 28 § 1). The Dalits seem to possess all these elements, which will justify their claim for a separate "Dalit Rite" within the Catholic communion. On the possibility of new rites, see the contribution of a canonist author, Frederick R. McManus, "The Possibility of New Rites in the Church," in *The Jurist* 50 (1990) 435 – 458.

38   Samuel Huntington, *The Third Wave. Democratization in the Late Twentieth Century* (Norman and London: Oklahoma University Press, 1991), 76; see also J. Troy, "'Catholic Waves' of Democratization? Roman Catholicism and Its Potential for Democratization," in *Democratization* 16, no. 6 (2009): 1093–1114; Fabio Bolzonar, "A Christian Democratization of Politics? The New Influence of Catholicism on Italian Politics since the Demise of the Democrazia Cristiana," in *Journal of Modern Italian Studies*, 21 (2016), 445–463.

39   Mary John, *Indian Catholic Christians and Nationalism. A Study Based on the Official Catholic Journals of the Period 1857-1947* (Delhi: ISPCK, 2011), 42.

40   Cf. Mario Prayer, "The Vatican Church and Gandhi's India 1920-1948," in *Social Scientist* 37, no. 1/2 (2009): 39–63.

41   On the controversy over the papal negation of the audience to Gandhi, see Chandra Mallampalli, *Christians and Public Life in Colonial South India, 1863-1937* (London: Routledge, 2004), 96–98.

42   Cf. Mary John, *Indian Catholic Christians and Nationalism, op.cit., passim.*

43   Cf. Julius Bautista, "Catholic Democratization: Religious Networks and Political Agency in the Philippines and Timor-Leste," in *Sojourn: Journal of Social Issues in Southeast Asia* 35, no. 2 (2020): 310–342.

44   There was a laudable exception – Archbishop Arockiasamy of Bangalore.

45   Archbishop of Bangalore P. Arockiasmay, as quoted in M. Roekaerts, *Christians and Emergency in India* (Brussels: Pro Mundi Vita Dossiers, 1980), 24.

46   https://www.indiatoday.in/india/story/delhi-archbishop-s-letter-turbulent-political-atmosphere-let-s-pray-for-new-govt-in-2019-1238564-2018-05-22 [accessed on 31 May 2021].

47   Cf. John Romus Devasahayam, *Human Dignity in Indian Secularism and in Christianity* (Bangalore: Claretian Publications, 2007).

48   Cf. John Kulandai E., *A Saint for Our Times. Martyr St Devasahayam. A Comprehensive Historical Research* (Nagercoil: Asssi Press, 2022).

49   Well-known is the involvement of Fr Stan Lourdusamy, a Jesuit priest who spent all his life for the democratization of the Indian polity and in defence of the poor and the marginalized and stood for their rights. Precisely the priests, nuns and laity who are in the forefront appear to be the beacon of hope for the future of Catholicism in India, and they are champions of democracy.

50   The Catholic Church also runs several TV stations. These serve as an extension of Church-activities with almost no public impact. The programmes are designed to cater to the pietism of the Catholics. They transmit mass, rosary recitation, way of the cross during Lent, and such religious activities, and occasionally preaching by Church-leaders and the clergy. See, for example: https://catholicmediaindia.blogspot.com/p/catholic-media-india.html.

51   Cf. Mary John, *Indian Catholic Christians and Nationalism, op.cit.*

52   See the official website of *Indian Currents*: https://www.indiancurrents.org/.

53   The Indian Catholic Association appears to have been an Indian version of "*Action Catholique*"(Catholic Action), which was vigorously promoted in Europe and other parts of the Christian world to safeguard Catholic identity in the public realm and protect Catholics from modern and secular influences.

54   See the official website www.aiuc.in [accessed on 28 May 2021].

55   Chandra Mallampalli, *Christians and Public Life in Colonial South India, 1863-1937*, 90.

56   The role of Basic Christian Communities introduced in India in the 1980s is ambiguous as to their impact on the larger society and their contribution to democratic values. In many instances, they simply function as an extension of the institutional Church and its management of spiritual goods.

FURTHER READING

Bautista, Julius. "Catholic Democratization: Religious Networks and Political Agency in the Philippines and Timor-Leste." *Sojourn: Journal of Social Issues in Southeast Asia* 35, no. 2 (2020): 310–342.

Beal, John. "Toward a Democratic Church: The Canonical Heritage." In Eugene C. Bianchi and Rosemary Radford Ruether, eds., *A Democratic Catholic Chuch*, 52–79. New York: Crossroad, 1992.

Berger, Peter. "Christianity and Democracy. The Global Picture." In *Journal of Democracy* 15, no. 2 (April 2004): 76–80.

Berryman, Philip. "Other Experiences, Other Concerns: Latin America and the Democratization of the Church." In Bianchi, Eugene C, and Rosemary Radford Ruether, eds. *A Democratic Catholic Church. The Reconstruction of Roman Catholicism*, 128–138. New York: Crossroad, 1992.

Bokenkotter, Thomas. *Church and Revolution: Catholics in the Struggle for Democracy and Social Justice.* New York: Image, 1998.

Bolzonar, Fabio. "A Christian Democratization of Politics? The New Influence of Catholicism on Italian Politics since the Demise of the Democrazia Cristiana." *Journal of Modern Italian Studies* 21 (2016): 445–463.

Brueggemann, Walter. *The Prophetic Imagination.* Minneapolis: Fortress Press, 2001.

Campenhausen, Hans von. *Ecclesiastical Authority and Spiritual Power in the Church of the First Three Centuries.* London: Adam & Charles Black, 1969.

Coleman, John. "Not Democracy but Democratization." In Eugene C. Bianchi and Rosemary Radford Ruether, eds., *A Democratic Catholic Church.* New York: Crossroad, 1992.

Congar, Yves. "Quod omnes tangit, ab omnibus tractari et approbari debet." *Revue historique de droit français et étranger* 35 (1958): 210–259.

Congar, Yves. *Power and Poverty in the Church.* London: Geoffrey Chapman, 1964.

Corrin, Jay P. *Catholic Intellectuals and the Challenge of Democracy.* Notre Dame: Notre Dame University Press, 2002.

Curran, Charles. "What Catholic Ecclesiology Can Learn from Official Catholic Social Teaching." In Eugene C. Bianchi and Rosemary Radford Ruether, eds., *A Democratic Catholic Church,* 94–112. New York: Crossroad, 1992.

Curran, Charles. *Catholic Social Teaching 1891 – Present.* Georgetown: Georgetown University Press, 2002.

Demel, Sabine. "From Junior Helpers to Valued Collaborators: Giving the Laity Their Rightful Place in the Clergy-Centred Church." In *Concilium* 2016/5, 78–89.

Devasahayam, John Romus. *Human Dignity in Indian Secularism and in Christianity.* Bangalore: Claretian Publications, 2007.

Douglass, R. Bruce, and David Hollenbach. *Catholicism and Liberalism. Contributions to American Public Philosophy.* Cambridge: Cambridge University Press, 1994.

Fenton, Elizabeth A. *Religious Liberties: Anti-Catholicism and Liberal Democracy in Nineteenth-century U.S. Literature and Culture.* New York: Oxford University Press, 2011.

Forrester, Ducan B. *Caste and Christianity. Attitudes and Policies on Caste of Anglo-Saxon Protestant Missions in India.* London: University of London, 1979.

Frykenberg, Robert Eric, and Alaine M Low, eds. *Christians and Missionaries in India: Cross-cultural Communication since 1500, with Special Reference to Caste, Conversion, and Colonialism.* Grand Rapids, Mich.: W.B. Eerdmans Pub., 2003.

Grasso, Kenneth L, Gerard V Bradley, and Hunt P Robert, eds. *Catholicism, Liberalism, and Communitarianism: The Catholic Intellectual Tradition and the Moral Foundations of Democracy*. London: Rowman & Littlefield, 1995.

Hagopian, Frances, ed. *Religious Pluralism, Democracy, and the Catholic Church in Latin America*. Notre Dame: Notre Dame University Press, 2009.

Hehir, J. Bryan. "Roman Catholicism and Democracy: The Post Conciliar Era." In George E. Demacapoulos and Papanikolau, Aristotle, eds., *Christianity, Democracy, and the Shadow of Constantine*. New York: Fordham University Press, 2016.

Huntington, Samuel. *The Third Wave. Democratization in the Late Twentieth Century*. Norman: Oklahoma University Press, 1991.

John, Mary. *Indian Catholic Christians and Nationalism. A Study Based on the Official Catholic Journals of the Period 1857-1947*. Delhi: ISPCK, 2011.

Karambai, Sebastian S. "Consultative Bodies in the Particular Churches Revisited in the Light of *Evangelii Gaudium*." In Adrian Loretan and Felix Wilfred, eds., *Revision of the Codes. An Indian-European Dialogue*, 283-292. Zürich: LIT Verlag, 2018.

Koilparampil, George. *Caste in the Catholic Community in Kerala: A Study of Caste Elements in the Inter Rite Relationships of Syrians and Latins*. Cochin: St Teresa's College, 1982.

Koshy, Ninan. *Caste in the Kerala Churches*. Bangalore: The Christian Institute for the Study of Religion and Society, 1968.

Küng, Hans. *The Church*. London: Search Press, 1968.

Leclercq, Jean. "Introduction." *Pseudo-Dionysius. The Complete Works*. New York: Paulist Press, 1987.

Lohfink, Gerhard. *Jesus and Community. The Social Dimension of Christian Faith*. London: SPCK, 1985.

Loretan, Adrian, and Felix Wilfred, eds. *Revision of the Codes. An Indian-European Dialogue*. Zuerich: LIT Verlag, 2018.

Louis, Prakash. "A Prophetic Evangelization for Dalit Salvation." In Felix Wilfred and John Romus, eds., *Local Churches in South Asia and Evangelization*, 384-401. Kolkata: Morning Star Regional Seminary, 2020.

Mallampalli, Chandra. *Christians and Public Life in Colonial South India, 1863-1937*. London: Routledge, 2004.

Mathew, C.J. "Empowerment and Agency of Dalit Catholics of Kottayam District, Kerala." Unpublished PhD dissertation, University of Madras, 2012.

McManus, Frederick R. "The Possibility of New Rites in the Church." *The Jurist* 50 (1990): 435–458.

O'Malley, John W. *What Happened at Vatican II*. Cambridge MS: Harvard University Press, 2008.

Oftestad, Bernt T. *The Catholic Church and the Liberal Democracy*. Oxford: Routledge, 2019.

Paul, Vinil Baby. "Onesimus to Philemon: Runaway Slaves and Religious Conversation in Colonial Kerala, India, 1816-1855." *International Journal of Asian Christianity* 4. no. 1 (2021): 50–71.

Perreau-Saussine, Emile. *Catholicism and Democracy: An Essay in the History of Political Thought*. Princeton: Princeton University Press, 2012.

Philpott, Daniel, and Ryan T Anderson, eds. *A Liberalism Safe for Catholicism? Perspectives from the Review of Politics*. Notre Dame: Notre Dame University Press, 2017.

Prayer, Mario. "The Vatican Church and Gandhi's India 1920-1948." *Social Scientist* 37, no. 1/2 (2009): 39–63.

Pro Mundi Vita Dossiers. *Christians and Emergency in India*. Brussels: 1980.

Schillebeeckx, Edward. *Church. The Human Story of God*. London: SCM Press, 1990.

Schuck, Michael J, and John Crowley-Buck, eds. *Democracy, Culture, Catholicism: Voices from Four Continents*. New York: Fordham University Press, 2016.

SDSA Team. *State of Democracy in South Asia*. Delhi: Oxford University Press, 2008.

Sebasti L, Raj, and G.F. Xavier Raj, eds. *Caste Culture in Indian Church: The Response of Church to the Problem of Caste within the Christian Community*. New Delhi: Indian Social Institute, 1993.

Troy, J. "'Catholic Waves of Democratization? Roman Catholicism and Its Potential for Democratization." *Democratization* 16, no. 6 (2009):1093–1114.

Weigel, George. *Catholicism and the Renewal of American Democracy*. New York: Paulist Press, 1989.

Wilfred, Felix, and Cosmon Arockiaraj. "Towards an Indo-Dalit Individual Church and Rite: A Proposal." *Journal of Indian Theology* xiv, no. 2 (2021): 8–30.

Wilfred, Felix. "Catholics." In Kenneth R. Ross et al., eds., *Christianity in South and Central Asia*, 211–222. Edinburgh: Edinburgh University Press, 2019.

Wilfred, Felix. "Dalit Future: Future of the Nation." *Vidyajyoti Journal of Theological Reflection* 73 (2009): 325–336.

Wilfred, Felix. "Theology and Canon Law: Journeying Together." *Concilium* 2016/5, 41–52.

Wilfred, Felix. *Christians for a Better India*. Delhi: ISPCK, 2014.

CHURCH RENEWAL

CROSSING A MILLENNIAL THRESHOLD
CHURCH IN INDIA ON THE SYNODAL PATH

Synodality has emerged as a prominent ecclesiastical discourse since the advent of Pope Francis. His prominence has only grown with the announcement of a synod on synodality scheduled for October 2023, a significant event expected to conclude in October 2024, allowing nearly three years of extensive preparation. The theme of the synod is aptly articulated as "For a Synodal Church: Communion, Participation, and Mission," a reflection of its profound significance. Pope Francis underscores the epoch-making nature of the synod, envisioning it as the guiding path for a Church in the third millennium - a grand scale vision indeed.[1] In his view, the synod represents a transformative process, reshaping the hierarchical structure of the Church into a more inclusive and participatory model. It is a process of making the Church an inverted pyramid.[2]

A preparatory document for the synod (*instrumentum laboris*) along with a Handbook (*vademecum*) with questions to facilitate reflections and discernment at the local Churches was released by the Vatican on 7 September 2021.[3] Further, on the basis of national reports, National and continental assemblies have already completed pooling together the reflections of the people of God. To facilitate continental assemblies, Vatican published in October 2022, a *Working Document for the Continental Stage*.[4] This was created collating the insights from the national reports.

As for theological reflections in the country, quite early on, in March 2022, St Peter's Pontificate Institute, Bengaluru, took the initiative to organize a mammoth national conference on synodality with over six hundred participants and presentation of close to sixty papers analyzing synodality from various angles, with emphatic reference to the Indian context.[5] With so much of serious preparations, there is hope that the Synodal Assemblies in October 2023 and in October 24 will bring about tangible results. Expectations are high among the people for a real turning point in the life of the Catholic Church and in its governance. We can only hope that the projected two assemblies of the Synod will not belie the increased expectations of the people to see a real change leading to the renewal of the face of the Church.

The present chapter intends to reflect on the ecclesial and social contexts in which the discourse on synodality is taking place, the shift of accent and expansion that have occurred in its understanding, and the dynamics involved in synodality for the life, communion, governance, and mission of the Church. It also highlights the need to be attentive to the anthropological foundation for the functioning of synodality. Pope Francis is concerned about beginning the right processes and not excessively preoccupied reaching a priori-set goals. This approach is important in any group or community of people for fostering unity, cohesion, and synergy. In that sense, synodality will be the beginning of a new process that eventually should lead to radical changes, as we will see in the proposals in the concluding reflections of the present chapter.

From Synod of Bishops to the Synod of the Church – Tracing the Theological Trajectory

In 1870, when the German bishops returned to their homeland after the abrupt end of Council Vatican I, which proclaimed the universal supremacy of the pope and his infallibility, the then-German Chancellor Otto von Bismarck mocked them. In a statement, he said that the bishops had become simply minions and officers of the pope with no power of their own.[6] The following one hundred years of history until Vatican II bore witness to the juridically diminutive role of bishops. Balancing the power of papal office and that of bishops was one of the crucial tasks of Vatican II, which, following the New Testament data and early Christian tradition, banked on the concept of collegiality.

The pope and the bishops stand in a collegial relationship just like Peter and the other apostles, and they jointly bear the responsibility for the entire Church. The bishops are not executives of the pope but have the power of their own to govern the local Churches. The ecumenical councils are the most intense expression of collegiality. But then ecumenical councils happen once in a couple of centuries. How can we translate the grand idea of collegiality and co-responsibility into everyday ecclesial life? Paul VI found a response in the ancient practice of synods. In 1965, he instituted the synod of bishops as a permanent body. From time to time, a select number of bishops gather together and counsel the pope on issues affecting the Church globally and sometimes locally.

Now, what Pope Francis has done is to expand further the idea and practice of the synod into a principle of synodality. In simple terms, there is to be not only the synod of bishops; the whole Church needs to be on the synodal path in everyday life and at all levels. Therefore, he has projected a synod of the entire Church, going beyond the synod of bishops. Some of the participatory structures like the pastoral council, parish council, parish/diocesan financial council, and presbyteral council proposed by Vatican II contained embryonically the idea of synodality, which has been a central organizing principle of the Orthodox Churches throughout the centuries. Therefore, the synod on synodality has a great task of reflecting on a principle that has far-reaching consequences for the reform and renewal of the Church.

The Conciliar Hermeneutics and Expansion of Synodality

How did this expansion come about from the synod of bishops to the synod of the Church? Pope Francis does not quote Vatican II as often as one may expect. What he does, instead, is to make a new phase in the reception of the Council, projecting its significance far beyond its texts and the context of its emergence. The meaning of any text, to adopt a distinction by Paul Ricoeur, is not exhausted by bringing out what the author meant by employing historical-critical method. The text has not only a meaning "behind" it, but also "in front of it."[7] It means that we pay attention not only to what Vatican II said but also to what it points to. This seems to be the hermeneutical path of Pope Francis. He is deeply interested in discovering with the entire Church the future to which Vatican II can lead us. He has made his own the method, process, and style of Vatican II. Here is a novelty.

Pope Francis' announcement of a synod on synodality is to be seen in the light of his new reception of Vatican II and his hermeneutics of the Council. He has made a new appropriation of *Gaudium et Spes* – The Church in the Modern World, and rightly so. For, as Massimo Faggioli observes, "the Future of Vatican II in the Church cannot be separated from the future of *Gaudium et Spes*."[8] For Pope Francis, synodality is not only an intra-ecclesial matter but also a mode of relating the Church with society, with the larger world.

It is precisely to continue the spirit of collegiality into the life of the Church as a permanent feature that Pope Paul VI instituted the Synod of Bishops, which would gather from time to time to discuss issues and questions of great importance for the life of the Church and advice the pope on the same. However, the concrete experiences of synods since Vatican II have shown that whether it is an issue of justice, family, or youth, each of those synods revolved around the bishops because all of them were simply named synods of *bishops*. Let me recall here my experience with the Plenary Assembly of FABC in Tokyo (1986), where I had the privilege of delivering the keynote address. The Assembly was in preparation for the Roman Synod on the laity. When I suggested why not a large number of laypeople participate in a synod on the laity, Archbishop Jan Schotte (later cardinal), Secretary General of the Synod of Bishops, Rome, who participated in the Assembly, responded by saying that it was a synod of *bishops*. He repeated it twice. He meant to say that others do not have much place in the synod since it is supposed to be a gathering of bishops alone.

Synods happen once in a while, and ecumenical councils once in centuries. Synodal way of life cannot be once in a while; it is a matter of every day. The life of the Church and its mission involves all the faithful who are equal disciples of Jesus by virtue of baptism. The Synod on synodality wants to reinforce the fact that the Church is larger than the bishops, and the issues that affect its life, governance, and mission have to do with all the faithful, requiring also their own active participation. How do we ensure such participation? Pope Francis has come out with a bright idea that the concept of synod need not be restricted only to the case of bishops but should become a general principle for the life and future mission of the Church. It is remarkable that he has invited no less than seventy people in the pew - laymen and women - to participate in the forthcoming synod, who will also have *voting right*.[9]

The experience of the Church community since Vatican II and the functioning of the many participative structures have contributed to deepening the synodal nature of the Church. Even more, we begin to see that collegiality itself is an expression of synodality at the ministerial level. The bishops and the pope walk together to serve the Church and its mission.

Rehabilitating the Ecclesiology of the People of God

The synodal approach involving the entire Church also means a new reception of the definition of the Church as the "people of God" by Vatican II, which brought about a "Copernican revolution." Here is another novelty of the present pope. When people became active through significant new movements in the Church and initiatives like Basic Christian Communities, it was feared that the Church could become "populist." Hence under the previous two papacies of John Paul II and Benedict XVI, the definition of "people of God" by Vatican II was downplayed. Instead, one sought to foreground the definition of the Church as communion, which came across for many people as vague, and they could not draw out practical consequences for the everyday life and mission of the Church.

The rehabilitation of the people of God ecclesiology by Pope Francis is based on its deeper biblical meaning, namely the Church as *qahal* Yahweh - assembly or community of the people convoked by God, and it is not based on populism. They are a people characterized as being on the way. That is precisely what the word "synod" - derived from Greek – means: to be together on the way. In this sense, synodality could be best correlated to the definition of the Church as the people of God than any other description. The people of God are endowed with the sense of faith instinct (*sensus fidelium*) which is an embodied trigger for synodality.

Communion, indeed, is a crucial concept bringing out the nature of the Church. However, it should not be divorced from but brought in close relationship to the reality of the Church as the people of God. The life of the people of God is characterized by communion, and its governance is facilitated by structures of communion proposed by Vatican II, such as the pastoral council, presbyteral council, parish council and so on. The Eucharist, the sacrament of unity and communion, should animate and nourish the functioning of these institutional structures of synodality. In this way, these bodies, far from being bodies of power and power conflict, will be facilitating means for learning from one another and will serve the community's common good and mission to the world and society.

The Ecclesial Context

Let us first look at the changing ecclesial scenario clamouring for synodality. There is an unmistakable disaffection among the people. For, the expectations of Vatican II are not met in the practice of the Church and its administration. They observe a glaring discrepancy between the grand Conciliar vision of the Church as people of God and the ground reality. Further, there is also an unease regarding the centralized mode of administration and awareness of the disastrous situations it can bring about. Moreover, one could sense increasing disappointment with decisions taken arbitrarily without discernment and consultation by the clergy, telling upon the Church's credibility and witnessing potential.

This general mood is exacerbated by the global exposition of clerical sexual abuse, raising critical questions on how the Church of Christ could be trusted when managed by clerics. In India, numerous cases of sexual abuse by priests and even some bishops are increasingly brought to public attention. At bottom, such abuse is a matter of abuse of power and "a structural betrayal of trust."[10] It has opened up the urgent necessity to revise the understanding of power and its exercise in the Church.

Further, experiences in different parts of the world, including the central offices of the Roman Curia, have exposed financial corruption among the hierarchy and clergy.[11] Sexual scandals and financial corruption at the highest level of the Church called for severe censoring and even scaling down some cardinals from their exalted positions by Pope Francis.[12] Do not the pope's ecclesiastical sanctions point also to the need for a human rights-derived criminal law in the Church?

Two recent acts of the pope confirm the earnestness with which he views the synodal approach. First, on 6 August 2020, he appointed six women to the top Council overseeing the Vatican's finances. Are we to think that he trusts women in financial matters more than high-ranking clerics? Second, on 6 February 2021, Sister Nathalie Becquart was appointed as undersecretary of the Synod of Bishops, making her the first woman to have the right to vote in the Catholic Synod of Bishops. Both the above events augur well and are to be viewed as examples set for the local Church in India - of course, all the three present rites included - and other churches worldwide.

Moreover, with all their teething troubles and limitations, the participatory structures instituted by Vatican II[13] have contributed to self-confidence and proactive role among the believers triggering their involvement. Furthermore, experiences with these structures and other bodies have increased the expectations of the faithful for a synodal Church. Thus, Synodality has become not an optional possibility but an urgent necessity.

The necessity is all the more when we note the disastrous consequences of leadership in the Church that is not fed from the bottom up and has lost touch with ground realities. The danger is that those in authority and leadership position, acting alone and on their own, could end up in the wrong assessment of men and matters with costly and devastating consequences. Not being in touch with the actual situation on the ground and failing to take counsel from the people of God, Church leaders could be intrigued into believing even the well-staged theatre-like performances.

In this connection, we could recall here at least two recent examples. The one is that of Marcial Maciel, the founder of the Congregation of the Legionaries of Christ. He took the highest Church authorities for a ride by inducing them to believe, thanks to the triumphal display of wealth, power, and ability to attract "vocations" and build massive institutions, that he and his congregation are Christianizing the world and are in the forefront to defend the Church. The second case is that of the elevation of the prolific fundraiser Theodore McCarrick as archbishop of Washington and then the creation of him as a cardinal of the Roman Catholic Church. In both cases, there were voices from the bottom trying to unveil the underlying monstrous moral corruptions and criminality and calling for caution, which were, sadly, disregarded, set aside, and even covered up. It is a sober reminder that in the Church, as history and experience testify, even the highest authority can suffer from error of judgment of men and matters.

If such things could happen at the highest level of the Church authorities, how much more should the local Churches and their leaders be attentive to the sane voices from the bottom – from the people of God on important issues affecting the Church. This will save the authorities in the Church from being blinded and committing grave errors. Moreover, it will hold them accountable and protect the Church from tarnishing its image and credibility.

The call to tread the synodal path has come at a critical juncture when it is facing several burning issues that might seriously affect the whole Church and its imminent future. This means the end of the monarchical mindset and mode of functioning in the Church, influenced partly by the eighteenth-century European political monarchy where the will of the sovereign became the law. The synodal path helps the Church cleanse itself of the past remnants and come out of the bunkers of self-isolation. In the synodal functioning of the Church, taking advice from the people of God, from the grassroots, becomes an obligation the Church leadership cannot shirk anymore.

The situations described above have cumulatively exposed *a structural failure* in the Church. As a result, there has been an "enormous loss of credibility suffered by the clerical system," as Hervé Legrand puts it.[14] Like in a building, when beams and columns crack, clearly indicating that there is a *structural failure*, we are experiencing in the current system of the Church sure signs of structural failures that cannot be repaired simply by sanctimonious exhortations and appeal to conscience. The dismal and critical situation calls for new practices in the Church. One such important practice is synodality, an ancient institution of the Church indeed, but reappropriated and reaffirmed in the spirit of *ressourcement* by Vatican II.

Synodality Responding to Epochal Changes

We live in an age in which people are increasingly aware of their freedom, autonomy, and agency in every realm of life and conscious of their dignity. They have passed on from a pre-modern world of heteronomy of letting others decide in matters concerning them to a modern conception of the world in which they can think and decide for themselves and hold their views and opinions. Anyone who recognizes the agency of the people and is sensitive to their aspiration will not treat them as objects of command. Well-meant patronizing also takes away people's agency which they value and cherish. Freedom is at the core of the gospel and not alien to it. The analysis *Gaudium et Spes* makes of the modern world, its dynamism, and the changes occurring all around also apply to Catholics who are part of this contemporary world and not alien to it. The document observes how "the people of our time prize freedom very highly and strive eagerly for it."[15] The Christian faithful refuse to be simply cogs in an ecclesiastical system controlled by a clerical hierarchy in which everything is preordained and decided, with no freedom. Their only role appears to be that of assisting in the functioning of this system.

Further, there is a general perception that the Church operates with a pre-modern rural mindset and feudal mode of exercising authority and has not addressed the transformations of culture, values, and ways of behaviour, with fast pace of urbanization. This is quite intriguing since freedom, dignity and agency of the people upheld by modernity belong to the core values of Christianity itself. Furthermore, the early Christian communities were profoundly aware of the freedom Jesus brought to them from the narrow confines of Judaism, its laws, customs, and traditions. "It is for freedom that Christ has set us free" (Gal 5:1). Christians breathed the air of freedom within their communities.

There is also a significant second development. We have passed on from a mechanistic and deterministic worldview of Newtonian physics to a new quantum conception of the universe. In the mechanical vision, all the parts are moved by a motor, and any part is replaceable. As a result, in this conception, everything moves along predictable lines. On the other hand, in the quantum conception of the universe, everything moves everything else in a chain of interdependence where every part is in a dynamic process with the rest, allowing for surprises in the absence of total predictability.

Moreover, there is something called the *butterfly effect*. It means even the tiniest element can, in the end, produce a significant effect, as in weather conditions where even the flapping of wings by butterflies could completely change the direction of a cyclone. This new integral and interdependent worldview has become sharper with growing attention to ecological reflections.

The above two approaches of science also affect how leadership is conceived and exercised today in the Church. There is a rightful aspiration that the mechanistic leadership model gives place to an organic model that is sensitive to the butterfly effect and hence takes into serious account every member of the Church community, involving the synergy and cooperation of everyone. This modern scientific intuition of reality was theologically expressed by St Paul when he figured the Church as a body- and indeed the body of Christ in which all the members are bound in a relationship of interdependence, and each member is indispensable and plays its unique role (I Cor. 12: 12-27; Rom 12: 3-8). There is no high and low – a worldly casteist parameter -but everyone is of equal dignity with different functions even as they are endowed with different charisms and gifts. The ones considered "smallest" in the Church community could significantly affect its life and mission. What affects the tiniest member affects everyone. "If one member suffers, all suffer together" (I Co. 12:26). Hence, nothing could be neglected and sidelined. That is why the Church is not a democracy where only the majority decides; much less is it a monarchy where one person decides, but rather it is a communion of minds and hearts united in faith, love, and hope for the attainment of common goals and goods. In this sense, the Church resembles more *republicanism* (*res publica*) than democracy. Not all voices speak with the same volume in a republic, and it is, therefore, imperative to create space and time, especially for the little voices to be heard. God was not in the strong wind, earthquake, or fire but in the 'still, small voice (I Kings 19:12). In the Rule of Benedict for monastic life in chapter three, there is a very striking passage on consulting the community:

> As often as anything important is to be done in the monastery, the abbot shall call the whole community together, and himself explain the business is … The reason why we have said all should be called for counsel is that the Lord often reveals what is better to the younger.[16]

It appears that synodality reflects both a modern scientific view of the world and the best Christian tradition of what the Church should be in its life and mission. On the other hand, a Church conceived in clerical mode with a hierarchical mindset of high and low – *secundum sub et supra* – could engender a pathology of ecclesial sclerosis causing many parts of the body of the Church to be numbed and become dysfunctional. Moreover, it can harm the Church by disregarding what its most neglected members could contribute to the Church community. A case in point is the role of women in the Church, which needs to be rethought in new terms and framework than the contraposition of male and female. The current discourse is bound to change the question of women if we adopt a different frame of interpretation. In any case, it has become increasingly clear that clericalism can be sustained only at a hefty cost to the credibility of the Church.

Synodality Flowing from Sound Christian Anthropology

Synodality is to be based on sound Christian anthropology. Accordingly, human beings are a mystery. They participate in the divine mystery with their knowledge, intellect, freedom, and will. Hence, any ecclesial community should respect the fundamental truth that the Christian faithful, as human beings, are a mystery.

Mysterious and inscrutable are the ways in which the unfathomable human mind and heart work. What distinguishes human beings from animal behaviour is that a person has the capacity to give a description and account of her intentions and actions.[17] Hence no person could be treated as an object lacking agency. The exercise of people's mind and heart in terms of their perspectives, views, opinions, and intentions need the highest respect and should be approached with a sense of sacredness and reverence.

Synodality will evoke among the faithful and the ministers a sense of wonder at everyone around them. It should be viewed as an opportunity to value everyone in their unique identity and difference. This mystical and aesthetic experience goes far beyond mere cooperation and consensus-building exercises, as part of best managerial practices.[18] Real happiness appears on our human horizon when we can experience truth, goodness and beauty (*satyam, sivam, sundaram*) of human persons, the image of God and, indeed, of the entire creation. Karl Rahner famously stated, "the devout Christian of the future will either be a 'mystic', one who has 'experienced' something, or he will cease to be anything at all."[19] Rooted this way in deep Christian anthropology, synodality will create in the faithful and the ministers – a new way of thinking – *novus habitus mentis*.[20]

We can identify another important anthropological foundation for synodality in the very nature of human beings, created for communion. It is in forging relationship with others the identity of a person is constituted. The other is an absolute condition for the unfolding of the self and its expressions. In other words, the other is part of the definition of one's very self. The fact that human beings are created in the image of God tells us not only about their dignity, but also about their being a reflection of the mystery of the Trinity – a mystery of perfect communion among three persons – Father, Son, and the Spirit. Human persons reveal the traces of the Trinity and our life in community needs to be guided and nourished by this mystery. Synodality is an invitation to live and give expression to that deeper communion to which human beings are called.

Argumentative Jesus

Jesus was in continuous encounter and conversation with people, desirous of knowing what they thought and discovering their yearnings and dreams. He was on a synodal path with the people and with the disciples.[21] The gospel presents *"an argumentative"* Jesus who listens attentively to people. Amazed by their words, he reasons with them, with the crowd, and is always ready to let others challenge him and respond sincerely and in the most original ways to their probing interrogations. Most striking are the examples of his conversations with the Samaritan woman (Jn 4: 1-27), the Syrophoenician woman (Mk 7:24-30), and the Centurion (Mt 8: 5-13) – all of them from entirely different backgrounds and experiences from his own. The early Church, in the footsteps of Jesus, throws light on what it means to govern communities and pursue mission in the spirit of synodality and co-responsibility.

The Process and Dynamics of Synodality

The Preparatory Document distinguishes three levels of synodality: First, it should be the enduring style in the day-to-day functioning of the Church, namely a style reflecting its nature as the people of God on a journey together. It is a journey bearing joint responsibility in exercising the diversity of ministries and charisms. A second level is the institutional embodiment of this interconnectedness and mutuality in the various participatory structures in the form of different councils and bodies. A third level is a formal convocation of synods following due theological and canonical procedures as in diocesan synod or the synod of bishops, or ecumenical councils, the most intense expression of collegiality.

Whichever the level, we should keep in mind that they all require a procedure through *discernment*. Synodality is an ongoing form of cooperation, facilitating the flow of communion. In a democracy, decisions are made going by the majority. The majority can go wrong, and experience shows they have gone terribly wrong, indeed. A single voice may have greater validity and be closer to the truth. This one single person need not be the leader but a simple member of a body. Her voice may have greater reason than the majority and even the leader. Hence, her voice should not be lost. I mean that we need to listen and take into account every voice, even the feeblest one in the Church community and decide things by consensus rather than imposing the will of a brute majority or of the leader as often happens in political praxis. But often, the aphorism "Church is not a democracy" is conveniently interpreted as a license for authoritarian practices in the name of God. In a pre-Vatican II world, it could be argued that knowledge, experience, education, and inclination to voice one's views were more or less stimed. But in an Internet world, there is much more 'democratization' of these; therefore, it could hardly be argued that wisdom and insights should flow only from a highly centralized body. Now more than ever, the furthest members on the fringes have access to a lot of information and they desire to contribute to a synodal Church.

Decisions are to be made through a process of discernment. Part of the discernment process is mutual respectful listening without the blinkers of prejudices and prejudgments. Listening is a psychologically conducive means for the community's life and a theological necessity. For, we believe the Church is the temple of God with many gifts and charisms, and these should not be lost or silenced but instead channelled towards the growth and flourishing of all. The fact that the Church as the people of God is the work of the Spirit demands that there be respectful listening, mutual learning, and common discerning of the path to journey together. That is indeed the meaning of the word "synod" – from *synodos* which means being together on the way, on a journey.

Again, listening is not to be viewed as an act of charity or courtesy extended to the faithful. Instead, as equal citizens in the Church through baptism, members of the ecclesial community individually and collectively have the right to be heard. Even more, the listening should go to the extent of ascertaining the views and seeking the advice of the faithful again for the common good of the Church community and its mission. Seeking advice expresses the respect given to the people.

True discernment happens when the members have the community's common good as the goal and not selfish motives and interests. Personal agenda and self-centeredness can replace the common good, which could also happen to the ministers and the faithful in the Church. Hence, we stand in need of continuous conversion in order to practice synodality.

There are three basic requirements for the effective practice of synodality. First, there should be a circulation of information resulting in transparency. It means one should not take refuge under the cloak of secrecy, which has been disastrous, as experience has shown in many cases of clerical sexual abuse. Second, Information is a prerequisite for taking enlightened decisions with a sense of co-responsibility. Third, synodality calls for openness. So, there are no reservations about what could be discussed. Felicitously, canon 465 for the diocesan synod lays down that "all questions proposed are to be subject to the free discussion of the members in the sessions of the synod."[22] Pope Francis has set an example at the universal level by removing all restrictions on discussions in the Roman synods.

Today's experiences make it increasingly evident that conflicts and dissent cannot be resolved by enacting new laws or requiring oaths and professions of faith. This very dated and unreliable practice reveals a mindset that cannot carry the Church forward into the future. This means there should be a willingness to embrace a process that could be messy, at times ugly and frustratingly slow. The temptation for quick solutions and invoking "obedience" could only hamper the overall atmosphere of dialogue and genuine listening.

Mission through Synodal Discernment

Communion and synodal participation affirm the fundamental equality of all Christian faithful and enliven the life of the Church-community by letting the Spirit-given charisms flourish for the common good. But the Church is not an end in itself. It is a sacrament, i.e., a sign and an instrument for the unity of the entire human family[23] whose service is its primary mission. As *Evangelii Gaudium* reminds us, "the principal aim of these participative processes should not be ecclesiastical organization but rather the missionary aspirations of reaching everyone."[24] In a fast-changing world, the mission must be identified and addressed in every context with its own specificities. The cooperation of everyone is required to respond to the political, social, economic, and cultural challenges of the time and fulfil the mission of the Church in context. Synodality is an essential means to generate and nourish the necessary cooperation for the work of the mission.

For, the mission takes place today through dialogue with the life of the world in its manifold facets. It is bolstered up through joint efforts to make the world a habitable home for humans and all creatures. It is also a journey with brothers and sisters of other faiths. Therefore, the synodal spirit practised in the Church community with its attendant values will help the Christian faithful to carry on the mission in context through dialogue and cooperation.

Synodality and Conflicts

Conflicts, power struggles, and polarization of views in the larger society get also reflected in the life of the Church. To be guided by the principle and spirit of synodality involves coming to terms with conflicts and controversies. There is then an *agonistic* aspect to synodality. A practice of synodality without taking into account the often-conflictual nature of inter-human relationships may sound too idealistic. The conflicts may take an ideological tone or could be caused by the differences in value espousal or, as often is the case, by conflicts between the various personal interests.

Like in other groupings, the Church-community also may need to deploy means and methods for conflict resolutions drawn from human sciences. More than that, the effort to overcome divergence of opinions, on whichever basis they may be voiced, needs to be guided by faith and by invoking the resources from the scriptures and tradition. There should be a process of discernment - different from the decision of the majority – in which every voice, especially the weaker ones, will have space and recognition. As we noted earlier, contrary to a brute majority which could decide in a democracy by imposing its will and sidelining the minority voices, the Church community is guided by discernment, by the Spirit. Here is an important difference between democracy and synodality. Synodality embodies germane democratic values while trying to overcome its limits.

To cite some examples, we find two instances in the Acts of the Apostles depicting the way the early community sought to overcome conflicts. One is the conflict of interest between the Jewish Christians and Hellenistic Christians regarding the treatment of widows.

The Hellenistic Christians felt that their widows were overlooked, discriminated against, and sought redress (Acts 6:1-7). Though we do not know how the issue was discussed, we could infer that the early Christian community arrived at a consensus from the fact that a new institution of the diaconate was created to take care of the discriminated group in the community.

The other example of conflict resolution is the mission for the gentiles with two opposing views. Again, we hear from Acts 15 something of the fuller discussion that might have taken place, along with the consensus arrived at by their synodal practice. "It has been decided by the Holy Spirit and by ourselves" (Acts 15:28). The good of the Church is so important that it cannot be left to the goodwill of an unenlightened and misguided leader. Active participation of the Church community is indispensable.

Insulated Bishops and Dioceses

In the early Church and early medieval period, synodality flourished, thanks to the communion and exchange and mutual support among the bishops of the region or province sharing the same cultural/linguistic world and facing common issues of mission in the same socio-political conditions. History records numerous councils of bishops and the decisions they arrived at through consensus. Much of the governing was done by the provincial councils which also framed common policies and directives for the Churches of a particular region.[25]

This contrasts with the present situation in our country where each bishop and each diocese seem to function as monads, insulated from the rest of the Churches around. Most bishops feel threatened by any collegial or collective directives and policies taken at the provincial level. They think that they would lose control and authority over their respective dioceses and hence do not want to be bound by the decisions of the provincial bishops. Decisions taken jointly at the provincial or national level of bishops' conferences are often not implemented in the diocese on the plea that they do not apply to one's diocese! This is, indeed, a sad situation.

Synodality is a wake-up call to the leaders of the Church in India that they live the communion with other Churches of the province or region and increase co-responsibility at that level. This is also important given the socio-political situation in the country/region. The challenges of today are such that no single diocese could by itself respond to them. Collective and cooperative engagement is required.

We could only expect that the country's bishops set a good example for synodality by first increasing the spirit of cooperation among themselves which will have repercussions on common pastoral choices. But unfortunately, the juridical status of intermediary bodies of collegiality such as the national bishops' conference and provincial or regional bishops' council, is far from what the spirit of synodality would require.[26] Unless there are provisions to bind the bishops through collegial decisions at the national or provincial level, the danger of even total disregard for these bodies and their recommendations and policies by individual bishops will continue.

Concluding Reflections - Towards Implementation

Pope Francis has programmed the event of the synod in such a way that there be three intervening years of preparation from the bottom up. Therefore, it is a great opportunity for the Church in India to think through some of the critical issues in relation to synodality, while discussing the preparatory document of the synod already released.

Our discussions in India should assess the quality of synodal participation in the Church today at different levels. How have the various participative structures, like diocesan/parish pastoral councils, finance councils, and senate of priests, functioned? What has been their impact? What are the difficulties encountered in their functioning, and how could they be redressed?

Synodality could become a tour de force for the renewal of the Church in India. However, it calls for some radical transformations. We shall go into them, with implementation in view.

There is an intriguing theological issue to be faced in the transition from the synod of bishops as an institution to synodality as a way of being and relating of the Church. The institution of the synod of bishops in its theology and intent was meant to facilitate the primatial role of the pope in a collegial manner. The step from here to strike a synodal path for the Church involving the entire people of God would mean deep structural changes. It is unclear what role the synod of bishops, originally meant to facilitate the exercise of the primacy of the pope, could now play unless we move decisively from the synod of bishops to the synod of the Church. This is a major theological issue to be addressed.

As we noted, in the vision of Pope Francis, synodality practised in its true spirit would make the Church an "inverted pyramid." If this image is to be translated into practice, we will need to rethink how canon law sees the power of governance in the Church. The present code states explicitly in canon 129 that the power of governance is reserved to those in sacred orders, and the other Christian faithful are excluded from it. They are expected only "to co-operate in the exercise of the same power" by the clergy, and they do not have any participation in it. This is the elephant in the room. The issue needs to be addressed for the common synodal journey of the entire Church, without which it is difficult to imagine the Church as an inverted pyramid.

Besides, there is a deeper and more critical question in India regarding governance in the Church. Why does the synodal structure of governance apply only to the two Oriental Rites in India? The synodal structure is not a matter of divine law (*jus divinum*), but positive law, and hence could be legislated for adoption also for the Churches at the level of the regional council of bishops or national conference in the Latin rite. This difference is striking. In the absence of synodal structure, the Latin Catholics living in identical socio-political conditions in the same nation are disadvantaged, especially in such crucial matters as the choice of bishops, while the Orientals enjoy autonomy. To begin with, the provincial councils should be strengthened. In fact, in early centuries and even in Middle Ages most issues were transacted in the provincial or regional councils.

There is yet another question of great import to consider. The clerical sexual and property scandals that have rocked the Church in India and in other parts of the world teach us the need for reasonable legal restraints on the exercise of the clerical power, and not to blindly rely on their apparent goodwill and moral rectitude. It calls for a fundamental canonical reform and adoption of fundamental or constitutional Church law – *Lex Ecclesiae Fundamentalis* in the Church – a proposal made by Pope Paul VI himself but unfortunately failed to materialize.[27] Synodality is, at the same time, a clarion call to revise the present Code and to get back to the proposal of Paul VI on *Lex Ecclesiae Fundamentalis*. Along with it, the Church will need to earnestly address its legal system in which legislative, executive and judicial powers are concentrated in a single office. This does not appear to be a viable form of governance anymore and certainly does not contribute to synodal practice in the life of communion, participation, and mission. Nor does this system respond to the signs of the times. Here lies the Achilles' heel.

We saw how regional and provincial councils were important bodies in the early centuries of Christianity. Vatican II speaks of true equality "with regard to the dignity and to the activity common to all the faithful for the building up of the Body of Christ" (LG 32; cf. can. 208 CIC). All the baptized Christian faithful do indeed share in the three offices of Christ of sanctifying, teaching and governing - according to their own position and task (LG 10-12/can. 204 CIC). Implementing this in practice would require binding structural procedures to be laid down for participation of the faithful and for joint deliberation. I propose that before convening any meeting of the body of bishops – national, regional, or provincial – there take place a meeting of the synod of the Church with representatives of the people of God, which will provide the main agenda for the discussion of the episcopal bodies - provincial regional and national - and this agenda will be based on ground realities. To avoid this becoming anything merely ritual, a canonical provision should be made that any decision of the episcopal bodies will be null and void if it was not preceded by a gathering of the synod of the people of God. This would perfectly fit into the ecclesiology of Vatican II on the people of God.

The participation of the lay faithful in the governance of the Church could be implemented even under present conditions. Several offices in the Church administration do not require clerics but could be fulfilled by the qualified Christian faithful. For example, to be a financial administrator of a diocese does not require ordination; rather a person competent in managing the economy and accounts! Similar is the office of the chancellor of the diocese, judges in ecclesiastical tribunals, assessors, auditors, notaries, promoters of justice, defenders of the bond, and parish pastoral administrators. Synodality will become credible if the regional or national episcopal bodies decide that within the next ten years, in all the dioceses, the offices mentioned above will be filled by lay Christian faithful and not clerics. It would require that steps be taken and financial provisions are made to train qualified lay faithful from the community to fulfil these ministries.

In view of the fact that in the past years there have been too many financial scandals in the dioceses tarnishing the image of the Church and its evangelizing potential, it is indispensable to bring about reforms both in the regular financial administration as well as in property management with checks and balances so that financial matters are not dealt secretively by a closed circle of bishops and a few handpicked clerics, but that there be greater transparency and credibility. This is another critical reason for enlisting the active participation of the Christian faithful in the financial management of diocese, parishes, and other institutions.

The reflections on synodality bring in the need to radically revise the present procedure in the appointment of bishops in which the participation of the Christian faithful at present is almost nil which is highly regrettable. For the past three decades or so, the most important criteria in the appointment of bishops seem to have been orthodoxy. As a result, there are ultra-orthodox leaders who, as experience has demonstrated, are not capable of handling critical situations in the Church. Extensive consultation with the Christian faithful would help identify candidates with the necessary skills for Church-leadership in the present conditions of the Church and with the ability to dialogue with society and the wider world today. The current canon law indeed speaks of two modes of appointment: "The Supreme Pontiff freely appoints bishops or *confirms those legitimately elected*" (Can. 377 §1). The synodal path increasingly calls for giving concrete expression to the second mode, which allows room for active participation of the Christian faithful in electing their bishops. Necessary structural and procedural reforms are to be established for the realization of the second mode, which will include enforceable participation right of the concerned Christian community of the faithful in the choice of the suitable candidate for the leadership role as bishop.[28]

From the functioning of the participative structures in the Church, we know there is a conflict between the *consultative* and the *deliberative*. It is unclear, when there is a general consensus of the community, how a Church leader could justify a different binding decision than what the community has discerned. How could one, in this case, save the Church from being thrown into the jaws of crass authoritarianism? Pope Paul was, indeed, a wise person with a lot of prescience.

While instituting the synod through the document *Apostolica Sollicitudo*, he said that it would be an advisory body. But then, he did not stop there. He added that this participatory body – the synod - could be empowered so that it "also can enjoy the power of decision making," and its deliberations and decisions only need to be ratified by the pope.[29] This is a great model as it provides an opening to get out of the dilemma of these structures functioning as toothless consultative bodies. Empowering these structures, in the spirit of synodality, also to be deliberative and decision-making, will foster greater communion, participation, and joint involvement for the gospel mission.

Finally, synodality could be put into effective practice by the Church in India by implementing in a stable form the already instituted "lay" ministries which will contribute to the self-confidence of the "lay" faithful and their participation in the life and mission of the Church. The opportunities for participation are there, and the Church in India should avail them.

Lector and Acolyte for "Lay" Faithful

With a Motu Proprio *Spiritus Domini*, released on 11 January 2021, Pope Francis established that from now on, the ministries of Lector and Acolyte are to be open to women in a stable and institutionalized form through a specific mandate.

There is nothing new about women proclaiming the Word of God during liturgical celebrations or functioning as altar servers or as Eucharistic ministers. In many communities worldwide, these practices are already authorized by local bishops. However, up to this point, this has occurred without a true and proper institutional mandate, as an exception to what Pope Paul VI had established on 17 August 1972 through his Motu Proprio *Ministeria Quaedam*. For, even while abolishing the so-called "minor orders," he decided to maintain that access to these ministries be granted only to men. Presently, Pope Francis gives a clarion call that *women* also should be instituted/installed as lectors and acolytes through a prescribed liturgical act. What prevents the Church in India from implementing this? Is it the case of the Tamil proverb, which says, even if God grants, the *poojari* will not permit?

Ministry of Catechists for the "Lay" Faithful

Pope Francis instituted the ministry of catechist in the Catholic Church by publishing the Apostolic Letter issued as Motu Proprio *Antiquum ministerium* ("Ancient ministry") on 10 May 2021. In this apostolic letter, Pope Francis traced the history of the catechist, beginning with the New Testament's First Epistle to the Corinthians, which refers to "teachers" within the early Christian community. The newly instituted ministry of the catechist is for "lay" people who have a particular call to serve the Church as teachers of the faith. The ministry is "*stable*," meaning that it lasts for the entirety of life, independent of whether the person is actively carrying out that activity during every part of his or her life. The catechist is dedicated to transmitting the faith through proclamation and instruction.

As we can see, there are large spaces open even within the present canonical framework for participation of the "lay" faithful in an official way. However, the conviction and the will to implement the available provisions appear to be lacking. We hope that the synodal path initiated by Pope Francis will open the eyes of the Indian Church leaders to give flesh and blood to the synodal vision of the Church. This is an important stepping stone towards overcoming the deep crisis the Church is going through due to clericalism. It is increasingly demanded by the abuse of power. This should go beyond treating the symptoms and identify deeper structural causes that inhibit the emergence of a genuinely synodal Church.[30]

NOTES

1   The address on the occasion of the 50th anniversary of the institution of the synodofbishops.Seehttps://vaticana.va/content/franceso/en/speeches/2015/ october/docuements/papa-franceso20151017_50-anniversario-sinodo. html [accessed on 11 September 2021]. Other documents to be studied: Motu Proprio of Pope Paul VI "*Apostolica Sollicitudo,*" and the document of the International Theological Commission on "Synodality in the Life and Mission of the Church" (2018). https://www.vatican.va/roman_curia/ congregations/cfaith/cti_documents/rc_cti_20180302_sinodalita_en.html [accessed on 11 September 2021].

2   This is the image he used speaking on the occasion of the 50th anniversary of the institution of Synod. For the text, see the site cited above footnote no.1. See also Ormond Rush, "Inverting the Pyramid. The *Sensus Fidelium* in a Synodal Church," *Theological Studies* 78 (2017): 299–325.

3   For the Preparatory Document and the Handbook, see the official Synod website: http://www.synod.va/en.html [accessed on 10 August 2023].

4   For the text of the document see https://www.synod.va/en/highlights/ working-document-for-the-continental-stage.html [accessed on 16 May 2023].

5   The papers and proceedings of the conference has been published. See Antony Lawrene, et al., eds., *Church in India on the Synodal Path* (Bengaluru: Asian Trading Corporation, 2022).

6   The German bishops reacted to Bismarck's comments through a collective statement which foreshadowed the teaching of Vatican II on episcopate in relation to papacy. The bishop's statement declared: "It is in virtue of the same institution upon which the papacy rests that the episcopate also exists. It, too, has its rights and duties, because of the ordinance of God himself, and the Pope has neither the right nor the power to change them." Leonard Fernando and John Romus, eds., *The Christian Faith in the Doctrinal Documents of the Catholic Church* (Bengaluru: Theological Publication in India, 2022), 841.

7   Paul Ricoeur, *Interpretation Theory: Discourse and the Surplus of Meaning* (Fort Worth: Texas Christian University Press, 1976), 87.

8   Massimo Faggioli, "Reading the Signs of the Times through a Hermeneutics of Recognition: *Gaudium et Spes* and It's Meaning for a Learning Church," https://www.cambridge.org/core/journals/horizons/article/reading-the-signs-of-the-times-through-a-hermeneutics-of-recognition-gaudium-et-spes-and-its-meaning-for-a-learning-church/9C0CF42CA3598AA04F0A6A-4CBC96F87B [accessed on 4 August 2023].

9   https://www.vaticannews.va/en/vatican-city/news/2023-04/synod-synodality-general-assemblies-laypeople-eligible-vote.html [accessed on 16 May 2023].

10   The matter was discussed almost two decades ago in a special issue of *Concilium* 2004/3, entitled "The Structural Betrayal of Trust."

11   The Preparatory Document alludes to this situation and states why "the Church herself must face the lack of faith and the corruption even within herself" (no. 6).

12   The sexual scandal relating to Cardinal Theodore McCarrick invited a thorough investigation by the Vatican, resulting in a lengthy report of over four hundred pages. See https://www.vatican.va/resources/resources_rapporto-card-mccarrick_20201110_en.pdf [accessed on 10 September 2022]. The financial scandal involving Cardinal Angelo Becciu, one of the highest-ranking curial officials, invited a historic trial in the Vatican on the allegations made. See, https://www.bbc.com/news/world-europe-57706618. [accessed on 10 September 2022].

13   Cf. Sebastian S. Karambai, "Consultative Bodies in the Particular Churches Revisited in the Light of *Evangelii Gaudium,*" in Adrian Loretan and Felix Wilfred, eds., *Revision of the Codes. An Indian-European Dialogue* (Zürich: LIT Verlag, 2018), 283–292.

14   Hervé Legrand, "Synodality is a Matter of Practice: A Plea for Learning," *Concilium* (2021/2): Special Issue "Synodalities," 119–129, at 121.

15 *Gaudium et Spes* 17.

16 W.K. Lowther Clarke, trans., and preface, *Rule of St Benedict* (London: S.P.C.K., 1931).

17 Cf. Satya P. Gautam, "Normative Structure of Human Actions and Causal Explanations," in J.V. Narlikar et al., eds., *Philosophy of Science* (Shimla: Indian Institute of Advanced Study, 1992), 180.

18 Managerial principles are important in the governance of the Church and they must be deployed. However, the core of what synodality for the Church flows from its character of mystery. The International Theological Commission expressed it succinctly, stating that "the mystery of the Church is intrinsically synodal" https://www.vatican.va/roman_curia/congregations/cfaith/cti_documents/rc_cti_20180302_sinodalita_en.html [accessed on 17 May 2023] no. 38.

19 Karl Rahner, *Theological Investigations*, vol. 7 (London: Dorton, Longman & Todd, 1971), 15.

20 This is the expression used by Pope Paul VI, speaking of what is expected of the new Code.

21 Lucien Legrand, "At the Heart of Synodality: Jesus' Disciples as Partners in the Messianic Mission," in Antony Lawrence et al., eds., *Church in India on the Synodal Path* (Bengaluru: Asian Traditiong Corporation, 2022), 178–188. For synodality from Old Testament Perspective, see P. Joseph Titus, "Biblical Prophet's Concern for Journeying Together and Standing beside the Poor and the Least in Israel," in Antony Lawrence, et al., eds., *Church in India on the Synodal Path*, 137–148; and M. David Stanley Kumar, "Including Every One and Leaving out No One: Struggles for an Inclusive Community in the Exilic and Post-Exilic Hebrew Prophets - A Model for Synod," in Antony Lawrence, et al., eds., *Church in India*, 149–162. A good overview of the Biblical approach could be found also in the document of the International Theological Commission, "Synodality in the Life and Mission of the Church," https://www.vatican.va/roman_curia/congregations/cfaith/cti_documents/rc_cti_20180302_sinodalita_en.html [accessed on 4 August 2023].

22 This canon should be read in conjunction with some of the canons at the beginning of Book II, which speak about the rights of the faithful, such as the right to express their opinion (c. 212), and "a lawful freedom of inquiry and of prudently expressing their opinion on matters in which they have expertise" (c. 218).

23 See *Lumen Gentium* 1.

24 *Evangelii Gaudium* 31.

25 On provincial councils and their mode of functioning in the early Church, see Francis A Sullivan, "Provincial Councils and the Choosing of Priests for Appointment as Bishops," *Theological Studies* 74, no. 4 (2013): 872–883;

Ramsay MacMullen, *Voting about God in Early Church Councils* (London: Yale University Press, 2008); see also Mary Pierre Wilson, and Mary Judith O'Brien, "Provincial and Plenary Councils: Renewed Interest in an Ancient Institution," *Jurist* 65 (2005): 241–267.

26   Cf. Felix Wilfred, "Episcopal Conferences - Their Theological Status," in Peter Fernando, ed., *Episcopal Conferences and Collegiality* (Madras: CBCI Commission for Clergy and Religious, 1989), 3–26.

27   On 20 November 1965, Pope Paul VI made this suggestion to the members of the consultors of the Pontifical Code Revision Commission. See also Felix Wilfred, Andres Torres Quieruga, and Enrico Galavotti, eds., "Revision of Canon Law," *Concilium* (2016/5), a special issue; Adrian Loretan and Felix Wilfred, eds., *Revision of the Codes. An Indian- European Dialogue* (Zürich: LIT Verlag, 2018).

28   This has been long the tradition of the Church. See Peter Norton, *Episcopal Elections 250-600: Hierarchy and Popular Will in Late Antiquity* (Oxford University Press, 2007).

29   See https://www.vatican.va/content/paul-vi/en/motu_proprio/documents/hf_p-vi_motu-proprio_19650915_apostolica-sollicitudo.html [accessed on 11 September 2021].

30   It is highly relevant to note here that in his Apostolic Exhortation *Evangelii Gaudium*, Pope Francis sees mission as the "principal aim" of participative bodies in the Church: "In his mission of fostering a dynamic, open and missionary communion, he [the bishop] will have to encourage and develop the means of participation proposed in the Code of Canon Law …and other forms of pastoral dialogue, out of a desire to listen to everyone and not simply to those who would tell him what he would like to hear. Yet, the principal aim of these participative processes should not be ecclesiastical organisation but rather the missionary aspirations of reaching everyone" *Evangelii Gaudium* no. 31.

FURTHER READING

Congar, Yves M. "Quod omnes tangit, ab omnibus tractari et approbari debet." Revue *Historique De Droit Français et étranger* 35 (1958): 210-59.

Faggioli, Massimo. Reading the Signs of the Times through a Hermeneutics of Recognition: *Gaudium et Spes* and It's Meaning for a Learning Church," https://www.cambridge.org/core/journals/horizons/article/reading-the-signs-of-the-times-through-a-hermeneutics-of-recognition-gaudium-et-spes-and-its-meaning-for-a-learning-church/9C0CF42CA3598AA04F0A6A-4CBC96F87B [accessed on 4 August 2023].

Fernando, Leonard, and John Romus, eds. *The Christian Faith in the Doctrinal Documents of the Catholic Church*. Bengaluru: Theological Publication in India, 2022.

Gautam, Satya P. "Normative Structure of Human Actions and Causal Explanations." In J.V. Narlikar, et al., eds. *Philosophy of Science*. Shimla: Indian Institute of Advanced Study, 1992.

Karambai, Sebastian S. "Consultative Bodies in the Particular Churches Revisited in the Light of *Evangelii Gaudium*." In Adrian Loretan and Felix Wilfred, eds. *Revision of the Codes. An Indian-European Dialogue*, 283– 292. Zürich: LIT Verlag, 2018.

Kumar, M. David Stanley. "Including Everyone and Leaving out No One: Struggles for an Inclusive Community in the Exilic and Post-Exilic Hebrew Prophets - A Model for Synod." In Antony Lawrence, et al., eds., *Church in India*, 149–162. Bengaluru: Asian Trading Corporation, 2022.

Lawrence, Antony, et al., eds. *Church in India on the Synodal Path*. Bengaluru: Asian Trading Corporation, 2022.

Legrand, Hervé. "Synodality is a Matter of Practice: A Plea for Learning." *Concilium* (2021/2): 119–129.

Legrand, Lucien. "At the Heart of Synodality: Jesus' Disciples as Partners in the Messianic Mission." In Antony Lawrence et al., eds., *Church in India on the Synodal Path*, 178–188. Bengaluru: Asian Trading Corporation, 2022.

Loretan, Adrian, and Felix Wilfred, eds. *Revision of the Codes. An Indian- European Dialogue*. Zurich: LIT Verlag, 2018.

MacMullen, Ramsay. *Voting about God in Early Church Councils*. London: Yale University Press, 2008.

Norton, Peter. *Episcopal Elections 250-600: Hierarchy and Popular Will in Late Antiquity*. Oxford: Oxford University Press, 2007.

Rahner, Karl. *Theological Investigations*, vol. 7. London: Dorton, Longman & Todd, 1971.

Ricoeur, Paul. *Interpretation Theory: Discourse and the Surplus of Meaning*. Fort Worth: Texas Christian University Press, 1976.

Rush, Ormond. "Inverting the Pyramid. The *Sensus Fidelium* in a Synodal Church." *Theological Studies* 78 (2017): 299–325.

Sullivan, Francis A. "Provincial Councils and the Choosing of Priests for Appointment as Bishops." *Theological Studies* 74, no. 4 (2013): 872–883.

Titus, P. Joseph. "Biblical Prophet's Concern for Journeying Together and Standing beside the Poor and the Least in Israel." In Antony Lawrence, et al., eds., *Church in India on the Synodal Path,* 137–148. Bengaluru: Asian Trading Corporation, 2022.

Vakayil, Prema. "Jerusalem Council (Acts 15: 1–35). A Paradigm for Synodality." *Word and Worship* 54, no. 1 (2023): 303–313.

Wilfred, Felix, Andres Torres Quieruga, and Enrico Galavotti, eds. "Revision of Canon Law." *Concilium* (2016/5).

Wilfred, Felix. "Episcopal Conferences - Their Theological Status." In Peter Fernando, ed., *Episcopal Conferences and Collegiality,* 3–26. Madras: CBCI Commission for Clergy and Religious, 1989.

Wilson, Mary Pierre, and Mary Judith O'Brien. "Provincial and Plenary Councils: Renewed Interest in an Ancient Institution." *Jurist* 65 (2005): 241–267.

Chapter 10

A LONELY CRUSADER?
A POPE'S STRUGGLES FOR A
SOCIALLY RELEVANT FAITH

The journey of a socially engaged faith is strewn with numerous obstacles and challenges. Even a pope's journey is no exception. Indeed, he is viewed by many in the larger world as a moral campus for humanity to navigate in a raging sea of crisis. Yet, on the other hand, Pope Francis, arguably, is the most hated person in the Catholic Church today and one of the most detested and reviled in the world among the traditionalist circles.[1] A war is being waged against him, and many invectives thrown on him. His critiques even ridicule him for being "*un papa pasticcione,*" meaning a messy pope sowing confusion in the Church.[2]

As for India, there is a lot of enthusiasm among the people about the pope and his many symbolic gestures and statements about commitment to the poor and the marginalized, about participation and synodality. But the same is not found among the non-descript and lukewarm Catholic hierarchy. Most Church leaders present themselves as ignoramus vis-à-vis what the pontiff does, and I wonder how many of them seriously read the encyclicals and statements of

Pope Francis. Why so? He seems to be a challenge and threat to their habituated ways of exercise of power and the traditional pomp, pageantry, and paraphernalia. Regrettably, these leaders do not allow themselves to be inspired by the teaching, gestures, and example of Pope Francis, especially his unswerving commitment to the cause of the poor, the oppressed and the marginalized and his commitment to a participatory and synodal mode of governance.[3]

The Siege Within

Does not the pope often appear as a lonely crusader? As we noted, there is hostility towards Pope Francis and resistance to him at the global level. The animosity began with his own most close collaborators. In 2016, four cardinals - Joachim Meisner, Walter Brandmüller, Carlo Caffara, and Raymond Burke raised critical questions regarding the pope's stand on family and morality expressed in *Amoris Laetitia.*[4] Pope was accused of heresy, and these cardinals wanted to make a "filial correction" of an errant pope through the infamous letter of "*dubia.*" Others go to the extent of accusing irregularities in the conclave and questioning the validity of his papal election. Cardinal George Pell characterized the present papacy as a "catastrophe."

A former papal nuncio to the United Nations, Archbishop Carlo Maria Viganò, in his explosive public statements, openly asked Francis to resign. Other prelates of no less influence and weight join him. There are many foul and petulant accusations hurled against Francis. For his revilers, his words and acts are not in keeping with the orthodox tradition of the Church. His teachings are found to be "ambiguous," "modernist," and "syncretistic." According to his detractors, he has disrupted the tradition of the Church and its teaching. One of the vicious narratives a small but potent minority of Church leaders and Catholic fundamentalists are trying to weave is that his pontificate is heading for a schism in the Church.

Viganò's Cassandric language characterizing the pontificate of Francis seems to present an impending apocalyptic doom. This is what he says,

> Now the Church is lifeless, covered by metastasis, devastated. The people of God grope, illiterate and robbed of their faith, in the darkness of chaos and division. In recent decades, the enemies of God have progressively burned two thousand years of tradition. With unprecedented acceleration, thanks to the sub-versive goal of this pontificate supported by the powerful Jesuit Apparatus, a deadly *coup de grace* is being prepared against the Church.[5]

For his detractors in the Church, Pope Francis woefully lacks deep theological knowledge and scholarly background. They contrast his teachings with that of John Paul II, in whom they find the embodiment of Catholic orthodoxy. Those beholden to Pope Benedict XVI, like the club of his disciples (*Schüller*), think that he is a theological giant, whereas Pope Francis is theologically a dwarf, a light-weight pussycat. For many such people, the theology of Francis is ephemeral and superficial.[6] Massimo Borghesi, in his book "*The Mind of Pope Francis*," challenges such commonly held views and presents the intellectual journey of the pope and the influences on his theology and philosophy.[7] Some in the Roman Curia think Francis is a transitional pope, hoping his successor will undo his forays in reform.

Finally, there is a legion of Catholic fundamentalists belonging to tribal and militant Catholicism who find the best only in the past and are wary of the surprises of God every new moment. They see the thoughts and ways of Francis abominable and abhorring. They even dare to warn the pope and hope for a natural biological solution – his death.[8] In 2021 an anthology of seventy essays by those opposing the pope – among whom several cardinals, archbishops and bishops - was published, which read: "From Benedict's Peace to Francis's War."[9]

Why this aggressive posture and passionate and full-blooded opposition to Francis in the Church? We need to dig deeper. Let me attempt. To begin with, opposition to the papacy is familiar as history amply attests. To cite examples from the modern period, when the pope was declared infallible at Vatican I, it met with stiff resistance against Pius IX. His anti-modernist views were expressed in his syllabus of errors. In the twentieth century, when there was a movement of theological renewal – *theologie nouvelle* - there appeared the encyclical of Pope Pius XII *Humani Generis*, which became the object of critique resulting in the ban on such theologians as Yves Congar, Dominque Chenu, Jean Daniélou and others, who ironically became some of the chief architects of reform in the Church at Vatican II.

What makes the difference in the critique of Pope Francis vis-à-vis the past is the fact that whereas the opposition to papal views in the past was in the name of them being anti-modern and closed, the resistance to Pope Francis is because of his openness to many areas in the life of the Church and society. To use a politically commonplace vocabulary, the "conservative" sections in the Church and society are up in arms against Pope Francis for his "progressive" views and his openness in exercising his papal ministry. He is trying to change "Vatican's Worldview," which explains the stridency of the critique he faces.[10] Even more, he is trying to reform the Roman Curia dislodging those entrenched there for years on end and who feel threatened about their dream careers. In his annual address to the Roman Curia in 2015, he was forthright about the "diseases" from which the Curia suffers – "spiritual Alzheimer" and "pathology of power." These were no flattering comments. They became ammunition to attack him.[11] What is remarkable is the resoluteness of Francis to weather the storm. No wonder his determination to change has earned him the title of "Dictator Pope" from his detractors.[12]

I think we may not be able to gauge the epochal significance of this papacy if we relate Francis to the teachings of Vatican II alone.

Under the past two pontificates (John Paul II and Benedict XVI), theological debates abounded on the reception and hermeneutics of Vatican II – whether Vatican II is to be interpreted in continuation with the Councils of Trent and Vatican I or whether it represents a caesura, a break with this tradition. This was the pivotal point at the Extraordinary Synod of 1985.

Further, there was a heated discussion on whether the Universal Church or the Local Church comes first. Western theological titans like Ratzinger and Kasper clashed on these points. Finally, the Congregation for the Doctrine of the Faith came out with a document that affirmed the *chronological* and *ontological* priority of the Universal Church. Theologians are racking their brains as to what all that means. Further, people from Asia, Africa, and Latin America were warned that their project of inculturation should not be at the risk of losing the Greco-Roman heritage, which, they were told, is an integral part of the Christian kerygma itself. Asian theologians and others from the Global South were flabbergasted.

Francis does not entertain any jugglery of theological concepts to awe his audience. He wants to avoid driving through the highway of theological debates about Vatican II, in which case the opposition to him may have been less fierce than we are witnessing. His would have been simply an inflexion within a basic theological model of Vatican II. One could debate with Francis on the significance of Vatican II, hoping that he would speak a conventional idiom and language and that any differences could be sorted out.

But the problem with Francis is that he treads the rough ground of everyday life and enters the byways and lanes of life. He relates the core of the gospel to the down-to-earth realities of life. This is something familiar to him. This was what he was doing as a shepherd in Buenos Aires. In short, he interprets Vatican II from the margins, from life at the periphery. He draws on his experiences. All this is unpalatable. He views his mission not only to put into practice the teachings of Vatican II. These teachings are now cramped by hermeneutical sophistry and minutiae. He also wants to come to terms with what did not emerge forcefully enough in Vatican II – the poor who make up the very heart of the gospel. The Good News to the poor, to whom Jesus promised the Kingdom of God, is the central agenda of Pope Francis.

He is not simply trying to do reforms and renewal but is attempting, against many odds, a paradigm shift in the life and engagement of the Church. The radical consequences of this commitment to the poor unsettle the establishment of the Church and the present world order. It challenges clericalism and careerism, the evils he never ceases to decry and denounce. No wonder he has become too unsavoury to the acolytes of a constricted tribal Catholicism ruled by an elitist clergy. Hence the high voltage of censure and resistance from within. While the support of his immediate predecessor Benedict XVI for Tridentine mass raised concerns about the Conciliar liturgical reform, Francis does not allow any compromise in the matter as he considers the Conciliar reforms as normative. Moreover, he has given up any centralization with regard to the translation of Roman liturgical texts, letting the local bishops' conferences, as the best judges, to decide upon translations in their respective languages. This firm commitment to the liturgical reform of Vatican II is also another point of resentment and furore on the part of his conservative critics.

I must add that what is at stake is not orthodoxy and tradition. In reality, it is the call of Francis for *greater accountability and transparency* (including financial transactions) in the Church and in its leadership, beginning from the curia. Naturally, this causes heartburn and stirs up fierce resistance. But there is an effort to camouflage these deeper issues as a matter of doctrine, of orthodoxy and try to strike Francis with this weapon of heterodoxy in the hope that it will garner support in their battle against him.

Capitalism Up in Arms

Francis garners strong disapproval due to his unrelenting critic of unrestrained capitalism and the global market. His actions and outspoken statements pose such a formidable challenge that they unsettle not only capitalists but also staunch market ideologues and practitioners. Pope takes on Wall Street and does not mince his words in chastising an impersonal and deterministic economy bereft of humanizing purposes. In this economy, values go into thin air. His call for equality and justice and denunciation of structures of injustice have infuriated the elites, the corporates, and the capitalist lobby. In his Apostolic Exhortation, *Evangelii Gaudium*, Francis called the market economy a murderous system which kills people.[13] It is capitalism that has caused increasing inequality in the world and impoverishment of developing countries. For him, unbridled capitalism and greedy accumulation of money and wealth are the "dung of the devil." No wonder he has gained many enemies in the capitalist world, and among them are many American conservative Catholics and even some ecclesiastics. Steve Bannon, the former adviser to Trump at the White House, is the leader who galvanizes the anti-Francis crusade. For him, Pope Francis is bad for business. Instead, he supports populist politicians masquerading as defenders of Christian West against migrants.

While Francis was flying to Maputo, Mozambique, a journalist told him, "Holy Father, the Americans hate you." His reply. It's "an honour that the Americans attack me."[14] It meant he was telling some uncomfortable truth about the capitalist system and its driving force in the market. The argument of his capitalist critics: First, the pope lacks knowledge of economics, so he should not venture into a realm which is not his. Second, he is a person of religion, and he should confine himself to his turf - the religious realm - and not meddle with issues of the economy that is not within his competence. We need to investigate deeper into the anti-Francis mood of capitalists. The arguments against the pope speaking about ecology – *Laudato Si* – are the same.

American capitalists see in this Jesuit Pope Francis the heritage, the legacy of the six Jesuits killed in El Salvador on the night between 15 – 16 November 1989. Fr Ignacio Ellacuría and his five companions at the Central American University in San Salvador were dragged out from their rooms in the middle of the night and brutally shot dead, along with the woman who cooked for the community and her daughter. After some years, I visited El Salvador at the invitation of my long-time friend, Jon Sobrino, who was part of that community but escaped death because he was away that night.[15] Sobrino showed me around, and I saw and was moved by the blood-stained clothes of these martyrs.

During the civil war, Ellacuría and his companions became the powerful voice of the powerless, the poor, the kidnapped, and the murdered. They were against unbridled capitalism and imperialism; they were against the violence unleashed by the imperial forces against the poor.

Ellacuría was the chief advisor to Archbishop (now Saint) Romero. The inspiration to stand up for justice for the poor led to the massacre of these exemplary Christian witnesses by the army personnel trained in the USA with the blessings of the US administration. Ellacuría, the rector of the Central American University, and his companions were branded as communists and as the inspiration behind the guerillas. In the minds of the imperialists, Pope Francis standing up for the poor and the marginalized evokes the image of the martyrs of El Salvador and their fearless commitment. Francis is the scapegoat on whom is heaped the long-harboured resentment of the USA's capitalism and militarism. They see the revival of the old enemy, the liberation Theology of Latin America in Pope Francis. As long as the popes painted in the darkest colours communism and projected it as a danger to Catholic teaching and morality, traditional Catholics were happy. Francis is the first pope to turn the tables. He points his finger at capitalism and the dehumanization of the poor for which he holds it responsible.

According to an assessment of the Franciscan papacy made by the Pew Centre of Research after the first five years, among the USA Catholics, the pope had, quite surprisingly, an 84 per cent of approval rating[16]- strikingly different from the position of the Church leaders in that country. Besides their conservative doctrinal position, some prominent members of the American Catholic hierarchy also seem to soft-pedal on capitalism and play second fiddle. But, as more than one American bishop stated, the critique of the pope does not apply to American capitalism, which is "soft- capitalism"! The capitalist economists, on their part, think that the pope does not appreciate enough the role played by market and that his views of capitalism is conditioned by his experience of the "crony capitalism" of his native Argentina.

A negative campaign against the papacy is unleashed in the public realm by several influential media and journalists like New York Times columnist Ross Douthat, who fears a schism in the Catholic Church,[17] and the politically right-wing journalist Philip Lawler. The title of the latter author's work is quite dramatic: *Lost Shepherd. How Pope Francis is Misleading His Flock.*[18]

Right-wing Populists – New Defenders of Christianity

Pope Francis is hated by right-wing populists and nationalists in Europe and elsewhere, just because he speaks out on the plight of the immigrants and refugees and appeals for a welcome policy towards them. In one of his addresses to the Pontifical Academy of Social Sciences, the pope said how he is concerned about the "re-emergence, somewhat throughout the world, of aggressive tendencies toward foreigners, and migrants, as well as that growing nationalism that disregards the common good."[19] He is opposed by right-wing political outfits like the Northern League party in Italy headed by Mateo Salvini - till September 2019, deputy prime minister and home minister of Italy. Salvini, a divorcee, is never known as a practising Catholic, but holds a rosary at public appearances on TV, holds a crucifix while addressing press conferences, and invokes the Virgin of Immaculate Conception for his political victory.[20] He staunchly opposes Pope Francis and his policies in the Church and the world. But, unfortunately, populists like Matteo Salvini are supported by people in the Church who oppose Pope Francis.

The far-right's recent victory in the European Union's parliamentary elections has further strengthened the increasing opposition to Francis. These right-wing politicians seem to enjoy the blessings and ecclesiastical patronage of some prelates since these politicians are viewed by them as defenders of western Christianity against the invasion of Islamic migrants. These populist politicians are projected in a favourable light among conservative Catholic voters.

Papacy with a Contextual Vision of Faith and Theology

Like all other ministries in the Church, papacy is in service of faith. This profound vision of faith inspired Pope Francis and led him to adopt a different approach of the Church to the world. The new relationship he envisages between faith-experience and mission also marks his dynamic theological orientation.

Faith is a way of seeing. Like the external eyes, faith is an inner or third eye. It lets us see reality in a different light. It is like the enlightenment of Siddhartha under the peepal tree. That experience made the enlightened one – the Buddha. Without narrating, let me allude here to the allegory of the cave in Plato's *Republic*, which is also a story of enlightenment. No wonder the early Church called the sacrament of faith – baptism – as *photismos* – illumination, enlightenment. Well-known is the transformation of Paul on the way to Damascus and the conversion of St Augustine. If we consider all these, we will understand what faith means as a new way of seeing. Everything looks different. Communicating from this experience of enlightenment is true evangelization.

This is very different from understanding faith as a set of propositions to believe in, to be preserved and transmitted. St Thomas Aquinas rightly reminds us, "*Actus fidei non terminatur ad enuntiabile sed ad rem*" (the act of faith does not end in propositions but in reality). When we conceive faith in terms of statements to be believed in, we will end up in a curious situation like the one that caused an infelicitous schism in the Church. I am referring to the theological dispute "*filioque*" which split Eastern Christianity from the West. The argument was whether the Spirit proceeds from the Father alone or the Father and the Son. A divided Christendom was the consequence. For any doctrine or faith tenet to be credible, it needs to refer to our life and concern for the salvation of the world.

For Pope Francis, faith and theology are dynamic and contextual. They need to be lived and practiced with reference to our experiences today and our struggles, hopes, and aspirations. Faith and theology are responses to God's continuous speaking. Through his deep engagement with all the burning problems and concerns that touch the people, especially those at the margins, the vision of Pope Francis' faith and theology acquire great vitality and dynamism.

Francis' Understanding of the Church and Its Ministry

The traditional image of the Church could be likened to a fortress – unassailable, unchanging. I am reminded about the episcopal motto of Cardinal Ottaviani, who played the leader of traditional Catholicism at Vatican II. It read: "*Semper Idem*" (ever the same!). Compare the fortress image with that of Pope Francis: Church as a field hospital – attending to the urgent needs of the people in critical situations.[21]

When I hear accusations that Pope Francis does not follow the traditional teaching, I am reminded of the words of the great Cardinal Bea, who immensely contributed to Vatican II. When he presented some of his views at the Council, he was opposed saying that what he was saying was not traditional teaching. Cardinal Bea is supposed to have answered, "Well, this is not traditional teaching, but life today is not traditional!" The expectation from the pope is that he keeps to tradition in his teachings. But these catholic fundamentalists do not understand that continuity has not always been the norm. There have also been instances of a breakthrough in tradition and traditional teaching. It is illuminating to see, for example, how the Church, from the negation of religious freedom, which was included as one of the errors in the Syllabus of Errors of Pius IX, came to uphold and defend religious freedom as it happened with *Dignitatis Humanae* in Vatican II. Some of the things Pope Francis speaks and does fall into this tradition of breakthrough and may not be fitted into the tradition of continuity. The breakthrough is painful for many, but like the birth pangs, it brings new life to the Church, society and the world. The breakthrough moments have been most significant in the growth of the Church and its mission. With Francis, we are experiencing such an upswing in the history of the Church.

Yes, A Different Papacy

I am not comparing popes. Indeed, each one is different. They come from different contexts and varied worlds of experience. These inevitably affect their way of thinking, their vision of the Church, and relationship to the world and society.

John Paul II, for example, took up his papal ministry as someone who had experienced first-hand the world of communism, atheism, and the Cold War tensions. He lived in a country of an oppressive totalitarian state with allegiance to Marxist ideology. No wonder he tended to see the rest of the world as facing similar danger of communism and exposed to Marxist atheism. He interpreted that communism and Marxism were insidiously at work in Latin America while people were actually struggling against dictatorships, oppression, kidnappings, tortures, and killings.

Pope Benedict XVI experienced painfully the revolution of 1968 and the student protests of the time, the sexual revolution of the 1960s. He witnessed in his own native Germany and all over Europe the decline of traditional Catholic Christianity with a mass exodus of people from the Church. He interpreted such developments as resulting from secularism and relativism and as signs of the absence of God. Hence, he needed to restore the traditional faith and Catholicism to their pristine glory. This was evident already when he was prefect of the Congregation of the Doctrine of the Faith, preceding his papal ministry. Before the conclave, he could warn the cardinals about the danger the "dictatorship of relativism" poses to the Church. All these experiences and thoughts influenced his decisions and policies as the pope.[22]

Orthodoxy has been the primary agenda of the Congregation for the Doctrine of the Faith (CDF). It has been known in history for ostracizing and castigating any shade of doctrinal deflection or woolly expression. This curial institution gave the impression of a tomb where the doctrines of the Church were embalmed and preserved. Things seem to have quite perceptibly changed with the advent of Pope Francis, who accords primacy to orthopraxis, namely following the path of the gospel and putting it into practice. The removal of Cardinal Gerhard Müller from the headship of this dicastery was a clear sign of a new line of thinking of the pope. The exaggerated importance this Congregation enjoyed under then-Cardinal Joseph Ratzinger has waned, and it is being downsized to its correct proportions. In the document on Reform of the Roman Curia – *Praedicate Evangelium* – CDF is no more the Congregation listed immediately after the Secretariat of State, as was the case with *Pastor Bonus*. Instead, it is the Congregation that deals with Evangelization.[23]

Pope Francis has both his feet on the ground and is not lost in the Platonic world of ideas. To say this does not mean that he has no vision. On the contrary, he is a pope of true gospel vision. With this vision, we hope the pope will introduce much-desired reform in communication with the local Churches and respond to their difficulties and experiences. The curia is a service apparatus, which should become evident in its attitude and how it deals with the local Churches and the bishops leading them.[24]

We can only pity the papal nuncios who are shunted from one country to the other without being able to strike root anywhere. Many of them, despite their best intentions, are not dexterous in assessing the situation of the local churches - often due to their lack of knowledge about and familiarity with the culture, social structure, language, life- condition and history of the local people - and yet expected to play a crucial role in matters of such gravity as the selection of bishops for the local Churches. This is true of some of the Roman Congregations.[25] Pope Francis has started to bring more and more pastorally seasoned bishops from the local Churches for leadership roles at Vatican curial offices. That helps avoid careerism in the Roman Curia. But then the Pope is bearing the brunt of all these moves.

The Roman Curia often projects the image of an institution meant for the self-preservation of the Church. The engagement of Francis for the Reform of the Roman Curia, on the other hand, stems from his vision of the gospel, from the dream of a purified and transformed Church. We could read between the lines his reformist agenda when he says in his very first Apostolic Exhortation, *Evangelii Gaudium*: "I dream of a 'missionary option', that is a missionary impulse capable of transforming everything, so that the Church's customs, ways of doing things, times and schedules, language and structures can be suitably channeled for the evangelization of today's world than for her self-preservation."[26]

A Burdensome Legacy

Before Francis appeared on the scene, what had happened in the Church for the past forty years constituted a problematic and complicated legacy. Many collaborators Francis inherited in the curia, many bishops appointed worldwide during the last few decades, unfortunately, do not chime with his spirit. They were trained and brought up in a different legacy. In the immediate post-Vatican period, the criterion for the choice of bishops was whether the candidate was open to dialogue, had the aptitude to put into practice the teachings of Vatican II, and had the skills to guide the local Church in the spirit of collaboration and co-responsibility. In the last few decades, the criteria have dramatically shifted to loyalty - whether someone adheres to doctrinal tradition and orthodoxy. People whose orthodoxy was tested, on the basis, for example, of their views on reproductive and sexual morality, their stance vis-à-vis liberation theology, communism, relativism, and their stance on communion for the re-married divorcees, and so on were appointed.

Another disturbing legacy Francis inherited is the clerical sexual abuse which continues to vex the Church and drain its energy and resources. I think we also need to ask whether the traditional theology of the holy order has not been responsible for the present predicament in which the Church finds itself with the issue of clerical sexual abuse. I mean the theology of *ex opere operato*. This theology, as is well-known, originated in the polemics against Donatists.[27]

It was a completely different context. Transported lock stock and barrel to our times, without discernment of changing times, this theology gave the impression that the sacramental seal trumps the failings and misdeeds of a cleric, even when these go manifestly against human dignity and rights as is the case with clerical sexual abuse.

We could identify a general template at work in handling this issue. Instead of taking to task the perpetrator of sexual abuse, the clerics were shunted from one place to the other in a bid to protect them. All these shoddy dealings were shrouded in secrecy with no room for transparency. This is because many ecclesiastics think that sexual abuse is a sin to confess in secret, repent from, and be forgiven, not a matter of public crime to be prosecuted. Sexual abuse is a serious matter of human dignity and violates fundamental human rights. Claiming that the Church is a different society with the implicit understanding that its clerics are not subjected to civil jurisdiction when they violate human rights is totally unacceptable. But this seems to have been the ideology behind the cover-ups of most cases of clerical sexual abuse.

Francis stepped into his pontificate with an enormous problem of clerical sexual abuse on his back. The media was pouring out embarrassing materials and outrageous cases from different parts of the world and even from unsuspected quarters in the Church. It was a moral pandemic Francis inherited, and he had to face a world that was becoming increasingly more critical of how clerical sexual abuses were handled under his predecessors. Pope Francis realized the gravity of the matter. But he does not think problems could be solved through magisterial statements and declarations. In trying to respond to the crisis, he took into confidence the entire Church and the world- episcopate. In February 2019, he convened a four-day extraordinary consultative meeting with the presidents of bishop's conferences on how to go about clerical sexual abuse, which was eroding the Church and its credibility. It was the most open step to address an issue which has been devastating the Church. Unfortunately, Francis continues to bear the brunt of the inherited policy failures in this matter.

Risks and Ambiguities

Pope Francis has set a model for Church leaders to take risks, as he said famously, "I prefer a Church which is bruised, hurting and dirty because it has been out on the streets, rather than a Church which is unhealthy from being confined and from clinging to its own security."[28] This open and courageous vision of the Church leads Francis to take risks and face puzzling and ambiguous situations. Let me illustrate this with some instances.

On 21 September 2018, Pope Francis signed a historic agreement with the Chinese state. Ever since the Chinese Communist Party (CCP) came to power, the relationship with the Vatican has undergone severe tensions and strains, causing an unfortunate split in the Chinese Church between the so-called underground Church and the open Church. Pope Francis faced a dilemma. If you give in to the Chinese government, then the freedom of the Church and its mission will be seriously hampered. On the other hand, if you refuse any negotiation with the CCP, then the split in the Chinese Church will continue and cause a lot of confusion among the faithful. It is a precarious situation. There was opposition. Cardinal Zen, emeritus bishop of Hong Kong, felt that a deal with the CCP would be to send "the flock into the mouth of wolves."[29] He even named it a betrayal of the loyal Chinese underground Church.

Pope Francis could have postponed a decision, saying it was not yet the opportune moment to take one. Most administrators do this in the Church – delay instead of engaging with complex problems. As it is said, for cowards, the opportune moment never comes! The pope is aware of the importance of the present moment and coming to a decision, which he took amid contestations. There is a risk. In hindsight, the agreement with China could be the most outstanding achievement of Pope Francis' papacy, but it could also be the most monumental blunder. Pope was aware of the risks and yet took a clear decision.

On 4 January 2019, Pope went to Dubai and met with the Great Imam at Al Azhar, with whom he made a joint historic declaration of peace and religious harmony. The meeting was historical, and so too was the content of the joint statement. This statement acknowledges the plurality of religion as willed by God - a revolutionary message. Henceforth, Christian relationship with other faiths takes on a new dimension and calls for a different approach. Let me quote from this statement:

> Freedom is a right of every person; each individual enjoys the freedom of belief, thought, expression and action. The pluralism and the diversity of religions, colour, sex, race, and language are willed by God in His wisdom, through which He created human beings. This divine wisdom is the source of the right to freedom of belief and the freedom to be different. Therefore, the fact that people are forced to adhere to a certain religion or culture must be rejected as too, the imposition of a cultural way of life that others do not accept.[30]

Far-reaching are the consequences of this joint declaration for the theology of religions. Here is a landmark in the Christian theology of religions. If religions are willed by God, like race, gender difference, and the colour of the skin, we need to take them very seriously and work with them (religions) for the salvation of the world. His encyclical "Fratelli Tutti" went deeper into fostering brotherly and sisterly solidarity.[31]

The significance of this meeting with the Imam of Al-Azhar and signing of the declaration on fraternity stands out in bold relief against the background of the controversial lecture of Benedict XVI in Regensburg (12 September 2006), which allegedly stated that Christianity is rational; in contrast, Islam is not (quoting the last Christian Byzantine emperor Manuel II). In Muslim perception, the claims made in this lecture insult Islam. Coming from none other than the head of the Roman Catholic Church, the claims added to the gravity of the issue. It caused colossal commotion and street protests in Islamic countries. A Pakistan-based Islamic body issued a fatwa against the pope. Thanks to the quick diplomatic moves of the Vatican, the situation was diffused, and the Church was saved from further embarrassment.

In any genuine dialogue, it is more than just a matter of whether what I am saying is right. It is crucial how what I am saying is perceived by my dialogue partner. The recent visit of Pope Francis to Al Azhar and the joint declaration with the Imam there have contributed to healing the wounds of the past and have helped to win back the trust of our Islamic brothers and sisters. His encyclical Fratelli Tutti cemented the inclusive fraternity.[32]

Pope Francis does not gloss over complex issues but takes the bull by its horn. One clear example is the issue of homosexuality which is not simply a moral issue but a humanistic issue. That there are people who have innate homosexual tendencies similar to heterosexuality is something no one can ignore. However, simply by possessing the bent and inclination, homosexuals automatically do not become sinners. In this case, the Pope showed that everything need not be subjected to moral judgement. We leave certain things to God to judge. Hence his reply to the journalist as he was travelling back from Brazil, "If a person is gay and seeks God and has goodwill, who am I to judge?" It implied that homosexuals should not be marginalized but integrated into society.[33]

Besides the issue of homosexuality, he has boldly confronted the long-standing pastoral problems connected with family. He convened two synods on this issue. One of the most disputed questions at these two synods was about giving communion to the re-married divorcees. It was an extremely sensitive issue with opinions very divided. He did not avoid this thorn in the flesh when he came out with his post-synodal exhortation. He faced it and made his view known with solid arguments. There is a footnote in *Amoris Laetitia,* where the pope expresses the possibility of communion to the divorcees and re-married due to mitigating situations.[34] His argument is in the spirit of the gospel. Quoting *Evangelii Gaudium* Pope says, "Eucharist is not a prize for the perfect, but a powerful medicine and nourishment for the weak." Eucharist is not only for the healthy and the holy but also has therapeutic or curing effects. Hell broke out from this footnote! Pope was accused of turning against the orthodoxy of the Catholic faith and tradition. His understanding of faith is much broader and deeper, and he stands his ground.

Let me cite one more instance that speaks volumes about Pope Francis' boldness to act amid uncertainties and ambiguities. I am referring here to the convocation of the Synod of Amazonia (October 6 – 27, 2019). Such a regional synod itself was a bold innovation. Pope created an environment of freedom of expression, giving the synodal reflections and proposals considerable attention and thought.

For example, he let such recommendations be made as the ordination of married men and women's ministry. But the synod was marred by controversy around the wooden statue of a lady (Pachamama) presented to the pope. The two-feet-high figurine became the focus of ire and vandalism. For those who presented it, the statue in question had multivalent meanings - mother Earth, Virgin Mary, fertility, life in Amazonia etc., whereas it was a provocation for people who saw just one thing in the statue – an idol!

If we analyze deeply, we will note that there was resistance to this synod by Euro-centric Catholicism which believes the legacy of Plato and Aristotle is an integral part of Christian kerygma. This Catholicism and *ancien régime* Christianity look cynically at efforts like that of indigenous peoples of Amazonia who live and understand faith according to their ethos and genius. The resistance, fear, and anger of Euro-centric Catholicism have discredited the synod and trivialized the initiative of Pope Francis. Through the Synod of Amazonia, Pope Francis allowed the face of another way of being Christian and Catholic be manifested at the very heart of Rome. It proved to be a provocation for Euro-centric Christianity.

Boldly, Francis has also led the Church in being more transparent than before in disclosing and being accountable for Vatican finances. It was a move that naturally upset those within the tightly controlled circle in Rome whose expenses and inflows had not seen such scrutiny before and naturally resisted this newfound openness.[35]

Conclusion

The Church is a tent; it moves with the people. It shifts. It is not a weakness. Faith in God makes the Church a pilgrim, always on the way. Hence there is no room for any sense of triumph as if one has reached the final goal. True to the pilgrim nature of the Church, we have a universal pastor who does not use his formal authority to impose. Here is a pope who listens to the local Churches and to Bishops' Conferences. Pope Francis listens to the voices of the indigenous peoples (Synod of Amazonia), representatives of the victims of clerical sexual abuse, prisoners, the physically challenged, the voices of peoples of other faiths, and the voices of refugees and migrants. The result is a different papacy. It is not a papacy of ermine cap, silk, and custom-made fine red shoes, cultivating a life of aloofness, and nestled in a cultural ambience of medieval nobility; no, it is a life lived in elegant simplicity residing in the community of Santa Marta, settling his own hotel bills, looking for his spectacles in an optical shop, and carrying his own bag on travel, like most people. As Leonardo Boff humorously remarked, it is difficult to poison Pope Francis because he stands in the queue with others to collect his food at his humble residence in Santa Marta![36]

Pope Francis is battling to carry forward the spirit of Vatican II and its legacy with a renewed and intensified focus on the poor and the marginalized. The major stumbling block he encounters on this journey is the stiff resistance to change among an influential segment within the Church. There is a fixated mindset among Church leaders and Church- institutions. Any radical reform occurs when a new mindset – *novus habitus mentis* - comes into being. To inculcate the flexibility of mind and openness to change, Francis refers to the words of Cardinal Newman, whom he recently canonized. "Here on earth to live is to change, and to change often is to become more perfect."[37] Francis' efforts at decentralization and synodal governance in the Church provoke a reaction. He encounters this difficulty both in the Roman Curia and in the leadership of local Churches, infected with feudal mindset and trappings.

From what I have said, it should be clear by now that to be Pope Francis is not a bed of roses but of thorns. It is a terrible experience of even isolation and loneliness. Marco Politi, a biographer of Pope Francis, has titled his work "*The Francis' Loneliness. A Prophetic Pope. A Church in Stormy Seas.*"[38] In his own house and Curia, Pope Francis is misunderstood and sidelined. Pope Francis needs the support of all of us. We support him by following his vision of faith, his path of the gospel, his image of the Church, and his continuing engagement with society and the world. His resoluteness to change and readiness for transformation are on account of his deep introspection and learning from his controversial leadership of the Society of Jesus in his native Argentina.[39]

The pope was working on the Reform of the Roman Curia. When I was president of the International Theological Journal *Concilium*, we prepared a special issue on the Reformation of the Roman Curia to support the pope in his reform initiative.[40] We released the volume in Rome. Copies in Italian and Spanish were reached to the Pope. Later, we concluded that to carry out the renewal of the Church, the existing code of canon law is inadequate. Hence, we brought out an issue on "Revision of Canon Law."[41] The idea proposed was to reshape the canon law to support the pope's initiatives for renewing the Church. The efforts to reform the Roman Curia have finally borne fruit in the recent document *Praedicate Evangelium*, issued on 19 March 2022.[42]

The voice of Asia, Africa and Latin America is not loud enough, though it is here that Catholicism is alive and vibrant. The European Catholics – from where most opposition against this non-classic pope stems, are just 21.5% compared to the rest of the world. It is time that the voices from the Global South resound. We need to tell the Euro-centric Christianity and the Catholic fundamentalists that we stand by the vision and praxis of Pope Francis because we see the splendour and joy of the gospel reflected in his words and actions. Our steadfast commitment to addressing the pressing challenges of our era will demonstrate that he is not merely a solitary crusader. Dose not what Francis both articulates and undertakes resonate deeply with our shared experiences in this region. Is he not indeed a pope from "the end of the earth"?

NOTES

1 On the other hand, Pope Francis is unprecedently popular and beloved more broadly among Christians and non-Christians, sought after by youth, women, social media influencers, rights and climate activists and civil society, political leaders and governments. One indication is that he has about 19 million followers on Twitter. Pew, 2021 found that apart from slight dips in popularity a few years ago, Francis's popularity has remained undiminished and if anything grown in recent years. In the US he is popular among well over 80% of Catholics. It is a different matter when it comes to the bishops. See https://www.aljazeera.com/features/2020/2/2/pope-francis-everyman-pontiff-profile [accessed on 26 May 2023]. https://polls.saintleo.edu/pope-francis-remains-popular-with-americans-new-saint-leo-poll-shows/ [accessed on 26 May 2023].

2 https://www.ilfoglio.it/chiesa/2022/12/03/news/un-papa-pasticcione-fa-perfino-simpatia-ma-e-mista-a-pena-4729653/ [accessed on 2 January, 2023].

3 It would appear that many Indian prelates are keen to get the pope to visit India and be part of a sweet spectacle. Still, his teachings on de-centralization of power, participation, and synodality seem to taste bitter for them.

4 https://www.ncregister.com/news/four-cardinals-formally-ask-pope-for-clarity-on-amoris-laetitia [accessed on 2 January 2023].

5 https://insidethevatican.com/news/newsflash/letter-65-2019-vigano-on-francis-and-mary/ [accessed on 2 January 2023].

6 In order to examine whether Francis is a pastoral pope lacking profound theology, a conference was organized by the University of Vienna, Austria, in October 2015, in which I had the privilege of participating and speaking. The conclusion of the conference is very different from the widely circulated perception. It brought out the depth of the theology of Pope Francis. For the papers of the conference, see Kurt Appel, and Helmuit Deibl eds., *Barmherzigkeit und zärtliche Liebe. Das theologische Progamm von Past Frazisus* (Freiburg: Herder, 2016).

7 Massimo Borghesi, *The Mind of Pope Francis* (Collegeville, Minnesota: The Liturgical Press, 2018).

8 For a deeper analysis of Francis's struggles, see Marco Politi, *Pope Francis Among the Wolves* (New York: Columbia University Press, 2015).

9   Peter A. Kwasniewski ed., *From Benedict's Peace to Francis's War* (Brooklyn, New York: Angelico Press, 2021).

10   Roland Flamini, "Is Pope Francis Shifting the Vatican's Worldview?" *World Affairs* 177, no. 2 (July / August 2014): 25–33.

11   For the text of the speech, see the Vatican website: https://www.vatican.va/content/francesco/en/speeches/2015/december/documents/papa-francesco_20151221_curia-romana.html [accessed on 5 August 2023].

12   Marcantonio Colonna [Henry Sire], *The Dictator Pope: The Inside Story of the Francis Papacy* (Washington DC: Regnery Publisher, 2018).

13   *Evangelii Gaudium* 53

14   https://www.nytimes.com/2019/09/04/world/africa/pope-americans-attack.html [accessed on 2 January 2023].

15   Cf. Robert Lasalle-Klein, *Blood and Ink: Ignacio Ellacuría, Jon Sobrino, and the Jesuit Martyrs of the University of Central America* (New York: Orbis Books, 2014).

16   James J. Bacik, *Pope Francis and His Critics: A Historical and Theological Perspective* (New York: Paulist Press, 2020), Introduction.

17   Cf. Ross Douthat, *To Change the Church* (New York: Simon & Schuster Paperbacks, 2018).

18   Philip Lawler, *Lost Shepherd. How Pope Francis is Misleading His Flock* (Washington DC: Regnery Gateway 2018).

19   https://www.vatican.va/content/francesco/en/speeches/2019/may/documents/papa-francesco_20190502_plenaria-scienze-sociali.html [accessed on 5 August 2023].

20   https://apnews.com/article/pope-francis-europe-ap-top-news-religion-international-news ef2b2fb43ed645c3a95107ad0646e1c5 [accessed on 3 January 2023].

21   On the ecclesiology of "field-hospital," see Massimo Borghesi, *Catholic Discordance: Neoconservatism vs. the Field Hospital Church of Pope Francis* (Collegeville, Minnesota: The Liturgical Press, 2021).

22   For the difference in character and approach between Benedict XVI and Francis, see Anthony McCarten, *The Two Popes: Francis, Benedict, and the Decision That Shook the World* (UK: Penguin Books, 2019).

23   "How Praedicate Evangelium Changes the Vatican's Dicasteries: A CNA Explainer," https://www.aciafrica.org/news/5478/how-praedicate-evangelium-changes-the-vaticans-dicasteries-a-cna-explainer - [accessed on 4 January 2023].

24   On what the reform costs Francis, see Austen Ivereigh, *Wounded Shepherd: Pope Francis and His Struggle to Convert the Catholic Church* (New York: Henry Holt and Company, 2019); see also Christopher Lamb, *The Outsider: Pope Francis and His Battle to Reform the Church* (New York: Orbis Books, 2020).

25   Felix Wilfred, "At Crossroads: Congregation for the Evangelization of Peoples," *Indian Currents* 7, no.13 (February 2022): 32 – 35.

26   *Evangelii Gaudium* no. 27. On the many initiatives of Pope Francis to reach out to the world with a message of peace, solidarity, and fraternity, see Mario L Aguilar, *Pope Francis: Journeys of a Peacemaker* (Delhi: Routledge, 2022).

27   For more on this point, see Chapter 14.

28   *Evangelii Gaudium* 49.

29   https://www.theguardian.com/world/2018/sep/22/vatican-pope-francis-agreement-with-china-nominating-bishops [accessed on 2 January 2023].

30   "A Document on Human Fraternity. For World Peace and Living Together," https://www.vatican.va/content/francesco/en/travels/2019/outside/documents/papa-francesco_20190204_documento-fratellanza-umana.html [accessed on 3 January, 2023].

31   For the text of the encyclical see: https://www.vatican.va/content/francesco/en/encyclicals/documents/papa-francesco_20201003_enciclica-fratelli-tutti.html [accessed on 4 January 2023]. See also, Michael Amaladoss, Antony Lawrence, and Joseph Victor Edwin, eds., *Fratelli Tutti. An Indian Reading* (Bengaluru: ATC Publishers, 2021); Felix Wilfred, "Fratelli Tutti as an Exercise in Subaltern Public Theology," *Vidyajyoti*, 85, no.4 (2021): 246–268.

32   https://www.vatican.va/content/francesco/en/encyclicals/documents/papa-francesco_20201003_enciclica-fratelli-tutti.html [accessed on 4 January, 2023].

33   Concilium reflected on the question in a special issue "Homosexualities," *Concilium* (2008/1).

34   *Amoris Laetitia* 305, footnote 351.

35   See https://www.americamagazine.org/politics-society/2022/01/28/vatican-budget-2022-242297#:~:text=A%20second%20source%20of%20income%20is%20from%20external,Works%20of%20Religion%20%28often%20called%20the%20Vatican%20Bank%29 [accessed on 26 May 2023].

36   Https://Leonardoboff.Org/2022/03/24/Merciless-Attacks-Against-Pope-Francis-Righteous-Among-The-Nations/ [accessed on 8 May 2023].

37   https://www.americamagazine.org/faith/2019/12/21/pope-francis-tells-roman-curia-do-not-fear-change-it-nature-missionary-church [accessed on 3 January 2023].

38   Marco Politi, *La solitudine di Francesco. Un papa profetico, una Chiesa in tempesta* (Roma-Bari: Editori Laterza, 2019); see also Austen Ivereigh, *The Great Reformer: Francis and the Making of a Radical Pope* (Bloomsbury: Atlantic Books, 2017).

39   On how his experiences in Argentina transformed him, see Paul Vallely, *The Struggle for The Soul of Catholicism: Untying the Knots*. Revised and Updated Edition (London, New York: Bloomsbury Publisher, 2015).

40   *Concilium* (2013/5).

41   *Concilium* (2016/5).

42   https://www.vatican.va/content/francesco/en/apost_constitutions/ documents/20220319-costituzione-ap-praedicate-evangelium.html [accessed on 4 January 2023].

FURTHER READING

Aguilar, Mario L. *Pope Francis Journeys of a Peacemaker*. Delhi: Routledge, 2022.

Amaladoss, Michael, Antony Lawrence, and Joseph Victor Edwin, eds. *Fratelli Tutti. An Indian Reading*. Bengaluru: ATC Publishers, 2021.

Amaladoss, Michael. "The Newness of Pope Francis." *Ignis Quarterly* LIII, no. 1 (2023): 82–93.

Ammiche-Quinn, Regina, et al. "Homosexualities." *Concilium* 2008-1.

Appel, Kurt, and Helmuit Deibl, eds. *Barmherzigkeit und zärtliche Liebe. Das theologische Progamm von Past Frazisus*. Freiburg: Herder, 2016.

Bacik, James J. *Pope Francis and His Critics: A Historical and Theological Perspective*. New York: Paulist Press, 2020.

Borghesi, Massimo. *Catholic Discordance: Neoconservatism vs. the Field Hospital Church of Pope Francis*. Collegeville, Minnesota: The Liturgical Press, 2021.

Borghesi, Massimo. *The Mind of Pope Francis*. Collegeville, Minnesota: The Liturgical Press, 2018.

Colonna, Marcantonio. *The Dictator Pope: The Inside Story of the Francis Papacy*. Washington DC: Regnery Publisher, 2018.

Douthat, Ross. *To Change the Church*. New York: Simon & Schuster Paperbacks, 2018.

Flamini, Roland. "Is Pope Francis Shifting the Vatican's Worldview?" *World Affairs* 177, no. 2 (July / August 2014): 25–33.

Gonsalves, Francis. "Pope Francis' Revolution of Tender Love." *Ignis Quarterly* LIII, no. 1 (2023): 9–25.

Ivereigh, Austen. *The Great Reformer: Francis and the Making of a Radical Pope*. Bloomsbury: Atlantic Books, 2017.

Ivereigh, Austen. *Wounded Shepherd: Pope Francis and His Struggle to Convert the Catholic Church*. New York: Henry Holt and Company, 2019.

Kwasniewski, Peter A. ed. *From Benedict's Peace to Francis's War*. Brooklyn, New York: Angelico Press, 2021.

Lamb, Christopher. *The Outsider: Pope Francis and His Battle to Reform the Church.* New York: Orbis Books, 2020.

Lasalle-Klein, Robert. *Blood and Ink: Ignacio Ellacuría, Jon Sobrino, and the Jesuit Martyrs of the University of Central America.* New York: Orbis Books, 2014.

Lawler, Philip. *Lost Shepherd. How Pope Francis is Misleading His Flock.* Washington DC: Regnery Gateway 2018.

McCarten, Anthony. *The Two Popes: Francis, Benedict, and the Decision That Shook the World.* UK: Penguin Books, 2019.

Pandikattu, Kuruvilla. "The Mission and Message of Pope Francis: The Moral Imperative for Equity and Fraternity." *Jnanadeepa* 27, no.1 (2023): 92–113.

Politi, Marco. *La solitudine di Francesco. Un papa profetico, una Chiesa in tempesta.* Roma-Bari: Editori Laterza, 2019.

Politi, Marco. *Pope Francis Among the Wolves.* New York: Columbia University Press, 2015.

Raupp, Klaus Da Silva. "Pope Francis' Call for a New Economy." *Concilium* (2021/2): 133–136.

Vallely, Paul. *The Struggle for the Soul of Catholicism: Untying the Knots.* London, New York: Bloomsbury Publisher, 2015.

Wilfred, Felix. "At Crossroads: Congregation for the Evangelization of Peoples." *Indian Currents* 7, no.13 (Feb. 2022): 32–35.

Wilfred, Felix. "*Fratelli Tutti* as an Exercise in Subaltern Public Theology." *Vidyajyoti* 85, no.4 (2021): 246–268.

PUBLIC THEOLOGY

Chapter 11

ASIAN THEOLOGICAL TRAJECTORIES AND NEW FRONTIERS OF PUBLIC THEOLOGY

Despite the western theology pursued in Asia in colonial times, there were laudable attempts for indigenous theologies. However, these were mostly focused upon relating Christian thought with Asian philosophy, culture, and tradition. A new ferment of liberative and transformative theology touching upon the lives of the people in context had to wait for the movements for national independence to pick up vigour. These provided a new impetus, fresh perspectives, and indigenous resources for original and liberative theological enterprises.

In the first part of this chapter, we shall go into an analysis of factors and forces at work in the post-colonial era that paved the way for Asian theologies. We will also present some of the salient features and characteristics of Asian theologies, despite regional differences in societies, cultures, and histories. The second and longer part of the chapter will highlight the importance of moving in a new direction of public theology focusing on the question and issues that touch upon the lives of the people. The presentation then goes on to sketch some of the features that will characterize Asian public theologies.

Part I: New Theological Discourses in the Post-Colonial Era

The emergence of fresh Asian theological perspectives and insights have to do with the social and political developments in the various regions of the continent. We can identify a few common factors: First, Asian countries experienced a surge of many movements for national independence which struggled against colonial powers – British, French, Dutch, Portuguese and American. The issue of liberation caught the imagination of the masses and the leaders involved in these struggles. These movements were propelled by the power deriving from indigenous resources and traditions of the people, and their past history. The liberative energies released in the anti-imperialist and anti-colonial struggles waged in different Asian countries, each in its own way, constitute a general point of reference for theological discourses in our societies.

Second, in the post-independence era, many of the Asian countries underwent the experience of repressive dictatorial regimes, for example, in Indonesia, the Philippines, Pakistan, and Korea. Fresh and prolonged struggles of the people for freedom and democracy brought new dimensions to the dynamic alignments in the common cause of the liberation of the people.

Third, there has been the sprouting of many voluntary and grassroots movements taking up particular issues at the local level and fighting for liberation. We have been witnessing the fast expansion of these groups to counter the situation of growing economic disparity, social discrimination, and political marginalization of the weaker sections in Asian societies. Through their involvement at the grassroots, they aimed at radical social transformation. These groups came into existence due to various reasons, chief among which are the betrayal of the promises of Asian states at the dawn of the post-colonial period to promote justice and equality and the general disillusionment with the state policy of development.[1]

Fourth, another critical force has been the awakening of the subaltern groups, marginal peoples, and ethnic and linguistic minorities within the different nation-states. This is true almost of all Asian countries, but particularly of South and South-East Asian countries. It has been a complex phenomenon, and they range from a demand for legitimate rights through democratic means to a violent and militant involvement in the cause of political freedom and cultural autonomy. We could think of the various tribal movements like the *Jharkhand* and *Dalit* movements of India, the *Suiheisha* movement for the liberation of the Japanese outcasts (Burakumin), and the prolonged and bloody conflict of the Tamils for their legitimate rights and autonomy in Sri Lanka. Some of these movements have a long history of dissent, resistance and struggle to win their freedom. In the post-colonial period, these movements have acquired considerable momentum.

Fifth, A further factor, closely connected with the above, is the re-reading of the history – the cultural, religious, social and political – of the subaltern groups. Through this re-reading, the subaltern groups and the backward castes and classes want to reclaim their heritage and their distinct historical and social identity. Notably, significant has been the reclaiming of folk-traditions and the religious heritage of the indigenous peoples and the marginalized.[2]

In India, for example, the ongoing debates on the nature of Hinduism has much to do with the claim by the subalterns of their distinctive religious universe. While the upper castes and classes want to see Hinduism as an all-encompassing cultural and religious reality, forming the basis for India's political unity, the marginal people maintain that what is known as Hinduism is, in fact, the amalgamation of many indigenous religious traditions and streams belonging to the tribals and many oppressed peoples. Similarly, in Korea, attention is being focused today on the relevance of Shamanistic tradition associated with people at the fringes, and especially women.

Such readings of history and reclaiming of traditions have contributed to the struggles of the marginalized against their long-standing oppression. Of particular significance for Asian theologies are the numerous ecological and feminist movements. Ecological questions in Asia, as in many other parts of the Global South, are also questions of *equality and justice.* For the over-exploitation of land, sea, forests, and other natural resources through modern technological means, and the resultant accumulation of wealth in the hands of a few causes hunger, misery, and deprivation of basic necessities of life to millions of Asians. Tribals, peasants, and fisher-people are among the most affected. Preserving the environment from degradation finds expression in the reclamation of the marginalized communities of their rightful, ancestral privileges concerning forests, lands, and oceans.

In the past few decades, there has been a spurt of actions and initiatives to liberate Asian women both from traditional as well as modern forms of slavery and oppression and uphold their dignity and freedom. There are many aspects of Asian cultural life that stand in the way of the liberation of women which need to be critically approached. Many women's groups and movements not only claim equal dignity, status, and opportunities but go deeper into the very system of patriarchy – both in its traditional and contemporary forms; both in the Church and in the society. Discrimination and violence against women are built into the dominant patriarchal mode of thinking and acting. Besides patriarchy, the prevailing market and capitalist culture of today has aggravated the oppression of women. We need to also highlight the violence against women, including state violence, by its police and military. Against the many experiences of oppression, there has emerged a vibrant Asian feminist theology which has its own unique and distinct marks.

We, therefore, conclude that there is a vigorous ferment of liberation sweeping through Asia. Though, liberation is not the monopoly of Christians, however, a Christian liberation theology makes sense in the Asian context of the general ferment of freedom in this continent. The birth of Christian liberation theology has been a response to this general mood of liberation in the various regions of Asia. This is something to take note of, since, there is a tendency even among scholars, to think that liberation theology in Asia is an extension and application of Latin American theology of liberation. What stands out from our above analysis is that liberation theology in Asia has its own historical roots and uniqueness.

These liberative theological articulations have a strong popular base as they reflect the experiences of some of the most oppressed sections in Asia, and their quest for freedom. Through these theologies, committed and socially conscious, Christians have been trying to contribute to the general project of liberation from their faith-perspective. Their reflections on faith and their attempts to re-read and re-interpret it led them to the formulation of Asian theologies of liberation, which can never be viewed independently of their context.

The Spirit of Asian Theology

Researching into the various theological efforts in Asia in the past decades and going through the documents of FABC and of Christian Conference of Asia (CCA), I find a certain convergence of concerns and shared perceptions. Asian theologising has a certain quality which may not always be explicitly articulated but could be found underlying. I wish to present here briefly the general spirit of Asian theologizing, instead of going into specific theological questions like Christology, ecclesiology, sacramental theology and so on. What we could safely state is that the following characteristics of Asian theologies provided inspiration for rethinking the various theological treatises and themes.

Sense of Divine Mystery

Asian theologies imply a sense of the inexhaustible mystery of God. This can be seen in the way Asian do Trinitarian Theology, Christology, mission theology or theology of religions. This sense of the divine mystery inspires Asian theologies not to follow paths of exclusion but of integration and inclusion. It is also behind the spirit of pluralism that characterizes Asian theologies. Pluralism here is not merely a reaction to dogmatism, but something born out of the realization that the mystery of God is inexhaustible and hence, innumerable are the ways in which it expresses itself – something to be rejoiced over. Asian theologies celebrate this pluralism and have tried to understand Jesus Christ and Christian faith from this perspective.

Reconceptualization of Mission

Asian approach to mission is inspired by the sense of divine mystery, as well as the dignity and freedom of human *subjects* in mission. Hence, mission is not simply a teleologically oriented project. Nor are people objects of mission, but subjects. It is they who in freedom appropriate faith, a process set in definite social, political, and cultural processes within their history. Therefore, it is crucial to enter into their world and understand their experience of faith and the multifarious expressions they give to it at various levels.

Moreover, the realization of the presence of God and the Spirit in peoples, cultures, religious traditions, etc., have contributed to reorient the traditional theologies of mission in Asia. It became very evident during the preparation as well as in the various interventions of bishops during the Asian Synod held in Rome in 1998. This broad vision of mission and evangelization is in stark contrast to the Christomonistic understanding of mission in Roman documents such as *Dominus Iesus* and *Ecclesia in Asia.* This was clearly seen in the response of the Japanese bishops to the *Lineamenta* for the Asian Synod, to which we referred in an earlier chapter.[3]

Asian theological efforts show more and more an integral understanding of mission and salvation. It means the wellbeing of the whole person without any dichotomy of body and soul, and the welfare of all without distinction of caste, class, religious belonging. Moving towards salvation implies progressive liberation from all that maims, corrodes or negates life in any form. It is a freedom from whatever binds the self as much as society and the world. Integral salvation and liberation imply that there are no two histories – one history of salvation and the other of the world moving on parallel lines. Some would even oppose one to the other. There is but one single history which all the peoples share across borders and boundaries, testifying to the universality of God's grace and dealings.[4] Here is an understanding of mission in a different key.

Recognizing Diversity and Pluralism

Few continents have such diversity in its composition of peoples, cultures, traditions, and the variety of gifts of nature as the Asian continent. The traditional recognition of pluralism and value of a life of harmony resist trends of uniformity and homogenization. For, among Asians, there is a mystical feeling that all the differences and plurality we experience meet somewhere and are somehow interconnected, though we are not able to identify clearly the bonds that bind us together. Asian theologies have cultivated this millennial spirit of diversity and pluralism of the continent. It is this which also inspires Asian theologies to recognize the infinite faces of the divine mystery.

Pluralism also derives from the fact that human beings are subjects and their perception of reality and their judgements are shaped by their differing world-views, experiences, diverse contexts, histories, and so on. This realisation has led Asian theologies to view the diversity of perspectives not as a hindrance but as a significant enrichment to the life of faith.

In this regard, we may recall here the *syadvada* heritage of Jainism. It was promoted at a time when there were many competing schools in conflict with each other. Syadvada does not approach the realm of truth assertively as if one has full control of it. Instead, a certain provisional character is recognised in our perception of reality. To put it in simple terms, we need to premise all our statements with a "May be…". This is an opening which lets the borders be porous and allows spaces of creativity, and most importantly, makes possible authentic dialogue. It is an attitude of a seeker, which should be the one characterising a true Christian and any believer at large.

There is today a feeling of threat whenever pluralism is talked about. It derives from a false conflation of pluralism with relativism. FABC has clearly distinguished the two.

> A pluralism which claims that all points of view of reality are of equal value surely ends up in relativism. When a point of view lacks a common reference to reality, it amounts to the mere opinion of the subject who holds that opinion. When each and every such point of view that is cut off from a common reference to reality is assigned an equal value, then it amounts to relativism. In other words, relativism holds that there are many truths which vary according to the subjects who hold different opinions of reality…. The affirmation of plurality rests on the human search for an underlying unity

that enables us to understand reality better. Many Asian philosophies and theologies have shown the unity and harmony behind pluralism.[5]

Partnership in Salvation and Liberation

If all the people in their diversity of cultures, traditions, and religious paths participate in the same process of salvation, they become partners in salvation and liberation. People of different religious traditions converge to experience and bear witness to the grace of God, and God's salvation. They engage themselves in bringing about ever greater freedom to the human family and in the protection and flourishing of nature and all of God's creation. Religious traditions are not opposed to each other but are partners in the project of God's salvation and liberation. The mystery about which all religions are concerned is not the possession of any particular religion. It belongs to the entire human family which participates in that mystery.

A Different Theological Methodology

Theology is not merely a learning of faith-propositions or interpretations of the same. Conscious of this fact, Asian theology follows a method of dialogue and mutuality. Its methodology is not aimed at simply communicating the truths of faith but dialoguing with the larger world. Asian theological orientation is not based on easily attained certainties, but rather is imbued with *the spirit of a movement*. The images of journey and pilgrimage characterise Asian theologizing than images of frames and architectures. In fact, Asian theologizing has broken the conventional frames and architectures as it moves into new avenues of reflection and travels on untrodden paths. We may recall here the words of a modern Indian philosopher, Jiddu Krishnamurti who captured the Asian spirit when he said that "truth is a pathless land" and indeed, a mapless territory to be explored creatively.[6]

Such being the nature and orientation of Asian theology, it called for also a significant transformation in theological methodology. This methodology can be characterized as dialogical and open-ended, experimental and transformation-oriented. The integral character of Asian theologizing has come out also in the fact that it does not simply rely on reason as it were the sole instrument of knowledge but involves other cognitive faculties and senses and the knowledge that comes through them.

As for the sources, they include the religious traditions of the neighbours of other faiths, the riches of cultures as well as the new forces at work in the life of the Asian peoples. These realities of the context, as rightly pointed out by the document of the Office of Theological Concerns (OTC) of FABC, form part of the resources of theology along with scripture and tradition. Asian theologians have been using these resources in their theological endeavours, and this has made a difference and given a distinctive character to their theologising. OTC sums up the Asian methodology when it states:

> The Asian way of doing theology is historically rooted and concrete, a method in which we learn to face conflicts and brokenness, a method we value as one of liberative integration, interrelatedness and wholeness, a method that emphasises symbolic approaches and expressions and is marked by a preference for those at the periphery and "outside the gate" (Heb. 13:3). [7]

Interdisciplinary approach to theology is indispensable since it does not have the means to mine the richness of truth which is multifaceted, nor has the tools to analyse and understand the various aspects of life - individual and collective. When theology interacts with other disciplines and is supported by them, it will be able to make its contribution to the people in a particular context and at a specific juncture of their history.

In concluding this part of the chapter, let me refer to a very interesting observation of the American-Vietnamese theologian

Peter Phan. Going into the expression "World Christianities" and its meaning, he points out how the Christianities in Asia, Africa and Latin America have contributed to a revision of the understanding of Christian history and missiology. According to him, the impact of the theologies emerging in these continents on systematic theology has not been sufficiently highlighted and recognized by most western theologians. According to Peter Phan, "One reason for this relative paucity of interest is that systematic theologians, whose field is doctrine, generally tend to be more concerned with permanence and less sensitive to historical changes than their colleagues in history and missiology." He then points out six broad areas of doctrine where developments in World Christianities have made an impact, and they are: experience, revelation, scripture, tradition, culture, and reason.[8] A similar overview of the Asian perspectives on some of the traditional theological issues was done earlier by Michael Amaladoss.[9]

What has been said about the lack of recognition to the creative thinking emerging from World Christianities, could be stated about the non-recognition of Asian theological contribution to rethink Christian doctrines and dogmas. This is unfortunate since the refreshing theological thinking coming out of Asia could help renew Christianity and the Christian Churches in other parts of the world, especially for the transformation of the dominant forms of western theology today. What is still worse is that the emerging Asian theological stirrings, like in the case of liberation theology in Latin America, were viewed as dangerous and attempts were made to suppress it by the Roman Curia, especially the Congregation for the Doctrine of the Faith. In general, the resistance to Asian theologies from the west were directed to their new openings towards other religions, understanding of mission, inculturation, dialogue, scriptures of other faiths, the mystery of Christ, Church, catholicity, and so on. This did not prevent Asian theologies making their impact felt through various international ecumenical bodies and find support and encouragement in the Ecumenical Association of Third World Theologians (EATWOT) that came into existence in Dar es Salaam, Tanzania in 1976.

Part II New Frontiers - Asian Public Theologies

Drawing Inspiration from Other Disciplines

It is a truism that theology today needs to necessarily relate to other disciplines, especially the ones that directly touch upon the lives of the people and society. We note that a discipline like sociology is challenged to come out of its world of data, analysis, flow charts, and statistical tables and state what is its contribution to society and its transformation, besides widening information and knowledge about it. It is the same challenge to theology to free itself from the narrow world of doctrines and dogmas and study what it could contribute really to the well-being of people, society, and nature by expanding its borders.

In recent decades, there is a movement to renew sociology and its impact by thinking in terms of its public role and contribution. Michael Buraoy was a pioneer in this field.[10] For him, society cannot take refuge in scientific and objective neutrality when the society it studies itself is under serious threat due to market forces, competition and so on. Such a social condition is a challenge to rethink reigning sociology in new terms by expanding its traditional borders and boundaries and turning it more critical, and thus undo the loss of public significance this discipline has suffered. The disengagement of sociology from public consciousness has caused its self-isolation. Any realm of knowledge today should have the transformation of society and nurturing of common good as its inspiration, and it applies eminently to sociology. Similar to sociology, also the discipline of philosophy is increasingly challenged to be public. In fact, the finest philosophical reflections are made by seminal thinkers and public intellectuals outside the closed environment of academia.[11] Public philosophy has the ability to stir the consciousness of the people to think in critical and unconventional ways which help transform particular situations, the society, and the larger world. In engagement with the community where the reflections take place, public philosophy brings in moral perspectives into public discourses and policies. The cultural revolution of 1968 in France, for example, was the result of philosophical engagement with public issues by such thinkers as Jean-Paul Sartre.

Some Contours of Public Theology

The turn in sociology and philosophy and similar disciplines to transform themselves into disciplines with relevance to the public and intersecting with common concerns, is a pressing invitation to theology to become public in its approach, method, and orientation. However, despite the innovative character of Asian theology, it is a fact that theological reflections have remained mostly internal to the Church and its pastoral needs. It does not mean that the concerns of the world and society are totally absent. But the point is that these are treated as realms or fields for the application of faith and theology. It has been more a theology in service of public life. The understanding of the nature of theology is basically the same, while the applications differ.

On the other hand, "public theology" understood rightly, represents a new genre in theology.[12] It affects the way theology is pursued. In the context of multireligious and multicultural societies with fast transformation in the field of culture, economy, politics, etc., theology needs to interrogate itself regarding its responsibilities to the larger world. Traditional theology tends to cut everything – the world, society, and culture – to its size, reminding us of the Procrustean bed. Asian public theological reflections need to be open-ended and should begin from the world and respond to the questions and issues thrown up from the life-situation of the people and societies. Such a theology can be characterized as public theology, which needs to be promoted increasingly.[13] According to one understanding,

> Public theology aims at making theology and religion relevant to the social order to help spiritualize or respiritualize it. In addition to, or in conjunction with, the resources of history and sociology, political theory, psychology, economic analysis, etc., public theology seeks to bring the resources of religion and theology to bear upon the goals, motivations, value judgements, and public policy to be promoted and striven for in the life of the nation.[14]

To understand more closely what is meant by public theology, it is better to see what it is not and how it distinguishes itself from other related forms of theologies.

As we noted in chapter three, we need to draw a distinction between *theology of public life*[15] and *public theology*. The former speaks about faith-motives and convictions for involving oneself as a believer in the affairs of the world – politics, economy, culture, violence, war and peace, and so on. It is a discourse within the Church about the world.

From a methodological point of view, in theology for public life, theology is already formulated and then applied to public life. Though it talks about issues in the world outside the boundaries of the Church, yet it is a discourse meant for consumption within the Church. On the other hand, in public theology, the concrete life-situation and the questions flowing from it are taken seriously, and an effort is made to respond to them in faith – a faith that understands itself in relation with others and not as a private matter. It is a theology firmly based on God's creation and on the Reign of God which have no walls.

Moreover, in public theology, we try to create a language and discourse which are understandable for others, and therefore can be shared with them. This new language breaks forth when we hold the truth of creation and the grand vision of the Reign of God aloft. We could cite here some classical examples in public theology. Such were *Pacem in Terris* (1963) by Pope John XXIII; the WCC document *Peace with Justice for the Whole Creation (1989)*; *Kairos Document* (1985) which addressed the crucial issue of apartheid and paved the way for its abolishment; *The Challenge of Peace* (1983) of the American Episcopal conference dealing with the issue of nuclear war; and *The Economic Justice for All* (1986) by the same conference.

How come that, even though theology speaks about the world, history and various issues affecting the society, yet it remains a discourse within the Church? How and why does this isolation occur? It could be explained partly by the clericalization theology suffers from. Theology is not only pursued by clerics but is also mostly oriented to the training and education of the clerics. Hence, it looks to me that the vision of the Kingdom of God needs to be accompanied by a process of de-clericalization, so that blinkers are removed and theology freed to see the presence and action of God in the society, world, and history. Then theology will not speak about these realities within the clerical or clerically-conditioned milieux but will become really a discourse about God in relationship to the world speaking a language the world understands and grasps, and indeed as something relevant and meaningful.

Public theology will necessarily be a pastoral theology. Here the "pastoral" is not to be understood in the limited sense of catering to the spiritual welfare of Christians, but an attitude and practice that concern the wellbeing of everyone across borders and boundaries. This is what would define also the pastoral presence of the Church in the world. It is enlightening to recall here the message addressed by Vatican II to the world at the time of its closing.

> Our concern is directed especially to the more humble, the more poor, the weaker, and, in keeping with the example of Christ, we feel compassion for the throngs who suffer hunger, misery and ignorance... For this reason, in performing our earthly mission, we take into great account all that pertains to the dignity of man and all that contributes toward the real brotherhood of nations.[16]

It is this open spirit to the plight of the world that prompted Vatican II to avail the support of disciplines like sociology for effective pastoral responsibility towards the world. "In pastoral care sufficient use should be made, not only of theological principles, but also of the findings of secular sciences, especially psychology and sociology." What will result is "a purer and more mature living of the faith."[17] Such an open pastoral orientation to the world necessitates a public theology, since the traditional forms of theology are not able to respond to the new challenges of the society and of the world.

Public Theology in Relation to Liberation Theology

The question commonly arises: How does public theology intersect with liberation theology? Historically, in the context of Europe one tried to respond to the privatization of religion, and critically review the way theology was concerned about individual's belief without having to refer to the condition of the society and world. St Thomas Aquinas could write volumes of theology without any reference to the feudal society in which he lived. Karl Rahner in twentieth century could awe the world of theology by his brilliant and masterful elucidation of traditional dogmas. Nevertheless, his interpretations refrained from making any reference to the devastating loss of life during the year of National Socialism, the horrors of concentration camps and the profound tragedy of the Holocaust. The attempt to forge a political theology by Johann Baptist Metz and Jürgen Moltmann and others were meant as a response to this manifest silence over the society and condition of the world in western theologies. Political theology broke the privatization of religion and made its way to the public realm.

Liberation theology of Latin America took seriously the critique of privatization of faith, but at the same time took stock of the oppressive condition under which people in that continent suffered by economic exploitation, militarization, dictatorship and so on. The motivation for the praxis of liberation came from Christian roots, and the methodology and tools of analysis were by and large Marxian in character. The people from where liberation theology sprung in Latin America had long Christian roots and tradition.

Public theology incorporates the concerns of political theology and liberation theology, but its approach is much more comprehensive, and its premises lie in the kind of relationship of religion to the common good. Some comrades may be sceptical of public theology and wonder whether it is an attempt to hijack liberation theology and even a conspiracy of capitalism![18]

We need to remember that liberation is the goal to which God's Word is beckoning us. Moving towards that goal calls for a continuous rethinking of our analysis of the society and the tools we use to uncover oppression and bondage. In today's world of globalization , we live in a much more complex society than was the case with the feudal society or industrial society of the past. The myriad forms of oppression today may not be adequately accounted for by a social analysis in terms of labour-capital conflict. Let us think of the issues of women's oppression, environmental degradation, discrimination against ethnic minorities, racism, casteism, migrants, refugee crisis, and so on. Consequently, the analysis of the past requires a thorough revision in present-day circumstances of globalization. Public theology will explore new methods to assess the nature of oppression about specific issues and questions, and seek a multipronged approach to overcome them.

Public theology, as we noted in the second chapter, is also different from a theology relating to public life propounded by Protestant radical orthodoxy or neo-orthodoxy - John Milbank, Max Stackhouse, Graham Ward, Stanley Hauerwas, Sebastian Kim and others.[19] Here we have a theology of Barthian inspiration, rather than a contextual theology bearing upon culture and society. This theology is centred on the transformation of public life to align with transcendental values, to the Kingdom of God, to God who is "totally the other" and who challenges and judges the world. It rests on the assumption that instead of God's Word coming in an encounter with the world, it is the world which needs to conform to God's Word.

The kind of public theology we are proposing is one that has a language inherently dialogical and is ready to cooperate with all forces contributing to the common good, something we understand when God's Kingdom becomes the point of reference. The ideal of God's Kingdom will also serve as the point of reference to distinguish a good theology from a mediocre one. Public theology firmly based on this ideal will serve to prune dominant theologies, and convert them to the core of faith and what is most essential. In the process, it frees itself from doctrinaire moorings that have no or little bearing on the shared life and history with others in society or polity. Since public theology needs to be done differently depending on the concrete situation, it cannot but be *contextual*. Public theology culls out from tradition and sacred sources those elements and insights that could contribute in the concrete context to the wellbeing of the people and of nature.

We highlighted a public theology that is concerned about the world, the history and what pertains to all. As such, it calls for some fundamental reflections. Since it is a theology through and through in dialogue with the world and history, we are led to the basic question of how to relate religion and the public realm. Public theology cannot escape this issue. As I noted earlier, to create a form of theology and a theological language which others can understand and perceive as relevant and meaningful, we need to clear the ground of this relationship of religion to society and public life. In other forms of theology, such a question may not figure, and if at all, only marginally. In public theology, it becomes a crucial issue. Even more, effective construction of public theology – whether in the East or the West – will depend on how this question of religion and public life is broached.

We shall begin from the case of the west which will help us understand why Asian public theology cannot but be different since the ways in which religion and public are related in Asian societies is much more complex, revealing different patterns. Moreover, in Asia public issues are also often issues of inter-religious relationships. It is difficult to separate them. Public issues are imbued with religious perceptions, traditions, and practices. The distinct nature of Asian public theology becomes particularly pronounced when we consider the issues and historical contexts that paved the way for the evolution of public theology in western contexts.

Efforts in the West

In the last couple of decades, there has taken place a shift in the perception of the relationship between religion and public life. With the decline of the thesis of secularisation and the progressive abandonment of the thesis of religion as private, there have come about new equations between religion and public life. In a certain sense, the public theology pursued in the west appears to be a response to secularization. At least some variants of western public theology gives the impression of being an attempt to translate the language of faith understandable in a secular/post-secular world. It is an attempt to make public issues theologically meaningful.[20] This form of public theology tries to speak both the language of faith and the language of the world and tries to bring them together in a common understanding. David Tracy, for example, speaks of three publics to which theology should be accountable – the Church, society, and the academia.[21] David Hollenbach, on his part, pursued, in practice, a public theology in relation to global common good and has done it with focus on ethical issues.[22]

Instead of going into tracing the birth of public theology in the west, what I intend to do is to examine two most influential voices in the West – Jürgen Habermas and John Rawls – whose position on the relationship of religion to public life has become the core issue in public theology in the west today, and at the same time most vigorously discussed and debated.

From Denial to the Recognition of Public Role for Religions

We could identify three phases in the thinking of Habermas concerning religion: a) Suppression of religion through communicative reason, b) co-existence of religion and reason, c) cooperation of both for upholding the gains of modernity. The new turn to the third phase can be identified in his works since 2001: *The Future of Human Nature, On Faith and Knowledge, Between Naturalism and Religion.* In the third phase of his thinking, Habermas shows his openness to the contribution of religion to the public sphere, challenging the claims of narrow secularity. He notes: "[S]ecularized citizens may neither fundamentally deny that religious convictions may be true nor reject the right of their devout (*gläubig*) fellow citizens to couch their contributions to pubic discussions in religious language."[23] By way of example, we may recall here how Habermas acknowledges the importance of Christian doctrine of creation for the strengthening of human dignity and rights. He also sees its importance in addressing biomedical technological issues such as genetic enhancement. Theological beliefs could throw light on such intricate questions and contribute to the present and future wellbeing of humanity.

The Question of "Comprehensive Doctrines"

John Rawls, on his part, speaks of "comprehensive doctrines" and "overlapping consensus." By comprehensive doctrines, he means articulated systems of thought or explanations that claim to give a full-range of ultimate explanation of the world, nature and society, bearing upon their origin, value, their future, and so on. And this is done by philosophy, religion, moral beliefs, etc. In simple terms, comprehensive doctrine means a theory of everything. Religions are habituated to present such a theory of everything – about God, the humans, and the world. These comprehensive doctrines shape the way we look at the world, others, and ourselves.

To be able to understand Rawl's political theory and his conception of the role of religion concerning public life, we need to grasp how he transforms Kant's ideal of moral autonomy *(Critique of Practical Reason)* in an inter-subjective manner. Here is a question of abiding by those laws and arrangements that find acceptance among all concerned in a polity based on their public use of reason. Moral autonomy is not merely a matter of freedom from coercion; it has a necessary reference to the other and the public. This moral autonomy is linked to political autonomy. A religious group is politically autonomous when it is able to abide by what the common good requires and what finds acceptance among all concerned in a particular society. In this sense, religious freedom today needs to be defined not in isolation from the other, but in relation to the other and to what concerns the general good of all concerned. I mean religious freedom is not simply a matter of conscience or of the individual – a framework of western interpretation. In Asia, there is a community dimension of religious freedom. One's religious freedom is not independent but inextricably bound with the freedom of religion of the other.[24]

Religion and Public Reason

In the context of the discussion on public theology, a question of paramount importance is the relationship of religion to public reason. Here is an issue that allows a broad interpretation but also raises many complex questions. Contribution to public reason means that religious traditions do not get bogged down by their internal convictions and belief-system but raise their heads above and hold before their eyes the general interest of the people. It would also involve a kind of translation into the secular language of these beliefs that have public significance. In other words, the beliefs and convictions held by religious groups require to be supported by public reason if they are to have any role in public life, so it is argued. The creation narrative of the Bible, for example, can support the equality of woman, which is a secular issue in the polity. The same creation story can be deployed to support the cause of human rights. According to Christian belief, human beings are endowed with dignity since they have been created in the image of God.

The question then is, should religions be stripped off their beliefs to reach a common ground of neutrality where they could enter into conversation with other similar religious groups. Don't we lose, in this way, the richness the religious beliefs, myths, and symbols contain? Why not the religions carry these roots with them and enter into conversation with others, and thus through a mutuality that touches more resonant chords reach consensus and understanding? This is a point which some western theologians like Linda Hogan and Nigel Biggar contend when responding to the position of Rawls and Habermas concerning public reason or overlapping consensus. Linda

Hogan notes, for example: "[A] fundamental flaw in the ideal of the public reason lies in the manner in which it requires the speaker and listener to believe both the self and the other to be, or to act as though he or she is *rootless*."[25]

The position of Rawls and Habermas are at the level of the normative and are abstracted from concrete context. They follow procedural reasoning in determining the relationship between religion and the public sphere. However, the factual reality does not correspond to this theorizing. Even in many European countries, there are so-called established religions. The clearest example is that of the UK. There, the bishops sit in the House of Lords.[26]

Situation in Asia

We do not want to begin the discussion from a normative and procedural plane, instead start from the empirical situation of differences in the relationship of religion to public life, as it obtains in Asia. Whether India, China, or other countries of Asia, we need a different public theology that is set in our unique contexts. The Chinese scholar, Alexander Chow has expressed this uniqueness of Asian public theology and its distinctness from efforts done elsewhere.

> Public theology looks very different whether we speak of mainland China or the United States or the United Kingdom—let alone Latin America or South Africa or Palestine. Undoubtedly, theological arguments related to the separation of church and state and the freedom of religion, at least in the ways they are conceived in many Western societies, have little relevance to the Chinese political and religious situation. I cannot labour the point that public theology—indeed, Christian theology—must be understood and expressed in unique ways that are attentive to the manifold contexts in which Christians live and congregate.[27]

To be able to understand the uniqueness and diversity of Asian public theology, we need to grapple with the concrete political and social situations. Looking at the empirical reality, we could identify three basic types regarding the relationship of religion to the public sphere, calling forth different kinds of public theologies in Asia.

Religion Controlled by Centralizing State Authority

This is the model we could identify in the so-called "socialist countries" (China, Vietnam, North Korea, etc.). While religions are allowed freedom for worship and for carrying out certain limited activities, they are strictly controlled, so that they do not become any threat to the centralized authority. Such a situation allows little room for religions to play any influential role for common good and the welfare of the whole society.

In the case of China, we need to refer to the cultural revolution of Mao Zedong. One of the ideological components of this revolution is the belief that religions are counter-revolutionary forces and against national goals. Along with the bourgeoisie, religion also need to be suppressed for the growth of the country, so it was argued. The ideology of the Cultural Revolution viewed religion as an enemy to be fought against. Senseless destruction of religious places of worship and symbols followed. The reforms of 1978 in that country allowed, indeed, some space for the existence of religions, but under the watchful eyes – panopticon - of the state authorities. The vicissitudes in the relationship of the Chinese state with Vatican illustrates the various shifts in the position of the state.

Zhibin Xie, who has researched on the public role of religion in China enumerates three crucial reasons for a greater role of religion in public life, in the future.[28] First of all, there is the traditional religious character of Chinese societies which is to be seen today also in the revival of religion in that country. Secondly, religious groups show increasing interest in participation in public life, which also involves dissent and protest. Thirdly, according to Zhibin Xie, with greater democratization in Chinese political life, there will be room for the voices of different religious groups to be heard. The view of this author may sound optimistic. Nevertheless, what is important to note is that even in a centralized Asian country like China, the prospects of religion playing any public role has become increasingly more significant. This calls for a theology of public life attuned to this new situation. The historically inherited models from the West may not respond to the unique nature of the relationship between religion and public life in China.

Christians in China and other countries with centralized rule are in a dilemma, of having to contribute to the common good and public life and at the same time not conforming uncritically to the state and its politics. It is from this situation that we need to think of Christianity vis-à-vis the public life. It is a very complex situation. However, for some Christian groups, especially from among the Protestant Churches, things seem to be rather simple. Religion contributes to public life by aligning with the state and its programmes, and one speaks about "common ground" of national goals where state and Church converge.

The common ground is made up of three principles: self-governing, self-supporting, and self-propagating. This state-policy should also become the policy of the Church, something adopted by many Protestant Churches. It is a theology uncritical and accommodative to the state for the survival of the Church.[29] Not that the three self-movements are wrong, but what lurks behind it has proved, in practice, a state-control of the Church and silencing any prophetic critique of the state and its functioning. The public role of religion here ends up in endorsing and promoting uncritically the programmes of the state and the goals of the society it defines. What is expected of the Church is that it cooperate with the state seamlessly in building up a socialist society through a united front. The three principles may be meant to free the Church from outside forces and foreign domination, but not independence from the communist party and the state. The world bore witness to the brutal quelling of dissenting voices and the tragic massacre that unfolded at Tiananmen Square on 4 June, 1989. We realize how crucial and complex and at the same time urgent is a critical reflection on pubic theology in such contexts.

Established Religions

We have in Asia also situations in which religions openly determine politics and public life. There are many variants to this model. Severe conditioning of politics and public life by Islam can be seen in Pakistan, Indonesia, Malaysia, Bangladesh, and so on, and relatively less rigorous intervention of Buddhism in politics and public life in Thailand and Sri Lanka. In these countries, one could hardly separate majority religion from public life. On the contrary, in many respects the majority religion defines public life. Sri Lanka has not made Buddhism the state religion, but the constitution gives it "foremost place." In some of these countries with established religion, like in Pakistan, certain public offices cannot be held by any person other than a Muslim. The state support and preferential treatment of a particular religion condition the scope for other minority religious groups. The highly conflictual nature of the issue became evident in the controversy surrounding the election of a Christian Governor in Jakarta.[30] It is, often, the case that the role in public life is reserved to the established religion, and other religious minorities are tolerated in the practice of their religion, and they may not claim to intervene in the public sphere.

Principled Distance

In this model, the "secular" is understood as non-privileging of any one religion by the state. Religions are allowed the freedom of worship and the freedom to propagate and be engaged in social and developmental activities, without prejudice to public order, morality, and hygiene. We have such a model for example, in India, the Philippines, Taiwan, and South Korea. This model allows, in theory, the possibility of religions converging together and jointly contributing to the promotion of common good. But, in reality, this does not seem to happen. For, religions and religious bodies are often in conflict with each other to secure greater power and privileges for their own groups. Therefore, there is an endless discussion and debate on secularism, for example, in India. However, in a positive sense, the secular in Asia could provide a common basis or platform for the various religious groups and humanistic ideologies to engage themselves for common good and public goals.[31]

All the three models and the underlying situations we have reviewed leads us to the conclusion that we in Asia urgently need a public theology in new terms, in unique contexts. Even though, the expression "public theology" was not used, however, thinkers like M.M. Thomas actually opened up Asian Christian theology to the larger issues of Asian nations. The independence from the colonial powers and the urgent task of rebuilding the once colonized Asian nations prompted Christian theology, like the one pursued by M.M.Thomas and others, to think in terms of Christian contribution to nation-building. Obviously, the situation has changed vastly in India and other countries with the advent of religious nationalism and the imposition of cultural uniformity adversely affecting minority communities. Christ-centred approach of M.M. Thomas with a tinge of evangelism may not be helpful for an open and dialogical public theology. The general environment is such that Christians are forced to reflect on what their role in public life is without too much of a priori Christological and other doctrinal preoccupations. This will help shape the kind of public theology required in context. In this regard, we need to widen the discourse of religion in public life in Asia.

Asian Debate on Religion in Public Life

Unlike in the west, there has been relatively little debate in Asia on religion in relation to public life in its various aspects and dimensions. The discussion, as we noted, has been almost exclusively focused on religious freedom and the understanding of secularism. This is clearly the case of India. Some intellectuals like Ashis Nandy, T. N. Madan debate this point often in a polemical manner against the western concept of the secular. They maintain that in India, religion has an important role to play. But then, there are few constructive theories and suggestions coming out from these circles as how to and in what manner religion could play a role in public life in a multireligious society. The discourse in this matter needs to be initiated and advanced. The issue becomes all the more difficult and complex with religious nationalism in the country. Let me put forward a few thoughts and views in this regard by way of a methodological foreword to Asian public theology.

The Understanding of Public – The Cultural and the Subaltern

When we speak of public theology in Asia, we need to be also conscious of the way "public" is understood and defined. This has consequences for the role of religion in general, and Christianity in Particular, vis-à-vis the Asian societies. Here is something that distinguishes the Asian approach to the understanding of the public and public theology. Hence, not only the Asian history of the relationship of religion to state is different from the West, but different also is the way the public comes across to peoples of the continent. Everyday experience shows that what the western cultural world would consider private is blatantly public for Asians, and the reverse is also true. The cultural determination explodes the conventional demarcation between the public and the private. We may recall in this regard one important and far-reaching contribution of the feminist movement: "The Personal is Political."

Without going into the details of the cultural determination, we may say that religion in Asia is *both public* and *private.* In a certain sense, it is private; in another sense, it is public. When a Hindu devotee does puja in his home, religion is private, and it is public when he participates in a temple procession passing through the main street and byways of the city. One would be at a loss to understand here what is the "wall of separation" of the religious and the secular or public. It is the unique kind of intermingling and crisscrossing of the two that is characteristic of Asia.

Of grater significants, particularly in the context of Asia, is the imperative to unequivocally acknowledge and amplify the voices of the marginalized and the subalterns, along with the profound significance they embody. For, as it is, in many Asian countries, especially in South Asia, the public space is pervaded by the values of dominant castes to which the rest of the society is expected to conform. The public here is not neutral and independent coffee shops, and salons, and clubs of the West. In South Asia, the public is imagined and shaped by the groups and castes that wield power. Unless one accommodates to the perspective and value system of the dominant castes, the backward castes and Dalits will be fully excluded from the public. Hence, Rajbharat Patta, in his doctoral dissertation, and Gnana Patrick in his work on Indian public theology have brought out well the subaltern deficit in the western public theologies and the need in India and Asia at large to focus on the subaltern public which needs to shape our public theologies.[32]

> Both political and apologetic public theologies have not recognised subalternity as a site and method of doing theology. In other words, power analyses and the contesting of demons in public have not been given their due place in these theologies.... To further public theology as a theological discourse relevant to the twenty-first century therefore requires a public theology originating from the sites of subalternity, and with the role of contesting the power and privilege of the powers and principalities of the public.[33]

This shift of public theologies in Asia from the centre to periphery, focusing on subalternity, will provide a new direction to them. It will also free them from becoming a bourgeois enterprise, and indeed from colonial epistemology. K.C. Abraham has pointed out the need of a subaltern approach to Asian public theology. As he stated,

> Public theology in Asia/India should come with resounding affirmation of its subaltern perspective. The epistemological break in theological paradigm by our commitment to praxis is a sheer achievement. In fact, this perspective should help us build bridges with other disciplines and also develop a critical and ecumenical theology.[34]

Difference in the Understanding and Approach to Religion

Public theology, as already noted, presupposes the current debate on the role of religion in the public realm. The discussion in the West on this question may trigger our reflections, but may not be able to render help to our unique Asian situation. One important reason for this is the fact that the concept of religion in Asian traditions has been quite different from the dominant conception of it in the West. To cite an example, religion is not viewed in Asia as a set of beliefs or doctrines but as a way of life – a path, a journey. Religion is embedded in the culture, and daily life of the people as the folk traditions of Asia manifests. This makes it already extremely difficult to create any "wall of separation" between religion and public life.

On the other hand, many Constitutions of States do not reflect this Asian reality of religion, but seem to be attuned to the western understanding of religion. Moreover, the relationship of religion to state and public life has had a different historical trajectory in the West, which may not be replicated in Asia. This trajectory, to put it summarily, had three stages: the distinction between the Church and the state; separation of the two; and finally, marginalization of the Church and religion from public life as of no consequence.

Public theology will go deeper into the relationship of religion and public life in Asian societies and their histories. This history is by and large one of the accommodations of religion in public life as the development of Indian secularism shows. This type of Asian accommodation cannot be fitted into any three stages of the western trajectory I mentioned above.

Political Justice

In the context of our present discussion, by political justice, we mean the rightful participation of various segments of the society with their different conceptions of the good life in the construction of the common good. Since religions in a very significant way determine the outlook on life and values, it is crucial that religious groups also play a role in contributing to the common good which means that they go beyond the interests of their respective groups. This way of considering breaks the framework of *minority and majority.*[35]

A second related question concerns specifically Christianity and its participation along with other religious groups for public good. The difficulty with Christianity is that it is viewed as a religion "foreign" to Asian societies. So, the question is: Should a foreign religion like Christianity be considered on par with other religious traditions of local origin and therefore having a share with others in deliberating on public good? This issue gets accentuated, where there is an established religion. The fact is that in Asia, Christianity is not viewed as a partner in the deliberation for the common good. Such being the case, how could Christians and Christian communities bring to bear upon public life, the values and ideals which they believe are essential and necessary for the general welfare of the people?

It has been observed that Christianity faces exclusion in public affairs, even in countries like India which have a secular Constitution. This attitude and practice of exclusion is a cause for concern. The principles of democratic governance which recognise equal rights to individuals and groups would go against any such exclusion. But then, here historical memory overtakes any theory of equal participation. The alleged connivance of Christians with the colonial rule makes many citizens sceptical about the participation of Christians and their contribution to the welfare of the nation. "Foreignness" and being "different" alone do not seem to be the only reasons for the exclusion of Christianity from being part of a national dialogue on the common good in different countries of Asia. For, the same societies have had no difficulty to accept western (foreign) science and technology as contributing to the welfare of the nation. And in the case of China, it is not only science and technology; its ideology of Marxism too was a western import upheld (in name, though) in China, ironically, when socialist systems have been abandoned in the West itself – its place of origin.

Public Accountability of Religions

Public theology calls for an internal critique within Christianity. It raises a crucial question: What is being discussed as theology in the Churches, how relevant is it to the public? For any religion, to have significance beyond the community of its believers, it needs to demonstrate what contribution it could make to the wellbeing of all. Public theology, on its part, makes theology answerable to the people, and in this way justifies its interpretation of God's Word for today. When theology does not bear upon public life, it is a failed theology, no matter how well it explains the truths of religion. Such a theology is not only irrelevant but could be most dangerous. Views maintained at a theological level have serious social and political consequences.

Sometimes the claim is made, as was done often by Pope John Paul II and Benedict XVI, that by the very announcement of its faith, Christianity contributes to humanity. In other words, announcing the gospel is the best thing Christianity can do to humanity. That could be a well-meant. But often, this is stated as a protective shield against undergoing any influence from society and the world. It could also be a sign of a refusal to learn from the world. What must be emphasized is that Christianity should not confine itself to the mere repetition of doctrines and beliefs as universal concepts directed to all humanity. Instead, it should demonstrate how these beliefs tangibly influence communitarian existence within the public sphere and actively contribute to the collective welfare. The central enquiry thus becomes: What social and public impact do the creeds, doctrines, and dogmas that Christians adhere to have?

Prophetic Character of Public Theology

Asian Public theology should envisage more than advocacy. The kind of public theology we are discussing here is the one that not only relates to the wider issues and questions of society, but also one that would speak out and take a stand. It is a public theology in its most intense and dense expression and is far from being accommodative to the existing order. The prophetic character of public theology should come to expression in its critical posture vis-à-vis the political and economic order, and in its challenge to all forms of authoritarianism and populism. It is clear that the Church leadership could be often easily swayed by pragmatic considerations and give in to the pressure of authoritarian political forces and exploitative market forces.[36]

In this regard, we have a unique case in the Philippines. Under the dictatorial Marcos regime, the then Cardinal of Manila, James Sin, gave the impression of being diplomatic and reluctant to challenge the dictator under whose regime the poor were oppressed, and tortured. A lot of people resisting the regime simple disappeared. It became a public scandal when on a birthday of Marcos, Cardinal Sin embraced the dictator in public while wishing him. I was in the city of Manila on the day it happened and could sense the public mood of surprise and dejection. But then, slowly, the cardinal began to realize the need to be prophetic, and the dictatorship came to an ignominious end, thanks to the decisive involvement of the peoples' movement, and people power. The public theology relentlessly pursued by the Filipino theologians of the time animating the grassroots had a decisive influence in the conversion of the cardinal and change of the political situation in the country. This is an example of the prophetic contribution a prophetic public theology could make.

Conclusion

We charted the exclusionary path that culminated in the rise of Asian theologies, elucidating their principal attributes. Venturing into uncharted territories entails immersing ourselves in a subaltern and prophetic public theology within Asia's multicultural and multireligious societies, all under the expansive umbrella of the Reign of God's overarching vision. In these societies, there is a need to foster communion and build inclusive communities. Theology will help in this project by reflecting on common interests that affect everyone. This, on its part, will help theology be truly catholic in its original sense of comprising all. Theology will not be a sectarian enterprise limited to the Christian community's faith-life. Asian Public theology will tell us what it means to live and understand the Kingdom of God in dialogue with the realities and experiences of this continent with peoples of different faiths.

The public theology in Asia is a real challenge since it needs to be pursued under such difficult conditions as authoritarianism, populism, and religious fundamentalism. Further, the Christian community is viewed in most parts of Asia as "foreign" and is not permitted to be active participants in the shaping of the society and nation and make its contribution to common good. In these circumstances, there is no easy way than continuous dialogue with all stakeholders of public life.

Even in these difficult circumstances, public theology in Asia should never lose its focus on the subalterns – the Dalits, tribals, women, children, migrants, unorganized labourers, domestic workers, and others at the margins. Issues of ecology will also be an integral part of subaltern public theology. For, the subalterns have close affinity to nature – land, sea, forest, and water. The subalterns and nature are intertwined in such a way that the defence of one is defence of the other. To begin theological reflection from the periphery of the subalterns is to cut across religious, linguistic, caste, and regional boundaries. It will indeed be an inclusive, public, and prophetic theology.

Finally, when public theology is to be subaltern and prophetic, it cannot be pursued simply in traditional theological institutions. It is a wider project in which public intellectuals across religious affiliation could join and contribute. Thus thinkers, poets, novelists, public intellectuals and those engaged in the fields of art, literature, public sociology and philosophy could become catalysts of creative public theology focused on the subalterns. The social location of fostering any subaltern public theology will be the margins.[37]

NOTES

1   Felix Wilfred, "Harbingers of Hope - Action Groups in India Today," *Vidyajyoti Journal of Theological Reflection* 49 (1985): 539–563.

2   For example, the Indian subaltern theology has drawn inspiration and resources from the so-called "Subaltern Studies" – an academic venture that has highlighted through so many micro-studies the liberative streams among the subjugated and oppressed peoples and groups. There is a series of volumes entitled "Subaltern Studies," published by Oxford University Press, Delhi since 1986.

3   "Jesus Christ is the Way, the Truth and the Life, but in Asia before stressing that Jesus Christ is the Truth, we must search much more deeply into how he is the Way and the Life." Peter Phan, *The Asian Synod. Texts and Commentaries* (New York: Orbis Books, 2002), 27–32.

4   Felix Wilfred, "A Matter of Theological Education - Some Critical Reflections on the Suitability of 'Salvation History' as a Theological Model for India," *Vidyajyoti Journal of Theological Reflection*, 48 (1984) 538-556.

5   Vimal Tirimanna, *Sprouts of Theology from the Asian Soil.* Collection of TAC & OTC Documents [1987-2007] (Bangalore: Claretian Publications, 2007), 258.

6   https://jkrishnamurti.org/about-dissolution-speech [accessed on 7 December 2020].

7   Vimal Tirimanna, *Harvesting from the Asian Soil. Towards an Asian Theology* (Bangalore: Asian Trading Corporation, 2011), 353.

8   Cf. Peter C. Phan, Asian Christianities. History, Theology, Practice (New York: Orbis Books, 2018), 76–78.

9   Michael Amaladoss, "Asian Theological Trends," in Felix Wilfred, ed., *The Oxford Handbook of Christianity in Asia* (New York: Oxford University Press, 2014), 104–120.

10   See Michael Burawoy, "Public Sociology: Contradictions, Dilemmas and Possibilities," *Social Forces* 82 (2004):1603–18. "For Public Sociology," *American Sociological Review* 70 (2005): 2–28. For a critical view on Burawoy's position, see Avi Goldberg and Axel van den Berg, "What Do Public Sociologists Do? A Critique of Burawoy," *The Canadian Journal of Sociology* 34, no. 3 (2009): 765–802.

11   Cf. Michael J. Sandel, *Public Philosophy. Essays on Morality in Politics* (Cambridge MA: Harvard University Press, 2005). Jack Russell Weinstein, "Public Philosophy: Introduction," *Essays in Philosophy* 15, no.1 (2014): 1–4; James Tully, *Public Philosophy in a New Key, Volume II: Imperialism and Civic Freedom. Ideas in Context series* (Cambridge, UK: Cambridge University Press, 2008); especially Chapter 9. James Tully, *Public Philosophy in a New Key: Volume 1, Democracy and Civic Freedom.* (Cambridge, UK: Cambridge University Press, 2008).

12 The expression has gained wide currency since its use by Martin Marty, *The Public Church* (New York: Crossroad Press, 1981). A related expression is "civil religion" originally used by Jean-Jacques Rousseau, and taken up in contemporary times by Robert Bellah.

13 Martin Marty distinguishes between ceremonial and cultic kind of public theology, the kind of theology implied for example in manifestation of one's faith while taking oath for public office placing one's hand on Bible, Bhagavadgita or other sacred scriptures, or in public celebration of religious festivities like Christmas, Ramzan, Krishnajanti and so on. This is different from 'prophetic' public theology which takes on critically the practices and policies in realms of politics, economy, culture and so on.

14 Interestingly this is a definition by an Islamic scholar which can serve as a point of reference in inter-religious theological discourses. See Ausaf Ali, "Public Theology," *Islamic Studies* 34, no. 1 (Spring 1995): 67–89, at 67.

15 Charles Mathews, *A Theology of Public Life* (Cambridge: Cambridge University Press, 2007).

16 https://vaticaniiat50.wordpress.com/2012/10/20/text-of-councils-message-to-world/ [accessed on 30 March, 2023].

17 Vatican II. *Gaudium et Spes* 62.

18 Cf. Gabriele Dietrich, "The Quest for Socialism in Times of Crisis: A Challenge for Public Theology," in *Theology to Go Public,* ed., Felix Wilfred (Delhi: ISPCK, 2013), 98–128.

19 Max Stackhouse, *Public Theology and Political Economy: Christian Stewardship in Modern Society* (Grand Rapids: William B. Eerdmann's Publishing Company, 1987); Sebastian Kim, *Theology in the Public Sphere: Public Theology as a Catalyst for Open Debate* (London: SCM Press, 2011); Sebastian Kim, Katie Day, ed., *Companion to Public Theology* (Leiden: Brill, 2017); Max L Stackhouse, Deirdre King Hainsworth, and Scott Paeth, eds., *Public Theology for a Global Society: Essays in Honor of Max L. Stackhouse* (Grand Rapids, Mich.: Edinburgh: William B. Eerdmans; Alban [distributor], 2010).

20 Cf. Katie Day and Sebastian Kim, eds., *A Companion to Public Theology* (Leiden: Brill, 2017); see also Elaine Graham, *Between a Rock and a Hard Place: Public Theology in a Post-Secular Age* (London: SCM Press, 2013); We must also refer here to growing literature from different parts of the world on public theology.

21 David Tracy, *The Analogical Imagination: Christian Theology and the Culture of Pluralism* (New York: Crossroad Publisher, 1981).

22 Cf. David Hollenbach, *The Global Face of Public Faith: Politics, Human Rights, and Christian Ethics.* Moral Traditions Series (Washington, D.C.: Georgetown University Press, 2003); Stephanie Ann Puen, "Public Theology and the Common Good: The Contribution of David Hollenbach," *Political Theology: The Journal of Christian Socialism* 19 (2018): 157–58.

23 Maurine Junker-Kenny, *Habermas and Theology* (London-New York: T & T Clark International, 2011), 137; Butler, et al., *The Power of Religion in the Public Sphere* (New York: Columbia University Press, 2011).

24 Felix Wilfred, "Religious Freedom in Asia," *Concilium* (2016/2): 63–74; see also Felix Wilfred, *Religious Identities and the Global South: Porous Borders and Novel Paths* (Cham, Switzerland: Palgrave Macmillan, 2021).

25 Nigel Biggar and Linda Hogan, *Religious Voices in Public Places* (Oxford: Oxford University Press, 2009), 223.

26 Cf. Felix Wilfred, *Religious Identities and the Global South. Porous Borders and Novel Paths* (Cham, Switzeland: Palgrave Macmillan, 2021), Chapter 12, 280.

27 Alexander Chow, *Chinese Public Theology: Generational Shifts and Confucian Imagination in Chinese Christianity* 1st ed. (Oxford: Oxford University Press, 2020), 161.

28 Zhibin Xie, *Religious Diversity and Public Religion in China* (Burlington: Ashgate, 2006).

29 Cf. Philip Wickeri, *Seeking the Common Ground. Protestant Christianity. The Three-Self Movement, and China's United Front* (Maryknoll, NY: Orbis Books, 1988).

30 Andang Binawan, "The Case of a Christian Governor in Jakarta as a Sign of Times for Catholics (and Christians) in Indonesia," in *International Journal of Asian Christianity* 1, no.1 (2018): 135–142.

31 Cf. M.M. Thomas, *The Secular Ideologies of India and the Secular Meaning of Christ* (Madras: Published for the Christian Institute for the Study of Religion and Society, by the Christian Literature Society, 1976).

32 Rajbharat Patta, "Towards a Subaltern Public Theology for India" (PhD Dissertation, University of Manchester, 2018). https://pure.manchester.ac.uk/ws/portalfiles/portal/156331169/FULL_TEXT.PDF [accessed on 6 April 2023]; Gnana Patrick, *Public Theology. Indian Concerns, Perspectives, and Themes* (Minneapolis: Fortress Press, 2020).

33 Rajbharat Patta, *op. cit.*, 72.

34 K.C. Abraham, "Asian Public Theology. Its Social Location," in *Theology to Go Public,* Felix Wilfred, ed. (Delhi: ISPCK, 2013), 25.

35 The critical condition of Christians being a minority in Asia, especially in India, China, and Myanmar has been well brought out in a recent article by Chandra Mallampalli, "Minority Vulnerability in South Asia and China," in *International Journal of Asian Christianity* 6, no.1 (2023): 29–50; see also his recent work: *South Asia's Christians. Between Hindu and Muslim* (New York: Oxford University Press, 2023).

36 Cf. Wilibaldus Gaut, "Steep Path Toward a Synodal Church," in *The International Journal of Asian Christianity,* 1, no 1 (2023): 99–121. The

author brings up a case of a bishop in Indonesia who stood with the people against the exploitation by a multinational company, but then gave in to pressure to make a turnaround and support the company.

37   See Felix Wilfred, *Margins. The Site of Asian Theologies* (Delhi: ISPCK, 2008).

FURTHER READING

Abraham, K.C. "Asian Public Theology. Its Social Location." In Felix Wilfred, ed. *Theology to Go Public*. Delhi: ISPCK 2013.

Ali, Ausaf. "An Essay on Public Theology." *Islamic Studies* 34, no. 1 (Spring 1995): 67–89.

Amaladoss, Michael. "Asian Theological Trends." In Felix Wilfred, ed. *The Oxford Handbook of Christianity in Asia*, 104-120. New York: Oxford University Press, 2014.

Ana, Julio de Santa. *Good News to the Poor*. Geneva: World Council of Churches, 1977.

Biggar, Nigel, and Linda Hogan. *Religious Voices in Public Places* Oxford: Oxford University Press, 2009.

Binawan, Andang L. "The Case of a Christian Governor in Jakarta as a Sign of Times for Catholics (and Christians) in Indonesia." *International Journal of Asian Christianity* 1, no.1 (2018): 135–142.

Burawoy, Michael. "For Public Sociology." *American Sociological Review* 70 (2005): 2–28.

Burawoy, Michael. "Public Sociology: Contradictions, Dilemmas and Possibilities." *Social Forces* 82 (2004):1603–18.

Butler, Jürgen et al. *The Power of Religion in the Public Sphere*. New York: Columbia University Press, 2011.

Chow, Alexander. *Chinese Public Theology: Generational Shifts and Confucian Imagination in Chinese Christianity*. Oxford: Oxford University Press, 2020.

Day, Katie, and Sebastian Kim, eds. *A Companion to Public Theology*. Leiden: Brill, 2017.

Dietrich, Gabriele. "The Quest for Socialism in Times of Crisis: A Challenge for Public Theology." In Felix Wilfred, ed., *Theology to Go Public*, 98–128. Delhi: ISPCK, 2013.

Freitag, B. Sandria. "'The Public' and Its Meanings in Colonial South Asia." *Journal of South Asian Studies* 14, no.1 (1991): 1–13.

Gandhi, Rajmohan. *Revenge and Reconciliation. Understanding South Asian History.* Gurgaon: Penguin Books, 1999.

Gaut, Wilibaldus. "Steep Path Toward a Synodal Church: An Indonesian Case." *International Journal of Asian Christianity* 6, no.1 (2023): 99–121.

Goldberg, Avi, and Axel van den Berg. "What Do Public Sociologists Do? A Critique of Burawoy." *The Canadian Journal of Sociology* 34, no. 3 (2009): 765–802.

Graham, Elaine. *Between a Rock and a Hard Place: Public Theology in a Post-Secular Age.* London: SCM Press, 2013.

Hollenbach, David. "Public Theology in America: Some Questions for Catholicism After John Courtney Murray." *Theological Studies* 37, no. 2 (1976): 290–303.

Hollenbach, David. *The Global Face of Public Faith: Politics, Human Rights, and Christian Ethics.* Washington, D.C.; Georgetown University Press, 2003.

Junker-Kenny, Maureen. *Habermas and Theology.* London and New York: T & T Clark International, 2011.

Kairos Theologians. *The Kairos Document, Challenge to the Church: A Theological Comment on the Political Crisis in South Africa.* Grand Rapids: Eerdmans, 1986.

Kim, Sebastian. *Theology in the Public Sphere: Public Theology as a Catalyst for Open Debate.* London: SCM Press, 2011.

Mallampalli, Chandra. "Minority Vulnerability in South Asia and China." In *International Journal of Asian Christianity* 6, no.1 (2023): 29–50.

Mallampalli, Chandra. *South Asia's Christians. Between Hindu and Muslim.* New York: Oxford University Press, 2023.

Martinez, Gaspar. *Confronting the Mystery of God: Political, Liberation, and Public Theologies.* New York: Continuum, 2001.

Marty, Martin. "Foreword." In Robin W. Lovin. ed., *Religion and American Public Life. Interpretations and Explorations.* New York: Paulist Press, 1986.

Marty, Martin. *The Public Church.* New York: Crossroad Press, 1981.

Mathews, Charles. *A Theology of Public Life.* Cambridge: Cambridge University Press, 2007.

Metz, Johann Baptist. "Religion and Society in the Light of a Political Theology." *Harvard Theological Review* 61, no. 4 (1968): 507–23.

Metz, Johann Baptist. *Faith in History and Society: Toward a Practical Fundamental Theology.* New York: The Crossroad, 2007.

Metz, Johann Baptist. *Theology of the World.* New York: Herder, 1971.

Moghadam, Valentine M. "Violence, Terrorism and Fundamentalism: Some Feminist Observations." *Global Dialogue* 4, no.2 (1996): 66–76.

Moltmann, Jürgen. *God for a Secular Society: The Public Relevance of Theology.* London: SCM Press, 1999.

Pandian, M. S. S. "One Step Outside Modernity: Caste, Identity Politics and Public Sphere." *Economic and Political Weekly* 17, no. 18 (2002): 1735–41.

Patrick, Gnana. *Public Theology. Indian Concerns, Perspectives, and Themes.* Minneapolis: Fortress Press, 2020.

Patrick. Gnana. *Wings of Faith: Towards Public Theologies in India.* New Delhi: ISPCK, 2013.

Patta, Rajbharat. "Towards a Subaltern Public Theology for India." PhD Dissertation, University of Manchester, 2018.

Phan, Peter C. *Asian Christianities. History, Theology, Practice.* New York: Orbis Books, 2018.

Phan, Peter C. ed. *The Asian Synod. Texts and Commentaries.* New York: Orbis Books, 2002.

Sandel, Michael J. *Public Philosophy. Essays on Morality in Politics.* Cambridge MA: Harvard University Press, 2005.

Scott, J. Barton, and D. Brannon Ingram. "What Is a Public? Notes from South Asia." *Journal of South Asian Studies* 38, no. 3 (2015): 357–70.

Stackhouse, Max L, Deirdre King Hainsworth, and Scott Paeth, eds. *Public Theology for a Global Society: Essays in Honor of Max L. Stackhouse.* Grand Rapid: William B. Eerdmans, 2010.

Stackhouse, Max. *Public Theology and Political Economy: Christian Stewardship in Modern Society.* Grand Rapids: William B. Eerdmanns Publishing Company, 1987.

Ranajit Guha, et al., eds. *Subaltern Studies.* Delhi: Oxford University Press, 1986-…

Thomas, M.M, *The Secular Ideologies of India and the Secular Meaning of Christ.* Madras: Christian Literature Society, 1976.

Tirimanna, Vimal, ed. *Sprouts of Theology from the Asian Soil. Collection of TAC & OTC Documents [1987-2007].* Bangalore: Claretian Publications, 2007.

Tirimanna, Vimal. *Harvesting from the Asian Soil. Towards an Asian Theology.* Bangalore: Asian Trading Corporation, 2011.

Tiwari, Badri Narayan. *The Making of the Dalit Public in North India: Uttar Pradesh, 1950 - Present.* New Delhi: Oxford University Press, 2011.

Tracy, David. *The Analogical Imagination: Christian Theology and the Culture of Pluralism.* New York: Crossroad, 1981.

Tully, James. *Public Philosophy in a New Key, Volume II: Imperialism and Civic Freedom*. Cambridge, UK: Cambridge University Press, 2008.

Tully, James. *Public Philosophy in a New Key: Volume 1, Democracy and Civic Freedom*. Cambridge: Cambridge University Press, 2018.

Weinstein, Jack Russell. "Public Philosophy: Introduction." *Essays in Philosophy* 15, no.1 (2014): 1–4.

Wickeri, Philip. *Seeking the Common Ground. Protestant Christianity. The Three-Self Movement and China's United Front*. Maryknoll, NY: Orbis Books, 1988.

Wilfred, Felix. "Action Groups: Harbingers of Hope." *Vidyajyoti Review of Theology* 49 (1985): 539–563.

Wilfred, Felix. "Religious Freedom in Asia." *Concilium* (2016/2): 63–74.

Wilfred, Felix. "Theological Perspectives on Mission and Political Engagement." In Simon Pinto et al., eds., *Politics and Mission in Critical Times: Local and Global Perspectives*, 26–55. Bangalore: Theological Publication in India, 2020a.

Wilfred, Felix. "Theological Perspectives on Mission and Political Engagement." In Simon Pinto et al., eds., *Politics and Mission in Critical Times: Local and Global Perspectives*, 33–58. Bangalore: Theological Publication in India, 2020b.

Wilfred, Felix. *Beyond Settled Foundations. The Journey of Indian Theology*. Delhi: ISPCK, 1993.

Wilfred, Felix. *Margins. The Site of Asian Theologies*. Delhi: ISPCK, 2008.

Wilfred, Felix. *Religious Identities in the Global South. Porous Borders and Novel Paths*. London and New York: Palgrave Macmillan, 2021.

Xie, Zhibin. *Religious Diversity and Public Religion in China*. Burlington: Ashgate, 2006.

Chapter 12

INTERSECTING FAITH AND SOCIETY SUBALTERN PUBLIC THEOLOGY OF *FRATELLI TUTTI*

In the previous chapter, we reflected on the Asian theological trajectory and the need to open new frontiers of a subaltern public theology, and reviewed some of its characteristics. The present chapter wants to carry forward these reflections by studying the encyclical *Fratelli Tutti*, a very timely document by Pope Francis. The approach and method this document follows and its underlying thought reveal a truly subaltern theology. We shall try to unravel the subaltern public theology at work in the thought of Pope Francis. For him, this theology is focused on those on the margins of the society – the poor, the migrants, the refugees, the prisoners, women, children, the physically and mentally challenged, the transgender, and those whose basic human rights continue to be violated.

His previous encyclical *Laudato Si,* and the present one have catapulted him as a 'global actor' of great impact. The "dark clouds" hovering over humankind and the environmental crisis make one realize more than ever the interdependence of human beings and their bondedness. Further, the outbreak of the pandemic Covid-19 brought out the urgent need to reflect on the survival of human beings and their future.[1]

> The pain, uncertainty and fear, and the realization of our own limitations, brought on by the pandemic have only made it all the more urgent that we rethink our styles of life, our relationships, the organization of our societies, and, above all, the meaning of our existence.[2]

All this poses a challenge to theology and calls for a new method and approach to it that would be increasingly open and public in reflecting on and addressing issues shared by humankind across borders, including religious, ideological, ethnic, and national. If *Laudato Si* dealt with the ecological crisis, *Fratelli Tutti* grappled with the social crisis and underlines the importance of social ecology. As common issues facing humankind, they become central questions of public theology today.

Situating the Public Theology of Pope Francis

To be able to better capture the nature and spirit of the public theology of Pope Francis, it is important to situate it in the context of the different types of public theology being discoursed and practiced. Even at the risk of simplification, let me classify five possible models of public theology.

The first type could be characterized as a *translation model*. Within this framework, individuals endeavour to articulate their religious convictions in public or secular language, thereby imbuing their beliefs with relevance and resonance for those who might perceive them as disconnected or outdated. In this model, one does not use confessional language. This is an attempt to make faith and Christian doctrines in tune with public reasoning on issues affecting everybody in society. The second type is *leaven model* of public theology. It tries to motivate religious believers to engage themselves in the world and society, inspired by their faith. The Vatican II document on the

Church in the Modern World would be an example of this model. This theology could be designated more appropriately as theology for public life rather than public theology. We have an echo of this theology in an address of Barrack Obama on religion, referring to the history of his country:

> Frederick Douglass, Abraham Lincoln, William Jennings Bryan, Dorothy Day, Martin Luther King—indeed, the majority of great reformers in American history— were not only motivated by faith, but repeatedly used religious language to argue for their cause.[3]

The third model could be called radical orthodoxy or *neo-orthodoxy model*. Besides some Protestant authors we mentioned in the previous chapter, we could add also representatives of integralist Catholicism such as Cardinal Joseph Ratzinger, later Pope Benedict XVI.[4] For this stream of public theology, ecclesiology would be the model for society that should be brought in line with the ideals the Church teaches. Beneath this orientation, one could identify the Augustinian paradigm of two cities – the city of God and the city of man. This kind of public theology could assume an apologetic tone in as much as it seeks to defend the Christian faith against the developments in the public sphere of the modern world.

The fourth is the *signs of the times model*. In this frame, public theology begins from the world, analyzes its condition with the help of many other disciplines, and then tries to reflect on how faith resources could illumine the situation and contribute to its transformation. This theology, far from being a conceptual exercise, addresses public issues or "common good" with deep concern and a sense of urgency and acts in collaboration with many other forces.

Finally, the fifth model is one that critically interrogates the "public" in public theology. It can be named as *subaltern model*. The public here is not identified with the bourgeois public or public as an amorphous general category. Instead, this type of public theology begins from those who are not visible and absent in the conventional public realm. They are the poor, the marginalized, the discriminated against, the physically and mentally challenged, the migrants, the refugees, asylum seekers, the elderly, the homeless, and others. A most glaring example are the Dalits, who are prevented from claiming what is their due and from occupying public spaces. Similar is the case of the migrants and refugees who are discriminated against and refused citizenship rights even in a modern democracy. This hidden public of our society and their issues become the centre from where public theology begins its reflection, and faith resources are brought to bear upon the transformation of their lives and instill hope for the fulfilment of their aspirations and trampled-upon dreams.

The public theology of Pope Francis would fall under the fourth and fifth models. He does not speak in generalities. The fraternity and friendship, he speaks about begin by observing the situation at the periphery, at the non-public represented by the marginalized and those discriminated against. The moral significance and the global impact of Pope Francis' public intervention is captured so well by Zygmunt Bauman when he said that Francis is, one of the very few public figures alerting us to the threats of following Pontius Pilate's gesture of washing hands of the consequences of the current trials and tribulation of which we all are, simultaneously, in one degree or another, victims and culprits.[5]

Subaltern Twist to the Concept of "Public"

The term 'public' means what pertains to all, what is common, and what is shared by a community. In this sense, we speak about 'public park' or 'public space.' It can also refer to various realms of life in common such as politics and economy. Hence, we could talk about "public policies." Public could also refer to governance and the activities and departments connected with the state. Thus, we speak of "Public Works Department" or "public concerns." Further, when a book is published or an artistic performance is enacted, we refer to the readers and to the audience as "the public." The "public" in public theology has all these layers of meaning and connotations. However, there is another dimension to 'public' where not *issues*, but *people* are the focal point. In fact, etymologically, the word "public" derives from *populus* – people; or *plebs*, the general populace.

In Pope Francis' public theology a discernible pattern emerges as he consistently directs his focus towards both pertinent societal concerns and often-overlooked segments of people - the hidden public. The issues are not abstracted from the condition of the discriminated against public. Since the subaltern public's condition in every context is different, the encyclical could not go into details. However, its basic orientation offers a significant impetus for a public theology from the margins. When the people at the margins get highlighted as the public, naturally, the issues of public concern will also be primarily the issues that concern these excluded groups of people, the outcasts and the "leftovers" of the society. Francis calls for a bending, a transformation of the public order – political, economic, cultural, etc. - in such a way that they address the condition of those absent from the bourgeois public because of oppression, negation, discrimination, and cultural hegemony. In fact, a subaltern public sphere is crucial now because forces of caste and class continue to colonize the bourgeois public, civil society, and media through their power.[6]

As is evident, public theology, far from being an endeavour to come to terms with the privatization of religion as in Europe, becomes in Asia, Africa, and Latin America an issue of the subalterns. The subaltern orientation in public theology marks *Fratelli Tutti*, the reason why it has great appeal in the Global South. If we trace the pope's intellectual journey, we will discover that in his native

Argentina, he was deeply immersed in the theology of the people. He has been able to capture all those experiences and beautifully weave those insights of the South into the encyclical – a departure from his Euro-centric predecessors.

The subalterns are not to be treated as passive subjects requiring our attention and compassion. The pope speaks of the contribution the subalterns and the vulnerable groups could make for the common good, for public life, using their rich and unique talents. He spells it out most clearly, here speaking specifically of the migrants. He sees in them a gift to be valued.

> The arrival of those who are different, coming from other ways of life and cultures, can be a gift, for the stories of migrants are always stories of an encounter between individuals and between cultures. For the communities and societies to which they come, migrants bring an opportunity for enrichment and the integral human development of all.[7]

The message of universal fraternity stands out in bold relief when the discourse begins from those who are deprived from being part of the public. For Francis, public theology begins from praxis and involvement. The pope brings to visibility those whom human selfishness hides from the eyes of the world; he becomes their voice because he continues to listen to them and knows their pain. In this way, the pope's public theological contribution is loaded with aspirations and dreams of the subalterns for greater humanization, dignity, acceptance, recognition, and equal treatment.

The disintegration of persons, communities, social relationships, and nature caused by the present order of things poses the challenging task of rebuilding the world and societies inspired by an alternative vision and a different set of values other than the reigning ones. Walter Brueggemann calls this the "disruptive grace" which came to Israel through the ministry of prophets aimed at an alternative community.[8] "The task of prophetic ministry is to nurture, nourish, and evoke a consciousness and perception alternative to the consciousness and perception of the dominant culture around us,"[9] This is what Pope Francis has attempted to do in *Fratelli Tutti*. He shows how important it is for humankind to pursue the utopia of another world where the common good will define politics and not struggle for acquiring self-serving power. The pursuit of the common good in the community of peoples needs to take place with compassion, generosity, and with charity in its more profound and comprehensive sense. Religions will sustain this project by drawing inspiration from their rich spiritual resources and by transformative engagement.

Public Issues and Religious Resources

There are arguments for and against the use of religious motives while addressing public issues. It is a question still lingering from the private/public debate within the frame of secularization theory.[10] The pope, as his habit, does not enter into such debates. Instead, he simply throws new light, with an original and insightful interpretation, on the parable of the Good Samaritan from the gospels, which commends itself for universal appeal. The parable of the Good Samaritan is an inspiration, a paradigm for an inter-religious and inter-cultural public theology as it is a story manifesting the spirit of fraternity to a stranger transcending the borders of religion, ethnicity and social standing. The parable is truly a *classic* that has a transcultural and trans-religious quality and compelling appeal as it portrays some universal truth both about human vulnerability and compassion. In this parable, as a classic, "we recognize nothing less than the disclosure of a reality we cannot but name truth."[11] Most fitting is, then, that the pope has deployed this classic as a hermeneutical guide for his public theology.[12] The very way he interprets this parable would convince anyone that so much new energy and dynamism for transformation could be unleashed for public life by interpreting religious resources.

Religious resources not only buttress a humanistic vision but often seem to be even necessary for the effective realization of a transformed world. To cite an example, the regime of fundamental human rights, as is well-known, often suffers from a lack of implementation even when the best humanistic arguments are set forth. Today, the human rights regime seem to require legitimation from transcendental grounds. In fact, *Gaudium et Spes* rightfully expressed this need, even though some what condescendingly, when it said, "by no human law can the personal dignity and liberty of human beings be so aptly safeguarded as by the gospel of Christ which has been entrusted to the Church…By virtue of the gospel committed to her, the church proclaims the rights of human beings."[13]

The story of human beings created in God's image, as portrayed in the Jewish Christian scriptures, only reinforces the humanistic and rational foundation of universal human rights. This narrative could help uphold with greater conviction and rigour every human person's dignity. There is no other unique Christian content to human dignity and rights as these are general issues affecting the entire humankind requiring joint and concerted involvement by everyone. However, the openness to a transcendental point of reference helps ensure the solidity of the foundation and free it from any transgression due to human infirmities and limitations. This echoes the classical teaching of St Thomas Aquinas, according to whom, "*Cum enim gratia non tollat naturam, sed perficiat* – grace does not take away nature but fulfills it."[14]

It is interesting to observe how Pope Francis harmoniously blends humanistic and rational arguments with faith-motives while addressing public issues. According to me, this is an important methodological contribution he makes to public theology. There is a parallel to the way he combines "public reason" with faith motives in *Laudato Si* and *Fratelli Tutti*.

The public theology of Pope Francis is the fruit of a close reading of the ministry of Jesus of history integrated into his own experience and formation in native Argentina. The pope puts at the service of the entire humankind the theology of the people which shaped him, and which he, on his part, contributed to shape, something evidenced by the Aparecida document (2007). Jorge Bergoglio was its chief architect.[15] He acknowledges that the word "people" could be abused and exploited.[16] At the same time, however, he is aware that it is a concept that can grow and expand, assuming new aspects and dimensions.[17]

A New Stage in the Social Teaching – Method and Issues

Francis is trying to do a public theology, whereas his immediate predecessors – John Paul II and Benedict XVI - seem to have done more of theology for public life by bringing out the fruitfulness of faith for life in the world. Just as in the tradition of the social teachings, the methodology employed by these predecessors have remained markedly influenced by neo-scholastic theology, notable for its a contrast of the natural order and the supernatural order. They have followed a model of public theology that understands its task as translation, namely translating the social and ethical implications of Christian doctrines in a language understandable and accessible to the general public. This kind of approach goes with the claim that the Christian faith has a humanizing effect. Hence, preaching the Christian faith is held as the best contribution to humanization.

In reality, however, the relationship of religion to public life is more complex than one of translation. In the neo-scholastic approach, there lurks a certain dichotomy between faith and the secular world. In Francis' theology, we find a fusion between faith and the world, the divine and the human.[18] Though he does not state this explicitly, his vision is that of a *perichoresis* (interpenetration) of the divine and the human in the realities of the world. Does not Gaudium et Spes tell us that "the earthly and the heavenly city penetrate one another?"[19] Francis, it seems to me, follows the orientation of Gaudium et Spes in seeing faith and world as interpenetrated, whereas his predecessors, by and large, follow the tradition of natural vis-à-vis the supernatural. This is true even of *Pacem in Terris* of John XXIII. It is well-known that it was the first time a papal document addressed all people of goodwill, breaking the tradition of speaking only to the Catholic faithful even when issues and questions pertaining all were presented.

To address all people of goodwill, John XXIII obviously could not merely use Christian doctrines and motives. He needed a methodology that would be inclusive and will find resonance among all people of goodwill and all people of faith or none. He argued from the order of nature and reason for the establishment of peace. The perspective of faith is added at the end of the encyclical in as much as the efforts of the reason may not be effective without the contribution of faith. The same observation could also be made of the way Pope Paul VI addressed the common theme of development in his *Populorum Progressio* (1967), in which one could identify the influence of the French neo-Thomist Jacques Maritain.

In the vision of Gaudium et Spes, followed by Francis, the world is not merely a pure nature. This is because we live already in a graced world through the creation and God's continuous presence and action in it. This vision can be identified as the undercurrent of *Fratelli Tutti* and his other writings, speeches, and interventions. Moreover, like in the case of Gaudium et Spes, we could notice in Francis a certain dynamism in the faith-world relationship, taking into account the fact that the world is evolving continuously and is not in a static situation that could be defined in terms of natural law; hence the importance of the reading of the signs of the times for relating faith and the world more relevantly and appropriately.

This dynamism can help the Church open up further in its dealings with issues of public nature.

For a long time, the primary agenda in Catholic social teachings, almost to the exclusion of other social issues, was workers' plight in the capitalist system. Later, the social teachings included in its scope also issues of social justice, peace, solidarity, private property, economy, politics, and issues of human dignity and rights. Pope Francis carries this tradition forward, as I noted earlier, by rethinking the relationship of faith and the world, gospel and culture in a different key which allows the poor, the marginalized, and the discriminated against to become the focal point. It is a vision of public issues from the margins contributing substantially to a subaltern public theology that leaves behind the dichotomous approach of the natural and the supernatural.

Some Innovative Principles for a Subaltern Public Theology

The subaltern character of Pope Francis' public theology comes out in greater relief when he elucidates certain principles as supporting universal fraternity and friendship. First and foremost, love is laid out as the principle cementing human relationships. It is not a vague and abstract love. It is a love that manifests in wishing the good of the other, of the society, and detached from any benefit that may accrue to oneself. Love expressing itself as compassion is the garden through which one reaches the mansion of truth.[20] This love is based on the realization of the dignity and value of the other – persons and communities - in themselves and not what they could bring to oneself. Against the general temptation of using calculus and pragmatism in human relationships, Pope Francis presents the principle of gratuitousness. This supports the cause of the subalterns. If one is guided by calculative reasoning, the poor and the subaltern will be left behind in their poverty and helplessness. Today, the worth of a person is regrettably still heavily influenced by birth, sex, race, caste, and gender, often on par with considerations of the productive abilities and consumption habits. For the salvation of the poor and the subalterns, I think it is indispensable that the "other" be viewed and treated non-teleologically and in a non-utilitarian manner. This will help reorder the world and society and create space for a dignified life for the poor.

A second innovative principle we find in *Fratelli Tutti*, is the expansion of the universal destiny of created goods and its application to include the political institution of the nation. As is well-known, in recent social teachings of the Church, one has drawn on early Christian tradition to state that the goods of the earth and the resources of nature are meant for the entire humankind. This sharing, however, needs to be done without any prejudice to the environment and the right of all God's creatures to have their own legitimate place on our planet. It is a common inheritance. The ownership of private property is subordinate to this primordial principle of the common destiny of earthly goods. This is laid out very clearly in Gaudium et Spes.[21] Today, nations assert their identity and ownership of their territory and erect borders and boundaries, which become problematic while facing issues of migration, or refugee-crisis resulting from war, poverty, and deprivation. Just as private property, the national ownership, according to Francis, cannot be absolute since the goods of the earth are shared and everyone has the right to have the resources of it for conducting a dignified human life.

Francis applies this principle to challenge the nations and tell them that one cannot deprive other human beings of their dignity and rights in the name of sovereignty. The resources a nation possesses is relative, and it may not claim absolute ownership. Francis is forthright and radical on this matter. "We can then say that each country also belongs to the foreigners, in as much as a territory's good must not be denied to a needy person coming from elsewhere."[22] We cannot but be struck by the far-reaching implications of this statement in such issues as international relationships, human trafficking, and in providing for the immigrants and refugees, not out of charity but as their rightful entitlement.

A third important principle relates to reconciling the richness plurality represents with the need for unity. Both are to be held in balance. There are numerous models of relating diversity with unity. The images we form and use influence significantly our conceptual universe. Knowing the complexity of the problem, the pope presents the geometrical image of a polyhedron. It has several facets, surfaces, and angles, and each one is unique, and together they form one unity. On the other hand, the image of the sphere leads us to think of homogenous condition of uniformity, where specificity and individuality are lost. According to the pope, polyhedron is an image applicable to globalization, Christian unity, unity of the human family, church-unity, and so on. He frequently uses this image in his speeches, and it is also found in *Evangelii Gaudium, Querida Amazonia,* and *Fratelli Tutti.*[23]

Critical Nature of Francis' Public Theology

Any public theology, especially subaltern public theology, cannot but be critical of our world and its various systems, especially the ideology of neoliberalism sustaining the present world-order. Pope Francis' vision of a fraternal society goes along with his pungent critique of neoliberalism. In particular, his thought challenges the neoliberal theories of "spill-over" and "trickle-down."[24] According to spillover theory, "a rising tide lifts all boats," meaning that growth and expansion of the economy help everyone – small and big.[25] According to "trickle-down" theory, the benefits of economic growth percolate down to benefit all. But history and experience have proved that these theories do not help bring about greater justice and equality in the world. On the contrary, they have increased inequality and have made oppression unbearable.

The pope is critical as well of political liberalism based on the individual and his or her freedom and rights. This kind of freedom, according to him, is concerned about expanding the spaces of the individual without serious concern for people, their aspirations and dreams. Unfortunately, when the community is drawn into the picture and ways are sought to reach them at least some benefits of growth, it is dubbed as "populist" by those who profess neoliberal ideology. In this context, the pope underlines the importance of social movements and popular movements, which will help create alternatives. Without the contribution of these movements, democracy can get atrophied.[26]

As could only be expected, Francis' critical stand on momentous public issues like the economy and political order has provoked severe critique.[27] The general pattern of resistance to religion playing a public role could also be seen in the reaction to Francis' addressing of economic and environmental issues.[28] Standard arguments against any public role of religion is losing steam. Increasingly people see the importance of drawing resources and inspirations from all possible quarters in the face of the catastrophes humanity and nature are facing.

Theological Presuppositions in Public Theology

The public theology of Pope Francis is deeply rooted in the genuine Catholic tradition, which is inclusive – faith and works, scripture and tradition, Jesus and Mary and so on, and it does not operate with the dichotomic split of either-or.[29] This is also true of the relationship of faith and the world, nature, and grace, to which I alluded above. They are not seen as opposed to each other but as one seamless reality in the divine dispensation. They blend in harmony.[30]

When public theology, methodologically, begins from the world, it becomes a theology rooted in the belief in creation. There is no surrender of faith, but its fresh re-appropriation through the realization of God's presence and action in the world and created realities. We may recall here that St Augustine saw even the traces of the Trinity in creation.[31] Francis leads us to a deeper understanding of faith and the *Word of God*, beginning from the *World of God*. He does it in *Laudato Si*, starting from nature and environment imbued with God's presence, and in *Fratelli Tutti*, he begins from the social and communitarian reality of human beings. We could identify in his approach, as a Jesuit, the spirituality of Ignatian discernment, asking what God wants in a particular concrete moment and circumstance and how one could respond to the promptings of God through the world, society, and creation - in short, discerning and responding to the signs of the times.

Further, deep down in Francis' public theology, we could recognize a sacramental dimension. The world, its human and material realms are God's signs and sacraments, mediating God's presence and action. This comes out in the ritual, sacramental celebration with material elements such as bread and wine, water and oil. In light of all this, faith and the world cannot be viewed as opposed to each other. This vision permeates the thinking of Pope Francis and is evident in his latest encyclical *Fratelli Tutti*. Such a vision also underlies his public theology.

Interreligious Public Theology

The analysis of the method and content of *Fratelli Tutti* clearly shows that Pope Francis is doing public theology, which is inter-religious in approach and spirit. The encyclical assumes that religions with their rich theological, humanistic, and moral resources can and should intervene for the common cause of fraternity. Here is an example of how a genuine public theology will take on interreligious character. People of goodwill belonging to other religious traditions, on their part, are inspired by their conviction and symbols to address all those issues affecting human life and fraternity.[32] In Pope Francis' vision, there should be an "overlapping consensus" of religions on cooperating for peace, justice, and transformation of societies. In this process, each one of them will draw inspiration from its resources. "Others drink from other sources," and he adds, "For us the wellspring of human dignity and fraternity is in the gospel of Jesus Christ."[33]

The pope is keen that the rich religious resources are not lost but are harnessed for the common good. Religions need to step in as voices for the common cause and not shy away from a public role.

> It is wrong when the only voices to be heard in public debate are those of the powerful and 'experts'. Room needs to be made for reflections born of religious traditions that are the repository of centuries of experience and wisdom [34]

We can see a new theology of public life at work in this encyclical. The new dimension to interreligious dialogue Pope Francis brings in *Fratelli Tutti* flows from his ecclesiology or the image of the Church. It is not a Church *incurvata in se* - bent on itself. From the beginning of his pontificate, Pope Francis has projected a centrifugal Church that would be right in the midst of the world and reach out to the conditions of society and the aspirations and dreams of people. The kind of inter-religious dialogue he promotes echoes his ecclesiological orientation directed to the world and its pastoral situation, very much in line with Gaudium et Spes. In his words and deeds, Pope Francis blends interreligious dialogue with a pastoral practice oriented to the world. He bridges so beautifully *Nostra Aetate* and Gaudium et Spes. From a theological point of view, what he does is indeed a public theology.

Solidarity of All Religions against Terrorism and Violence

Contribution of religions to peace is one of the chief concerns of *Fratelli Tutti*. After treating in chapter seven about peace and its relationship to justice and truth, the pope reflects in chapter eight, how religions today could contribute to peace. The pope knows the ambiguous character of religion relating to peace. In history and in present times, religion is being misused and interpreted for violence and terror. However, the same religions possess abundant sources for the promotion of peace, and hence the pope underlines the importance of believers of all religions joining together to promote peace.

He had already stated clearly in *Evangelii Gaudium* how interreligious dialogue could contribute to the promotion of peace. In the present encyclical, the pope props up the same point by citing from his joint statement with the Grand Imam of Al-Azhar: "Religions must never incite war, hateful attitudes, hostility and extremism, nor must they incite violence or the shedding of blood."[35] During his visit to Iraq, at an inter-religious meeting in the ancient city of Ur, he invoked the same message saying, "We believers cannot be silent when terrorism abuses religion .... Indeed, we are called unambiguously to dispel all misunderstandings. Let us not allow the light of heaven to be overshadowed by the clouds of hatred."[36]

Building peace is no easy task. The pope speaks about the importance of cultivating the "art" and "architecture" of peace. Further, genuine religiosity and worship of God will shun all forms of violence. For, "sincere and humble worship of God bears fruit, not in discrimination, hatred and violence, but in respect for the sacredness of life, respect for the dignity and freedom of others, and loving commitment to the welfare of all."[37] One significant way to promote peace is to build trust. Trust is the glue for reconciliation and peace. In many instances, religious leaders are in a position to be trusted more than politicians in facilitating and advancing the cause of peace.

Peace is not achieved through "normative frameworks and institutional arrangements" (FT 213), which is named as "architecture" of peace. There is also an "art" of peace that involves meeting, encounter, dialogue, fostering of friendship and fraternity. Through the "art" of peace, even complex issues of conflict could be faced and sorted out. In post-conflict situations, the establishment of peace becomes very challenging, as it involves a delicate balance between memory, forgiveness, and reconciliation.[38] A peace established at the cost of setting aside memory will not be lasting. On the other hand, forgiveness and reconciliation can never be prescribed or demanded but are to take place in all freedom as these are truly gratuitous. Religions do have immense resources for cultivating the spirit of forgiveness and leading to the path of reconciliation.

By going deep into the issue of peace, conflict, forgiveness, and reconciliation, the pope has shown how important it is for theology to become increasingly public. More than anyone, it is the poor and the marginalized who are deeply affected by conflicts. In fact, today's world situation tells us that wars and conflicts are taking place mostly in the poorer parts of the world where the poor are struggling with issues of justice, social equity, discrimination, and marginalization.

Changing Public Theology – War and Capital Punishment

Yet another example of how theology could enter into a rethinking on public issues is seen in how the pope treats the issue of war. Here again, he is taking into account the vastly changed circumstances of today, and has proposed something that departs from traditional teaching and theology on just war. The traditional arguments in defence of just war is well-known. Even Gaudium et Spes of Vatican

II with all its caveats does not rule out just war; so too the Catholic Church's Universal Catechism. John XXIII raised serious doubts about whether the traditional condition for just war could be found in current circumstances. *Fratelli Tutti* takes us farther than this position and seems to think that there can be no legitimacy for the so-called just war in today's circumstances. In *Pacem in Terris*, John XXIII considered it "contrary to reason to hold that war is now a suitable way to restore rights which have been violated." (PT 127). This was also the view of Pope John Paul II. For Pope Francis, today, the arguments like armed intervention for humanitarian reasons or for prevention of greater evil appear so weak that there is the danger of them being exploited to enter into war to promote self-interests.

Today's changed circumstances have also led Pope Francis to come out emphatically against capital punishment for its many aporias. He encourages promoting action for its abolition worldwide. The abolition of the death penalty is really a test on how firm and deep our conviction about human dignity is. The abolition needs to be upheld regardless of the moral rectitude of a person. Any religion concerned about the security and wellbeing of all people will need to respond to such public issues as war and capital punishment. In taking up these issues and dealing with them in detail, Pope Francis has contributed an important page to the development of public theology in the contemporary world.

Conclusion

"Bergoglio is, in his apparent simplicity, a complex figure."[39] Massimo Borghesi has shown admirably in his research how the "simplicity" of the theology of Francis is *a point of arrival* behind which lies a long and arduous intellectual journey with many influences that went into the shaping of his thought in Argentina. A closer reading of his programmatic Apostolic Exhortation, *Evangelii Gaudium*, and especially the encyclicals *Laudato Si* and *Fratelli Tutti*, reveal the depth of his theological thinking. Far from being a "populist" or lacking in theological depth – allegations often made against him - he shows the way to do theology today.[40] It is not a shadow-boxing with concepts in an insulated and illusionary world of cerebral sophistication, but struggling in a real-world of everyday life in its manifold expressions, increasingly complex and complicated. His theology emerges from the experience of navigating often between a rock and a hard place, between Scylla and Charybdis.[41] It bears upon the issues and questions affecting humankind and nature in a language that appeals to all people of goodwill and hence acquires a public character.

Pope's public theology is not one that attempts to come to terms in a post-secular society of the West. His public theology begins from the margins – the excluded public, the public who have no voice or whose voices are muffled.[42] Hence his public theology has a clear stand-point. Responding to public issues calls for cooperation among the various religious traditions as well as people of goodwill who do not believe in God or religion.[43] Dialogue is crucial to sustaining the spirit of cooperation and joint engagement to transform society and its present order.

For faith to address the contemporary issues of humans and nature meaningfully, it needs the support of the Church community that should be centrifugal in its orientation. Francis reimages the Church as a body, a community-oriented to the world, present "out on the streets" and truly active right amid the world and society.[44] The effectiveness of public theology and faith-inspired intervention in public life will depend upon the credibility and transparency of the Church. Public theology cannot be done by a Church of unthinking self-righteousness, lacking in humility and lost in the idolatry of verbal formulation of doctrines and orthodoxy; a centripetal Church cannot do it, preoccupied all the time about itself, its establishments, and its benefits.[45] No real public theology could come out of such a Church community.

Francis' favourite image of the Church as field-hospital characterizes a centrifugal, humble and open Church without walls that makes the concerns of the people and wounds of humanity its own, and tries to respond to them. Church, after all, is not an end in itself, but only a sign, and an instrument,[46] and a bridge to cross over to the Reign of God. From such a Church, we could expect the emergence of genuine public theology, and indeed a subaltern public theology addressing the concerns of the poor, the non-public, to whom Jesus promised the Kingdom of God. Pope Francis is a trailblazer of such a theology, and his encyclical *Fratelli Tutti* is a significant landmark in the social teachings of the Church.

NOTES

1 Cf. Felix Wilfred, "Disclosing and Concealing. Human Fallibility and Civilizational Upheaval," *Jeevadhara* 51, no. 305 (January 2021): 7–25.

2 *Fratelli Tutti* no. 33. https://www.vatican.va/content/francesco/en/encyclical s/documents/papafrancesco_20201003_enciclica-fratelli-tutti.html [accessed on 9 April, 2023].

3 *New York Times*, 21 June 2006. https://www.nytimes.com/2006/06/28/us/ politics/2006obamaspeech.html [accessed on 9 March 2021].

4 Cf. *Ratzinger Report. An Exclusive Interview with Cardinal Joseph Ratzinger with Vittorio Messori* (San Francisco: Ignatius Press, 1985).

5 Zygmunt Bauman, *Strangers at Our Door* (Cambridge: Polity, 2016), 20.

6 I think the city and village streets are the best symbols of the Indian public sphere. For actual socializing – political, religious, cultural, and entertainment events, including processions - takes place in the streets, and where people also exchange goods and services. This is a very different public sphere than the coffee shops of England, salons of France and table-societies of Germany. Now those who dominate the public space symbolized by streets also impose who has access or not to the streets – the public space, and it is here the caste-domination and subjugation is played out. We know how much violence is involved in numerous instances where the Dalits are

forbidden to transit and even carry their dead for burial. Numerous statues of Baba Saheb Ambedkar, erected on the streets have been vandalized all over the country – yet another sign of hegemony of the "public" by upper castes and classes. See Felix Wilfred, "Smart City vs Compassionate City," *Jeevadhara* 49, no.289 (January 2019): 11– 38.

7   *Fratelli Tutti* 133.

8   Cf. Walter Brueggemann, *Disruptive Grace. Reflections on God, Scripture and the Church* (Minneapolis: Fortress Press, 2011).

9   Walter Brueggemann, *The Prophetic Imagination* (Minneapolis: Fortress Press, 2001), 3.

10   Cf. Nigel Biggar and Linda Hogan, eds., *Religious Voices in Public Places* (Oxford: Oxford University Press, 2009).

11   David Tracy, *The Analogical Imagination* (New York: Crossroad, 1986), 108.

12   See *Fratelli Tutti*, chapter 2.

13   *Gaudium et Spes* 41.

14   *Summa Theologica* I, q.1, art. 8, ad 2.

15   Cf. Paul Christopher, "How the Theological Priorities of Pope Francis Inform His Policy Goals," in Alynna Lynn et al., eds., *Pope Francis as Global Actor* (Cham, Switzerland: Palgrave Macmillan, 2018), 22 – 40. For the shaping of Jorge Mario Bergoglio's mind, see Massimo Borghesi, *The Mind of Pope Francis. Jorge Mario Bergoglio's Intellectual Journey* (Collegeville: Liturgical Press, 2018). See also, Austen Ivereigh, *The Great Reformer: Francis and the Making of a Radical Pope* (London: Allen & Unwin, 2014); see also Paul Vallely, *Pope Francis: Untying the Knot* (London: Bloomsbury, 2013); Marco Politi, *Pope Francis among the Wolves. The Inside Story of a Revolution* (New York: Columbia University Press, 2015); Walter Kasper, *Pope Francis' Revolution of Tenderness and Love* (New York: Paulist Press, 2015).

16   Probably it is this fear often connected with liberation theology that led increasingly to a shift from the "People of God" ecclesiology of Vatican II, to communion ecclesiology. *Abusus non tollit usum* – abuse does not take away legitimate use. Pope Francis does not abandon the concept of "people" because of its ambiguity, but rather he re-appropriates this Vatican II concept drawing from the theology of the people, as developed in Argentina.

17   On the Argentinian theology of the people which had great impact on Jorge Bergoglio, see Ciro Enrique Bianchi, *Introduzione alla teologia del popolo: Profilo spirituale e teologico di Rafael Tello* (Rome: Editrice missionaria italiana, 2015). It has an introduction by Bergoglio.

18   A very revealing intellectual biography of Bergoglio and the influence of several Latin American thinkers on him tells that he does not polarise, instead tries to see a more profound unity and convergence beneath

what appear to be polar opposites. I think this is an important insight to understand Francis' thinking.

19 *Gaudium et Spes* 40.

20 I think it is important to realize how love and truth are interrelated in Pope Francis's vision. He sees truth as a relational reality and intertwined with love. It is this vision that led him to make a radical statement: "I would not speak about 'absolute' truths, even for believers…Truth, according to the Christian faith, is the love of God for us in Jesus Christ. Therefore, truth is a relationship. As such, each one of us receives the truth and expresses it from within, that is to say, according to one's own circumstances, culture, situation in life etc." http://www.vatican.va/content/francesco/en/letters/2013/documents/papa-francesco_20130911_eugenio-scalfari.html [accessed on 10 March 2021].

21 *Gaudium et Spes* 69.

22 *Fratelli Tutti* 124.

23 *Evangelii Gaudium,* 236; in *Querida Amazonia* 29-32; and in *Fratelli Tutti,* 145, 190, 215.

24 *Fratelli Tutti* 168.

25 This aphorism is generally attributed to John F. Kennedy.

26 *Fratelli Tutti* 169.

27 On this point see Chapter 10

28 For more details on the critique, see Andrea Tornielli and Giacomo Galeazzi, *This Economy Kills: Pope Francis on Capitalism and Social Justice* (Minnesota: Liturgical Press, 2015). Francis's critique is based on what he saw and experienced in his country, Argentina. See also Marco Politi, *Pope Francis among Wolves…op. cit.,* 109–113.

29 Cf. Charles Curran, *Catholic Social Teaching 1891 – Present. A Historical, Theological, and Ethical Analysis* (Washington D.C.: Georgetown University Press, 2002), 21.

30 It is important at this juncture to recall the intellectual formation of Bergoglio influenced by his teachers, who were both Latin American and European. Under their influence, Bergoglio, far from subscribing to a dialectical tension leading to conflict, learnt to bring the opposites together in harmony – *coincidentia oppositorum.* This matrix of his thought gets applied also to theological issues of grace and nature, which he brings in a harmonious relationship and applies this harmony in addressing issues and questions of great public relevance today.

31 St Augustine, *De Trinitate,* Book 15.

32 Cf. Felix Wilfred, *Religious Identities and the Global South. Porous Borders and Novel Paths* (Cham, Switzerland: Palgrave Macmillan, 2021).

33 *Fratelli Tutti* 277.

34 *Fratelli Tutti* 275.

35   *Fratelli Tutti* 285.

36   https://www.bbc.com/news/world-middle-east-56302173 [accessed on 7 March 2021].

37   *Fratelli Tutti* 283.

38   Cf. Felix Wilfred, "Dilemmas and Trajectories of Peace," *Concilium* 2015/1 (A special issue on: Religion and Identity in Post-conflict Societies), 13–20.

39   Massimo Borghesi, *The Mind of Pope Francis. Jorge Mario Bergoglio's Intellectual Journey* (Collegeville: Liturgical Press, 2018), xxvii. Unfortunately, Pope Francis's "populist" and "superficial theology" is often contrasted with the "theological genius" of Benedict XVI. But it looks to me that, despite his disciples' (*Schülerkreis*) adulation, even while he was alive, Benedict XVI's theological legacy was getting buried. History will remember him, probably, not so much for his integralist and doctrinaire theological views as for his wise and honest decision to resign when he felt that physically and mentally, he could not carry on with the leadership of the Church. Cf. Felix Wilfred, "The Resignation of Pope Benedict XVI," *Concilium* 2013/2, 123–127.

40   See Kurt Appel – Jakob Helmut Deibl, eds., *Barmherzigkeit und zärtiliche Liebe. Das theologische Programm von Past Franziskus* (Freiburg: Herder, 2016).

41   Suffice it to recall here the challenging situation Bergoglio faced as a leader of the Society of Jesus at a critical time of dictatorial regime and martial law in Argentina. He was even accused of "betraying" his confreres involved in the ministry of liberation.

42   His approach from the margins and his taking a stand from the subaltern' perspective has unleashed a "tempest" of opposition in the Church. See Marco Politi, *La solitudine di Francesco: Un papa profetico, una Chiesa in tempesta* (Roma: Editori Laterza, 2019).

43   The pope acknowledges respectfully the valuable contribution of humanists who do not believe in God. "As believers, we also feel close to those who do not consider themselves part of any religious tradition, yet sincerely seek the truth, goodness and beauty which we believe have their highest expression and source in God. We consider them precious allies in the commitment to defending human dignity, in building peaceful coexistence between people and in protecting creation" (EG 57). For a very insightful appraisal of Pope Francis' humanism, see Shoshana Ronen, "What Do We Share? A Secular-Humanist Response," in Harold Kasimow, and Alan Race, *Pope Francis and Interreligious Dialogue* (Cham, Switzerland: Palgrave Macmillan, 2018), 279–300.

44   "I prefer a Church which is bruised, hurting and dirty because it has been out on the streets, rather than a Church which is unhealthy from being confined and from clinging to its own security" (EG 49). In the face of the environmental crisis, Pope Francis wants to address "every person living on

the planet" (LS 3), and they include not only people professing belief in God but also non-believers.

45 Reaching out to the other, and addressing the problems of society and human suffering, presupposes a humble self-understanding. Humility and awareness of one's limitation make one a perpetual learner from others and capable of dialoguing. It is remarkable that Pope Francis, when he was posed the question "Who is Jorge Mario Bergoglio?" his straightforward answer was, "I am a sinner. This is the most accurate definition." http://www.vatican.va/content/francesco/en/speeches/2013/september/documents/papa-francesco_20130921_ intervista-spadaro.html [accessed on 8 March 2021]. Whatever he is, Francis attributes it to divine mercy and compassion. His episcopal motto was precisely this: "Miserendo atque eligendo" (having mercy and choosing) – an expression taken from the Homilies of Bede the Venerable.

46 *Lumen Gentium* 1

FURTHER READING

Alva, Reginald. "The Need of Global Social Nearness in Light of the Teachings of the Encyclical *Fratelli Tutti.*" *International Review of Mission* 110 (2021): 312–26.

Amaladoss, Michael, Anthony Lawrence, Joseph Victor Edwin, eds. *Fratelli Tutti. An Indian Reading.* Bangalore: Asian Trading Corporation, 2021.

Appel, Kurt, and Jakob Helmut Deibl. eds. *Barmherzigkeit und zärtiliche Liebe. Das theologische Programm von Past Franziskus.* Freiburg: Herder, 2016.

Bauman, Zygmunt. *Strangers at Our Door.* Cambridge: Polity, 2016.

Bianchi, Ciro Enrique. *Introduzione alla teologia del popolo: Profilo spirituale e teologico di Rafael Tello.* Rome: Editrice missionaria italiana, 2015.

Biggar, Nigel, and Linda Hogan. eds. *Religious Voices in Public Places.* Oxford: Oxford University Press, 2009.

Borghesi, Massimo. *The Mind of Pope Francis. Jorge Mario Bergoglio's Intellectual Journey.* Collegeville: Liturgical Press, 2018.

Brueggemann, Walter. *Disruptive Grace. Reflections on God, Scripture and the Church.* Minneapolis: Fortress Press, 2011.

Brueggemann, Walter. *The Prophetic Imagination.* Minneapolis: Fortress Press, 2001.

Christopher, Paul. "How the Theological Priorities of Pope Francis Inform His Policy Goals." In Alynna Lynn et al., eds., *Pope Francis as Global Actor,* 22 – 40. Cham, Switzerland: Palgrave Macmillan, 2018.

Curran, Charles. *Catholic Social Teaching 1891 – Present. A Historical, Theological, and Ethical Analysis.* Washington D.C.: Georgetown University Press, 2002.

De Oliveira, Roberto Jelson, and Clovis Ultramari. "The Eutopian City: The Challenge of Urban Conviviality in the *Laudato Si'* and *Fratelli Tutti* Encyclicals." *International Journal of Public Theology* 16, no. 2 (2022):154–173.

Fernandes, Stany C. "A Missionary Response to a Technocratic Paradigm." In Michael Amaladoss, Antony Lawrence, and Joseph Victor Edwin, eds., *Fratelli Tutti. An Asian Reading,* 307-321. Bangalore: Asian Trading Corporation, 2021.

Irudayam, Charles. "The Abolition of the Death Penalty – Pope Francis: An Advocate Par Excellence." In Michael Amaladoss, Antony Lawrence, and Joseph Victor Edwin, eds., *Fratelli Tutti. An Asian Reading,* 225–239. Bangalore: Asian Trading Corporation, 2021.

Ivereigh, Austen. *The Great Reformer: Francis and the Making of a Radical Pope.* London: Allen & Unwin, 2014.

Karunanidhi, Yesu. "A Subaltern Reading of *Fratelli Tutti.*" In Michael Amaladoss, Antony Lawrence, and Joseph Victor Edwin, eds., *Fratelli Tutti. An Asian Reading,* 95-107. Bangalore: Asian Trading Corporation, 2021.

Kasper, Walter. *Pope Francis' Revolution of Tenderness and Love.* New York: Paulist Press, 2015.

Machado, Felix. "*Fratelli Tutti* and Mahatma Gandhi." In Michael Amaladoss, Antony Lawrence, and Joseph Victor Edwin, eds., *Fratelli Tutti. An Asian Reading,* 69-73. Bangalore: Asian Trading Corporation, 2021.

Messori, Vittorio. *Ratzinger Report. An Exclusive Interview with Cardinal Joseph Ratzinger.* San Francisco: Ignatius Press, 1985.

Mulligan, Suzanne. "'Builders of a New Social Bond': *Fratelli Tutti* on Good Politics and the Challenge of Inequality." *The American Journal of Economics and Sociology* 80 (2021): 1173-203.

Politi, Marco. *La solitudine di Francesco: Un papa profetico, una Chiesa in tempesta* Roma: Editori Laterza, 2019.

Politi, Marco. *Pope Francis among the Wolves. The Inside Story of a Revolution.* New York: Columbia University Press, 2015.

Ronen, Shoshana. "What Do We Share? A Secular-Humanist Response." In Harold Kasimow and Alan Race, eds. *Pope Francis and Interreligious Dialogue,* 279–300. Cham, Switzerland: Palgrave Macmillan, 2018.

Titus, A Joseph. "Do Away with 'False Universalism': Pope Francis' Call for Adequate Understanding of Universal Love." In Michael Amaladoss, Antony Lawrence, and Joseph Victor Edwin, eds., *Fratelli Tutti. An Asian Reading,* 176–198. Bangalore: Asian Trading Corporation, 2021.

Tornielli, Andrea, and Giacomo Galeazzi. *This Economy Kills. Pope Francis on Capitalism and Social Justice.* Minnesota: Liturgical Press, 2015.

Tracy, David. *The Analogical Imagination.* New York: Crossroad, 1986.

Vallely, Paul. *Pope Francis: Untying the Knot.* London: Bloomsbury, 2013.

Wilfred, Felix. "Dilemmas and Trajectories of Peace." *Concilium* 2015/1,13–20.

Wilfred, Felix. "Smart City vs Compassionate City." *Jeevadhara* 49, no. 289 (January 2019): 11– 38.

Wilfred, Felix. "The New Humanism of Pope Francis." *Jeevadhara* 52, no. 313 (2023).

Wilfred, Felix. "The Resignation of Pope Benedict XVI." *Concilium* 2013/2, 123–127.

Wilfred, Felix. *Religious Identities and the Global South. Porous Borders and Novel Paths.* Cham, Switzerland: Palgrave Macmillan, 2021.

POST-PANDEMIC THEOLOGY

Chapter 13

DISCLOSING AND CONCEALING
THE MANIFEST AND THE HIDDEN IN COVID-19 SAGA

Covid-19 has exposed some harsh truths about the present trajectory of humankind and its inherent fallibility. The response to the pandemic, however, has tried to bury many other truths of vital importance for a transformed world and humanity. This chapter starts questioning the use of martial metaphor to refer to the pandemic and reflects on how populist and totalitarian mode of governance has failed to come to grips with the pandemic situation and how inequality characterizes the way Covid-19 has affected some of the most vulnerable segments of the society.

The Covid-19 crisis has also exposed how our world is divided by race, caste, gender and religion. The ideological projection of a world of limitless progress has been brought to its knees to face the actual human condition of uncertainty and vulnerability. It is an opportunity to imaging a different world, not driven by greed, competition, and accumulation, but inspired by the sense of compassion, love, altruism, and solidarity. The chapter also reflects on the failure of social sciences, religious studies, and theology to respond creatively to such critical situations.

A Singular Experience for Present-day Humanity

The year 2020 turned out to be *annus horribilis*. The pandemic situation has prompted humanity to engage in profound soul-searching and deep thinking. It has caused panic, consternation, insecurity, angst, fear of the unknown and unmitigated suffering. Never before in history has humankind given such a serious thought to its survival and the shape of its future as it has happened since the outbreak of this contagion. A pandemic like this one is indeed capable of transforming history, societies, nations, politics, economy and culture, in short, human civilization. The end of the pandemic is not vaccination, but the challenge to humanity to turn over a new leaf with far reaching implications for its future, and the future of the planet. What may often look absurd and senseless could, with due reflection, become the beginning of a new fruitfulness. Myopic would it be, on the other hand, were we to brush aside the magnitude of the present civilizational crisis and hope to return to business as usual.

We know from history that the Black Death, the plague that spread in medieval Europe through flourishing Crimean trading ports was devastating; it decimated half the population of European cities.[1] Once the crisis was surmounted, there was no return to the routine life. The plague profoundly transformed Europe, its attitudes, values, way of life, its society, culture, and economy, with far-reaching consequences for the entire world and the course of history. The world today is in a similar situation of having to learn many a lesson from Covid-19 pandemic and move in a new direction.[2] We need to bring to an end the ideologically coloured lethargy of the Thatcherian TINA ("There is no Alternative") syndrome and explore new paths.

The pandemic revealed to us many truths – some of them very unsavoury – while the response to it is concealing many facets of reality and truth. This disease is a microcosm in which the state of our world and society is reflected. It uncovers the systemic fault-lines in global and national politics, economy, culture wherein inequality has got embedded. In the following reflections, we shall try to understand what is being disclosed and what is being concealed. Ultimately, the pandemic reveals radical limits of the human and radical human fallibility, a situation from which we need to image and construct a post-Covid-19 world and civilization of solidarity and compassion.

Martial Metaphor and Governance-Failure

I am struck by the militarist language employed, especially by the politicians, to describe the pandemic situation. A most frequent image is that of *"enemy."* We saw in the media – print and digital – the same kind of portrayal. This virus is an enemy to be defeated and conquered. Everyone becomes in the nation a soldier in the war against Covid-19. Those who are caring for the victims of this pathogen become frontline *"warriors."* It reminds us of the expression *"exam warriors,"* describing in a martial fervor the children going through an evaluation of their study and learning. The metaphor of enemy and war is appealing. One speaks of war on terror, war on drugs.

> The narrative of Trump's belligerent "wartime presidency" for instance, personifies the medical concept "virus" by calling doctors and nurses "frontline soldiers" fighting an invisible "intruder." Medical workers, together with other indispensable personnel in service industries, are hailed as "brave warriors." Panicked utterances of this ilk are perilous because of the destructive imprint they leave on public life, not to mention calls "for an arms race" to combat *The Virus.* Performatives like these together with the declaration of a "national competition" to produce a vaccine to eradicate the pandemic might deflect feelings of fear and frustration. However, the language of war does little to comfort an ambient, intangible sense of all-pervasive helplessness on the part of an abandoned people.[3]

The association of martial language with contagion and epidemy is not something new altogether. In ancient times, in some parts of the globe, infecting the enemies with diseases was a war stratagem. Expressed in a refined modern idiom, it is bio-war. Diseased cadavers were thrown into the citadels of the enemy so that the militia and even civilians were disabled from fighting. The Mongols did this when they could not break through any fortified city and were forced to lift their siege.

The use of such a language in India reveals what is happening in the country socially and politically. The bellicose language seems to cheer a lot of people because it echoes the enemies of the nation – Pakistan, China, the secularists, the communists, and all those who endanger, according to them, the security of the nation. There are paramilitary organizations and clandestine armies of all kinds - some of them wielding lethal weapons - purportedly to defend the nation, caste, cow and tradition. This militarist language also applies to the enemies within – the Muslims, Christians, lower castes and classes, migrant labour, inquiring commentators, media who speak truth to power, rights activists and other minorities.

When governance follows the militia model, then the leaders turn themselves into generals and commanders, and the people become foot-soldiers. This does not require any coup. It is happening in democratic nations and set-ups. Any deviation or divergence of thought or opinion becomes a threat to the security of the nation and *laesa majestas,* a high treason. Like the army commanders, the despots know what is best, and there is no time or inclination to listen. Their word becomes law.[4] In The Philippines, where people lived under fascist populism, President Duterte deployed soldiers with firearms to make the people keep social distancing and wearing of masks. Many people disappeared, others were arrested, and some were even shot dead for not complying. In Indonesia, retired army generals were recruited to enforce discipline.[5] What is strange is that this militarist approach is practised in countries claiming to function democratically and under Constitution.

Hannah Arendt has masterfully analyzed the origin of the historical phenomenon of totalitarianism, and we can only wonder how actual it is also in the present-day situation.[6] Today totalitarianism has donned the mantle of populism. A populist leader represents machismo – the strong man image. He creates the impression of acting decisively while caring least for democratic institutions and procedures, and breaking norms at every turn for his heroic exploits. An iconic image is cultivated through rhetoric, manipulation of media, and the fabrication of lies for widespread consumption. Reflecting on the way governance responded to Covid-19 crisis, Fareed Zakaria observes,

> Authoritarian regimes – always and everywhere – want to control information tightly. It is a source of their power. Looking at all epidemics recorded since 1960, *The Economist* found that dictatorships often mishandle outbreaks. In general democracies have dealt with them better, resulting in significantly lower death rates compared to autocracies of the same income level...It is also unclear that China's heavy-handed approach with total lockdowns and closures was the only path to success. Other countries managed the disease as effectively with far less coercive methods.[7]

The magnitude of this political course stands out when we note that in one-third of all democratic countries, their leaders have taken their respective nations on the populist path. Statistics about how many were infected, recovered or died depended on the political need of the hour. Giorgio Agamben has argued that the crisis of Covid-19 was mostly socially constructed or manipulated for states to usurp exceptional executive powers. A state of emergency helps the state power to act in an authoritarian manner. For the wielders of state power there is a temptation to use exceptional and emergency powers as normal, which is what happened, according to him with Covid-19.[8]

Logically, totalitarian and populist leaders are involved in one-way communication and centralized action. They consider civil society organizations and voluntarism as a thorn in their flesh and a challenge to their insulated planning and coercive mode of governance.

NGOs, largely built around philanthropist or private money, are in effect standing in for inefficient or absent state involvement (poor, indebted farmers, lower castes, disabled, children, women, sick etc.) and are forced to depend on foreign funding to sustain operational costs let alone project work for beneficiaries.

When the Tsunami disaster of 2004 struck, we could notice how individuals and voluntary organizations were at the forefront to listen and attend to the plight of the victims. The contrast with what has happened with Covid-19 is very striking. Sure, there were many instances of grassroots involvement in responding to the health crisis. However, the involvement of civil society and voluntary groups and organizations was drastically reduced this time. They were either shunned, demonized or did not find the proper climate for addressing the traumatic situation of the Covid-19 victims. Often NGOs were prevented from exposing the facts on Covid deaths to hide government mismanagement.

As elusive as the virus itself, the political establishment constructed the pandemic from time to time swaying and bending it to political expediency. The reactions of the populists ranged from giving assurance to extirpate the virus from the country within days and weeks; concocting conspiracy theories on its origin and spread; dismissing and even ridiculing the views of experts in the field of epidemiology as Donald Trump did; humouring the people for life as usual as if nothing had happened; and even encouraging them most irresponsibly to move around with least regard for physical distancing or masks, as Bolsonaro did in Brazil. In the eyes of the establishment, more than a medical issue threatening the lives of millions of people,

Covid-19 became primarily a "spectacle"[9] choreographed by the acolytes of power, not to mention an opportunity to make quick money.

In India, the Hindutva encouraged demonizing of Muslims by misleading the public and alleging a superspreader event around a meeting of Tablighi Jamaat to divert attention from the state's ignorance, incompetence, high-handedness and unilateralism around diagnosis, treatment and prevention of spread and fatalities.

The pandemic has also highlighted the real state of public health care in different countries. It exposed the absence of any long-term system, infrastructure, and allocation of adequate funds. Such a challenging health crisis as Covid-19 required robust structures, especially to be able to embrace within health safety net the poor and the disadvantaged. Studies show how our system in India, for example, lags far behind other South Asian neighbours which could be seen also in the mortality caused by Covid-19.

Experts say that the real scale of deaths by Covid-19 in India could be as high as six times the publicly accepted state figure, not only because of poor recording but also because of notorious fudging and undercounting across the country with little/no oversight by India's Ministry of Health. According to India's government the country ranks 105/201 countries in terms of highest Covid-19 deaths, but experts clarify that a more truthful record will put India at 15/201 countries, making it one among 15 countries with the highest death toll.

The WHO confirmed that India has had the highest number of deaths worldwide and ranks number 1 in Covid-19 death count; at 4.7 million deaths by 2021.

It is clear that a significant number of deaths could have been prevented if the state had not been an obstacle to delivery of health by private institutions and individuals. Millions of selfless volunteers filled the vacuum left by the state health system in 2020 and 2021 but they were often hamstrung by obstructive, unscientific, unilateral state policies around testing, lockdown, quarantine, vaccination and treatment. So, thousands of NGOs and volunteers could not perform as effectively as they otherwise might have.

Experts say that when Ebola struck Sierra Leone and Liberia, it was not the one billion dollar foreign aid (for hospital infrastructure) that beat it back but community participation and community-led efforts. India's monumental failure is as much a failure of the state as the state failing to at least facilitate selfless volunteering by individuals cutting across caste, class, religious and geographical lines.

> Reckoned in terms of any health indicator, India compares poorly with its neighbours. Based on the World Health Statistics, it is evident the per capita health spending of India ($62) is only 40% of that of Sri Lanka ($ 153), and total health spending as a percentage of the gross domestic product (GDP) is only 0.93%, as against 1.17% for Nepal and 1.68 for Sri Lanka…In all health outcomes, India is far below Sri Lanka and, in regard to life-expectancy at birth, neonatal morality, etc., India has a poor record compared to Bangladesh, Nepal and Sri Lanka.[10]

India stands among a mere 15 nations worldwide that allocate less than 1.2% of the GDP towards healthcare. Interestingly, some officials combine expenditures for water and sanitation with healthcare resulting in a dubious figure of 1.4%. However, the international benchmark of maintaining a reasonable standard healthcare encompassing primary care, communicable disease management, disease surveillance, hovers around the 5% mark.In spite of its vast poor populations, successive governments have allowed the private sector to represent 70% of India's healthcare sector, both in terms of private institutions meeting health needs and individual families spending disproportionate amounts of individual/household incomes on health (diagnosis and treatment). Even allowing for some of the state's tall claims of India as an IT superpower, precious little of that was used to provide timely and appropriate healthcare to those in need.

Disclosing a Humiliated Truth in a World of Inequality

The pandemic situation discloses the humiliated truth of the poor and the inequality they have been suffering from. One sudden realization the medieval European plague brought about was that all humans are equal and share the same mortality – from emperor and popes down to the smallest peasant tilling the ground. We could imagine the profound impact this realization brought about in a society entrenched in feudal and hierarchical thinking and practice. That the virus has no caste or creed is to state a plain truth. In India, it exposed most glaringly the existing social divisions and inequality, which got also reflected in the difference in the way people responded to it.

The virus is the same for all, but the degree of threat and danger depended on one's caste and social location. It affects disproportionately women, African Americans, Hispanics, Dalits, tribals, among whom occurred also the highest number of deaths. Speaking specifically of women, a study concludes,

> Women are vulnerable not just to the direct impact on their lives because of their disproportionate presence on the frontlines and increased rates of domestic violence, but also indirect socio-economic impacts such as economic insecurity and an increase in their burden of care ... These vulnerabilities are further amplified for women living in complex emergency situations. As such, a gendered perspective on the impacts of COVID-19 is vital.[11]

The prevailing inequality based on caste and class had its repercussion on the way people were exposed to the danger of Covid- 19. People from the lowest rungs of the society doing sanitation work, scavenging, drain-cleaning were in fatal risk of contagion. The whole of India saw visuals of millions of migrant labourers of unorganized sector trudging across the country on foot hundreds and even a thousand miles to reach home, while those with white-collar jobs were working in the safety of their homes online, or in the protected environment of modern offices.[12] Many of these migrant labourers were lynched, stoned, and harassed on their way including by state police forces manning state roads, inter-state highways, and others reached to be quarantined under trees because they did not have homes.[13] We need to remember that these migrant labourers are the ones who contribute today significantly to the building and upkeep of our cities through their blood and sweat, and it is a fact that they belong mostly to Dalit, Adivasi or nomadic communities. Yet another mostly affected group was those in slums. Inequality is compounded by the sheer lack of means in the slums for health-care and constraint of space for physical distancing.

The way Covid- 19 bore on the livelihood of the people was not also the same. Daily wage-earners, petty traders, small teashop owners, street vendors, domestic workers and many others in the informal sector of the economy – and they are several million - were badly hit as they lost the small occupations that ensured their livelihood.[14] Nor did they have any reserve to fall back on in times of crisis. The pandemic struck them at the very root of the means of survival. Many of them were already in deep debt with accumulating interest and no way to pay back.

The pandemic also exposed the global inequality affecting developing nations the most. Antonio Guterres, the General Secretary of the United Nations, in a speech honouring Nelson Mandela, highlighted inequality as one of the major revelations of the pandemic.

> COVID-19 has been likened to an X-ray, revealing fractures in the fragile skeleton of the societies we have built. It is exposing fallacies and falsehoods everywhere: The lie that free markets can deliver health-care for all; The fiction that unpaid care work is not work; The delusion that we live in a post-racist world; The myth that we are all in the same boat. Because while we are all floating on the same sea, it's clear that some of us are in superyachts while

> others are clinging to the floating debris…More than 70 per cent of the world's
> people are living with rising income and wealth inequality. The 26 richest
> people in the world hold as much wealth as half the global population.[15]

Covid-19 has added to the situation of global inequality by rendering the economically already vulnerable even more so, and adding about 580 million people who will face extreme poverty and will suffer hunger and malnutrition in Sub-Saharan Africa, Asia, Latin America, Oceania and elsewhere. The world is going to experience the fallout of Covid-19 with more children going to bed hungry. The poor face also another deprivation. Even as many brands of vaccine were getting readied, there was a gross disparity as to who got it and how soon. The Global South and its poor have been the disadvantaged ones. With economic clout and political power, the rich nations grabbed the vaccines for themselves, letting some crumbs for the poor, and that too at the fag end of the day.

A Divided World by Race, Caste, Gender, and Religion

I mentioned about the "enemy" image being used in the context of the pandemic. Covid-19 crisis has also exposed the religious prejudices. It reinforced traditional stereotyping and added new ones. In this country we have seen in the initial stage of the spread of the contagion how the Muslims were targeted as if they were responsible for the fast spread of the virus. We already referred to the Islamic gathering of Tablighi Jamaat in Delhi early March 2020. Any number of other religious festivals, pilgrimages and meetings took place in the same period with the confluence of thousands of people, and yet only the Muslims became easy scapegoats and were stigmatized as super-spreaders of the virus.

One cannot but be struck by a parallel from medieval times. While facts are clear from where the plague came and spread, however, given the long history of hostility towards the Jews in Europe conspiracy theories were floated scapegoating the Jews, an already persecuted tiny minority community. In nineteenth-century America, there was the tragic case of the Irish-born Mary Mallon, an ordinary woman – a domestic help and cook - who was blamed for spreading typhoid among the wealthy families. She was forcibly quarantined and was derogatorily referred to as "Typhoid Mary."

It is interesting to note that in responding to the Covid-crisis, in India, one took some pages from the book of communalism and casteism. The same kind of spread of rumour found in communal riots could also be observed in the case of Covid-19.[16] Rumours and fake-news spread faster than the disease! There was much stereotyping that associated the spread of Covid- 19, not only with Muslims but with migrant labourers, those living in slums and in the poorest quarters of cities and towns.

Moreover, in the construction of the disease and its spread, the basic caste- structure of the Indian society with its social stigma and discriminatory behaviour raised its ugly head. Social distancing is something which the upper caste has been doing for millennia to keep themselves sufficiently away from the impure and "untouchable" Dalits, so that they are not contaminated. Now, when with the pandemic one is advised to keep "social distance" it is no new language. In India, this language has a sinister connotation, and I would strongly advocate that we use the expression *"physical distancing"* rather than *"social distancing."*

The anti-Dalit and anti-Muslim rhetoric and posture vis-à-vis Covid-19 was kept up as this could bring about political dividends. Unfortunately, there are numerous sad instances all over the country, especially in the North, where Muslims, Dalits, people of lower castes, and other vulnerable groups - milk vendors, vegetable vendors and others - were physically attacked for allegedly spreading the disease.

Sadly, deep religious prejudice and stereotyping led even to segregation of Muslim, Dalit and tribal patients in hospitals.

Realism vis-à-vis the Ideology of Unbound Linear Human Progress

Faith in science and technology was shaken when the experts themselves were, in the initial stages of the pandemic, gripped by uncertainties and were struggling to understand the nature and complexities of the disease. There has been no consensus on this. The technology that could take human beings to the moon and the mars was brought to its knees before the tiny corona. Science has been viewed as a solid rock, a sure point of reference, given its normativity, as an unfailing guide and beacon of light for the future of humanity. However, science, like money, cannot answer all human problems. It cannot forecast every possible scenario of the future – something we realized acutely with the outbreak of Covid-19. To say this is not to run down the important role science plays in our lives and the tremendous innovations it has created, but only to acknowledge that it has its limits, especially if it is tied to the ideology of limitless human progress.

In the western tradition, ever since Aristotle, rationality was viewed as the defining characteristics of the humans, and the humans as the yardstick to measure everything else. This is a tradition continued in the European Renaissance and the period of Enlightenment and modernity. The tragedies of the twentieth century of two world wars, the Holocaust and other horrendous experiences raised grave questions about a narrowly defined reason and its ability to come to grips with situations of inhumanity and brutality. Far from taking one to the realm of truth, motivated reasoning could construct arguments to reinforce inherited and deeply entrenched prejudices and can become a source of barbaric violence.

Today, we view human beings in a more complex way given their multidimensionality which cannot be boxed into rationality. Moreover, reason itself is seen not as an abstraction but as embedded in different cultures in innumerable forms and expressions, and hence the need to speak of a plurality of rationality.[17] Against the situation of crisis and affliction, scientific rationality which pretends to control everything and even what is not controllable requires a complete rethinking.

The problem with the paradigm of development and scientific rationality is that they are so cocksure of themselves that there is little space for human vulnerabilities, the imponderables, and the unpredictables of history. And when these do occur – as happened with the outbreak of Covid-19 - the conventional frames of linear development and rationality are no more able to cope with the situation with the already existing means and instruments. It is an irony that Europe and the USA, which consider themselves as scientifically and technologically most advanced nations are the ones which found themselves counting most bodies as a few hundred thousand of their citizens were falling dead with recurring new waves of the pandemic. The pandemic has demonstrated that history is made not simply through human agency– but also by non-human forces.

The Deficit of Social and Religious Sciences

The positivist approach to knowledge and science spearheaded since the nineteenth century continues to condition the various disciplines. Social sciences have fallen into the trap of such an understanding of knowledge. For many practitioners of social sciences, what matter are data, tables, and figures. But it became clear that in the face of the crisis, we lack purposive social sciences oriented to providing a framework of meaning within a broader holistic vision. Human and societal life does not always move along predictable trajectories.

Many disruptions and inscrutable puzzles characterize it. These are not simple exceptions as amply borne out by facts in the course of human history. Confronted with the pandemic, social sciences dished out many facts which, as Shiv Visvanathan observes, do not add up to "insights and perspectives," as for example, in the case of literature with its narrative language.

> The social science lacked such a language to capture the nature of suffering and the demands of ethics. The breakdown of concepts and categories created too many black boxes and silences. The crisis of the social sciences around COVID – 19 stems from the flatness of language and emptiness of concepts. One required a different language for ambiguity, ambivalence, for folds and hyphens, linking disparate worlds.[18]

Further, in the western Enlightenment tradition in which social sciences grew up, nature took a back seat. The study of society meant investigating the dynamics of its functioning, its structures, patterns of human relationships, and interaction. Through empirical study and interpretation, social sciences made progress. What the present crisis teaches us is that human and societal behaviour and interrelationships are governed as well by what happens in nature. The outbreak of a virus has revolutionized the way people relate to each other and how societies and nations interact with each other.

What about disciplines focused on the study of religion? One would naturally expect more from religious studies and theology to grasp the present civilizational crisis and help humankind come to terms with it.[19] But, alas, religious studies, not unlike the social sciences, are lost in ethnographic data of religious phenomena – beliefs and rituals.[20] In the absence of an enlightened approach on the part of religious studies and theology, what has come to the fore is the magical consciousness. Covid-19 is demonized, and religious practitioners were seen busy exorcising it through all kinds of rituals. The religious agents deeply resented the inability to perform rituals and sacraments.[21]

A New Brave World of Uncertainties

There are diseases like cancer and HIV/AIDS which kill every year more people than Covid-19 as the statistics tell us. However, what causes deep worry is that unlike many other diseases, Covid-19 spreads very rapidly, given the swift means of travel and communication in our globalized world. From where this pathogen comes and where it moves are most difficult to ascertain, even with stringent measures to control the disease and contact-tracking. Even more worrying is the uncertainty surrounding the nature of the disease and the volatile behaviour of the virus that causes it. At one point of the crisis, a new strain of Covid-19 in the UK erupted which left the world panicking once again. No wonder, there are so many views, even contradictory ones, among the medical and epidemiological experts. As a scholar put it, "Epidemiologists are like the blind-folded men trying to guess what the elephant was in Gandhiji's favourite fable."[22] Though humanity has known epidemics, the frequency of new epidemics and viruses is on the increase since the crisis of influenza in the early twentieth century, especially in the last two or three decades. This should be a matter of grave concern as we envisage the future of human life.

Covid-19 has led us to the realization of something basic, namely, uncertainty is woven into our very fallible human existence.[23] Our gaze was deflected from this fundamental truth by the glamour of the power to control everything. Covid-19 has broken the backbone of self-confidence on which humans were riding since the time of the Enlightenment followed by the advent of science and technology. It has exposed the vulnerability of human beings navigating in totally unchartered waters without campus of direction and amidst threatening storms.

Ancient Greeks had a very expressive term as to how tragedies happen. *Hubris* in the Greek tragedy refers to the fatal flaw in the character of the hero who becomes so infatuated by his powers and prowess that he dares to step out of human bounds but then is humbled and punished by the gods who remind him of his vulnerability and human mortality. The excessive confidence to be able to face any situation and bring it under control, and master, in principle, all things by means of calculation,[24] has experienced a deadly blow from nature in the form of a pandemic for which the twenty-first century humans were not prepared. Yes, the human pretence of having mastery over nature has been torpedoed by a tiny creature which is a few thousand times smaller than the head of a pin.

Human ingenuity bolstered by science controls the world by its ability to predict and forecast the shape of things to come. Scientists could already see decades ahead, if not centuries, of any asteroid that may pass by the earth or could cause potential damage. But nothing of that happened with coronavirus. It arrived unannounced and took the scientists and the entire humanity by surprise. No exit paths and emergency measures could be prepared before its arrival as it happens with many natural disasters like earthquakes, cyclones, and typhoons.

The total unpreparedness could be seen even in developed countries where the health-care infrastructure could not cope with the extent of the pandemic. Thousands were pouring into hospitals, as doctors and medical personnel were struggling to save precious human lives for which ventilators were in short supply. What happened with the advent of this pandemic is not the end, but the beginning of an era in which human beings will be living in increasing insecurity, and with existential angst vis-à-vis what could befall them. This is painful against the background of an obsession with security in the current order and establishment. On the other hand, is it not true that insecurity is what characterize all along history the lives of millions of poor and marginalized people?[25]

From Profit to Compassion and Solidarity

What the crisis of humanity at the present juncture reveals is that despite the crass selfishness and quest for one's advantage and profit, there are islands of selflessness and marvellous courage and altruism. Amid the pandemic, a fifteen-year-old young girl, Jyoti Kumari, daughter of a migrant worker, peddled a cycle 1200 km from Gurugram to Bihar, carrying her ailing father to reach home. Is this not a story of courage, resilience, hope and resurrection?

We could not fail to notice how, in the past few decades, the medical profession has suffered the same lot as other departments of life, namely commercialization. It has been deprecated for its profit-motive. And yet what we saw right at the heart of the pandemic was hundreds and thousands of medical personnel donning protective gear and pulling many helpless victims from the jaws of death. Probably many of these healthcare persons were reluctant and certainly had concerns about their safety and of their families. Here was not a question of money but a question of life and death - their own and of their patients.

What we have been witnessing is a transformation of the medical practice from an opportunity for profit to a selfless service. It represented an oasis of humaneness in the desert of profit-oriented medical business. The wellsprings of compassion, solidarity and care gushed forth in numerous hospitals and centres of care where the victims of coronavirus were treated. The doctors, nurses, and other medical, health care and sanitary personnel who toiled day in day out to save the lives of people did not speak the language of the enemy, war and conquest. Their language was that of care, love, compassion, the dignity of human persons, sacrifice, selflessness, and altruism. Here is a different life-giving language and practice. I am reminded of the words of Albert Camus in his celebrated novel, *The Plague*:

"To simply say what we learn from the plagues, [is] that there are more things in men to admire than things to despise."[26] Admiration could be undoubtedly said of the dedication of all the health-care and medical personnel, of which 70% are women, who stuck their neck out amidst most trying adversity.

What has happened in the field of health care should become a model for other critical domains of life – economy, politics, culture and so on. All of them are badly in need of a modicum of idealism and spirit of service to the common good. Political order, for example, is meant for the attainment of justice and the common good. In the absence of this noble goal, as St Augustine put it so very perceptively, governance becomes the business of a band of robbers.[27] Economy insensitive to the needs of the poor and the victims but concerned only about profit becomes murderous.

In Conclusion

Covid-19 exposed some of the stark realities of our world, which those in power and those who reap benefits from the status quo tried to conceal. Now, these naked realities are in the open. The inequalities characterizing our world and the belief in unending development and progress of humanity by exploiting nature have come under critical scrutiny. Similarly, the bankruptcy of the reigning paradigm of accumulation of wealth through the capitalist economy and market – the engines of the liberal order – stands exposed. The liberal order and market-centric thinking are incapable of coming to grips with a highly critical situation as the pandemic. They cannot create a situation of social, economic and cultural justice and equality for all, which, of course, includes health-care.

I think Covid-19 is but a foreshadowing of things to come, which are shrouded in great uncertainty. Whatever certainty we have now are only "provisional."[28] We do not know which pathogens are waiting to wreak havoc on humanity in future. This insecurity is compounded by new factors and forces, and these lead us to be more and more conscious of the radical limits of the human. Think of the fact that we are entering an era of Artificial Intelligence (AI), robotics, hyperloop transportation, ChatGPT, and "editing" of the human species through biotechnology and genetic manipulation.

What it took extremely ingenious work and application of human rationality and logical thinking in the past are done increasingly within the fraction of a second by the digital means and Artificial Intelligence. Reasoning, logic, coherence and calculation do not qualify any more as uniquely human as once imagined. Further, what we call human freedom, autonomy, and "free" decisions have become predictable and foreseeable through complex algorithms. The privacy of the human is open to total surveillance to the minutest details (panopticon); so too the functioning of economy.[29] In short, we are at the threshold of many implausible uncertainties and ambiguities, and the Enlightenment paradigm of reason and human development is ripped to shreds, and rock-like certainties of the past are collapsing like a pack of cards. Humankind needs to shed a lot of its assumptions and enter with a deep sense of humility and awareness of human fallibility in this new era, which is important for its own flourishing and the wellbeing of the entire creation.

A new civilization is in the making. The future is not evermore the same – more science and technology, more money and power. Money cannot buy everything.[30] Machines today, as we noted, can do infinitely better reasoning, logical and coherent calculations than the humans. What is left for the humans of the future is but a world of love, friendship, a sense of purpose in life, contemplation of beauty, solidarity, and compassion. What will stand out will not be the ability to compete, calculate, create more technology, accumulate wealth and grab power, but the care and effective concern for others, greater trust, generosity, and undying hope for a different world. These will be the pillars of a new civilization to come. Thousands of victims of Covid-19 who succumbed to death all over the world beckon us to cultivate a sense of more profound and shared humanity.

NOTES

1   Cf. Norman F. Cantor, *In the Wake of the Plague. The Black Death and the World It Made* (New York: Simon & Schuster Paper Back, 2015).

2   Cf. Fareed Zakaria, *Ten Lessons for a Post-Pandemic World* (London: Penguin Random House, 2020).

3   Reingard Nethersole, "Language in Limbo: Being Suspended between Consolation and Control," in *Philosophy and Rhetoric* 53, no. 3 (2020): 306–311, at 309.

4   I am reminded of the despot Hastings Banda of Malawi who ruled his country for more than three decades (1963 – 1994), and could state unabashedly that his word was law!

5   Cf. "The Pandemic has given armies in Southeast Asia a Boost," https://foreignpolicy.com/2020/06/15/coronavirus-pandemic-army-military-southeast-asia-boost-indonesia-philippines-jokowi-duterte-authoritarianism/ [accessed on 2 January 2021].

6   Cf. Hannah Arendt, *The Origins of Totalitarianism* (London: Penguin Random House, 1994).

7   Zakaria, *Ten Lessons for a Post-Pandemic World*, 33.

8   Cf Giorgio Agamben, "L'invenzione di un' epidememia" https://www.quodlibet.it/giorgio-agamben-l-invenzione-di-un-epidemia [accessed on 17 April 2023]; see also Id., *State of Exception* (Chicago: Chicago University Press, 2005).

9   Cf. Farhana Latief and Reyazul Haque, "Spectacle as a Response. The COVID–19 Pandemic," *Economic and Political Weekly* 55, no. 34 (2020): 28–33.

10   M.A. Oommen, "Covid-19 in the Indian Context and the Quest for Alternative Paradigms," *Economic and Political Weekly* 55, no. 34 (2020): 18–21, at 18. See also Amartya Sen and Jean Drèze, *An Uncertain Glory. India and Its Contradictions* (London: Allen Lane – Penguin Books, 2013). For more statistics on the poor performance of India in tackling Covid-19 in comparison to other South Asian neighbours, see Editorial, *Economic and Political Weekly* 31 October 2020 (with reference to reports of World Bank and International Monetary Fund).

11   S Nanthini and Tamara Nair, "Covid-19 and the Impacts on Women," S. Rajaratnam School of International Studies. https://www.jstor.org/stable/

resrep26875 [accessed on 24 November, 2020]. See also Guidorzi, Brianna. "The 'Shadow Pandemic': Addressing Gender-based Violence (GBV) During COVID-19," in *COVID-19 in the Global South: Impacts and Responses,* eds., Carmody Pádraig et al. (Bristol: Bristol University Press, 2020), 117–26.

12   Felix Wilfred, "No Return to the Normal: Church after Covid-19," in *Corona of Thorns? Or Corona of Life?* eds. Francis Gonsalves and Vinod Victor (Delhi: ISPCK, 2020), 25–32. Politicians like Trump, Giuliani, Boris Johnson and many of them in India tested positive but were quickly brought to their feet with best possible care. So too actors and actresses in Bollywood and Kollywood, because they possessed enormous wealth and influence; not so the poor immigrants, labourers and slum dwellers. Who gets out of Covid-19 has become a matter of money and influence?

13   The pathetic story of the migrants after the lockdown is portrayed and analyzed in a recent publication by Migrant Workers Solidarity Network with a telling subtitle: Citizens and the Sovereign: Stories from the Largest Human Exodus in Contemporary Indian History, November 2020. See https://mwsn.in/assets/front/pdf/resource/Citizens_and_the_Sovereign. pdf [accessed on 25 November, 2020]. See also S.K. Singh et al., "Reverse Migration of Labourers amidst Covid-19," *Economic and Political Weekly* 55, no. 32/33 (2020): 25–28.

14   Cf. Tripti Lahiri, *Maid in India. Stories of Inequality and Opportunity inside Our Homes* (Delhi: Aleph Book Company, 2017).

15   https://www.nelsonmandela.org/news/entry/annual-lecture-2020-secretary-general-guterress-full-speech [accessed on 26 November, 2020]. See also Gerard McCann and Chrispin Matenga, "COVID-19 and Global Inequality," in *COVID – 19 in the Global South: Impacts and Responses,* eds., Pádraig Carmody, et al. (Bristol: Bristol University Press, 2020), 161–171.

16   In his classical study, Paul Brass has gone deep into the role of rumour in communal conflicts in North India. See *Theft of and Idol. Text and Context in the Representation of Collective Violence* (Princeton: Princeton University Press, 1997).

17   Cf. Felix Wilfred, "Christian Faith and Socio-Cultural Rationalities: Reflections from Asia," *Concilium* (2017/1): 101–110.

18   Shiv Visvanathan, "The COVID-19 Pandemic and the Crisis of the Social Sciences," *Economic and Political Weekly* 55, no. 42 (2020): 29–33, at 29.

19   For more on this, see Chapter 14

20   Cf. Felix Wilfred, *Religious Identities and the Global South. Porous Borders and Novel Paths* (Cham, Switzerland: Palgrave Macmillan, 2021).

21   There has also been another tradition in which epidemy was associated with gods and goddesses. The most well-known example is the connection of smallpox with goddess *Mariamma* or *Sitladevi*. The deadly disease of smallpox killed millions of people throughout history in India and elsewhere.

22   Suranyua Aiyar, "Covid-19: Dodgy Science, Woeful Ethics," *Seminar* (2020): 33–41, at 39.

23   Cf. Helga Nowotny, *The Cunning of Uncertainty* (Cambridge: Polity Press, 2015).

24   Cf. Steve Bruce, *God Is Dead: Secularisation in The West* (London: Blackwell Publishing, 2002), 26–27. This is what Max Weber had elaborated with his concept of "disenchantment of the world."

25   On the ambivalence of security, Cf. Regina Ammicht Quinn, "A Mighty Fortress is Our God: The Needs and Limits of Security," *Concilium* (2018/2): 26–35.

26   Albert Camus, *The Plague* (London: Penguin Books, 2010), 237.

27   St Augustine, *The City of God* IV.4: "Without justice, what are kingdoms [states] but great bands of robbers? And what is a band of robbers but such a kingdom in miniature? It is a band of men under the rule of a leader, bound together by a pact of friendship, and their booty is divided among them by an agreed rule. Such a blot on society, if it grows, assumes for itself the proud name of kingdom [state]."

28   Cf, Helga, Nowotny, The *Cunning of Uncertainty* (Cambridge: Polity Press, 2015).

29   Cf. Shoshana Zuboff, *The Age of Surveillance Capitalism. The Fight for a Human Future at the New Frontier of Power* (London: Profile Books, 2019).

30   Cf. Michael J. Sandel, *What Money Can't Buy: The Moral Limits of Markets* (London: Penguin, 2012).

FURTHER READING

Aiyar, Suranyua. "Covid-19: Dodgy Science, Woeful Ethics." *Seminar* (September 2020): 33–41.

Ammicht Quinn, Regina. "A Mighty Fortress is Our God: The Needs and Limits of Security." *Concilium* (2018/2): 26–35.

Arendt, Hannah. *The Origins of Totalitarianism.* London: Penguin Random House, 1994.

Brass, Paul. *Theft of an Idol. Text and Context in the Representation of Collective Violence.* Princeton: Princeton University Press, 1997.

Bruce, Steve. *God Is Dead: Secularization in The West,* 26–27. London: Blackwell Publishing, 2002.

Camus, Albert. *The Plague,* 237. London: Penguin Books, 2010.

Cantor, Norman F. *In the Wake of the Plague. The Black Death and the World It Made.* New York: Simon & Schuster Paper Back, 2015.

Delanty, Gerard, ed. *Pandemic, Society and Politics.* London: Routledge, 2021.

Guidorzi, Brianna. "The 'Shadow Pandemic': Addressing Gender-based Violence (GBV) During COVID-19." In *COVID-19 in the Global South: Impacts and Responses,* edited by Carmody Pádraig et al., eds.,117–26. Bristol: Bristol University Press, 2020.

Horton, R. *The Covid-19 Catastrophe.* Cambridge: Polity Press, 2020.

Lahiri, Tripti. *Maid in India. Stories of Inequality and Opportunity inside Our Homes.* Delhi: Aleph Book Company, 2017.

Latief, Farhana, and Reyazul Haque. "Spectacle as a Response. The COVID–19 Pandemic." *Economic and Political Weekly* 55, no.34 (2020): 28–33.

McCann, Gerard, and Chrispin Matenga. "COVID-19 and Global Inequality." In *COVID–19 in the Global South: Impacts and Responses,* edited by Pádraig Carmody et al. 161–171. Bristol: Bristol University Press, 2020.

McMillen, C. *Pandemics: A Very Short Introduction.* Oxford: Oxford University Press, 2016.

Nethersole, Reingard. "Language in Limbo: Being Suspended between Consolation and Control." *Philosophy and Rhetoric* 53, no. 3 (2020): 306–311.

Nowotny, Helga. *The Cunning of Uncertainty.* Cambridge: Polity Press, 2015.

Oommen, M.A. "Covid-19 in the Indian Context and the Quest for Alternative Paradigms." *Economic and Political Weekly* 55, no.45 (2020): 18–21.

S. Nanthini, and Tamara Nair. "Covid–19 and the Impacts on Women." 2020, 10. https://www.jstor.org/stable/resrep26875 [accessed on 24 November 2020].

Sandel, Michael J. *What Money Can't Buy: The Moral Limits of Markets.* London: Penguin, 2012.

Sen, Amartya, and Jean Drèze. *An Uncertain Glory. India and Its Contradictions.* London: Allen Lane-Penguin Books, 2013.

Singh, S.K. et al. "Reverse Migration of Labourers amidst Covid-19." *Economic and Political Weekly* 55, no. 32/33 (2020): 25–28.

Snowden, F. *Epidemics and Society: From the Black Death to the Present.* New Haven: Yale University Press, 2020.

Visvanathan, Shiv. "The COVID – 19 Pandemic and the Crisis of the Social Sciences." *Economic and Political Weekly* 55, no.42 (2020): 29–33, at 29.

Waltner-Toews, D. *On Pandemics: Deadly Disease from Bubonic Plague to Coronavirus.* Vancouver: Greystone, 2020.

Wilfred, Felix. "Christian Faith and Socio-Cultural Rationalities: Reflections from Asia." *Concilium* (2017/1):101–110.

Wilfred, Felix. "No Return to the Normal: Church after Covid-19." In *Corona of Thorns? Or Corona of Life?* edited by Francis Gonsalves and Vinod Victor, 25–32. Delhi: ISPCK, 2020.

Wilfred, Felix. *Religious Identities and the Global South. Porous Borders and Novel Paths.* London and New York: Palgrave Macmillan, 2021.

Zakaria, Fareed. *Ten Lessons for a Post-Pandemic World.* London: Penguin Random House: 2020.

Žižek, S. *Pandemic! Covid-19 Shakes the World.* Cambridge: Polity Press, 2020.

Zuboff, Shoshana. *The Age of Surveillance Capitalism. The Fight for a Human Future at the New Frontier of Power.* London: Profile Books, 2019.

Chapter 14

THEOLOGY IN A PRECARIOUS WORLD

At the height of Covid-19, Arundhati Roy made a thought-provoking reflection.

> Whatever it is, coronavirus has made the mighty kneel and brought the world to a halt like nothing else could… Historically, pandemics have forced humans to break with the past and imagine their world anew. This one is no different. It is a portal, a gateway between one world and the next.[1]

What does that mean for theology?[2] With the outbreak of Covid-19, theology is provoked to re-examine itself radically and rethink faith in whose service it defines itself. A theology that does not let itself be challenged by such momentous social and cultural shifts caused by Covid-19 runs the risk of becoming obsolete. The present chapter has the modest scope of reflecting on a few theologically significant issues which Covid-19 has triggered: 1. Revisiting traditional Christian anthropology and redefining theology today as cosmology 2. The limits of the rational and the play of the magical 3. The precarity of everyday human life and salutary disruptions vis-à-vis human hubris and self-conceit. 4. The ambivalence of human security and insecurity and its implications, including for the Church community. 5. The theodicy question and human suffering as the starting point of theology 6. Rethinking traditional sacramental theology, especially the Eucharist and the sacrament of order.

Revisiting Traditional Christian Anthropology

Revisiting traditional Christian anthropology shifts our perspective away from portraying humans as the pinnacle of creation and the ultimate goal of the universe. Instead, it invites us to envision humanity as an integral component of an ever-evolving cosmos, where our presence represents only a small fragment, a minuscule narrative. In fact, Yuval Harari, a historian from Israel, points out that humans are late-comers in the universe and on earth, which were shaped by other forces than human. The Anthropocene, namely the period humans appeared on the scene as actors, is relatively much smaller – about 70, 000 years compared to the 13.5 billion years of the universe. The relatively a very small period of the Anthropocene is the time when human beings exacted a heavy toll on flora and fauna of the earth. As Harari says, "since the appearance of life, about 4 billion years ago, never has a single species changed the global ecology all by itself…An insignificant ape became the ruler of the planet earth."[3]

What Covid-19 has taught us is that any anthropology without cosmology is faulty and inexorably bound to fail. Anthropology and cosmology should be the two lungs with which theology should breathe. But unfortunately, theology has been breathing but with one lung. It is time to realize that cosmology is as important to theology as anthropology.

There was a turning point when theology came to be defined as anthropology, as Karl Rahner did, for example. In this approach, anthropology and theology were interchangeable and harmoniously blended. One enquired into the a priori transcendental structures in the human spirit corresponding to divine revelation.[4] This methodological orientation and approach brought about great innovation in theology, buried in the world of doctrines far removed from the world of human experience, and made traditional dogmas meaningful to human mind. The anthropological approach provoked also a sharp critique from conservative quarters for fear that the divine would be reduced to the human.

Theology needs to keep evolving as we move forward with new discoveries and insights. The last few decades have brought about profound awareness of the inextricable relationship of the humans with nature and a vision of interdependence of all creatures. As a result, the human is not to be separated from the lot of the earth, its flora and fauna, and indeed from the whole universe. Theology needs to be seized by this integral vision. I think in our times it is crucial to define theology as also cosmology and cosmology as also theology. For the God-question is intertwined with the question of nature and the universe, which in some philosophical currents was portrayed as the body of God. Today, theology faces the task of redefining itself with a cosmological framework.[5]

Moreover, what Milan Kundera wrote in his novel *Immortality* gives a lot of food for thought on the decisive turn theology needs to make with a vision of the human "in the image of woman" and let us add, 'in the image of nature, since these images are intertwined.

> Woman is the future of man. That means that the world which was once formed in man's image will now be transformed to the image of woman. The more technical, cold and metallic it becomes, the more it will need the type of warmth that only the woman can give. If we want to save the world we must adapt to the woman, let ourselves be led by woman, let ourselves be penetrated by the *Ewig-Weibliche*, the eternal feminine.[6]

Theology of the future, in short, will find its right axis and sustenance the more it becomes cosmological and feminine. The issue goes much beyond taking up ecology and feminism as part of theological discourse. Rather ecology and feminism need to shape the theology that is to come and that which the pandemic Covid-19 has already adumbrated. In short, the eternal cosmic and the "eternal feminine" will be the future of theology. They will free it from the Anthropocene, within which it seems to be caught now.

A Theology Bereft of Body and Emotions

Covid-19 has further helped us revise the conception of human person in Christian anthropology in another important respect. Traditional Christian anthropology defines a human person as someone endowed with the capacity for reasoning, possessing freedom, and autonomy. This was held in antiquity by Stoics and by the European Enlightenment thinkers. The identification of the person with reason and freedom or with *"psyche"* (soul) in the Stoic parlance has conditioned Christian theology. Body, emotions, suffering, negations, deprivations were viewed as *contingent* to the human, defined in terms of reason and freedom. We are led to review the Stoic idea of *human invulnerability* on which much of the traditional Christian anthropology was built.

Covid-19 was an occasion to realize how crucial our bodies are for inter-human relationships. Our social perceptions and our perceptions of the world are profoundly embedded. We realize that the body is the symbol of our being through which our thoughts and emotions get expressed.[7] The English language has retained something of this bodily character with its expressions like no-*body*; some-*body*; every-*body*. The absence of bodily expressions created a void. Even more, the body – the axis of our being - became a source of fear, a threat as the carrier of virus.

Since social categories get inscribed onto the body, the body is a crucial site for studying social interactions. The body is also the site of exercise of power, control and surveillance, as

Michael Foucault has shown through empirical observations and historical studies.[8] Moreover, the body plays a significant role in the acquisition, dissemination, and transmission of knowledge – hence its epistemological role and significance. Feminists were the trailblazers in theorizing the body. Recent developments in cultural studies, feminist studies, and sociology of knowledge have brought to the fore the importance of proper theorizing on the body from which theology can benefit.

The pandemic has challenged us to develop a theology of the body for our times. Reflections on human vulnerability should start from the body.

Human beings are embodied entities whose texture is made up of the material fibres of the universe – the *panchabudha*. Moreover, the search or quest for the wellbeing of bodily existence is an integral part of salvation – *Salus* (wellbeing). There is a neglected stream in theology that saw body as the hinge of salvation – *caro cardo salutis*. Rice, water, shelter, the care and wellbeing of the body are all an integral part of salvation, though they do not exhaust salvation.[9] In the infection by the virus, suffering, death, bereavement, loss and pain, care for and succour to the victims – in all these salvations were in process.[10]

Without going into elaboration, let me simply state that the pandemic is an invitation to a theology that attends to the embodied condition of the poor, the unemployed, the refugees, the migrant workers, homeless, in short, victims of all kinds. The plight of these subalterns during the pandemic presented a challenge to our moral and ethical consciousness. We may recall here the reflections by Emmanuel Levinas on the face of the other. For him, the experience of the infinite is not the result of the realization of our finitude. Rather the experience of the infinite takes place through the face of the suffering other appealing and challenging us.[11] Theology could become a metanarrative explaining everything and conceptually absorbing everything – conceptual imperialism – forgetting the down-to-earth experiences of everyday. Covid-19 is an invitation for theology to be critical of its own comprehensive schemes of explanation vis-à-vis the lives of the marginalized. Was not theology in deep slumber during Covid-19 in the face of the struggles of the migrants making their way hundreds and even thousands of miles to reach home and safety?

The Irrational and the Turn to Magical Thinking

Theology needs to attend to both poles. It needs to challenge the hubris of the rational on the one hand and the irrational or the magical consciousness on the other. Reconciling human reason and faith has been a perennial theological theme. This heritage was recaptured in the encyclical of Pope John Paul II, entitled - *Fides et ratio*. The pandemic has led us to critically reflect on the fallacy of relying on human reason alone. Moreover, experience and history show that reason is not always a trustworthy ally of humans. The reason was in deep slumber at critical moments, for example during the horrendous experience of two World Wars and genocides in the twentieth century. Further, there are multiple approaches to reason itself, due to difference in cultural worlds and epistemologies.[12]

Over against the Enlightenment-driven human arrogance and hubris of unending progress, the limits of human prowess have been exposed through this pandemic. It has exploded the teleologically oriented history and development and has disclosed our radical human frailty, vulnerability and impuissance. It has punctured the sense of human omnipotence and big-headed attitudes and has brought humanity to its knees, shaking it to its very foundations.

After Covid-19, our grandiose plans and the self-confidence we trumpet around stand in fact, on the clay feet of uncertainty and extreme frailty.

On the other hand, the pandemic has also exposed the absurdity of not listening to reason and to experts in due measure and the disastrous efforts to resolve the crisis through charlatanism and applying apocalyptic solutions.[13] These obscurantist forces of magic consciousness of the radical religious right were very active churning out new theories. It happened not only in the poorer parts of the world – since often irrationality and superstition, thanks to colonialism, have been associated with colonized people – but also in affluent and technologically advanced countries. There have been several violent protests against vaccines and precautionary measures like wearing masks. No small number of people stoutly refused to be vaccinated in the USA, Canada, Denmark, Germany, Belgium, and so on. Hardened by esoteric irrationality, authoritarian rulers like Jair Bolsonaro of Brazil and far-right evangelical Christians were opposed to vaccination. The anti-rational and magical elements were to be seen also in how conspiracy theories were introduced, with unfortunate social effects of stigmatization and exclusion.[14] We are reminded here, of the scapegoating of the Jews for the medieval plagues. The non-scientific and irrational approach were to be seen also in the manipulation of data regarding the number of Covid-19 deaths.[15] In many instances there was a stunning discrepancy between the facts and the official figures, as in the case with the Communist Party of China.

In this context, we are also reminded of the process of the introduction of western medicine in India and other colonies. It is significant to recall here that opposition to modern medicine and especially preventive inoculation against smallpox in India came from high castes, whereas the Dalits and lower castes had recourse to modern medicine and readily accepted inoculation.[16] Moreover, thanks to these marginalized people, modern medicine spread slowly all over the country. There are numerous case studies that illustrate this historical truth.[17]

The Precariousness of Everyday Life and Impermanence

Covid- 19 is an awakening to precariousness. Life is always and necessarily an endangered one. Insecurity is woven into our very fallible existence. A secure life is an oxymoron. During the pandemic, personally, I realised the deeper implications of what our Muslim brothers and sisters mean when they say: *In sha' Allah – God-willing*. It is to be premised on every plan, project and promise. It is a humble confession of the precarity of human life shot through with intractable unpredictability. There is a difference between precarity and risk. Risk is when we can reasonably predict something – the possible danger that could befall us. On the other hand, precarity hangs in the balance as something capricious and volatile. Imponderable as it is, precarity strikes us like lightning and makes sudden irruption into our lives and leaves us flabbergasted.

While the traditional Christian reflections focused on the transitory character of the world and life - a reason for us to turn our gaze towards heaven - the pandemic may not be responded to by turning our back on the immensity of suffering. It could be resolved only by immersing into the world. Here I see a point of intersection with the Dravidian secularity. It is a secularity not a la French *laicité* but a secularity that is conscious of the transitory and impermanent character of all that is. Because everything is precarious and impermanent, the Dravidian thought, as found in classical Tamil *sangam* literature and in Thirukkural, does not advocate negation or abdication of the world rather its enjoyment. Even Dravidian religious expressions are secular in character, dissociated from temple worship and priests.[18] The secularity is expressed poignantly in its vision of life. Life is fleeting. If you do not take the fleeting moment seriously and seize every opportunity it offers, you will not have the joy of life anymore.

Thirukkural has a chapter on impermanence (*nilayamai*). One couplet of Tiruvalluvar says "*nerunal uḷaṉoruvaṉ iṉrillai eṉṉum perumai uṭaittu'iv vulaku.*"[19] It means, our world is renowned for the fact that the one who was there yesterday is not there today. It would appear that Tiruvalluvar spoke of Covid-19! For, precisely, this was the experience, especially with the second wave. The one whom we saw a day ago was not there anymore. Covid- 19 is an invitation to cherish and engage ourselves every moment of our lives, taking a coaching from the butterfly. Let me cite the arresting and inspiring words of Tagore in this connection: "the butterfly counts not months but moments, and has time enough."[20]

The words of poet Thiruvalluar has another profound message, namely nothing is permanent in the world; everything changes. This is a critique against the infatuation of power which begins to believe that its position is secure and permanent; so too those who uphold caste, thinking it is an immutable divinely sanctioned structure. Covid-19 exposed the futility of such thinking and it should help theology to think in terms of continuous change that take place around us and not equate claims of permanence with truth.

The best way to make sense of the impermanence of life is to subdue the thirst for planning and progress with a salutary interruption from time to time. Covid-19 was a mega interruption. For, during Covid-19, there was a massive disruption in the process of production, distribution, and consumption of goods and services. Every human achievement seemed to plummet from the dizzy height it occupied. Yes, everything was disrupted; regularity and routine broken; the rhythm of human life came to an abrupt halt. And came the dishevelled dance of the chaos. Dreams were trampled upon. Covid-19 infused a visceral fear as men and women oscillated between life and death. Damocles' sword of infection and death was hanging over the head of *every-body* without distinction.

In the biblical view, disruption brings salvation; it takes us to something we could never have imagined or planned. It starts with the Sabbath. Sabbath is a disruption of what is the habit, custom, and work-plan of the week.[21] Let me say, it is a planned and voluntary disruption that helps renew, rethink, and look back. Chaos, as the pandemic is, is an unsettling and traumatizing irruption. We would have learnt too little if chaos and disruption were simply responded to by getting back to the old and normal. In the case of the pandemic, we should not neglect its overwhelming innovative potential in our anxiety to quickly get back to the old.

In Christian tradition, disruptions of the human trajectory are a way God uses to enter into history and reminds us of the human precarity against the inflation of human hubris. The disruption of the pandemic should help theology to rethink and renew itself. Mary Douglas, a great cultural anthropologist, notes rightly, "though we seek to create order, we do not simply condemn disorder. We recognize that it is destructive of existing patterns; also that it has potentiality. It symbolizes both danger and power."[22] What is the theological potentiality flowing from the experience of Covid-19 is something we need to reflect upon deeply.

Human Security and Insecurity - A Key for the Reform of the Church

Our preceding reflections on the precarity of life take us to the issue of insecurity and security.[23] Theology is both a critique of pathological and obsessive security of the powerful who want to have everything under control and, at the same time, a critique of the abyss of insecurity and precariousness into which the poor are constantly thrown. We need a radical shift and focus of attention from a security conception overlapping with nation and territory to people, especially the vulnerable ones. Covid-19 showed us concretely that the security of the people, especially the marginalized, is not guaranteed by the security of state or nation.

> The world is entering a new era in which the very concept of security will change-and change dramatically. Security will be interpreted as: security of people, not just territory. Security of individuals, not just nations. Security through development, not through arms. Security of all the people everywhere - in their homes, in their jobs, in their streets, in their communities, in their environment.[24]

No one is secure if all are not secure. This is a profound lesson Covid-19 has driven home. It gave the opportunity to the rich and the powerful to discover that their security depends on the security of the poor. To get back to history, one sudden realization that dawned on the plague-ridden mediaeval Europe was that all humans are equal and share the same mortality – from emperors and popes down to the smallest peasant tilling the ground.

Covid-19 was impartial. It struck the Brahmins, Dalits, and Shudras in an equal measure; it did not discriminate between cardinals, bishops, priests and simple faithful. All are equal when it comes to biology and succumb to death when the plague strikes. Yet I do not see that covid-19 shook India's caste and hierarchical-structure. Strangely, it has continued to remain impenetrable even to the lethal attack of the virus. I wish deeper reflection on caste and hierarchy took place as a sequel to the experience of Covid – 19. That this has not happened is regrettable.

Securing basic needs like food, water, shelter, and education trumps the neurotic insecurity of the powerful and the ideology of national security. The pandemic laid bare the frenzy with which the affluent wanted to get back to the security zone, while the insecurity of the poor was exacerbated. There is no proper national security when the poor are not sheltered and secured. Security is an ambivalent concept. We know how much violence could be unleashed and freedom suppressed in the name of national security on the part of states.

Similar to national security, there is something like Church security. The Church could become pathological and unleash moral violence for fear of insecurity. One of the most leading psychologists of the twentieth century, Abraham Maslow made a very telling statement. He said, "I suppose it is tempting, if the only tool you have is a hammer, to treat everything as if it were a nail."[25] The fear of insecurity could make the Church see nails everywhere. The Congregation for the Doctrine of the Faith (now renamed Dicastery for the Doctrine of the Faith) symbolized this kind of perception prompted by fear and threat. Under Pope Francis, the situation of fear in the Church has come down considerably, thanks to his commitment to the Church as people of God and as a field-hospital.

The pandemic has offered an opportunity for the Church to become aware of its own vulnerability. The Church is a community on the path of discovery, search, not knowing everything right from the beginning. St Augustine in his *De Vera Religione* spoke about the graduality of truth. For him, truth is an object of quest and not a matter of possession.[26] To recall the immortal verse of John Henry Newman in his "Lead Kindly Light" written amidst encircling gloom, he prays to God, saying, "Keep Thou, my feet; I do not ask to see the distant scene; one step enough for me."[27] We could say that the Church, and every believer, should be happy and content with one right step just now and without arrogating the security of the distant future, which is not a possession but the destination towards which we need to move, making infinite discoveries on the path.

The lack of the Church's awareness of its own vulnerability stems from its deep-rooted fear of making mistakes, a fear of imperfection, brokenness, frailty of which real life is made of. No wonder the Church gets alienated from real-life situations characterized by risks, ambiguities, frailty, and insecurity. But these are the features of everyday life. The fear of making mistakes leads it to a hysteric level of self-defence.

In India, we have too many "goody-goody" Church-leaders who act in evasive and "touch-me-not" fashion. If these prelates make any mistake, instead of honestly owning it, they pretend that they are unblemished and perfect and pass on the blame to someone else. I am reminded of an old saying. *"senatus non errat et si errat non corrigit ne videatur errasse"* (The senate does not make any mistake, and if it does, it does not correct itself so that it is not seen to have made a mistake!). It is the fear of making mistakes that prevent many Church-leaders from taking bold decisions. It requires much courage to own mistakes. It takes much courage to speak out. Here Pope Francis has set a model for Church-leaders to take risks, as he said famously, "I prefer a Church which is bruised, hurting and dirty because it has been out on the streets, rather than a Church which is unhealthy from being confined and from clinging to its own security."[28]

Human Suffering and the Theodicy Question

Covid- 19 brought about unmitigated suffering, pain, loss, and death. In the past, in the face of natural disasters like earthquakes, or man-made warfare, one raised the question of how one could reconcile an omnipotent and benevolent God with the presence of the evil of human suffering. Theodicy is an attempt to justify and defend God in the face of evil and suffering.

The classical theodicy question sounded thus: If God is all-powerful, why does he not remove evil? If evil exists, then it can only mean that God may be powerful but merciless. If God is merciful and yet evil exists, it would mean that despite being merciful, God is powerless. Theology on its part, tried to explain suffering as something God lets be and there lurks some ultimate good for the one who suffers. It was also explained as the will of God to which the suffering person needs to submit herself or himself. Both theodicy and theology assume that the existence of God and the presence of evil are not contradictory.[29] As scholars have pointed out, modern society is far from being devoid of disasters; rather with modernization there has come about what is called a "risk society" with unpredictable turn of events and occurrence of disasters.[30] In that sense, the issue of evil and suffering dealt by theodicy is still an issue of our times.

However, theodicy should not attempt to reconcile everything so easily, including suffering and too quickly justify God, turning one's back on evil and human suffering. If we go by the gospels, we see the historical Jesus was seriously concerned about human suffering rather than sin. A theology of atonement has sadly neglected the reality of human suffering, especially the suffering of the innocent, the existence of injustice, and inequality, and had focused its attention on sin and redemption from sin. But in reality, salvation is also a liberation from human suffering, especially of the innocent.[31] Evil was explained away by several arguments - as part of the mysterious design of God, as the product of free human will, as a pedagogical means for the growth of humanity and so on.

What the Covid-19 has taught us is that human suffering should be the fulcrum of theology and the hinge on which it should turn. It needs to leave behind the frozen zones of dogmatism fomenting stereotypes and statutory concepts, attitudes and values. Genuine theology will be the one imbued with the *pathos* for the suffering ones. For, the God question is inextricably linked to the question of human suffering, which has no easy answer. To bolster with arguments and justify the compatibility of evil and the existence of God, is an attempt to justify the unjustifiable, and indeed a trivialization of the suffering of the victims.[32]

In recent decades, there has been a lot of theology about God's suffering and the death of God and the cross. The attempt to explain away theologically human suffering stating that God is also someone who suffers, as done, for example, by Jürgen Moltmann and Hans Urs von Balthasar in the West and the Japanese theologian Kazoh Kitamori in Asia – is gnostic and mythical.[33]

I think there is no point and no consolation in knowing, amidst extreme human suffering, that God also suffers. Reduplicating suffering in God does not help. The real problem is with the question of the very conception of God. An eschatological and apocalyptic conception of God as the one who comes implies a conception of justice to come, the Kingdom to come, a promise to be yet fulfilled. It sustains the hope that the suffering of the victims and the innocent are not in vain. The poor and the victims of today will be vindicated. God and justice are where we move towards. There is then a convergence of the search for God to come and search for justice with firm faith in the future. This approach explodes the way traditional theodicy posed the question of God and evil – *unde malum*. Let me express the apocalyptic hope of the innocent in the projection of the Kingdom to come, through a beautiful verse of the medieval fourteenth century Dalit Bhakti poet Ravidas – a chamaar, a leather- worker by profession.

> The regal realm with the sorrowless name:
> they call it Queen City, a place with no pain,
> No taxes or cares, none owns property there,
> no wrongdoing, worry, terror, or torture,
> Oh, my brother, I've come to take it as my own,

> my distant home, where everything is right.
> My imperial Kingdom is rich and secure,
> where none are third or second-all are one.[34]

The other pole of the quest for God and God's Reign is the movement to *alleviate suffering*. The suffering of the other is a challenge for an ethical response, an appeal for responsibility towards the other.[35] We have two parables, rather master-narratives, in this regard, one that has been the bedrock of altruism and moral consciousness in western civilization, and the other one the master narrative of the East. I mean the parable of the Good Samaritan and the parable of Buddha about the man wounded by an arrow hitting him from nowhere. Both critique established theologies – one pharisaic theology and the other Brahminic theology. Neither of these theologies provide assistance to the victim or addresses human suffering. Does not salvation lie in reaching out to others during times of trauma, vulnerability, and helplessness, as demonstrated in the parables of the two victims? The pandemic witnessed many Samaritans and many Bodhisattvas who postponed their own safety and wellbeing for the survival and salvation of others.

Rethinking Traditional Sacramental Theology

History tells us that God and religions have served as a means of *contingency management* in the face of crises and disasters. As Zygmunt Bauman, graphically formulated, "God will exist as long as does human existential uncertainty, and that means forever. Or rather God will die together with human species and not a second earlier."[36] Religions have used two sources to come to terms with the precarity of life – theological and ritual. The theological reasoning went in several directions. For example, for the prophets of doom, sinfulness and transgression of the victims and their suffering are punishment from God. Earthquakes, tsunamis, fire, war, violence, and pandemic are interpreted as divine punishment. "Rabbi, who sinned, this man or his parents, that he was born blind?" (Jn 9:2). This was the question disciples posed to Jesus. In the context of the pandemic, we could observe a return of this theological reasoning of sinful humanity given to consumerism, sensuality, and moral depravity inviting divine wrath. This theological approach was quite widespread and took different forms and expressions, often adopting the apocalyptic idiom, especially in the right-wing Christian movements. This seems to have been how Christians addressed great calamities, persecution at times of great anxiety.

Along with theological explanations, religions set in motion the symbolic realm for contingency management. However, the restrictions and social distancing prevented many people from availing of ritual means to respond to the crisis of the pandemic. Religious worship, pilgrimages, devotions etc. which traditionally served as contingency management mechanism, were dramatically disrupted. Being deprived of the ritual means was a severe blow.

Restlessness among priests and bishops during the pandemic was palpable. Numerous bishops and priests who had been pontificating became, all of a sudden, clueless about the situation of lockdown. Their voices fell silent. Once the familiar world of ritual ebbed out, they became like fish out of water. So also, the laypeople felt simply lost since they could not attend masses in the churches. They were just awaiting to flock to the church and participate in the eucharist and feel genuinely Christian. These people could not think of Christian identity without the celebration of the eucharist. This prompted me to reflect on the roots of this kind of sentiments and thoughts that underlie the deep unease felt by most Christians. Why this? The following section of this chapter, will try to throw some light on the deeper reasons for the shock, sense of loss, and disruption felt by many Christian faithful during the pandemic as they could not access eucharistic celebration in the churches.

Vatican II – Eucharistic Theology and Its Consequences

Under the influence of Orthodox theology – Russian Orthodox theologians Nicholas Afanasiev, John Zizioulas and others – a definition of the Church was formulated in terms of the eucharist. This Orthodox eucharistic theology entered into Vatican II through the *resourcement* theologians - Henri de Lubac, Yves Congar, Jean Daniélou and others. Here it is the eucharist that makes the Church. Instead of seeing the eucharist as part of the ecclesial reality, Church itself came to be defined by the Eucharist. For the Russian Orthodox theologians like Nicholas Afanasiev and John Meyendorff, the eucharist is the basis and nucleus of Orthodox ecclesiology.[37] According to this theology, the eucharist is the *event* of the Church. According to John Zizioulas, Church happens in the act or event of gathering for the eucharist.[38]

Vatican II defined liturgy – especially the Eucharist – as the *fons et culmen*, namely, it "is the summit toward which the activity of the Church is directed; it is also the fount from which all her power flows."[39] I think, if there is a passage in Vatican II documents that, perhaps, needs to be reviewed and reformulated, it is this sentence in SC 10. I was pleasantly surprised to find that my intuitions were confirmed from the history of discussion on this point at Vatican II. Joseph Andreas Jungmann, in his commentary on the discussion about the above statement in the aula of Vatican II observes thus:

> In the assembly many Fathers raised their misgivings against this which recurred several times in the form of proposed amendments during the final vote on the chapter. In the text which came from the Central Commission and was placed before the Council the sentence had been modified. Yet, according to it, the liturgy is "in its centre, that is, in the divine sacrifice of

the eucharist", the summit and fountain. But in spite of this new version, misgivings about the sentence were expressed in the assembly: in the view of the opponents, one could not say even of the Eucharist that everything without exception was ordered in relation to it and proceeded from it.[40]

The Local Church happens when the bishop and the clergy, along with the faithful, celebrate the eucharist. This is how the particular or local Church is depicted in *Sacrosanctum Concilium* – Vatican II document on liturgy. Eucharistic assembly around the bishop is the fundamental unit of the Church – the local Church. There is little talk about *culture or context* in defining the local Church. Local Church is viewed the same everywhere. Eucharist is the same everywhere. In *Sacrosanctum Concilium*, the understanding of the Church as liturgy and eucharist comes out most eloquently.

> Therefore, all should hold in very high esteem the liturgical life of the diocese, which centres around the bishop, especially in his cathedral church. Let them be persuaded that the Church reveals herself most clearly when a full complement of God's holy people, united in prayer and in common liturgical service (especially the Eucharist), exercise a thorough and active participation at the very altar where the bishop presides in the company of his priests and other assistants.[41]

This eucharistization of the Church came in handy in the Catholic Church at the time of the Council of Vatican II, when the Church was also faced with devotionalism and innumerable expressions of popular piety. The intention was to restore the central place of the eucharist as a sacrament and let it not get submerged under practices of popular piety. But when you define Church by liturgy and Eucharist, then there is no way of being Church except participating in the eucharist.

A second motive that prompted the widespread acceptance of the eucharist defining the Church derives from the critique of the Church as a universal entity – a "perfect society" as Bellarmine defined it at the time of counter-reformation. The local Church would be a unit, a portion of the universal Church. This was countered by projecting every local Church as reflecting the universal, and the universal Church itself is made of local Churches, each one celebrating the eucharist and presided over by a bishop and his clergy. This was a contribution of Vatican II.[42]

Today, with a double crisis affecting the Church - widespread clerical sexual abuse and the pandemic - we need to rethink the definition of the Church in terms of the eucharist. The Church is first and foremost *a community of faith, love and hope.* Eucharist is but *one* expression of faith, love, and hope - albeit a crucial manifestation - and is not everything of the identity of the Church. In this way, we overcome a sacramental reduction of the Church to eucharist and open up Christian life and involvement in the light of the most fundamental theological realities – faith, love and hope. Further, the eucharist is not something amorphous but is concrete and is celebrated in a particular space, with a particular community. The *social context and cultural reality of the community* should be in the very texture of the eucharist which consequently becomes unique in every place it is celebrated.

Let me illustrate the point with reference to a personal experience. When I had the privilege of serving as secretary of the Theological Advisory Commission of the Federation of Asian Bishops' Conferences (FABC), we prepared a document on local Churches.[43] A small minority in the commission under the influence of the American theologian Joseph Komonchak – who also was invited to the meeting of the Commission - held a "field-theory" for the local Church and went hammer and tongs in maintaining that the local Church derives everywhere its identity solely from the eucharist. However, the majority of the members of the Commission were of the view that, without undermining the place of the eucharist, one should consider also culture as an integral and an inalienable part of the understanding of the local Church, and that the eucharist may not be conceived in the abstract, but in the concrete with reference to particular communities from whom each eucharist will acquire its unique character. In short, in the approach to the local Church one should not limit simply to a de-territorialized understanding of the eucharist. This could have other consequences.

From Eucharistization and Liturgization to Clericalism

Eucharist is where the sacramental power of the clergy is expressed most potently. Anthropologists tell us how the social reality gets reflected in the ritual. According to one definition, "ritual is the repetitive spontaneous or prescribed symbolic use of bodily movement and gesture to express and articulate meaning within a social context."[44] Ritualization reproduces and cements the prevailing social order, in this case, the Church order. For example, a pontifical mass reflects the Church hierarchy - archbishop, bishops, priests, deacon, religious, and a large mass of people. In the Church, the eucharist not only reflects back the hierarchical order, but it is also, according to Orthodox and Oriental theology, a reflection of celestial liturgy. The divine hierarchy - God the Father, Son, the Spirit, archangel, angels, cherubim, seraphim –gets replicated in the eucharist.

As it is, performance of eucharist and other sacraments give legitimacy to the sacred and hierarchical order in the Church. Therefore, the priest begins to occupy a central place in the identity of the Church and the consciousness of the people. With the claim of being the minister of eucharist, there comes a certain sacredness to clerical claims of entitlements, privileges; so also loss of any sense of cooperation and co-responsibility involving the people of God in the affairs of the Church-community. All this opens the way to gross abuse of power.

On the other hand, if the identity of the Church is based on *faith, love, and hope,* instead of eucharist and sacraments, then, the minister's pastoral role would be that of celebrating eucharist and sacraments to transform the community into the body of Christ living by faith, love, and hope. Thus, the community of the faithful gets highlighted in the approach to the eucharist, and not the minister. "For where two or three gather in my name, there am I with them" (Mt 18:20). The gathering of the community need not be exclusively for eucharist which would mean an overlap of the Church and eucharist. We need to pay attention to other forms of Jesus' presence in the gathering of the community which are also constituents in the identity of the Church.

Further, baptism is the primordial sacrament in the Church. Christian faith, love, and hope professed in this sacrament gets expressed and deepened through other sacraments, including the eucharist. First and foremost, it is through baptism that a faithful gets incorporated into the body of Christ (1 Cor 12:27) which is the Church, and the members "grow up in every way into him who is the head" (Eph 4:15-16). Here is the basis of ecclesial communion deriving ultimately from the Trinitarian communion. As Henri de Lubac brough out so well in his seminal historical study, for a long time – beginning from Augustine to the end of the first millennium - both the Church community and the eucharist were referred to as the body of Christ (*corpus Christi*). Subsequently, the eucharist came to be referred to as the mystical body (*corpus mysticum*).[45] This was apparently for the reason that some sects tried to over-spiritualize the eucharist leading to Church emphasize eucharist as body of Christ, similar to the reference to the historical body of Jesus of Nazareth born of Virgin Mary. In a reverse development, the mystical body of Christ referring to the eucharist came to be transferred to the Church as the corporate body of believers.

Theology of Ministry

Covid -19 has led us also to rethink radically the traditional theology of ministry bearing unmistakable marks of the Church's polemics against the Donatists, dominant in North Africa at the time of St Augustine. Church, for the Donatists, is a community of the holy. For Augustine, Church is a community in which both holy and sinners are there – like the two cities he developed in his *City of God*. This had its impact on the issue of sacraments. For Donatists, the sacramental validity depends upon the minister's holiness. An unholy minister or a minister in sin cannot perform the sacraments validly. It is against this, there arose the famous axiom: *ex opere operato* (not *ex opere operantis*). As Augustine put it, whether Peter baptizes or Judas baptizes, Christ baptizes.[46] So, there took place the development of a theology of ministry in the key of *alter Christus* – other Christ. The minister stands in the place of Christ, whether he is holy or a scoundrel.

The sacralization of ministers, often without due consideration of their holiness and faithfulness, gave rise to the bestowal of unique privileges upon the clergy both in the Church and in the civic society of Christendom. First, one spoke of the seal of the sacrament of order by which one is a cleric irrevocably. There was, then, the *privilegium clericale* (which became part of the medieval canon law) which ensured that a bishop, abbot or any cleric was not prosecuted in civil courts. The disastrous consequence of this theology of sacred order is exposed in the case of clerical sexual abuse of today.

We could draw some inspiration from the early Church for today's crisis. The legitimacy to preside over the eucharist does not derive simply from ordination, which would be a sacerdotalizing of ministry. Could we think of the right to preside over eucharist as deriving from the minister's role to facilitate the exercise of their priesthood by the Christian faithful – the community?[47] The inextricable link between the minister and the community comes out clearly in the words of St Cyprian who stated, "no bishop is to be imposed on the people whom they do not want."[48] This is something to be pondered upon in our times.

According to Cassel's Latin dictionary, *ordo/ordinare* means to arrange, appoint, settle, dispose, classify and so on.[49] The word ordination is derived from the Roman imperial tradition. The *senators* were ordained means that they were set in a particular higher slot in the hierarchy of the society. By adopting this term, the Church wanted to say that by ordination, a person is set in a particular position of ministry in the community of the Church. However, over time, the word ordination got sacralized and got equated with the sacral ritual of laying of hands. It created an easy passage to absolute ordinations – wandering bishops and priests - without reference to a community, which would be later prohibited by the Council of Chalcedon.

Since the eucharist is the sacrament of unity, this unity is best represented when the community approves their leader, who will also preside over the eucharist. It could help remove much of the magical consciousness around the eucharist and the ordained minister. Let me quote a controversial and disputed passage from Tertullian.

> But where no college of ministers has been appointed, you the laity must celebrate the Eucharist and baptize; in that case you are your own priests, for where two or three are gathered together, there is the church, even if these three are lay people.[50]

Do not Tertullian's words appear in a new light after the experience of Covid-19, when ministers were not able to celebrate the eucharist in the Churches for the public? We know of domestic Churches in the early Christian period, where probably also eucharist took place. Could people celebrate at home and in small communities the eucharist? Things would not be so tragic as has been experienced by many Christians with the closing of the churches and the inability of priests to function as ministers of the eucharist. These are issues to be reflected upon in depth, thanks to the critical experience of Covid-19.

To conclude our reflections on this point, the Church is a community of faith, love and hope. It does not overlap with the eucharist. Eucharist is a *symbolon,* namely identification, mark of the community. In ancient Greece, a clay plate or a clay ring or pottery is broken and then the pieces were held by the members of the same family. It was transmitted, and when the broken pieces match with each other, then the identification of the family takes place. Symbolon was the pledge and guarantee of identity. Coming together of the community is like where the broken pieces are all put together and the shared identity is discovered.

The pandemic gave us an opportunity to overcome the magical consciousness regarding the sacrament of the eucharist and the holy order. What has happened is an eucharistization of the Church, and sacerdotalizing of ministry. The presbyterial ministry (let us remember *Presbyterorum Ordinis* of Vatican II, which employed the term presbyter rather than *sacerdos*) is multi-layered. It may not be reduced only to the priestly role -*sacerdos* (*sacrum+facere*) – of making things holy.

General Conclusions

We could anticipate many more pandemics, even more severe than the one experienced. Covid-19 is only an exemplar of what could continue to happen in the years and centuries to come if there is no course-correction. Hence, the importance of bringing human societies to a balance through the practice of justice and equality. A society of justice and equality will also seek to balance it with human relationship to nature and ensure its flourishing, which means also human flourishing. Theology needs to get into these dynamics to be able to play a constructive role for the future of humans and of nature. Breathing with both lungs of anthropology and cosmology is essential.

Covid-19 provided an opportunity to take up for consideration several issues of high importance for human life – individual and collective. We have been confronted with the issue of the precariousness of life, the importance of the security of the people over that of state and nation, the mixture of the rational and the irrational in responding to crisis situation and so on. We also saw how crucial it is to start theology from the experience of suffering.

Finally, the Covid-19 experience has led us to rethink the traditional understanding of the sacraments and priestly ministry in the Church. In the pre-Covid period, the whole life of the Church seemed to veer around priests and eucharist. The disruption caused by Covid-19 in access to eucharist and priests has challenged us to see them in a new light, with the help of history. In short, it has brought about a shift of focus from eucharist to the fundamental Christian reality of baptism which all Christian faithful share. Further, faith, love, and hope appear in their primacy for the life of individual Christians and Christian communities. They also help the Christian faithful and ministers free themselves from a kind of magical consciousness and misrepresentation of sacraments in the Church.

NOTES

1   Arundhati Roy, "The Pandemic Is a Portal," in *The Financial Times,* 2020, https://www.ft.com/content/10d8f5e8-74eb-11ea-95fe-fcd274e920ca [accessed on 20 April, 2022].

2   Pandemic is a challenge to many areas of human and societal life and the disciplines dealing with them – political science, sociology, economics, medicine and health care and so on. Here we raise the question of the significance of Covid-19 for theology and its future course.

3   Yuval Noah Harari, *Homo Deus, A Brief History of Tomorrow* (London: Vintage, 2017), 85 and Id., *Sapiens. A Brief History of Humankind* (London: Vintage, 2015). See also E. Horn, and H. Bergthaller, *The Anthropocene: Key Issues for the Humanities* (London: Routledge, 2020); J. R. McNeill, and P. Engelke, *The Great Acceleration. An Environmental History of the Anthropocene since 1945* (Cambridge, Mass.: Belknap Press of Harvard University Press, 2016); W. Steffen, et al., "The Anthropocene: Conceptual and Historical Perspectives," *Philosophical Transactions of the Royal Society A: Mathematical, Physical and Engineering Sciences* 369, no. 1938 (2011): 842–867; W. Steffen, et al., "The Trajectory of the Anthropocene. The Great Acceleration," *Anthropocene Review* 2, no.1(2015): 81–98.

4   Cf. Anton Losinger, *The Anthropological Turn. The Human Orientation of the Theology of Karl Rahner* (New York: Fordham University Press, 2020).

5   Cf. Felix Wilfred, "Theological Significance of *Laudato Si:* An Asian Reading," *Vidyajyoti Journal of Theological Reflections* vol.79 (September 2015): 645-661.

6   Milan Kundera, *Immortality* (London: Faber & Faber, 1992), 380.

7   Cf. Felix Wilfred, "Novel Ways of Being Religious," in *Religious Identities and the Global South. Porous Borders and Novel Paths* (Cham, Switzerland: Palgrave Macmillan, 2021), Chapter 6, 105–126.

8   Cf. Vernon W. Cisney, and Nicolae Morar, eds., *Biopower: Foucault and Beyond* (Chicago: University of Chicago Press, 2020); Katia Genel, "The Question of Biopower: Foucault and Agamben," *Rethinking Marxism* 18, no. 1 (2006): 43–62; Sujatha Raman, and Richard Tutton, "Life, Science, and Biopower," *Science, Technology, & Human Values* 35, no. 5 (2010): 711–734.

9   Cf. Masao Takenaka, *God is Rice. Asian Culture and Christian Faith* (Eugene, Oregon: Wipf & Stock Publishers, 2009); Felix Wilfred, "What is Wrong with Rice Christians," in *UCAN*, https://www.ucanews.com/news/a-dalit-cardinal-can-help-end-casteism-in-indian-church/97446. [accessed on 6 August 2023].

10   There was universal recognition of the heroic dedication of health workers during the pandemic at constant risk of their own life. Wendy Lipworth, "Beyond Duty: Medical 'Heroes' and the COVID-19 Pandemic," *Journal of Bioethical Inquiry* 17, no. 4 (2020): 723–730. There is another side to the issue. The discourse on heroism should not absolve the responsibility of the state and health structure which could demand heroism to cover up their failures. See Rochelle Einboden, "SuperNurse? Troubling the Hero Discourse in COVID Times," *Health* 24, no. 4 (2020): 343–347.

11   Cf. Emmanuel Levinas, *Totality and Infinity* (Dordrecht, Boston, London: Kluwer Academic Publisher,1969); *Time and the Other,* trans. Richard A. Cohen (Pittsburgh: Duquesne University Press, 1987); *Humanism of the Other* (Urbana and Chicago: Illinois Press, 1972).

12   Cf. Felix Wilfred, "Christian Faith and Socio-Cultural Rationalities," in *Concilium* (2017/1): 101–110.

13   Fareed Zakaria speaks of the need for the people to listen to experts and experts listening to the people, see *Ten Lessons for a Post-Pandemic World* (New York: W.W. Norton & Company, 2020), 75–96.

14   Studies show that the social quarantine and lockdowns have increased belief in the magical and the pseudo-scientific. See Álex Escolà-Gascón, Jordi Rusiñol Francesc-Xavier Marín, and Josep Gallifa, "Pseudoscientific Beliefs and Psychopathological Risks Increase After COVID-19 Social Quarantine," *Globalization and Health* 16 (2020): 1–11; see also Ian Freckelton Qc, "COVID-19: Fear, Quackery, False Representations and the Law," *International Journal of Law and Psychiatry* 72 (2020): 101611.

15   Cf. Kiran Mahasuar, "Lies, Damned Lies, and Statistics: The Uncertainty Over COVID-19 Numbers in India," *Knowledge and Process Management* 29, no. 4 (2022): 410–417; Fatih Serkant Adiguzel, Asli Cansunar, and Gozde Corekcioglu, "Truth or Dare? Detecting Systematic Manipulation of COVID-19 Statistics," *Journal of Political Institutions and Political Economy* 1, no. 4 (2020): 543–557.

16   Cf. David Arnold, "Smallpox and Colonial Medicine in Nineteenth-Century India," In *Imperial Medicine and Indigenous Societies* (Manchester: Manchester University Press, 2017), 45–65; Poonam Bala, ed., *Medicine and Colonialism: Historical Perspectives in India and South Africa* (London: Routledge, 2014).

17   See for example, Satheesh Palanki, "'Clinical Christianity' as Philanthropy: Missionaries and Western Medicine in Colonial Travancore, 1813-1947," *International Journal of Asian Christianity* 5, no. 1 (2022): 136–152.

18   Cf. Ganapathy Subbiah, "Patterns in Religious Thought in Early South India: A Study of Classical Tamil Texts," (PhD diss., McMaster University, 1988).

19   *Kural 336*

20   Tagore, *Fireflies* https://www.best-poems.net/poem/fireflies-by-rabin drana th-tagore.html [accessed on 18 April 2023].

21   Cf. Walter Bruggemann, *Disruptive Grace. Reflections on God, Scripture, and the Church* (Minneapolis: Fortress Press, 2011).

22   Mary Douglas, *Purity and Danger: An Analysis of the Concepts of Pollution and Taboo* (London: Routledge, 1992), Chapter 6.

23   Cf. Taylor Owen, ed., *Human Security* (SAGE Library of International Relations, 2013); Sakiko Fukuda-Parr, and Carol Messineo, "Human

Security: A Critical Review of the Literature," *Centre for Research on Peace and Development (CRPD) Working Paper* 11 (2012): 1–19.

24 Mahbub ul Haq, *Reflections on Human Development* (New York: Oxford University Press 1995), 115.

25 Abraham Maslow, *The Psychology of Science* (Texas: Gateway Books, 1966), 15.

26 See the excellent research work by Denis Gabriel Veigas, *Graduality in Truth in the Light of St Augustine's De Vera Religione* (Bengaluru: ATC Publisher, 2022).

27 https://newmanu.edu/about-newman/history-of-newman/lead-kindly-light [accessed on 19 April 2023].

28 *Evangelii Gaudium* 49.

29 John Hick has analysed the various streams of theodicy and their roots. See John Hick, *Evil and the God of Love* (New York: Palgrave Macmillan, 1966).

30 Cf. Beck, U. *Risk Society. Towards a New Modernity* (London: Sage, 1992).

31 See Johann Baptist Metz, *Faith in History and Society: Toward a Practical Fundamental Theology* (New York: The Seabury Press, 1980); Id., *A Passion for God: The Mystical-Political Dimension of Christianity* (New York: Paulist Press, 1988); Id., "Suffering Unto God," *Critical Inquiry* 20 (1994): 611–22. http://www.jstor.org/stable/1343852 [accessed on 16 April 2023]; Johann Baptist Metz, *Memoria Passionis. Ein provozierendes Gedächtnis in pluralisticher Gesellschaft* (Freiburg: Herder, 2006); see also Janice Allison Thompson, *Theodicy in a Political Key: God and Suffering in the Post-Shoah Theology of Johann Baptist Metz* (Ph.D. dissertation, University of Notre Dame, 2004). Notre Dame: https://search.proquest.com/openview/761c52ea8a68450aed7f607f6f80e3f5/1?pq-origsite=gscholar&cbl=18750&diss=y [accessed on 16 April, 2023].

32 Cf. Manuel Losada-Sierra, "Memory and History: The Overcoming of Traditional Theodicy in Levinas and Metz," *Religions* 10, no. 12 (2019): 657. https://doi.org/10.3390/rel10120657 [accessed on 16 April 2023].

33 Jürgen Moltmann, *The Crucified God* (Minneapolis: Fortress Press, 2015) 40th anniversary edition; See Matthew Lewis Sutton, ed., "Does God Suffer? Hans Urs von Balthasar's Theology of Holy Saturday," in *Making Sense of Suffering: Theory, Practice, Representation* (Leiden, The Netherlands: Brill, 2011), 31–39; David Lauber, ed., "Hans Urs von Balthasar and a Theology of Holy Saturday," in *Barth on the Descent into Hell*, (London and New York: Routledge, 2017).

34 As quoted in John Stratton Hawley, *Three Bhakti Voices: Mirabai, Surdas, and Kabir in Their Times and Ours* (Delhi: Oxford University Press, 2005), 333.

35 Felix Wilfred, "Listening to the World: Prophetic Anger and Sapiential Compassion," in *Buddhist-Christian Studies* 34 (2014): 63–66.

36   Zygmunt Baumann, "Jerusalem Versus Athens Revisited," in Ulrich Beck, *Ulrich Beck: Pioneer in Cosmopolitan Sociology and Risk Society* (Cham – Heidelberg: Springer, 2014), 70–75.

37   Cf. Nicholas Afanasiev, *The Church of the Holy Spirit* (Notre Dame, Ind.: Notre Dame University Press, 2007); John Meyendorff, *Byzantine Theology* (New York: Fordham University Press, 1976).

38   Theodor Avramov, "Trans-Ecclesial Eucharist? An Exploration of Some Critiques of Eucharistic Ecclesiology and an Outline of a New Path," in *Astra Salvensis* 6 no.11 (2018): 385–401.

39   *Sacrosanctum Concilium* 10.

40   Joseph Andreas Jungmann, "Commentary on the Documents of Vatican II," in Herbert Vorgrimler, ed., vol.1 (London: Burns Oates, 1967), 15.

41   *Sacrosanctum Concilium* 41.

42   J.-M.R. Tillard, *Church of Churches. The Ecclesiology of Communion* (Collegeville, Minnesota: The Liturgical Press, 1980).

43   For the text of this document, see Vimal Tirimanna, Sprouts of Theology from the Asian Soil. Collection of TAC and OTC Documents [1987-2007] (Bangalore: Claretian Publications, 2007).

44   Gerald A. Arbuckle, *The Pandemic and the People of God. Cultural Impacts and Pastoral Responses* (New York: Orbis Books, 2022), 16.

45   Henri de Lubac, *Corpus Mysticum: Essai sur L'Eucharistie et l'Église au moyen âge,* Paris:Aubier, Paris, 1944.

46   Cf. *The Works of Saint Augustine. A Translation for the 21st Century - Part III —Sermons Volume 8: Sermons 273-305A* (Hyde Park, New York: New City Press, 1994).

47   J.-M.R. Tillard, "And although the Eucharistic celebration cannot be effected without the minister, it is important to repeat that the role of the minister is to permit the community *as such* to exercise *the* priesthood there," *op. cit.,* 187.

48   Cyprian, *Epist.* 4.5.

49   *Cassell's Latin Dictionary* (London: Cassell and Company Limited, 1957 – twenty-eighth Edition), 385.

50   Tertullian, *De Exhort. Cast.* 7.3.

FURTHER READING

Arbuckle, Gerald A. *The Pandemic and the People of God, Cultural Impacts and Pastoral Responses.* Maryknoll, New York: Orbis Books, 2022.

Adiguzel, Fatih Serkant., Cansunar, Asli., and Corekcioglu, Gozde. "Truth or Dare? Detecting Systematic Manipulation of COVID-19 Statistics." *Journal of Political Institutions and Political Economy* 1, no. 4 (2020): 543–557.

Afanasiev, Nicholas. *The Church of the Holy Spirit.* Notre Dame: Notre Dame University Press, 2007.

Arnold, David. "Smallpox and Colonial Medicine in Nineteenth-Century India." In *Imperial Medicine and Indigenous Societies*, 45-65. Manchester: Manchester University Press, 2017.

Avramov, Theodor. "Trans-Ecclesial Eucharist? An Exploration of Some Critiques of Eucharistic Ecclesiology and an Outline of a New Path." In *Astra Salvensis* 6 no.11 (2018): 385–401.

Bala, Poonam., ed. *Medicine and Colonialism: Historical Perspectives in India and South Africa*. London: Routledge, 2014.

Baumann, Zygmunt. "Jerusalem Versus Athens Revisited." In Ulrich Beck, *Ulrich Beck: Pioneer in Cosmopolitan Sociology and Risk Society*. Cham – Heidelberg: Springer, 2014.

Beck, U. *Risk Society. Towards a New Modernity*. London: Sage,1992.

Bruggemann, Walter. *Disruptive Grace. Reflections on God, Scripture, and the Church*. New York: Fortress Press, 2011.

Cisney, Vernon W., and Nicolae Morar, eds. *Biopower: Foucault and Beyond*. University of Chicago Press, 2020

De Lubac, Henri. *Corpus Mysticum: Essai sur L'Eucharistie et l'Église au moyen âge*, Paris: Aubier, 1944.

Douglas, Mary. *Purity and Danger: An Analysis of the Concepts of Pollution and Taboo*. London: Routledge, 1992.

E. Horn, and H. Bergthaller. *The Anthropocene: Key Issues for the Humanities*. London: Routledge, 2020.

Einboden, Rochelle. "SuperNurse? Troubling the Hero Discourse in COVID Times." *Health* 24, no. 4 (2020): 343–347.

Escolà-Gascón, Álex., Francesc-Xavier Marín, Jordi Rusiñol., and Gallifa, Josep. "Pseudoscientific Beliefs and Psychopathological Risks Increase After COVID-19 Social Quarantine." *Globalization and Health* 16 (2020):1–11.

Fukuda-Parr, Sakiko., and Messineo, Carol. "Human Security: A Critical Review of the Literature." *Centre for Research on Peace and Development (CRPD) Working Paper* 11 (2012): 1–19.

Genel, Katia. "The Question of Biopower: Foucault and Agamben." *Rethinking Marxism* 18, no. 1 (2006): 43–62.

Haq, Mahbub ul. *Reflections on Human Development*. New York: Oxford University Press, 1995.

Harari, Yuval Noah. *Homo Deus, A Brief History of Tomorrow*. London: Vintage, 2017.

Harari, Yuval Noah. *Sapiens. A Brief History of Humankind*. London: Vintage, 2015.

Hawley, John Stratton. *Three Bhakti Voices: Mirabai, Surdas, and Kabir in Their Times and Ours*. Delhi: Oxford University Press, 2005.

Hick, John. *Evil and the God of Love.* New York: Palgrave Macmillan, 1966.

Jungmann, Joseph Andreas. "Commentary on the Documents of Vatican II." In Herbert Vorgrimler., ed., Vol. 1. London: Burns Oates, 1967.

Kundera, Milan. *Immortality.* London: Faber & Faber, 1992.

Lauber, David., ed. "Hans Urs von Balthasar and a Theology of Holy Saturday." In *Barth on the Descent into Hell.* New York and London: Routledge, 2004.

Levinas, Emmanuel. *Humanism of the Other.* Urbana and Chicago: Illinois Press, 1972.

Levinas, Emmanuel. *Time and the Other.* Pittsburgh: Duquesne University Press, 1987.

Levinas, Emmanuel. *Totality and Infinity.* Dordrecht, Boston, London: Kluwer Academic Publisher,1969.

Lipworth, Wendy. "Beyond Duty: Medical "Heroes" and the COVID-19 Pandemic." *Journal of Bioethical Inquiry* 17, no. 4 (2020): 723–730.

Losinger, Anton. *The Anthropological Turn. The Human Orientation of the Theology of Karl Rahner.* New York: Fordham University Press, 2020.

Mahasuar, Kiran. "Lies, Damned Lies, and Statistics: The Uncertainty Over COVID-19 Numbers in India." *Knowledge and Process Management* 29, no. 4 (2022): 410-417.

Maslow, Abraham. *The Psychology of Science.* USA: Gateway Books, 1966.

McNeill, J. R., and Engelke, P. *The Great Acceleration. An Environmental History of the Anthropocene since 1945.* Cambridge, Mass.: Belknap Press of Harvard University Press, 2016.

Metz, Johann Baptist. "Suffering Unto God." *Critical Inquiry* 20 (1994): 611–22.

Metz, Johann Baptist. *A Passion for God: The Mystical-Political Dimension of Christianity.* New York: Paulist Press, 1988.

Metz, Johann Baptist. *Faith in History and Society: Toward a Practical Fundamental Theology.* New York: The Seabury Press, 1980.

Metz, Johann Baptist. *Memoria Passionis. Ein provozierendes Gedächtnis in pluralisticher Gesellschaft.* Freiburg: Herder, 2006.

Meyendorff, John. *Byzantine Theology.* New York: Fordham University Press, 1976.

Moltmann, Jurgen. *The Crucified God.* Minneapolis: Fortress Press, 2015.

Osada-Sierra, Manuel. "Memory and History: The Overcoming of Traditional Theodicy in Levinas and Metz." *Religions* 10, no. 12 (2019): 657.

Owen, Taylor. Ed. *Human Security.* SAGE Library of International Relations. 2013.

Palanki, Satheesh. "'Clinical Christianity' as Philanthropy: Missionaries and Western Medicine in Colonial Travancore, 1813-1947." *International Journal of Asian Christianity* 5, no. 1 (2022): 136–152.

Qc, Ian Freckelton. "COVID-19: Fear, Quackery, False Representations and the Law." *International Journal of Law and Psychiatry* 72 (2020): 101–611.

Raman, Sujatha., and Tutton, Richard. "Life, Science, and Biopower." *Science, Technology, & Human Values* 35, no. 5 (2010): 711–734.

Roy, Arundhati. "The Pandemic Is a Portal." In *The Financial Times*, 2020.

Steffen, W. et al. "The Anthropocene. Conceptual and Historical Perspectives." *Philosophical Transactions of the Royal Society* 369 /1938 (2011): 842–67.

Steffen, W. et al. "The Trajectory of the Anthropocene. The Great Acceleration." *Anthropocene Review* 2 (1) (2015): 81–98.

Subbiah, Ganapathy. "Patterns in Religious Thought in Early South India: A Study of Classical Tamil Texts." PhD diss., McMaster University, 1988.

Sutton, Matthew Lewis., ed. "Does God Suffer? Hans Urs von Balthasar's Theology of Holy Saturday." In *Making Sense of Suffering: Theory, Practice, Representation*. Leiden: Brill, 2011.

Takenaka, Masao. *God is Rice. Asian Culture and Christian Faith*. Eugene, Oregon: Wipf & Stock Publishers, 2009.

Thompson, Janice Allison. *Theodicy in a Political Key: God and Suffering in the Post-Shoah Theology of Johann Baptist Metz*. Ph.D. dissertation, Notre Dame: University of Notre Dame, 2004.

Tillard, J.-M.R. *Church of Churches. The Ecclesiology of Communion*. Collegeville, Minnesota: The Liturgical Press, 1980.

Tirimanna, Vimal. *Sprouts of Theology from the Asian Soil. Collection of TAC and OTC Documents [1987-2007]*. Bangalore: Claretian Publications, 2007.

Veigas, Denis Gabriel. *Graduality in Truth in the Light of St Augustine's De Vera Religione*. Bengaluru: ATC, 2022.

Wilfred, Felix. "Christian Faith and Socio-Cultural Rationalities." In *Concilium 2017/1*: 101–110.

Wilfred, Felix. "Theological Significance of *Laudato Si*: An Asian Reading." *Vidyajyoti Journal of Theological Reflections* vol.79 (September 2015): 645-661.

Wilfred, Felix. "Listening to the World: Prophetic Anger and Sapiential Compassion." In *Buddhist-Christian Studies* 34 (2014): 63–66.

Wilfred, Felix. "Novel Ways of Being Religious." *Religious Identities and the Global South. Porous Borders and Novel Paths*, Chapter 6: 105-126. Cham, Switzerland: Palgrave Macmillan, 2021.

Wilfred, Felix. "What is Wrong with Rice Christians." In *UCAN*, https://www.ucanews.com/news/a-dalit-cardinal-can-help-end-casteism-in-indian-church/97446

Zakaria, Fareed. *Ten Lessons for a Post-Pandemic World*. New York: W.W. Norton & Company, 2020.

APPENDIX:

SOURCES OF THE CHAPTERS

1.   The Mission of All Religions for Humankind and Nature

This chapter grew out of a lecture delivered online during the Covid-19 Pandemic to celebrate Mission Sunday, October 2020. The event was organized by Ishvani Kendra, Pune.

2.   Mission and Political Engagement

Keynote address delivered at a symposium organized by the Missiology Department, St Peter's Pontifical Institute, Bengaluru, during 16 &17 January, 2020.

3.   The Gospel Mission in South Asia. Today and Beyond

Keynote address delivered at a conference organized to commemorate the centenary of the mission encyclical *Maximum Illud* at Morning Star College, Barrackpore, Kolkata, in collaboration with St. Xavier's University, Kolkata (SXUK), India, during 14-16 February 2019.

4.   Social Exclusion in South Asia. Principles to Overcome It

An extension lecture delivered at St Xavier's University, Kolkota, on 11 March 2023. An earlier version appeared in *Vidyajyoti Journal of Theological Reflection*, October 2023.

5.   Women's Liberation in South Asia.

It is a reworked and expanded version of a contribution to a book on Kālidāsa's classic *Abhijñānaśākuntalam* edited by Namrata Chaturvedi and published in 2020.

6.   Smart City vs Caring City. Reflections on Urbanization with Focus on the Poor

The chapter goes back to a lecture delivered at a *Concilium* Conference held in Frankfurt a.M., Germany, in June 2018. An earlier version of the lecture appeared in *Concilium* 2019/2, in English, German, Italian, Spanish, Portuguese editions. Another expanded version appeared in *Jeevadhara* in January 2019.

7.   Evolving Human Rights and Engaging Christian Faith. Where Have All the Prophets Gone?

The chapter originated from my lectures for a group of M.Th. students. An earlier version appeared in *Jeevadhara* in September 2021.

8.   Christian Churches and Democratic Challenges. The Case of Indian Catholicism.

The beginnings of the chapter go back to a contribution on Indian Catholicism to a series on World Christianity, published by Edinburgh University, UK. An earlier and shorter version appears in a work on

Christianity and democracy edited by James Ponniah and Ashok Kumar Mocherla in 2023. The chapter is a reworked and expanded version.

9.   Crossing a Millennial Threshold. Church in India on the Synodal Path

This is an expanded version of the keynote address delivered at the National Conference on "Church in India on the Synodal Path" organized by St Peter's Pontifical Institute, 21-23 March 2022. A summary version appeared in Portuguese in the journal *UNISINOS* University, Brazil. https://ihu.unisinos.br/631021.

10.   A Lonely Crusader? A Pope's Struggles for a Socially Relevant Faith

Originally delivered as a keynote address at a conference organized by Jnana Deepa, Pune, 29 November 2019. An earlier version appeared as an online publication of the International Theological Review *Concilium*. A reworked and expanded version appeared in *Jeevadhara* in January 2023.

11.   Asian Theological Trajectories and New Frontiers of Public Theology

The chapter goes back to a keynote address delivered at an International Conference organized by the Indonesian Association of Philosophy and Theology Institutes, held in Yogyakarta, Indonesia, in March 2019. An earlier version was published by the International *Journal of Indonesian Philosophy and Theology* in 2020.

12   Intersecting Faith and Society. Subaltern Public
      Theology of *Fratelli Tutti*

The origin of the chapter goes back to a contribution to an edited volume on *Fratelli Tutti* by De Paul University, Chicago, USA. A reworked version appeared in *Vidyajyoti Journal of Theological Reflections* 2021.

13.   Disclosing and Concealing. The Manifest and the
      Hidden in Covid-19 Saga

The article goes back to reflections online made during the pandemic and shared with different audiences. An earlier version appeared in *Jeevadhara* in January 2021.

14.   Theology in a Precarious World

A paper presented at the annual conference and meeting of the Indian Theological Association (ITA), Bengaluru, during 26-29 April 2022.

INDEX

I

X

Y

Z